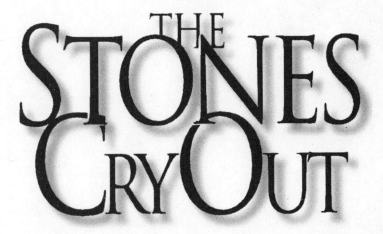

THE STONES CRY OUT

Dr. J. Randall Price

HARVEST HOUSE PUBLISHERS
Eugene, Oregon 97402

Scripture quotations in this book are taken from the New American Standard Bible, © 1960, 1962, 1963, 1968, 1971, 1972, 1973, 1975, 1977 by The Lockman Foundation. Used by permission.

Cover by Koechel Peterson & Associates, Minneapolis, Minnesota

For a free copy of Dr. Price's newsletter about biblical archaeology, biblical backgrounds, and biblical prophecy, write to:

World of the Bible Ministries, Inc.
P.O. Box 827
San Marcos, TX 78667-0827
(512) 396-3799, FAX (512) 392-9080
E-mail: wbmrandl@itouch.net

Pictured on the cover are actual artifacts from the periods discussed in this book. From left to right: fragments of an Early Bronze Age III storage jar from Bab edh-Dhra (possibly biblical Sodom); a Late Bronze Age I juglet (time of Joshua); Iron IIA oil lamp (time of King David); lower left—Roman period Herodian oil lamp (time of Jesus); lower right—Middle Bronze I (replica) cuneiform tablet from Ebla (time of Abraham); coins (left to right): shekel (first year of the Jewish War, A.D. 66/67), Roman period coin struck in time of Augustus (A.D. 6-9), Hellenistic coin of Alexander the Great (332 B.C.), Roman period coin of Herod Antipas (A.D. 38/39).

THE STONES CRY OUT
Copyright © 1997 by World of the Bible Ministries, Inc.
Published by Harvest House Publishers.
Eugene, Oregon 97402
www.harvesthousepublishers.com

Library of Congress Cataloging-in-Publication Data
Price, Randall.
    The stones cry out / Randall Price.
      p. cm.
    Includes bibliographical references and indexes.
    ISBN-13: 978-1-56507-640-2
    ISBN-10: 1-56507-640-0
    1. Bible—Antiquities. 2. Bible—Evidences, authority, etc. I. Title.
    BS621.P75 1997
    220.9'3—dc21   97-16947
                                                              CIP

Printed in the United States of America.

12 13 14 15 / BP / 17 16 15 14

To
DR. H.L. WILLMINGTON

A servant of Christ,
a minister to multitudes,
a model for many,
a friend to me.

and to

My Mother
Maurine Price

For cultivating my curiosity
and directing my devotion
that I might seek
both
the stones and the Savior.

About the Author

Dr. J. Randall Price received his Master's of Theology degree in Old Testament and Semitic Languages from Dallas Theological Seminary and his Doctor of Philosophy degree in Middle Eastern Studies and Archaeology from the University of Texas at Austin. He has also done graduate study in archaeology at the Hebrew University of Jerusalem and has participated in field excavation at Tel Yin'am in the Galilee as well as at Qumran, the site of the community that discovered the Dead Sea Scrolls. He has taught Biblical Archaeology at the University of Texas at Austin, is an adjunct Professor of Theology at the International School of Theology, and serves as President of World of the Bible Ministries, Inc., an organization specializing in biblical research on the ancient and modern Middle East. He is a certified tour guide to the State of Israel, having conducted 34 tours to the Bible lands and is author or co-author of nine books and three videos related to archaeological subjects, including *In Search of Temple Treasures* (Harvest House, 1994) and *Secrets of the Dead Sea Scrolls* (Harvest House, 1996). He also served as technical advisor to and appeared in several of the Ancient Secrets of the Bible television series as an expert on archaeology and biblical studies. He is married to Beverlee Shaw and has five children, who share his enthusiasm for the world of the Bible.

Acknowledgments

This book owes a great deal to many friends whose profession or passion is archaeology. First among these is Clifford Wilson, who kindly contributed the foreword. His lifelong contribution to biblical archaeology is appreciated by all who have studied under him or read his many fine works.

Because the first and last words of this book were written in Jerusalem, my gratitude is due to those in that country who shared their time, research, and photographic resources with me. These include Amihai Mazar, Avraham Biran, Trude Dothan, Sy Gittin, Gaby Barkay, Amnon Ben-Tor, Dan Bahat, Magen Broshi, Hanan Eshel, Hillel Geva, Ehud Netzer, Ronny Reich, Yitzhak Magen, Rami Arav, Bob Mullins, Steve Pfann, and Zev Radovan. Special thanks are also due to those in the United States and England who advised me and freely shared personal photographs and materials. First among these is Gordon Franz, whose assistance and counsel throughout this project were invaluable. Others include Leen Ritmeyer, Bryant Wood, Keith Schoville, David Merling, Sr., Eugene Merrill, David Livingston, James Strange, and Tom McCall.

I am again most grateful to Jack and Kay Arthur for the generous use of their apartment in Jerusalem during my initial research in October of 1996. I am also grateful to Dr. and Mrs. Weston Fields for use of their home, where this writing was completed in June of 1997. There were many others who assisted in transcription (Linda Winn, Debbie Smith), photography (Paul Streber, who took many of the photographs on location in Israel and Jordan), or provided technical support (Wayne House, Jim Fox, Gary Collett, and Ken Stanford). Thanks is also given to Richard Short, who prepared the chronology, and Steve Ando, who did the indices.

I must also pay special thanks to Professor Harold Liebowitz, who first invited me to excavate with him in Israel and offered me the opportunity to assist him in teaching a course on Biblical Archaeology at the University of Texas at Austin.

I am likewise grateful to Terry Glaspey, who suggested the idea for this book, Bob Hawkins, Jr. and Carolyn McCready of Harvest House Publishers, who offered me the project, to Steve Miller, who has served ably as its editor, and Barbara Sherrill for her expertise on the book's cover.

Appreciation also goes to my ministry supporters, who share in these earthly labors and their eternal rewards, and to Pastor Steve Sullivan, whose faithful prayers on my behalf have enabled the work to succeed. Finally, I must remember my family, whose hardships equaled my own in preparing the manuscript. To my mother, Maurine Price, who provided me a workplace and put up with piles of books for the majority of the typing; my wife, Beverlee, whose personal encouragement and insights into the proper presentation of this material have helped the work immensely; and my children Elisabeth, Eleisha, Erin, Jonathan, and Emilee, who prayed for their Dad and his writing and always greeted him with a hug when he came home.

Contents

Foreword

The Stones Cry Out by Dr. J. Randall Price is a scholarly, up-to-date and highly relevant survey of the major finds relating archaeology to the Bible. Every one of the 18 chapters includes gems that are a delight for the Bible-believing Christian—both scholar and layman.

As I personally have been for many years the "voice" on a widely heard radio program which is also called "The Stones Cry Out," I am delighted to recommend this book, which so capably brings together a vast amount of material that specifically endorses Bible backgrounds, incidents, and people. Moreover, Randall Price does not hesitate to tackle seeming problems, and answers them in ways that are acceptable to thinking people who are prepared to recognize that the Bible is not only a theological textbook but is also the greatest history record ever known to man.

For example, he tackles the controversy relating to the name "House of David" found in a monumental inscription at Tel Dan. As well as arguing cogently for his conviction as to the genuineness of the inscription and the correctness of the translation, he adds greatly to the value of his presentation by his personal contacts with archaeologists and other scholars who have been involved in finds such as these.

There are, of course, areas of controversy and debate, which will always be the case with the questions that history and archaeology raise. The contribution this work makes is toward informing reading audiences of the latest discoveries and discussions on the archaeological front. In addition, as Randall himself reminds us by quoting another author, the established "absolute truth in archaeology lasts about 20 years." No one can write a definitve book on the Bible and archaeology and be sure that all its interpretations and conclusions will be unquestioned in 20 years!

I recommend this book very highly. It has been a delight to read, and it is a privilege to pen this foreword. Dr. Price's work should be tremendously important in the ongoing process of today's scholarship in rejecting the far-too-prevalent criticisms of the Bible as history. He shows us that this Book, the Bible, is God's marvelous revelation of truth, set in historical contexts that are wonderfully reliable.

—Dr. Clifford Wilson
President
Pacific International University

Preface

The British politician and novelist Benjamin Disraeli once put the panorama of archaeology in perspective when he wrote concerning his first tour among the ruins of ancient Thebes:

> Conceive a feverish and tumultuous dream full of triumphal gates, processions of paintings, interminable walls of heroic sculptures, granite colossi of Gods and Kings, prodigious obelisks, avenue of Sphinxs and halls of a thousand columns, thirty feet in girth and of a proportionate height. My eyes and mind yet ache with grandeur so little in unison with our own littleness.[1]

Archaeology, in revealing the greatness of the past, helps us measure our present attainments in the progress of the ages. Every civilization in isolation from the past tends toward the exclusive claim that they are more advanced, more accomplished than their primitive descendants. However, it is a healthy awakening to see one's own "littleness" in light of the monumental cultures of antiquity. Empires have arisen, endured for millennia, and then crumbled into the dust from which they arose. Ours, in time, will do the same. In addition to this revelation of the past, biblical archaeology uniquely affords us a glimpse at a history whose direction is according to a design and attended by timeless lessons for life. By revealing for us the world of the Bible, it draws us also into the word of the Bible, where the rise and fall of nations is explained as part of a purposeful plan that incorporates our "littleness" and gives it meaning. This book was written to touch upon that meaning as we set the story of the Scripture into the setting of the stones.

Modern Challenges to Archaeology

Today, books on biblical archaeology face many challenges. As a result, one of the leading voices in the field, William Dever, has cautioned those who would publish: "You have to be very bold to venture into print now . . . you are certain to be attacked from all corners."[2] The first of these challenges is from the archaeologists' corner. Within this discipline there is widespread debate concerning the propriety of even using the term biblical archaeology. Indeed, the archaeology in those regions where biblical history unfolded reveals other peoples and cultures besides those that are relevant to the Bible. Therefore, some contend that the exclusive use of the term biblical undermines their significance. Furthermore, the trend in recent years has moved toward archaeological specialization and away from biblical studies. The school of "New Archaeology," rooted in cultural anthropology and renouncing the historical orientation of traditional archaeology, views biblical studies as the albatross of an older religiously oriented and less scientific generation. Lacking the biblical reference point that guided their predecessors, this new generation of archaeologists has proposed revolutionary origin theories and revisionist interpretations to replace traditional, biblically based models of Israel's history. This has especially been the case among the archaeological community in Israel. Today in "the Land of the Book," the Bible is regarded less as real history and more as religious history by the same archaeologists who reveal its rock record.

The second challenge comes from the opposite corner in this issue—those who are students and teachers of the Bible. For many of them, archaeology has lost its relevance to religion. In this age of moral relativism, where the focus in ministry training has shifted from being "biblically based" to being "socially significant," courses in biblical archaeology have largely disappeared from many Bible college and seminary curricula.[3] Those who do teach biblical archaeology often struggle against the system to do so, and if progressive education models persist, will probably not be replaced when they retire. Perhaps some of the present neglect of biblical studies in archaeology is a reaction to archaeology's having distanced itself from biblical studies. Whatever the cause, the divorce of these disciplines is producing a generation of abstract theologians and archaeological technicians who feel they have little in common. Without the synthesis that's necessary between the Scriptures and the stones, students in both fields will surely suffer.

My Involvement with Archaeology

My own introduction to and interest in archaeology was birthed by biblical studies. My enthusiasm to make the Bible relevant was tempered by the realization that every text had a context. In a twentieth-century (soon to be twenty-first-century) American context, I was separated from the biblical context by thousands of miles and years. It made sense to me that before I could apply the Bible to my own life and times, I needed to first understand the original lives and times to which its message was applied. This led me to move to Israel to learn about this context directly, first through graduate studies in biblical archaeology, and later through field work in archaeological excavations.[4]

Then during my doctoral work in the states, I had the rare privilege of teaching a course on Biblical Archaeology at one of our nation's largest secular universities. There I had students who had grown up in a public education system without access to the Bible, and they were amazed that during each class their instructor could stand before them with a Bible in one hand and an archaeology textbook in the other. In my opinion, their amazement came from their growing realization that the Bible was real history, attestable by the hard facts that attend every other historical subject. This highlights one of the contributions archaeology has made to an age in which the Bible has been reduced to the level of a literary legend.

The Popularity of Biblical Archaeology

In sharp contrast, while on the professional level biblical archaeology may be struggling, on the popular level it has never been more successful. The average person, whatever his beliefs, has a great fascination for archaeology, and especially archaeology of the Bible. The proliferation of archaeologically oriented specials on regular television and new series connecting the Bible and archaeology on cable channels, as well as numerous magazines featuring articles about biblical archaeology, have demonstrated this enormous groundswell of interest. We can hope that passion may prove to be the salvation of biblical archaeology in the academic arena. If enough people demand from their rabbis, pastors, and priests the same archaeological insights they receive from their television sets, then maybe the institutions that train such leaders will reconsider equipping them to teach the Scriptures with a knowledge of the stones.

It is for the popular audience, then, that I have written this book. My perspective comes from a high view of the Bible (what is called by archaeologists the "maximalist position"), which believes historical corroboration with the archaeological record is both possible and preferable. My purpose, however, is not to "prove" the Bible, which as an archaeological document is proof itself. Rather, it is to show from the stones that the Scriptures are reliable and reveal to us the Scriptures in a way impossible without them.

I have not planned this as a backward journey into the past, but as a forward journey in light of the past, which will illumine the present. If this effort has been successful, then that journey will provide for you a new appreciation and deeper desire for both the world and the Word of the Bible. Too, like Disraeli, may you find on this journey that your own eyes and mind ache with that uncommon grandeur that helps us measure our moments.

— Dr. J. Randall Price
Jerusalem (Shavuot, 1997)

AN INVITATION TO HEAR THE STONES

The stones cry out,
Long silent through the ages,
Unfolding now, a written scroll,
God's truth in dusty pages.

The stones cry out,
Their story tells with power,
Long hidden from the eyes of man,
God's truth for this hour.[1]

—Anne Moore

I can still remember the first time I climbed the Great Pyramid of the Pharaoh Cheops in Egypt. One of the seven wonders of the ancient world, it still remains the subject of mystery and controversy. As I ascended its massive height, each stone was a climb in itself. On the way up the view had been the millions of blocks of limestone used to build the pyramid. How many must have labored a lifetime here with no other sight than these stones! But at the summit the view changed. From this new vantage point could be seen the remains of the past in a way that could not be seen before. From here one could see the outline of the ancient causeway that connected the pyramid to the Valley Temple and the giant tombs of the pharaonic sun-boats. From here one could also catch a better view of the present. There, stretching out on the horizon, was the great metropolis of Cairo, which like the surrounding sands, had now encroached upon the pyramid city of Giza.

As my senses caught up with all the panorama before me, I began to reflect on this pyramid's place as a still point in the onward march of time. These stones, which had seen the flowering and fall of the Egyptian empire, were already 1,000 years old when Abraham passed through to claim his inheritance in Canaan. They were a symbol of refuge in the days of Joseph when he brought his father Jacob and his sons to settle in their shadow. The pyramids had witnessed the oppression of the Israelites and the exodus under Moses. They had watched the Hebrew prophet Jeremiah as he was taken from his captive Land of Judah, and beheld the infant Jesus in His flight from King Herod. If only these stones could speak, what stories they could tell!

In a manner of speaking, the stones do tell stories. The Bible uses the symbolism of speaking stones to remind us that God has left a witness to His works. In the case of the Babylonians, blinded to their own self-destruction, the prophet Habakkuk wrote, "Surely the stone will cry out from the wall, and the rafter will answer it from the framework" (Habakkuk 2:11). When the religious leaders sought to silence those praising Jesus' Messianic entry into the rock walls of Jerusalem, "He answered and said, 'I tell you, if these become silent, the stones will cry out!'" (Luke 19:40). Today, too, if men fail to receive the witness of the Word there is added the witness of the rocks. As the psalmist has said, "Truth shall spring out of the earth" (Psalm 85:11 KJV).

While I was standing on one of the great archaeological relics of the world, I was able to see more than I had before. The past gained a new perspective and the present was viewed in the greater light of history. Ever since, this has continued to prove true in my experience with the unearthed evidence of the Bible. But regardless of my experience, archaeology has provided us all with a better witness to the work of God as revealed in His Word. Should we not scale its mound of temporal treasures to attain an enhanced vision of eternal things?

Because I believe it to be a proper pursuit—even a holy quest—I have attempted in this book to remind us again how effectively the stones can shout. However, one can only shout so much, so I have had to be selective in my stories from the stones. Too, the attempt has been to present these stories as clearly as possible so that as many people as possible might hear. For this reason I have sought to address this book to the nonspecialist. Yet I have also tried to give professional archaeologists a voice through the many interview statements that have been included.

I am also aware that every book on archaeology is doomed, by virtue of ongoing digs, to be outdated before it goes to print. However, our ultimate focus here is not the stones, but the Scriptures, whose truths cannot be diminished by time.

To chart this course between layman and scholar and obsolescence and absolutes has not been easy. For this reason some specialists in the field may feel that I have overstated the value of their finds. However, we who have a stock in the sacred Scriptures have reason for our excitement over excavations. We acknowledge a God who heads up history, and as Christians believe, has even entered into history itself. To see stones which touch this history is to draw more deeply of the reality of Him who was and is and is to come. If you share this excitement, or even if you do not, I invite you to join me in listening to the stones speak once again. It will take you to new heights—I promise!

1. *Randall Price climbing the Great Pyramid.*

2. *Price atop the Great Pyramid.*

PART 1

What Can Archæology Prove?

1

THE ADVENTURE
OF ARCHÆOLOGY

Unveiling the Secrets of Ages Past

> *I believe in the spade. It has fed the tribes of mankind. It has furnished them water, coal, iron, and gold. And now it is giving them truth—historic truth, the mines of which have never been opened till our time.*[1]
>
> —Oliver Wendell Holmes

We live in an exiting time! New archaeological discoveries are being unearthed throughout the world faster than our newspapers can report them. And in what is surely good news for students of Scripture a great many of the finds are helping us to understand the Bible as never before. To illustrate how much and how quickly the past is invading the present, here are just some of the amazing discoveries, with relevance to the Bible, that were made near the time of this writing in early 1997:

- A hidden chamber was discovered in the King's Valley (Luxor, Egypt) next to the tomb of the famous King Tut. It may be the burial place of the firstborn sons of the Pharaoh Rameses II. If, according to one theory, he was the pharaoh of the Exodus, then these sons were those killed in the last of the miraculous plagues ordered by Moses.

• Beneath the waves off the coast of Alexandria, Egypt, thousands of artifacts from the years 670–30 B.C. have been discovered.[2] Among them was one of the seven wonders of the ancient world, the great Pharos lighthouse, which vanished from history over 2,200 years ago. Other finds include the royal palaces of famous figures such as Queen Cleopatra, Julius Caesar, and Mark Antony.[3] And somewhere in this underwater site of some five-and-a-half acres, archaeologists believe they will at last uncover the golden sarcophagus of Alexander the Great, who founded the city in 323 B.C. and whose conquest of the known world was predicted by the Hebrew prophet Daniel (see Daniel 11:3-4).[4]

• Just discovered, but still unpublished, is a 3,500-year-old cuneiform inscription on a clay prism from the Syrian kingdom of Tikunani. Early work on the translation of the text has led to the announcement that the text may finally contain the long-sought identity of the enigmatic Habiru, a people thought by some to be related to the biblical Hebrews.[5]

• News has come that through the use of a form of infrared satellite technology, the lost Pishon River has now been revealed. Long buried by the desert sands, its ancient course could be traced by the satellite in the riverbed Farouk El-Baz, which runs from Hijaz in western Arabia to Kuwait. It was this river, along with the well-known Tigris and Euphrates Rivers, that helped to define the location of the Garden of Eden in the Bible (Genesis 2:11).[6]

• And, speaking of the Garden of Eden, just in from Israel is the report of a fossilized snake with well-developed hind legs found in a modern stone quarry.[7] This first-ever discovery of such a legged snake gives new relevance to the story of a similar serpent described in the temptation account in the book of Genesis (Genesis 3:1-15).

• Heard of the mysterious Essenes? Fifty newly discovered tombs at Beit Safafa in southwest Jerusalem may be our first evidence of this lost community.[8] It's believed that a group of

Essenes may have settled at Qumran and produced the Dead Sea Scrolls. These tombs are from the same time period and just like those at Qumran. This find may provide the missing link between Jerusalem and Qumran, finally solving the riddle of the Dead Sea Scrolls authorship.

If these reports fail to stir excitement on your part, it may be because such news has become more and more commonplace in our age of 24-hour news networks and smorgasbord of multi-channeled educational television shows. To really appreciate the archaeological revelations arising in our modern age, we need to take a brief trip back to the days when such information was unknown to the world.

The Way It Was

In the late eighteenth century, no one could have dreamed what wonders archaeology was about to reveal. The world of the past was largely forgotten except for the historical parade of ancient names of people and places, but there was no physical evidence to prove they really existed. Typical of that time was the observation of Herder:

> In the Near East and neighboring Egypt everything from the ancient times appears to us as ruins or as a dream which has disappeared. . . . The archives of Babylon, Phoenicia and Carthage are no more; Egypt had withered practically before the Greeks saw its interior; thus, everything shrinks to a few faded leaves which contain stories about stories, fragments of history, a dream of the world before us.[9]

Such was the condition of our material knowledge of the ancient past only two centuries ago. The Bible stood as the only surviving testimony to itself. On the one hand the reader was blessed by its truths, yet on the other hand he was often left to wonder about the places and events it recorded. There were, of course, many ancient literary sources that offered commentary on ancient and biblical history, such as the Talmud, Josephus, and the Graeco-Roman writings, but these were available only to those trained in classical literature. All other people had to content themselves with their faith and imagine the world of the Bible with no other reference than the world in which they lived. And, even for those who mastered the classics the picture of the past remained dim and dreamlike.

For some people, the fact that the past had seemingly nothing to offer made it best suited for illustrating man's mortality and musing philosophically about his transitoriness. It was in this vein that Dunsany wrote his contemplative soliloquy:

> It was the spider who spoke. "The Work of the World is the making of cities and palaces. But it is not for Man. What is Man? He only prepares my cities for me, and mellows them. Ten years to a hundred it takes to build a city, for five or six hundred more it mellows, and is prepared for me; then I inhabit it, and hide away all that is ugly, and draw beautiful lines about it to and fro. . . . For me Babylon was built, and rocky Tyre; and still men build my cities! The work of the World is the making of cities, and all of them I inherit."

Unearthing the Past

Archaeology, however, boldly reclaims this heritage for man. It chases away the spiders of time and resurrects the faded glory of the past for a future generation to understand and enjoy. In some respects it has also chased away certain skeptical notions concerning the Bible, which were made popular by the invasion of Higher Criticism over a century ago. This has been made possible through the exciting discoveries of the spade, bringing to light and life insights from the world of the Word. Indeed, as Professor William Foxwell Albright, the dean of the old school of biblical archaeology, once proudly professed, "Discovery after discovery has established the accuracy of innumerable details, and has brought increased recognition of the value of the Bible as a source of history."[10]

While for many modern archaeologists Albright's aim of establishing biblical accuracy has changed or been challenged, the evidence of archaeology has continued to increase. A couple of decades ago Dr. Donald J. Wiseman could boast that "The geography of the Bible lands and visible remains of antiquity were gradually recorded until today more than 25,000 sites within this region and dating to Old Testament times, in their broadest sense, have been located."[11] Today, however, such remains number in the hundreds of thousands. With such an abundance of artifacts—and more surfacing all the time—it is difficult, if not impossible, for us who are students of the Scriptures to keep up on every important item from the field that has biblical relevance. Nevertheless, it is the goal of books like these to help us try, by taking us on an archaeological journey into the realm of reality out of which the words of truth were born— the lands, languages, and life-settings of the Book of books. In order to start our journey together, let us begin with a basic understanding of our subject.

What Is "Biblical" Archaeology?

Our English word archaic refers to some ancient thing from the past. The same Greek word that gives us archaic also forms the first part of our word archae-ology. The second part comes from another Greek word, *logos,* meaning "study of" (used to earmark fields of study such as bio*logy,* socio*logy,* anthropo*logy,* and so on).

The ancient Greeks used the word archaeology to describe their discussion of ancient legends or traditions. Its first known appearance in English was in 1607, where it was used to refer to the "knowledge" of ancient Israel from literary sources such as the Bible. Then in the nineteenth century, when ancient artifacts from Bible times began to be unearthed, the word was applied to these (apart from the written documents).

So, from the beginning, the idea of archaeology was linked to the Bible. Today, *archaeology* is understood as a branch of historical research that seeks to reveal the past by a systematic recovery of its surviving remains. However, as archaeology developed as a science and excavations included lands other than those having a biblical significance, there was a need for the more exclusive term *biblical archaeology*. Therefore, as a separate discipline within the larger field, *biblical archaeology* has come to refer to the science of excavation, decipherment, and critical evaluation of ancient material records related to the Bible.

The Birth of Biblical Archaeology

Archaeology first began when men wanted to recover the material past. The earliest "archaeologists," if we may call them that, were graverobbers who plundered the tombs of antiquity (usually not long after they were sealed) in search of buried treasure. Even though those with a knowledge of a tomb's entrance usually ended up being entombed with such treasure and a severe death was promised to those robbers who were caught, the profession apparently flourished. When discovered in our time, most of the great tombs of the past had already been visited by these ancient "archaeologists."

When in relatively modern times the past began to be explored by adventuresome Europeans, relics and souvenirs were carried home to enchant friends and enhance fame. Soon fortune hunters began to proliferate, sailing away to distant lands in search of the riches they envisioned waiting in vast unclaimed treasure troves among ancient ruins. Most of the "excavations" these archaeological mercenaries carried out destroyed as much as they discovered. Others of a different spirit, however, began to record their observations with ink and etchings, bringing news, although often romanticized, of long-forgotten lands and their material cultures.[12]

The first "scientific" attempt at archaeology was conducted under Napoleon Bonaparte in 1798. His interest in archaeology was implied when he addressed his troops after their invasion of Egypt, saying: "Fifty centuries look down upon you!" On the American continent, it is said that Thomas Jefferson, the third president, "scientifically explored" the tumuli (burial mounds) of Virginia. In the following century, other Americans, such as Edward Robinson and Eli Smith, joined a host of other scholars from England, Switzerland, France, Germany, and Austria in publishing topographical surveys, detailed maps, and the results of arduous explorations and excavations in the Bible lands.

For the most part, these early archaeological forays, undertaken at great expense, were financed by people whose primary concern was the Bible. Thus, biblical archaeology has most often been the compelling factor in the progress of archaeology as a whole. Yet, whatever the motivations, these "founders of the archaeological frontier" opened the way for a more scientific development of the discipline—to the advantage of us all.

History Made Tangible

As I mentioned earlier, before the birth of archaeology, no one really knew what the world of the Bible had been like. Everyone's concept of that world was imagined. In result rather than intent, accounts from the Bible were received in a fashion almost the same as the mythological tales of the Greeks and Romans. It was not that people did not believe the Bible was true; rather, the world of the Bible seemed like a different planet with alien folk, whose appearance and manner of life were the stuff of dreams, not reality.

I remember the shock I received when I first visited the Holy Land. Gone were my flannelgraph conceptions of Jesus in pressed linen walking on carpet grass! Before me in the archaeological trenches and in the many museums of the Land were real remains that changed my many preconceptions. My own imagined world of the Bible shrank even as the facts concerning the real world—and my faith—began to grow. However, after the initial awe of archaeology had passed, a new awakening arrested me. No longer could I excuse myself from behavior different than the biblical figures of the faith. They, too, had been real people, living in a real world. They struggled with the same concerns and doubts that I face today. If they lived by real faith in a real world, then so should I. The reality that confronted me when I first saw the "original context" of the Bible has continually been reinforced over the years through archaeological discoveries.

Archaeology has revealed the cities, palaces, temples, and houses of those who lived shoulder to shoulder with the individuals whose names appear in Scripture. Such discoveries make possible for us what the apostle John once voiced to authenticate his message: "What was from the beginning, what we have heard, what we have seen with our eyes, what we beheld and our hands handled, concerning the Word of Life . . . these things we write" (1 John 1:1,4).

Tangible things can assist faith in its growth toward God. Archaeology brings forth the tangible remnants of history so that faith can have a reasonable context in which to develop. It also allows faith to be supported with facts, confirming the reality of the people and events of the Bible so that skeptics and saints alike might clearly perceive its spiritual message within a historical context. Archaeologist Bryant Wood, director of the Associates for Biblical Research, makes this point in discussing the discovery of the name "House of David" on a monumental stele from Tel Dan (*see* chapter 9):

> We know he [David] is a historical figure because he is mentioned in the Bible, but that is not enough for scholars. They need evidence outside the Bible. So biblical archaeology can play a very important role in verifying the truth of Scripture in the face of the criticism that we are receiving today from modern scholarship.[13]

An Adventure for All Time

The archaeology of Hollywood is an endless adventure. The archaeologists of cinematic making are part scholar and part superman, capable of leaping across fiery chasms in pursuit of ever-fantastic finds. But archaeology, in its pursuit of the past, is nothing like this. It is methodological and often quite mundane. Even so, it is still an adventure—an adventure that transports us to the past and challenges us to change our perspective in the present. An adventure that sometimes forces us to replace our private opinions with the hard facts of history, and perhaps for the first time face the reality of the Word. And in light of the never-ceasing claims of critics, it also makes more adequate our answer to a doubtful age—an age that is technologically blessed but theologically bankrupt. With a sense of adventure, then, I invite you to join me on a trek through time, digging in soil and Scripture to discover what amazing things the stones cry out!

2

DIGGING FOR ANSWERS

The Story in Stone

The real business of archaeology is to establish factual benchmarks in the world of the Bible to guide interpreters.[1]

—Joseph Callaway

We live in an age eager for answers. Unlike the ages that have gone before, our age uniquely has access to an immeasurable storehouse of information previously unavailable. For instance, even while archaeologists dig for more answers, the general public can dig into a multitude of archaeological archives via the worldwide web. Through the Israeli Antiquities Authority database alone, armchair archaeologists now have access to more than 100,000 archaeological relics discovered in the State of Israel since 1948.

Among the more significant relics are those with inscriptions, for these give us immediate access to the knowledge of the past. Inscriptions are not found very often, but some of those which have been unearthed have offered us an important means of understanding the biblical record.

The Power of the Written Word

So Shall It Be Written . . .

Written words were important to the ancients; they were thought to symbolically carry a force that could accomplish the will of the speaker.[2] An example of this was dramatized in Cecil B. DeMille's production of the Ten Commandments. At pivotal points throughout the film was the pronouncement: "So shall it be written . . ." The script writer poignantly used this phrase to underscore the contest between the word of earth and that of heaven. The pharaoh of Egypt used these words to seal the decree spoken against Moses (and God). However, the pharaoh's use of these words had no power, for Moses returned to thwart both Egypt's king and her gods. By contrast, God's use of these words was powerful. Moses spoke them against pharaoh, and the king found he could do nothing but accept his fate. In case the point was missed, the film's final scene reinforced the power of God's Word by showing a picture of the Tablets of the Law over which this phrase "So shall it be written" was majestically superimposed.

. . . So Shall It Be Found

Nothing is more exciting to an archaeologist than to discover a written word from the past. Like voices from the ancient world, though rarely "heard," they speak volumes to those trained to "hear" their words. Those so trained are called *epigraphers* (from the Greek word meaning "written upon"). These written remains themselves are called *inscriptions* because they come from the Latin word meaning "to write upon").

Just as modern writing is preserved on everything from CDs to postcards, so inscriptions from the world of the Bible have come to us on various types of materials. And like today, the range of writing might be anything from a child's schoolwork to religious revelation. Then, as now, important announcements and documents were preserved on the most permanent of materials. Sometimes writing was done on various kinds of metals;

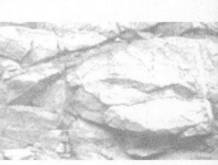

3. *Egyptian scribe in writing posture (2750 B.C.), Egyptian Museum, Cairo.*

however, except for coins, the use of metals was reserved for special texts and purposes. For example, the oldest portion of the Bible so far discovered was found inscribed on silver scrolls taken from a tomb in the Hinnom Valley, and a priceless record of buried treasure is preserved on one of the Dead Sea Scrolls known as the *Copper Scroll.*

In the biblical world, the best-preserved inscriptions are found on stone or clay materials. Inscriptions on stone are usually monumental inscriptions, such as those found in association with public buildings, to commemorate some special event (for example, a victory or dedication), or in connection with burials (to preserve a name or memorial). They may range in size from the huge obelisks, statues, and wall panels in Egyptian temples to smaller documents such as the oblong cylinders used for Mesopotamian records. The Ten Commandments fit into this latter category. And, contrary to the Hollywood conception, they were probably inscribed on a stone plaque or tablet about the size of a man's hand.

Inscriptions on clay are usually associated with diplomatic communications and royal archives. However, because clay was an inexpensive and durable writing material, it was also used for general purposes (such as inventories or economic record-keeping). Such clay inscriptions most often appear as small rectangular tablets. The earliest form of writing engraved on them looks like a series of interconnected wedges. The official name for this kind of writing is *cuneiform*. Another kind of clay product used for common writing was broken pieces of pottery known as *potsherds* (or sherds). The technical term used for these fragments when they contain writing is *ostraca*. As the most abundant form of writing material they were, in effect, the poor man's postcard. Inscriptions of this type are usually found scratched onto the sherds or written with ink (created from combining charcoal, gum arabic, and water).

Writings of sacred or other literature, as well as private and commercial letters, were written with ink on sheets of material roughly equivalent to our paper. One kind of material used was the prepared skins of animals (usually sheep or

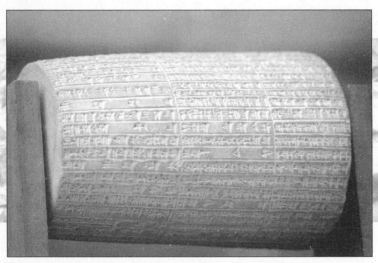

4. *Cuneiform text, Ashmolean Museum, Oxford, England.*

goats), known as *parchment.* There was also *vellum,* which was made from calf skin. The other kind of material, and the one most commonly used, was made from a reed plant that grew in marshes and along rivers. This delicate material was known as *papyrus,* which was also the name of the plant. Papyrus documents survive only if they are stored under exceptional conditions. They have been found only in dry areas, such as in sealed tombs, buried under hot desert sands, or stored in jars within caves like those in the Dead Sea region.

Such literary evidence, along with the vast array of other material remains, has built through more than a century of discovery into an impressive arsenal of evidence for the historicity and increased illumination of the biblical text. Let's now consider the valuable contribution these archaeological artifacts have made to biblical studies.

The Value of Archaeology to the Bible

The proper use of archaeology in relation to the Bible is to confirm, correct, clarify, and complement the Bible's theological message. Since the "Word" was announced to people in this world, at particular places and times, the historical, cultural, and religious context of those addressed must be understood. The better we are able to understand the original meaning of the message, as communicated in the ancient world, the better we will be able to apply its timeless truths to our lives in the modern world.

Archaeology can assist us in our understanding of this original context of the Bible so that the theological truth will not be misinterpreted or misapplied. Professor Amihai Mazar, director of the Hebrew University in Jerusalem's Institute of Archaeology, states this purpose for us when he says:

> I think the most important thing that we have to understand is that archaeology is our only source of information that comes directly from the Biblical period itself.... Archaeology can give us information right away from the period when things happened.... a

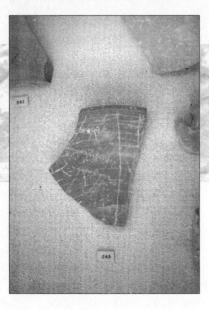

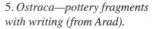

5. *Ostraca—pottery fragments with writing (from Arad).*

> whole picture of daily life from this period as well as inscriptions . . . which are the only written evidence that we have from the Biblical period, except the Bible itself.[3]

Because the biblical text describes people, places, and events that are foreign to the modern reader and as many as two or more millennia removed from the present, the information available from the archaeological record is vital to an improved knowledge of the context of the Bible text. Let us now look at the four ways in which archaeology contributes to a greater understanding of the Bible.

Confirming the Word of the Bible

According to Webster's English Dictionary, one of the meanings of the word *confirm* is "to give new assurance of the validity" of something. Archaeology provides a new assurance of the Bible from the stones to accompany the assurance we already have from the Spirit. This value is an apologetic one, and from the beginning of the science of archaeology it was a conrtibuting factor in both instigating and sponsoring excavations. Despite the recent shift in archaeological circles away from the confirmatory value of excavated evidence, almost all scholars still attest to the significant agreement between the stones and the Scriptures. For example, Amahai Mazar, though having an aversion to using archaeology as a biblical apologetic, nevertheless admits that a corroborating relationship between the Bible and the archaeological discoveries can be made:

> In certain cases, we can even throw light on certain events or even on certain buildings which are mentioned in the Bible. We can enumerate many subjects like this where the relationship between the archaeological finds and the biblical narrative can be established. The earlier we go, the more problems [we encounter] and the questions are more difficult to answer. With the later periods of time [the time of the Monarchy] things become more secure and better established.[4]

6. *Fragment of papyrus document from Judean desert.*

Although it is true that more evidence is available for confirming the latter periods of Israelite history, what has been uncovered from these periods may reflect positively on the earlier times. For instance, in 1979 Gabriel Barkay discovered tiny silver scrolls in a tomb in Jerusalem's Hinnom Valley. Containing a text of scripture from the Pentateuch (the Aaronic benediction of Numbers 6:24-26), it predated the Judean exile. This find posed a problem to critical scholars, who argued that priests had authored most of the Pentateuch after the Judean exile. As a result, critical scholars must now adjust or reformulate their theory concerning the authorship of the Pentateuch.

Archaeology has also given us a new assurance of the trustworthiness of the biblical account not only in matters of history, but tangently, in its uniqueness when compared with other ancient Near Eastern documents. The discoveries of the religious literatures of the Sumerians, Egyptians, Hittites, Assyrians, Babylonians, and Canaanites have all

7. *Excavation of tomb 25 at Ketef-Hinnom in Hinnom Valley, Jerusalem.*

highlighted the originality and elevated morality of the Bible (see next chapter). Therefore, archaeology is able to offer confirmation of biblical revelation by discrediting historical skepticism and, at the same time, demonstrating Scripture's theological distinctiveness.

Correcting Our Wording of the Bible

One of the first steps to understanding the Scriptures is to discern the meaning of the text as it was originally written by its authors. While it is unlikely that archaeologists will ever unearth one of the autographs (original texts of the Bible), the copies that have come to us have been preserved and passed down to us in such a manner as to give us confidence that we have the very "Word of God" in our hands. Even so, our many manuscript copies of the biblical text sometimes contain variations in wording. These ancient versions present the challenge of recovering the precise form, grammar, and syntax of Hebrew, Aramaic, and Greek words, as well as their exact meanings and nuances. Therefore, as Bryant Wood points out, "a very important contribution that archaeology makes is in the study of the language of the Bible."[5]

> We have had many discoveries of ancient texts, libraries
> and collections of documents that help us understand
> the Hebrew and Greek languages, which help us get a
> better translation of these languages into English.[6]

In most cases the discoveries of inscriptions in the biblical languages, as well as in cognate languages (languages having affinities with the biblical languages) have affirmed the integrity of the received (authoritative) texts. In addition, they have helped scholars understand the peculiarities of poetic sections and better interpret words that appeared only once *(hapax legomenon)* without any certain meaning for translation. As a result, we now have greater assurance of the validity of our texts in the original languages and an improved ability to translate the texts into our modern tongues.

Clarifying the World of the Bible

Before archaeology, the Bible stood supremely alone as a witness to what was then called "sacred history." But the Bible also seemed to be a foreign book, telling a history of an alien world unrelated to real people and events. With no access to the material past, the only way people could make sense of the biblical world was to make it like their own. Because much of the world's population was illiterate until modern times, art and architecture played the role of educating people concerning life in Bible times. The spiritual world was elevated through, for example, cathedral architecture, removing the common man even further from the real world known by the people of Bible times. From mosaics to paintings to sculptures, the lives of sinners and saints on the sacred pages were illustrated, but only in the limited light of the times and knowledge of the artist.

My first understanding of this prearchaeological dilemma was when I viewed a special exhibit at the Israel Museum entitled "Rembrandt and the Bible." I had degrees in both art and theology, so I was very interested in this unique showing of the Dutch master's collected works on biblical themes. One of the first scenes I viewed was a sketch dated 1637 of a man of obvious wealth standing on some stairs at the stately entrance of his mansion. Dressed in turban, robes with a sash, high-laced boots, and a fur-lined overcoat, the man had an obedient dog at his heels. The scene also included a boy outfitted in heavy travel clothing and boots, with a similarly dressed woman bearing a silk handkerchief. In the background were high stone buildings and tall green trees along with a woman who was watching as the man apparently said good-bye to the weeping woman and boy. The theme of the work was Abraham's sending out of Hagar and Ishmael. But, being acquainted with the world of the Bible, it would never have occurred to me that this was the scene before me! These characters were dressed for a cold climate, not the hot Negev desert. Where Abraham lived, there were no such trees, and probably not dogs—at least not as pets. The Patriarchs lived in tents, not elegant mansions. The contrast and irony really struck me when I left the exhibit room where these seventeenth-century misconceptions were being displayed. Only a few hundred feet ahead was the permanent exhibit of the archaeological section of the museum. In that room were archaeological remains from Abraham's day— remains that painted a very different picture than Rembrandt had! These artifacts rang true to the nomadic lifestyle and geographical surroundings of the Patriarchs.

Now Rembrandt couldn't have known how to paint a Mesopotamian Abraham and Sarah or an Egyptian Hagar living in a Canaanite setting. He had no reference for his art outside of his era. Archaeology changed this forever by providing both artist and spectator alike an accurate view of the original setting. Relief sculptures from Mesopotamian palaces, Canaanite pottery and artifacts, and painted murals from Egyptian tombs dating from the Patriarchal period have now made these biblical figures come alive. Had Rembrandt had our archaeological record to illustrate these for him, what paintings he would have made!

The world of the Bible as illuminated by archaeology has brought clarification to interpreting the Bible in a historical context as well. As Gonzalo Báez-Camargo has noted, "No longer do we see two different worlds, one the world of 'sacred history' and the other the world of 'profane history.' All of history is one history, and it is God's history, for God is the God of all history."[7]

The material finds from this God-governed history have produced for us an archaeologically enhanced world of the Bible in a new and more realistic detail than was formerly conceived possible. Professor Amihai Mazar explains:

> We can calculate even the population size in places like Jerusalem or the entire area of Judah, or the kingdom of Israel. We can imagine how many people lived there, in what type of settlements they lived, what type of town plan there was, what kind of vessels they used in everyday life, what kind of enemies they had and what kind of weapons they used against

these enemies—everything related to the material aspect of life in the Old Testament period can be described by archaeological finds from this particular period.[8]

As an example of how the world of the Bible has brought clarification to the Word of the Bible through archaeological discovery, let us consider the so-called "hard saying" of Jesus recorded in Matthew 8:22 and Luke 9:60: "Let the dead bury their own dead." These Gospels set this saying in the context of certain disciples making excuses about why they could not immediately leave their respective situations and follow Jesus. In this specific instance, one disciple asked permission to first go and bury his dead father. As understood by modern readers, Jesus' apparent denial appears as both unreasonable and unnecessarily harsh. Some commentators attempt to soften the statement by interpreting it to mean "let the *spiritual* dead bury the physical dead," but this would still contradict the fifth commandment in the Mosaic Law to "honor your father and your mother" and the Jewish responsibility of providing a proper burial as mandated in Deuteronomy 21:22-23.

However, when interpreted in light of the archaeological information concerning first-century Jewish burial practices, the disciple's request and Jesus' response are seen in a different light.[9] Jewish burial in the time of Jesus actually consisted of *two* burials that took place at least one year apart. The first was within the family burial cave (known as being "gathered to the fathers") and was followed by a period of mourning. The second was within a bone box (ossuary), usually with the remains of other family members, after the flesh had decomposed. What seems to be in view in the Gospel saying is this act of secondary burial (known as *ossilegium*). Jesus' retort to the disciple wanting an 11-month leave from service was not only with regard to this prolonged absence, but especially with respect to the unbiblical aspect of secondary burial.

The act of immediate burial ("gathered to the fathers") is reflected in the Bible (*see* Genesis 49:29; Judges 2:10; 16:31; 1 Kings 11:21,43), but by New Testament times this concept had acquired new theological meaning.[10]

According to rabbinic sources, the act of decomposition had a purifying effect, atoning spiritually for the deceased's sins.

The consummation of this spiritual process was the ritual of secondary burial. Since Jesus followed the biblical teaching that God alone makes atonement (on the basis of faith in His provided sacrificial redemption), His statement served as a correction of this improper practice. We could then render the saying in Luke 9:60 (in an amplified manner) as: "Look, you have already honored your father by giving him a proper burial in the family tomb. Now, instead of waiting for the flesh to decompose, which cannot atone for sin, go preach the Kingdom of God and tell of the only true means of atonement. Let the bones of your dead father's ancestors gather his bones and place them in an ossuary! You follow Me!"[11]

Complementing the Witness of the Bible

The 66 books of the Bible were written on at least three continents over 4,000 years of history by prophets, poets, peasants, shepherds, and statesmen. While a vast and diverse witness, the Scriptures mention only certain people and specific events that were necessary to their larger theological purpose. The Bible focuses on some details of ancient history and doesn't mention others. One of the great values of archaeology, then, is that it acts as a complementary witness that completes the outline drawn by the biblical authors. For example, although historically the Israelite King Omri (885–874 B.C.—he built up Samaria and made it the capital of the Northern Kingdom) was one of the most important rulers of his period, the biblical text grants him only a passing reference in a mere eight verses (1 Kings 16:21-28). The reason was because he was one of the most wicked Israelite Kings up to his time. Archaeology, however, has provided us with background information about Omri. This includes extrabiblical accounts of his exploits as recorded by some of his foreign foes.

This complementary witness has been especially helpful for understanding the Second Temple era, which includes the period during which Gospels were written. For instance, the Pharisees and Sadducees, who opposed Jesus, are well known from the

Gospel writings, but no contemporary witness to them was known to exist before 1948. It was then that the Dead Sea Scrolls came to light with numerous descriptions and accounts of Jewish sects, including the Pharisees and Sadducees.

The Limitations of Archaeology

While archaeology is of great help to the understanding of the Bible, those who use archaeology with this purpose in mind must avoid using material evidences to critique the authenticity or accuracy of the biblical text. A. Momigliano has correctly expressed this caution:

> Whether biblical or classical historians, we have also learned that archaeology and epigraphy cannot take the place of the living tradition of a nation as transmitted by its literary texts. At the same time we have been cured of early delusions that the reliability of historical traditions can be easily demonstrated by the spade of the archaeologist.[12]

One of the reasons that the evidence in the biblical text must be given priority over archaeological evidence is the limitations of archaeology. One limitation of archaeology is that, by nature, it is confined to the realm of the material. Professor Amihai Mazar, director of the Hebrew University of Jerusalem's Institute of Archaeology, affirms this when he notes:

> Archaeology is of course limited. Archaeology deals mainly with the material culture, not so much with ideas, philosophy, poetry, wisdom, etc. as we have in the Bible. The Bible is a rich, full world of intellectual thought. Archaeology is limited. It gives us pottery, buildings, fortifications, plans of cities, patterns of settlement, how many sites there were in each period, what was the population size.[13]

The primary limitation of archaeology, however, is the extremely fragmentary nature of the archaeological evidence that has been unearthed. Edwin Yamauchi, professor of history

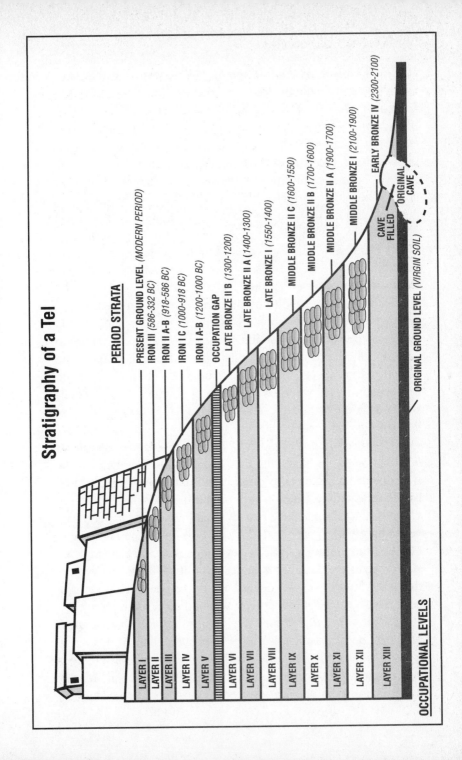

Stratigraphy of a Tel

PERIOD STRATA

PRESENT GROUND LEVEL (MODERN PERIOD)
IRON III (586-332 BC)
IRON II A-B (918-586 BC)
IRON I C (1000-918 BC)
IRON I A-B (1200-1000 BC)
OCCUPATION GAP
LATE BRONZE II B (1300-1200)
LATE BRONZE II A (1400-1300)
LATE BRONZE I (1550-1400)
MIDDLE BRONZE II C (1600-1550)
MIDDLE BRONZE II B (1700-1600)
MIDDLE BRONZE II A (1900-1700)
MIDDLE BRONZE I (2100-1900)
EARLY BRONZE IV (2300-2100)

CAVE FILLED
ORIGINAL CAVE
ORIGINAL GROUND LEVEL (VIRGIN SOIL)

LAYER I
LAYER II
LAYER III
LAYER IV
LAYER V
LAYER VI
LAYER VII
LAYER VIII
LAYER IX
LAYER X
LAYER XI
LAYER XII
LAYER XIII

OCCUPATIONAL LEVELS

at Miami University, Oxford, Ohio, has underscored this limitation by pointing out the fractional degree of evidence available from archaeology.[14] I have updated his points as follows:

1. *Only a fraction of what is made or what is written survives.* In the case of written materials, which add directly to our knowledge of the past, even though several great Near Eastern archives have been discovered, they are an infinitesimal number next to those that have been destroyed in the past. For example, the great library of antiquity located in Alexandria held almost one million volumes, many of these the only copies. All of these works were lost when it was burned to the ground in the seventh century A.D. The Land of Israel has yet to produce an archive from any period, even though correspondence between it and its neighbors is attested to by discoveries made in other lands. As we have already noted, this might be expected if the Israelites used perishable writing materials. If an archive were to be found, it would most likely date from the earlier Canaanite period. Already clay tablets discovered at Tel Hazor indicate this possibility; however, what might be found would still constitute only the smallest fraction of what had been produced by this people.

2. *Only a fraction of the available archaeological sites have been surveyed.* In Israel and the Near East there are still thousands of unexcavated tels. (A *tel* is an unnatural mound created by the repeated destruction and rebuilding of ancient cities and villages on the same site.) The few that have been properly surveyed barely keep pace with the new sites discovered each year. Many of these known sites, however, can never be properly surveyed because of lack of resources or political disputes over territories. Many more will never be surveyed because they have been destroyed by population growth and construction projects.

3. *Only a fraction of the surveyed sites have been excavated.* This may be surprising to some people, but archaeology, even in Israel—where it is tied to the national tourist economy—does not receive high priority. Israeli government budgets go mostly towards military applications, securing the country against

terrorism, or developing a still-young nation. Archaeologists, most of whom are not salaried as archaeologists but as professors, must raise their expedition money from private sources. And most of their workers are volunteers who must pay their own expenses to excavate. For these reasons, less than 2 percent of the surveyed sites in Israel have been excavated.

4. *Only a fraction of an excavation site is actually examined.* Again, funds are limited, so archaeologists seek to determine priority areas at any given tel in hopes of being able to unearth the most significant finds. Such prioritization is oftentimes necessary because in some cases, the provision of permits and future funds is dependent on the progress demonstrated in previous years. In addition, because there are so many unexcavated sites waiting to be explored, only a limited number of seasons can be allotted to any one dig. Therefore, many potentially important discoveries will be missed as a result of incomplete excavation. Even though the most strategic sites, such as Tel Hazor, may be repeatedly excavated by different groups, there is still much ground left untouched. In terms of proportion, given its immense size, Hazor still represents the largest unexcavated tel in Israel!

5. *Only a fraction of what is excavated is eventually reported and published.* Even the most significant finds, such as inscriptions, are not always published. The reasons for this have been the source of controversy, such as the 40-year delay in releasing just the *photographs* of the Dead Sea Scroll material from Cave 4. It also took about 30 years for Kathleen Kenyon's final reports from Jericho to be published. In addition, of the known 500,000 cuneiform texts lying in museum storage rooms, only about 10 percent have ever been published. The problem here has simply been lack of interest, expertise, time, and money.

Compounding the publication problem is the continual development of archaeology as a science. With more specialists in the field, more sophisticated methods, and more technological instrumentation, the amount of detail work done at an excavation site has exploded. At one time it used to take years to complete a field report for publication; now it may take decades. Therefore, professionals—and much less the public—rarely get to see the evidence excavated from sites during their careers. It might also be noted that another problem is the protection of excavated sites from archaeological theft. Each season, many sites are pillaged by the nomadic Bedouins and others who make their living off black-market antiquities. Thus even before some discoveries can be documented, they are lost forever.

These limitations in archaeology should caution historians, social scientists, and theologians from making premature judgments based on archaeological remains alone. It should also make unwarranted criticisms of the historicity or accuracy of the biblical text in comparison to the archaeological record. This, of course, goes against contemporary practice, which is voiced by those who feel that archaeology has grown beyond the biblical priority. But in cases where questions or doubts have arisen, time has usually proven the text correct against problems presented from the field.

The Bible—An Archaeological Document

In the final analysis, it must be remembered that the Bible itself is our finest example of an archaeological document. While we have only a limited number of archaeological artifacts from the biblical period, the Bible represents the most complete literary record we possess of ancient times. Surviving in one form or another since its first books were penned by Moses some 3,400 years ago, it remains the most accurate and trustworthy account of antiquity in the archaeological record. For this reason it is improper to elevate other archaeological inscriptions above the biblical text in order to challenge the latter's integrity. There are indeed instances where the information needed to resolve a historical or chronological question is lacking from both archaeology and the Bible, but it is unwarranted to assume that material evidence taken from the more limited content of archaeological excavations should be elevated above or used to critique the more complete content of the canonical Scriptures.

At the same time, while the Bible is a completed revelation, it is not an *exhaustive* one. Though its message can be readily understood in any age, it is still selective in its statements and set in ancient contexts. Therefore, despite its limitations, archaeology, as a handmaiden to the Bible, can enlarge the scope of its statements and make more understandable its settings. In the upcoming chapters, we will explore some specific examples of how archaeology has served the Scriptures in bringing to the present new knowledge of the past.

3

Digs That Made a Difference

Writings from the Past

Every area on the face of the earth, be it seemingly ever so waste and empty, has a story behind it which the inquisitive sooner or later will attempt to obtain.[1]

—Nelson Glueck

Museums today have thousands of amazing archaeological artifacts from the ancient Near East. These fabulous finds have significantly contributed to our understanding of the biblical world. Yet, it was not always so. In the eighteenth century, English author Samuel Johnson once stated with a note of finality that "all that is really known of the ancient state of Britain is contained in a few pages, and we can know no more than the old writers have told us."[2] Johnson could scarcely have imagined that as he talked in the George Inn of Fleet Street that the vast remains of Roman London lay just beneath his feet, or that part of its surviving wall was within a five-minute walk of his own house! At the same time in the land of Egypt, people in the city of Luxor fought for the "good ground" in the midst of the desert on which to build their mud-brick huts. This "good ground" was what they considered bedrock protruding from the sands. They never knew that these fine flat areas on which they had securely built were in fact the tops of massive pillars that formed the Great Hall of Columns at Karnak, a structure described by the Greek historian Herodotus in 450 B.C. when he walked at the bases of the columns *some 100 feet below!*

Up to the eighteenth century, then, people had not yet learned how to read the record of the rock. Their knowledge was shut up to the stories of the past. This was about to change.

As the eighteenth century came to a close, men began to dig, and those digs made a difference. Some of the discoveries finally taught people how to read the past—and even how to read present works in a new light.

Digs That Taught Us How to Read

The early explorers of the biblical world were amazed when they saw for the first time the monumental ruins of Egypt and Mesopotamia. Recording these sites in order to excite an eager audience at home, they returned with sketches of these rock wonders. All who viewed these pictures of another world were curious about the mysterious characters covering these majestic structures. Although researchers knew that these peculiar symbols represented the history of lost civilizations, they concluded for the most part that the clues for their decipherment were generally thought to be lost as well. Here were the cryptic languages of Egypt and Mesopotamia, the two great world powers of the past. How historians longed to unlock their secrets! But no one possessed the keys. Ironically, as archaeological discoveries continued to be made, the keys turned up on the stones themselves. Two of these discoveries literally taught us how to read these long lost languages, and as a result, opened up new wonders for the world. These were the Rosetta Stone and the Rock of Behistun, which were among the first great discoveries in archaeological history.

8. *Great Hall of Columns, Karnak, Egypt. When first discovered, native houses rested atop the columns, which were at ground level.*

The Rosetta Stone—Key to Egyptian Hieroglyphics

The ancient Egyptian writing called *hieroglyphics* (derived from two Greek words: *hieros* = "sacred" and *glypho* = "engrave")[3] was given a special aura of mystery by the European artists who romanticized the ruins of Giza and Thebes. For Europeans, who took fancy with them, they were regarded as either decorative motifs or as having some secret meaning known only to the pharaohs. Most scholars of that time agreed that the symbols held a mystical meaning for the Egyptians, but also realized that if they could be deciphered, then much of that lost culture could be recovered. However, the meaning of the hieroglyphs continued to be as elusive as a rain cloud in that desolate land.

Then in 1798, soldiers under the command of General Napoleon Bonaparte, who along with a corps of French scientists had invaded Egypt the year before, began amassing large numbers of freshly discovered Egyptian artifacts. As it would turn out, they were destined to be collectors only and not keepers. A year later, the treasures fell into the hands of the British, who routed the French fleet and drove Bonaparte's army from Egypt. Among this newly won collection of antiquities which the British sent back to their national museum in London was a large slab of black basalt stone inscribed from top to bottom with ancient writing. It had been found by the French army officer Lieutenant P.F.X. Bouchard while reconnoitering near the village of Rosetta on the left bank of the Nile River. Almost four feet high, 2fi feet wide, and one foot thick, the stone weighed 1,676 pounds! Aptly named the Rosetta Stone, it soon drew particular interest when it was observed that the writing on it was in different scripts. Further study revealed that the scripts were parallel texts, each recording the same account. The text at the top of the stone was written in hieroglyphs, the middle text in what appeared to be a cursive form of hieroglyphic (now called *demotic),* and the bottom text was in Koine Greek.

Because this Greek (the same as the Greek used to write the New Testament) was easily read by scholars, it was hoped

9. *The Rosetta Stone as it appears today in the British Museum, London.*

that someone could work from the known to the unknown. By first comparing the easily understood Greek words with the demotic text (which was thought to be readable), perhaps some light could be shed on the cryptic hieroglyphs (which were thought to be only symbolic). As the Greek text of the Rosetta Stone was translated, it was learned that the stone was a commemorative stela that had once stood in an Egyptian temple. It recorded a decree issued from Memphis (the ancient Egyptian capital) in 196 B.C. extolling the triumphs of King Ptolemy V Epiphanes. The inclusion of this name (the only royal name preserved in the hieroglyphic section of the stone) was to prove essential to finally cracking the code of the hieroglyphs.

The first successful attempt to read the Egyptian text was made by Thomas Young (better known as the author of the wave theory of light). He correctly identified a recurring group of hieroglyphic signs written with an oval (called a *cartouche)* with the name of King Ptolemy. Now that it was known that foreign names were written with these unique hieroglyphs, the meaning of the signs themselves had to be understood by scholars. Ironically, a young Frenchman by the name of Jean-François Champollion entered this drama of decipherment. A gifted linguist, Champollion energetically applied himself to the task at hand. He compared Young's hieroglyph for "Ptolemy" on the Rosetta Stone with a newly discovered (1819) obelisk from an Egyptian temple near Aswan, which contained the names of Ptolemy and Cleopatra in Greek. He was able to isolate the cartouche for Cleopatra and, working from this, to decipher other royal names. Finally, in 1822, at the age of 32, he announced triumphantly that he had solved the riddle of the hieroglyphs. To the surprise of many scholars, he demonstrated that hieroglyphics were not merely symbols, but signs with phonetic value—they formed a readable language! Therefore, because of the discovery of the Rosetta Stone, the hidden secrets of Egyptian language and through it, ancient Egypt's history, religion, and culture, was opened to the world.[4]

The Behistun Inscription—Key to Akkadian Cuneiform

What the Rosetta Stone did for Egyptian hieroglyphics a monumental inscription in Iran (ancient Persia) did for Akkadian cuneiform. Akkadian was the Semitic language of Mesopotamia, and its two principal dialects (Assyrian and Babylonian) were used to record the military triumphs and religious tales of the great world empires of Assyria and Babylon. Both of these empires figure prominently in the Bible as nations used by God to punish the Israelites for their unfaithfulness to the Mosaic Covenant.

For centuries, those passing along the old caravan trail at the foot of the 4,000-foot Iranian mountain known as the Rock of Behistun wondered in awe and curiosity at the strange figures carved into the side of the cliff some 300 feet above their heads. These ancient travelers considered this gigantic relief to be the work of God. Ancient records from around 500 B.C. reveal that the rock was called *Baga-stana* ("the Place of God"), hence the modern name of the site, Behistun (also Bisitun). On this massive relief (see next page) is a man with upraised hand. Ten men face the man and two more men stand behind him. Above their heads is suspended a bird-like image. Who were these strange men and what was the object hovering over their heads? Prior to modern times, the tour guide's answer was, "Christ, His disciples, and the Holy Spirit" (as a dove)!

Like a great wall rising behind the sculpted figures, the surface of the stone had been chiseled flat and appeared polished smooth. That is, until those who boldly scaled the face of the cliff reported that these "smooth" walls were actually engraved with thousands of tiny arrowheads! Were these some sort of ancient decoration? The scholars who studied them decided not. Rather, they were taken to be a form of ancient writing which, because of its shape, was given the name *cuneiform* (from the Latin, meaning "wedge-shaped").

Based on the discovery of similar writing at the ancient Persian capital of Persepolis, other scholars suggested that the figures were not from the New Testament but the Old, and that

10. *The Inscription of Darius the Great, King of Persia on the Rock of Behistun, Iran.*

they might include one of the Persian kings. This conjecture proved to be correct, for when the cuneiform characters were finally deciphered, one phrase boldly proclaimed, "I am Darius, Great King, King of Kings, the King of Persia." Once this had been read, it was clear that the central figure was none other than Darius the Great, who ruled the Persian empire from 522 B.C. to 486 B.C. Further decipherment also found the name of his sons, Xerxes, who succeeded Darius on the Persian throne. Here then, for the first time, was primary evidence for the monarch Darius I Hystaspes, who served as God's instrument for returning the Jews to Judah and helping them to rebuild the Temple in Jerusalem. Here, too, was testimony in stone to Xerxes (Ahasuerus), who had married the Jewess Esther, and has ever since been enshrined in the traditional Jewish festival of Purim. Not only had they left their kingly "calling cards" at Behistun, but also their "photographic IDs" for all to see! The secrets of the mysterious mountain were revealed at last.

The man who succeeded in reading the cuneiform writing and solving these "secrets in stone" was the British Major Sir Henry Rawlinson. At great physical risk, Rawlinson repeatedly scaled the sheer cliff of Behistun to copy the inscriptions. His normal precarious posture while copying the cuneiform text was to poise himself on the top rung of a ladder with no support other than one arm on the rock face! On one occasion the rope ladder he was using broke and left him hanging from a narrow ledge until he was rescued.

Thanks to the painstaking work of Rawlinson and other scholars, we've learned that the Behistun inscriptions preserved not one cuneiform language, but three—Old Persian, Babylonian, and Elamite. With the help of their work on the Rock of Behistun, the riddle of cuneiform scripts has been solved. This key in turn opened up to the world the abundant annals of ancient Assyria and Babylonia, throwing new light not only on their histories but also on the historicity of the Bible.[5]

Digs That Retold Ancient Tales

Have you ever wondered why the Bible should have all the good stories? If the great stories of the Creation and the Flood were real history, as the Bible portrays them, shouldn't other ancient cultures have known and told these stories as well? This assumption was confirmed when a number of ancient cuneiform texts were discovered that contained Mesopotamian parallels to these biblical accounts.

Technically speaking, these texts were not discovered by archaeologists in the field, but by scholars in the study. Although British archaeology in Mesopotamia was not the exact science it is today, it did unearth hundreds of tons of monumental sculptures and thousands upon thousands of cuneiform tablets. Most of these came through the efforts of Sir Austen Henry Layard, who dug in the ancient Assyrian capital of Nineveh in the 1850s. At the palace of the Assyrian king Ashurbanipal, he found thousands of clay tablets that had once been part of the royal archives. These had apparently been waiting for Layard since they had been abandoned to the elements when the palace was destroyed in 612 B.C.

He shipped these treasures back to the British Museum, and there they were dutifully stored away in the recesses of the museum's basement. In time scholars began to identify, catalog, and decipher many of these tablets. These scholars may have never dug in a foreign land, yet the writings they dug out of a basement in their own land proved to be some of the greatest archaeological discoveries of all! Three of the most ancient texts, the Atrahasis Epic, Enuma Elish, and the Gilgamesh Epic, are especially significant when compared to the Bible.

The Atrahasis Epic—The Babylonian Genesis

The discovery of the earliest Mesopotamian text with parallels to Genesis was made in the last century and named the *Atrahasis Epic* (Atrahasis is the principal character in the narrative). Although first published in 1876 by George Smith of the British Museum, it was found in 1956 that he had incorrectly ordered the damaged fragments of the text, and in 1965 that he had only one-fifth of the text itself! It was then that British scholar Alan Millard, for a time the Assistant Keeper of the Department of Western Asiatic Antiquities at the British Museum, was able to restore another three-fifths of the text from fragments in storage in the museum's basement. As he analyzed a text that had been unearthed more than a century earlier, he noticed that the wording sounded strangely like the book of Genesis. This epic story was preserved on a tablet of some 1,200 lines. The tablet itself probably dated to the seventeenth century B.C., but the story it retold went back centuries to the earliest Babylonian period. The story, although presented from the theological perspective of the Babylonians, contains many details that are similar to the biblical accounts of the Creation and the Flood. In the Babylonian tale, the gods rule the heavens and earth (cf. Genesis 1:1). They make man from the clay of the earth mixed with blood (cf. Genesis 2:7; 3:19; Leviticus 17:11) to take over the lesser gods' chores of tending the land (cf. Genesis 2:15). When men multiply on the earth and become too noisy, a flood is sent (after a series of plagues) to destroy mankind (cf. Genesis 6:13). One man, Atrahasis, is given advance warning of the flood and told to build a boat (cf. Genesis 6:14). He builds a boat and loads it with food and animals and birds. Through this means he is saved while the rest of the world perishes (cf. Genesis 6:17-22). Much of the text is destroyed at this point so there is no record of the boat's landing. Nevertheless, as in the conclusion of the biblical account, the story ends with Atrahasis offering a sacrifice to the gods and the chief god accepting mankind's continued existence (cf. Genesis 8:20-22).[6]

Enuma Elish—The Mesopotamian Creation

George Smith, who had first translated the Mesopotamian story of the Flood, was also the first man to reveal to the world the existence of a Mesopotamian creation account known as the

Enuma Elish. Like the Atrahasis Epic, fragments of this text had also come from Ashurbanipal's library at Nineveh, but other fragments were later found at Ashur (the old capital of Assyria) and Uruk. In the mid-1920s two almost complete tablets were also found at Kish. All told, seven tablets together comprise this epic tale. The most interesting section of this tale (for Bible students) is a retelling of the Creation from the Babylonian and Assyrian perspective. The text's strange name comes from the Assyrian words which introduce the text: *enuma elish,* which means "when above."[7] In the small portion of the text that mentions the Creation, we are told that the universe, in its component parts, began with the principal gods (who represent the forces of nature), and was completed by Marduk, who became the head of the Babylonian pantheon (assembly of gods). It is Marduk, not the Creation, who stands as the dominant theme in the epic.

When we look for parallels with the Genesis account we find few: the watery chaos is separated into heaven and earth (cf. Genesis 1:1-2,6-10), light pre-exists the creation of sun, moon, and stars (cf. Genesis 1:3-5,14-18), and the number seven figures prominently (cf. Genesis 2:2-3). Beyond this, however, the mythological context controls the content. The gods procreate other gods whom they in turn seek to destroy because of their loud parties. The mother of these gods, Tiamat, creates monsters to eat them up, but the strongest of them—Marduk— cuts her in half. It is from her two halves that the heavens and earth are formed. Mankind is created from the blood of the captured leader of the rebel gods (a sort of devil among the gods) in order to work as slaves for the lazy lower gods and feed the Babylonian pantheon. This mythological account has little in common with the early chapters of Genesis, which tells us God created man in His own image, gave him the world to enjoy, and cared for him and sought fellowship with him. Yet the discovery of the Enuma Elish provided our first knowledge that other Near Eastern cultures shared some aspects of the biblical cosmogony (account of Creation).

11. *Tablet 11 of The Gilgamesh Epic, which features an old Babylonian account of the Flood.*

The Gilgamesh Epic—The Mesopotamian Flood

Another of the important finds that came from Henry Layard's excavation was an old Babylonian account of the Flood called the Gilgamesh Epic. It was named after the principal character, King Gilgamesh, who is supposed to have ruled the Mesopotamian city of Uruk around 2600 B.C., and who in this epic story is searching for immortality. Because no copy of the entire text was discovered, scholars had to make a composite text based on fragments from periods separated by over 1,000 years (1750–612 B.C.)! While a date to the eighteenth century B.C. is conjectured for the original composition, if Gilgamesh material is confirmed in the Ebla tablets, the date could go back much earlier. The epic as we have it today is recorded on 12 tablets. The Flood story, which appears in tablet 11, seems to have been borrowed directly from the Atrahasis Epic (which is incomplete).

When the Gilgamesh Epic was first published in Europe in 1872, it caused a sensation rivaling Darwin's theories. Some people claimed it as historical proof of the Genesis Flood, while others said it diminished the Bible's claim to uniqueness and authenticity. In all the Mesopotamian literature, the account of the Flood in tablet 11 represents the foremost correlation with the biblical text. In the story recounted here, Gilgamesh is told about the Flood by Utnapishtim, a man who had gained immortality, and like the biblical Noah, had also passed safely through the waters of the Flood. In his account of the Flood, he says the creator god Ea favored him by warning him of the Flood and commanding him to build a boat (cf. Genesis 6:2,13-17). On this boat he brought his family, his treasures, and all living creatures (cf. Genesis 6:18-22;7:1-16), thereby escaping the heaven-sent storm that destroyed the rest of mankind (cf. Genesis 7:17-23). By his reckoning, the storm ended on the seventh day, and the dry land emerged on the twelfth day (cf. Genesis 7:24). When the boat came to rest on Mount Nisir in Kurdistan (rather than biblical Mount Ararat in Turkey), Utnapishtim sent out a dove, a swallow, and finally a raven (cf. Genesis 8:3-11). When the raven did not return he left the boat and offered a sacrifice to the gods (cf. Genesis 8:12-22). Although these selective elements of the Mesopotamian story appear strikingly parallel to the biblical story, a person who reads the entire translation of the story will find it extremely legendary in character; its tone differs dramatically from the Genesis account.

Where Did These Stories Come From?

Since the discovery of the Mesopotamian texts, questions have been raised about the origin of these stories that are similar to those found in the Bible. Three possible answers have been offered by scholars: 1) They were originally Israelite accounts that were borrowed and adapted for the Mesopotamian religion and culture; 2) they were originally Mesopotamian tales, which were borrowed and adapted by the Israelites to fit their religious purposes; 3) both the Mesopotamian and Israelite (biblical) accounts came from a common ancient source.

Concerning the first option, as far as we know, the biblical accounts were not written down until the time of Moses in the fifteenth century B.C. It seems unlikely, then, that the "older" (seventeenth-nineteenth century B.C.) Mesopotamian stories were derived from the Israelite account. As for the second option, it is possible that Moses used sources in compiling his accounts in Genesis (*see* Genesis 14). Moreover, it is possible that the biblical writers had access to the Gilgamesh Epic, as a fragment of the epic turned up in the 1956 excavations at Megiddo in Israel.[8] Does this mean there was a literary dependence on the Mesopotamian texts in compiling the biblical accounts? The use of extrabiblical sources does not conflict with the doctrine of biblical inspiration as there are numerous instances in which non-canonical works are cited in both the Old and New Testaments (*see* Joshua 10:13; 1 Samuel 24:13; 2 Samuel 1:18; Luke 4:23; Acts 17:28; Titus 1:12; Jude 14). However, neither the possession of nor occasional use of extrabiblical texts by the biblical writers demand that there was a literary dependence upon them. The biblical writers continually stress that their primary source was divine revelation. Secondary sources may have been used at times, but it does not appear that they were used in reference to Creation and the Flood.[9] The many significant differences and omissions between the accounts make it unlikely that either the Mesopotamian or biblical authors borrowed from each other.

But could there have been a "tradition dependence"? That is, could the biblical accounts simply be variations of Mesopotamian myths? Again, this is unlikely. One reason is that the biblical orientation is monotheistic (one God) and its characters are ethically moral. By contrast, the Mesopotamian orientation is polytheistic (many gods) and its characters are ethically capricious. This contrast is evident, for example, in the way the two texts treat the account of the post-Flood world. In the biblical text, God accepts Noah's sacrifice and promises to never again destroy the earth by a flood (Genesis 8:20-22). In the Atrahasis Epic, the gods discover to their chagrin that they have wiped out their only source for food (men's sacrifices). Because they

(Continued on page 70)

Major Inscriptions of Old Testament Significance

NAME	LANGUAGE	DISCOVERER	LOCATION FOUND	FOUND DATE (A.D.)	SUBJECT	DATE OF ORIGIN (B.C.)	BIBLICAL SIGNIFICANCE
Beni-Hasan Tomb Painting	Hieroglyphic	Newberry	Beni-Hasan	1902	Tomb painting of Khnumhotep II	1900	Pictures Semites in Egypt
Laws of Hammurabi	Akkadian (Old Babylonian)	deMorgan	Susa	1901	Collection of Babylonian laws	1725	Illustrates ancient Near Eastern law
Merenptah Stela	Hieroglyphic	Petrie	Thebes	1896	Military accomplishments of Merenptah	1207	First mention of the name "Israel"
Sheshonq Inscription	Hieroglyphic		Karnak Temple	1825	Military accomplishments of Sheshonq	920	Confirmation of raid against Rehoboam
"House of David" Inscription	Aramaic	Biran	Dan	1993	Syrian conquest of region	9th c.	Earliest mention of David in contemporary records
Mesha Inscription	Moabite	Klein	Dibon	1868	Military accomplishments of Mesha of Moab	850	Moabite-Israelite relations in 9th century

	Language	Discoverer	Location	Year Found	Description	Date	Significance
Black Stela	Akkadian (Neo-Assyrian)	Layard	Nineveh	1845	Military accomplishments of Shalmaneser III	840	Picture of Israelites paying tribute
Balaam Texts	Aramaic	Franken	Deir Alla (Succoth)	1967	Prophecy of Balaam about the displeasure of the divine council	8th c.	Connected to a famous seer known from the Bible
Silver Scrolls	Hebrew	Barkay	Hinnom Valley Tomb	1979	Amulet containing the text of Num. 6:24-26	7th c.	Earliest copy of any portion of the Bible
Siloam Inscription	Hebrew	Peasant boy	Jerusalem	1880	Commemoration of the completion of Hezekiah's water tunnel	701	Contemporary example of Hebrew language
Sennacherib Cylinder	Akkadian (Neo-Assyrian)	Taylor	Nineveh	1830	Military accomplishments of Sennacherib	686	Describes siege of Jerusalem
Lachish Ostraca	Hebrew	Starkey	Tell ed-Duweir	1935	18 letters from the captain of the fort of Lachish	588	Conditions during the final Babylonian siege
Cyrus Cylinder	Akkadian	Rassam	Babylon	1879	Decree of Cyrus allowing the rebuilding of temples	535	Illustrates the policy by which Judah also benefited

Major Tablets of Old Testament Significance

NAME	NUMBER OF TABLETS	LANGUAGE	DISCOVERER	LOCATION FOUND	DATE FOUND (A.D.)	SUBJECT	DATE OF ORIGIN (B.C.)	BIBLICAL SIGNIFICANCE
Ebla	17,000	Eblaite	Matthiae	Tell-Mardikh	1976	Royal archives containing many types of texts	24th c.	Provide historical background of Syria in late 3rd millennium
Atrahasis	3	Akkadian	Many found different parts	Different parts in different sites	1889 to 1967	Account of creation, population growth, and flood	1635 copy	Parallels to Genesis accounts
Mari	20,000	Akkadian (Old Babylonian)	Parrot	Tell-Hariri	1933	Royal archives of Zimri-Lim containing many types of texts	18th c.	Provide historical background of the period and largest collection of prophetic texts
Enuma Elish	7	Akkadian (Neo-Assyrian)	Layard	Nineveh (library of Ashurbanipal)	1848 to 1876	Account of Mara-duk's ascension to the head of the pantheon	7th c. copy	Parallels to Genesis creation accounts

Gilgamesh	12	Akkadian (Neo-Assyrian)	Rassam	Nineveh (library of Ashurbanipal)	1853	The exploits of Gilgamesh and Enkidu and the search for immortality	7th c. copy	Parallels to Genesis Flood accounts
Boghaz-Köy	10,000	Hittite	Winckler	Boghaz-Köy	1906	Royal archives of the Neo-Hittite Empire	16th c.	Hittite history and illustrations of international treaties
Nuzi	4,000	Hurrian dialect of Akkadian	Chiera and Speiser	Yorghun Tepe	1925 to 1941	Archive containing family records	15th c.	Source for contemporary customs in mid-2nd millennium
Ugarit	1,400	Ugaritic	Schaeffer	Ras Shamra	1929 to 1937	Royal archives of Ugarit	15th c.	Canaanite religion and literature
Amarna	380	Akkadian (W. Semitic dialect)	Egyptian peasant	Tell el-Amarna	1887	Correspondence between Egypt and her vassals in Canaan	1360 to 1330	Reflects conditions in Palestine in the mid-2nd millennium
Babylonian Chronicles	4	Akkadian (Neo-Babylonian)	Wiseman	Babylon	1956	Court records of Neo-Babylonian Empire	626 to 594	Record of capture of Jerusalem in 597 and history of the period

(Continued from page 65)

are hungry, they decide to put up with mankind (who can feed them). Another reason is that important details in the accounts differ (such as the sizes of the boat, the duration of the Flood, the sending out of the birds, and so on). A.R. Millard, who co-authored a book on the *Atrahasis Epic,* summarizes the question of alleged borrowing when he says:

> All who suspect or suggest borrowing by the Hebrews are compelled to admit large-scale revision, alteration, and reinterpretation in a fashion that cannot be sub-stantiated for any other composition from the ancient Near East or in any other Hebrew writing.... Granted that the Flood took place, knowledge of it must have survived to form the available accounts; while the Bab-ylonians could only conceive of the event in their own polytheistic language, the Hebrews, or their ancestors, understood the action of God in it. Who can say it was not so?[10]

In fact, literary clues in these Mesopotamian compositions imply the antiquity of the Genesis account. Scholars have long recognized that Genesis 2:1-4 is a *colophon* or appendix to the first narrative of Creation in Genesis 1.[11] The ancient tablets that contain an account of Creation likewise have a colophon. A comparison of the two reveals that the arrangement of the mate-rial in the Genesis colophon accords with the information given in the ancient colophons: 1) *title* ("the heaveans and the earth," Genesis 2:1a, 4a); 2) *date* ("in the day the LORD made earth and heaven," Genesis 2:46); 3) *serial number* ("six days" = series of six tablets); 4) *whether or not completed in series* ("seventh day [= after sixth tablet] ... completed," Genesis 2:1b-2); 5) *name of scribe or owner* ("the LORD God," Genesis 2:4b).

Therefore, it seems more likely that both the Mesopotamian and Israelite accounts reflect a universally preserved knowledge of events that occurred during earth's pre-Flood history. The variations in these stories were passed down by the different

Semitic cultures that developed after the division of the nations in the post-Flood ancient Near East (see Genesis 10–11).

Legacies Left from Antiquity

It is archaeological relics like the Rosetta Stone and the Rock of Behistun that have taught us how to read the past and to regard the Bible with a greater sense of history and uniqueness. Yet these are only part of the great legacy left to us from antiquity. In the next chapter we will continue our tour through the museum of time to see more of the discoveries from digs that made a difference.

4

MORE DIGS THAT MADE A DIFFERENCE

Pictures from the Past

It is today a truism to say that archaeological investigation in Palestine and in surrounding lands, which since the end of the First World War has been conducted on an unprecedented scale, has transformed our attitude towards, and our understanding of, ancient Israel and the Old Testament.[1]

—D. Winton Thomas

In the previous chapter we took a look at excavations that have represented the writing of new chapters in the annals of archaeology. These digs made a difference because they affected our perception of the Bible and the world in which its major events unfolded. In this chapter we will take a look at digs that have improved our understanding of the past by both preserving it in photographic fashion and changing current beliefs about it historically.

Digs That Photographed the Past

Before archaeological excavations opened up the world of the Bible, no one had any idea what the people who appeared on its pages really looked like. However, when discoveries began to be revealed, among them were statues, relief drawings, and paintings that gave us "snapshots" of the kind of people who lived during Bible times. Even more incredible was that archaeologists found "pictures" of the very people mentioned in the Bible. Among these were statues of pharaohs who met Moses, enemies who threatened Israel or conquered much of Israel, and Roman rulers mentioned in the New Testament, some of whom talked with Jesus and the apostle Paul.

The details included in these scenes depicting ancient daily life have made it possible for artists to correctly depict biblical scenes and filmmakers to accurately portray biblical dramas on television and in movies. From the archaeological "photo album" let's consider three famous "prints" that have offered us a rare glimpse into the unseen past.

The Beni-Hasan Mural—Picture Parade from the Time of the Patriarchs

Throughout the biblical period the Israelites continued political and economic contact with Egypt, one of the superpowers of that time. Israel's contact with Egypt spans the early period from the Patriarchs (Genesis 12,37–50) to Moses (book of Exodus), and the monarchy from King Solomon (1 Kings 9:16) to King Josiah (2 Kings 23:29-35) to the time of Jesus (Matthew 2:13-15). Since Jewish law (Exodus 20:4) forbids the making of human images (because man is created in the image of God), we should not expect any pictures made by the Israelis. However, on the Egyptian side, where the making of images was mandated, plenty of portraits have been discovered.

One famous example came from a small village known as Beni-Hasan, located south of Cairo on the east bank of the Nile. There, carved into the surrounding cliffs, is a large necropolis (city of the dead). As was often the custom inside Egyptian tombs, the walls were decorated in vivid colors with scenes depicting daily life. In one of these tombs, dating from about 1890 B.C., archaeologists found a splendid mural 8 feet long by 1fi feet high depicting a parade of foreigners: eight men, four

12. *The Beni-Hasan Mural, which pictures a group of people from Canaan entering Egypt, similar to the biblical Patriarchs.*

women, three children, and assorted animals, all being led by Egyptian officials. The hieroglyphic text at the top of the painting gave a description of the procession and its purpose. The text stated that these people were part of a group of 37 Asiatics from the region of Shut (which includes the area of Sinai and southern Canaan). They were being led by their chief, named Abishai, to trade with the Egyptians. Details such as physical features, hairstyles, clothing, shoes, weapons, and musical instruments are all clearly shown.

While it is still not known exactly who these people were or even why they were caravaning so far from the normal trade centers, the importance of the painting lies in its visual depiction of what people looked like in the time of the patriarchs. When we look at these images we can imagine Abram and Sarai's trip to Egypt (Genesis 12:10), and later, Jacob and his sons' journey to Egypt (Genesis 42:5; 43:11; 46:5-7). Some people have even suggested that the colorful patterns on the tunics of the Asiatics

13. *The Black Obelisk of Shalmaneser III, discovered in 1845.*

in the mural are like Joseph's "coat of many colors" *(see* Genesis
37:3). Even if, as other scholars have thought, a better translation
is "a robe with long sleeves," an example of this kind of garment
is also attested elsewhere in the archaeological "photo album."[2]

The Black Obelisk of Shalmaneser III—
Portrait of an Israelite King

One of the most exciting discoveries ever made in biblical
archaeology was of a large black stone extracted from a pit dug
at the ancient Assyrian city of Calah (modern Nimrud) in 1945.
This stone, however, almost wasn't unearthed. The British
archaeologist Henry Layard had been told by his workmen to
give up searching and close down the dig. It was winter, the
ground was extremely cold and hard, and the difficult job of
digging trenches to uncover artifacts had proved futile. Layard
didn't want to quit, but compromised and asked the men to work
for just one more day. They didn't have to wait that long!
Almost as soon as the men resumed their work they struck a
huge stone that we now know as one of the most important
Assyrian documents relating to the Old Testament.

The stone was a four-sided polished block (obelisk) of black
limestone 6fi feet high. On each side panel of the obelisk were
carved five registers of relief sculptures depicting various scenes of
tribute brought to the Assyrian court. In addition, above and below
the panels on all sides were almost 200 lines of cuneiform text.
Once the cuneiform text was translated it was found that they cata-
logued 31 military campaigns by the Assyrian monarch Shalmaneser III. The detailed relief sculptures of tribute and
tribute-bearers beautifully picture many different styles of clothing,
costly articles, and even exotic animals for the Assyrian zoo. However, the big surprise came when the lines above one register
showing a figure kneeling before the Assyrian king were translated:

> Tribute of Jehu, son of Omri.[3] Silver, gold, a golden
> bowl, a golden beaker, golden goblets, pitchers of gold,
> tin, staves for the hand of the king [and] javelins,
> [Shalmaneser] received from him.

14. *Israelite King Jehu (on left side) as depicted on the Black Obelisk of Shalmaneser III.*

Here, for the first time on any archaeological artifact, was a portrait of one of the kings of Israel![4] According to the Bible (2 Kings 9-10; 2 Chronicles 22:7-9), Jehu, a commander in King Joram's army, was "appointed by the Lord" to succeed to the Israelite throne. Instructed by the prophet Elisha to kill Joram, he became the ruler of Israel from 841–814 B.C. He served as God's final instrument of judgment against the house of the wicked King Ahab (including the infamous Queen Jezebel), and eradicated the idolatrous worship of Baal from the Land.

In the biblical account, however, there is no mention of King Jehu paying tribute to Assyria as depicted on the obelisk. The Bible does tell us that Jehu, toward the end of his 28-year reign, lapsed in his kingly responsibility to maintain the law of God (2 Kings 10:31) and instead followed again the henotheistic worship instituted by Jeroboam *(see* 1 Kings 12:28-29). Because of this the Lord removed Israel's protection and foreign enemies began to invade and conquer parts of the Land (2 Kings 10:32-33). Israel's weakness at this point may have influenced

Jehu to seek protection from Assyria. Once Assyrian hegemony was imposed, Israel would have been liable to pay tribute (cf. 2 Kings 17:3). If this was the case, the obelisk fills in a missing part of history not included in the biblical text.

The Siege of Lachish Reliefs—Panorama of Israel's Judgment

Finding the picture of an Israelite king mentioned in the Bible was indeed a surprise, but finding pictures of *hundreds* of Israelites in an ancient photo of an actual biblical event was no less than stunning! The "photo" was of Lachish, one of the most important Israelite cities in Judah during the biblical period. Lachish today is an excavated tel located about 25 miles southwest of Jerusalem. Though now silent and desolate, the ancient snapshot shows a very different picture. It not only depicts Lachish at the height of its glory, occupied and strongly fortified, but also vividly records what happened on the fateful day of its demise.

The "photo" itself did not come from Israel but from the far-off land of Assyria. It originated as a 90-foot-long mural decorating a ceremonial suite in the palace of the Assyrian king Sennacherib at Nineveh. The palace was excavated by Henry Layard, and the mural, made of panels of relief sculptures, is today housed in the British Museum. On the reliefs are accurate and realistic depictions of the battle between the Assyrians and the people of Lachish, which occurred during the Assyrian conquest of Judah in 701 B.C. *(see* 2 Kings 17:5-6; 2 Chronicles 32:1). The scene shows (from left to right) the Assyrian camp, their siege and conquest of the city with Assyrian troops storming the walls, the torture of some of the city's inhabitants, and finally the exile of the prisoners and their presentation before Sennacherib, who was seated on this throne in front of his camp. The Bible records this very event in the book of 2 Chronicles: "After this Sennacherib king of Assyria sent his

15. *Close-up of Assyrian siege as depicted on the 90-foot Lachish Reliefs. Note the siege ramp and battering ram.*

servants to Jerusalem while he was besieging Lachish with all his forces with him" (2 Chronicles 32:9, *see also* 2 Kings 18:13-14,17; 19:8; Isaiah 36:1-2; 37:8). While neither the Bible nor any Assyrian annals provide the details of this conquest, both do describe the brutality of the Assyrians and the horrible conditions of a siege—which we see pictured on the reliefs.

Excavations at Lachish have also confirmed the accuracy of various details found on the reliefs. From the charred layers of destruction at this site the fortifications of the city have been revealed—exactly as shown on the Assyrian reliefs.[5] The siege ramp pictured on the relief, up which the Assyrian soldiers took their battering rams and archers, has also been uncovered at Lachish. In addition, sling stones and arrowheads, unearthed in abundance, testify to the ferocity of the battle, just as shown in the reliefs. Once again, archaeology has made it possible to actually view one of the great historical events mentioned in the Bible.

Digs That Changed History

Many people today believe that by now, our knowledge of history is generally complete. They accept that some details are still missing, but they assume we know almost all there is to know about the great civilizations that ruled the past. The impressive coverage we see in history textbooks and on The History Channel seems to confirm this. Yet historians will admit that our present knowledge of the past is sorely limited. What we do know has come with major gaps and often with unanticipated revisions. This has also been true with respect to the history of the Bible. Even though Scripture presents historical information, that information is selective and incomplete. This fits with the theological purpose of the Bible, for it was not written to be a textbook of history. For this reason, historians have sometimes doubted certain historical facts in the Bible. This is not only because they suspect a religious view of history has altered the facts, but because some historical details in the Bible have no material evidence to support them.

However, archaeological surprises have now and then revealed historical peoples and places known in the Bible though unknown in any other source. Such discoveries not only give us a new perspective on what was already known, but also serve to affirm the historical integrity of the biblical narratives. Sometimes, too, excavations surface new facts, never known before, which shed light on both the Bible and ancient history. There are two archaeological digs that have done just that, expanding our appreciation for the accuracy of the Bible while forcing historians to rewrite chapters in their textbooks. These digs confirmed the former existence of the Hittites and the empire of Ebla.

The Hittites—Proof of a People of the Past

The Bible makes mention 47 times of a people called "the Hittites." They were listed among the nations inhabiting ancient Canaan when Abraham entered the land (Genesis 15:20). They were considered significant enough to have purchased chariots and horses from King Solomon (1 King 10:29). And they maintained such a powerful army that the king of Israel hired them to fight and put to flight the formidable army of the Arameans (2 Kings 7:6-7). Two Hittites particularly gained notoriety in the biblical account. One was Ephron the Hittite, who sold to Abraham his field and its cave of Mechpelah in Kiriath-arba (Hebron) to bury his wife Sarah (Genesis 23:10-20). It has since been known as the Tomb of the Patriarchs. The other was Uriah the Hittite, a soldier in King David's army. Though a foreigner, Uriah is portrayed in Scripture as a loyal servant in contrast to Israel's own son, King David. The book of 2 Samuel tells how David had an adulterous affair with Uriah's wife Bathsheba. The king's sin was compounded when Bathsheba was found to be pregnant and he had Uriah put to death to cover-up his crime (2 Samuel 11). And later, when the prophet Ezekiel denounced sinful Jerusalem, God declared that Jerusalem's moral mother was a Hittite (Ezekiel 16:3).

Yet despite the prominence of the Hittites in the biblical text, just over 100 years ago critical scholars doubted they ever existed. At that time no historical evidence of such a people had ever been found. They were simply part of the religious history of the Bible. However, this historical verdict was about to change. In 1876, the British scholar A.H. Sayce suspected that an undeciphered script discovered carved on rocks in Turkey and Syria might be evidence of the heretofore unknown Hittites. Then clay tablets were discovered from the ruins of an ancient city in Turkey called Boghaz-Köy. The locals were selling these tablets, and some got into the hands of experts. This prompted a German cuneiform expert, Hugo Winckler, to go to the site and excavate. There he uncovered five temples, a fortified citadel, and many monumental sculptures. Also, in one burnt storeroom he found more than 10,000 clay tablets. Once they were finally deciphered it was announced to the world that the Hittites had been found! Boghaz-Köy had in fact been the ancient capital of the Hittite empire (known as Hattusha). Other surprises followed, such as the revelation that the Hittite language should be classed with the Indo-European languages (of which English is a part), and that the form of their law codes was very helpful in understanding those described in the Bible. The rediscovery of this lost people,[6] one of the most outstanding achievements in Near Eastern archaeology, now serves as a caution to those who doubt the historicity of particular biblical accounts. Just because archaeology has not produced corroborating evidence today does not mean it could not tomorrow. The Hittites are just one example in which the Bible has been shown to be historically reliable. Thus it should be respected despite the present lack of material support for certain events or the chronological problems that remain unresolved.

Ebla—A Lost Civilization Discovered

Prior to 1968, scholars had known from their study of ancient Mesopotamian texts that there had once been an ancient Syrian empire called Ebla. The early Babylonian kings had claimed to have conquered this vast kingdom around 2300 B.C., but no one knew where it had been located. Then one day in 1968 an inscription was found at a prominent tel in Syria

16. *Piles of clay tablets, which once comprised the royal archives of the Eblaite empire.*

known as Tel Mardikh; this inscription appeared to identify the site as Ebla. But the greater discovery was yet to come. In 1975, as archaeologists were excavating underneath the city's temple, they found a small room that had served as a royal archive. There, some 17,000 clay tablets lay in piles! The shelves that had once held them had long ago been destroyed in a fire, but this same fire had also baked the clay tablets, hardening and preserving them against the ravages of time. These tablets confirmed the name of the place as Ebla and had introduced scholars to the empire's previously unknown language—Eblaite.

Decipherment of some of these texts revealed that Ebla had been a flourishing empire 4,500 years ago, centuries before the time of the biblical Patriarchs. Its citizens had traded for ages with Mari, another ancient Syrian city that had laws and customs that helped to clarify similar ones associated with the biblical Patriarchs. The sheer volume of the tablets recovered at Ebla (four times greater than all the previous texts from this period put together), made the discovery immensely important to those involved in ancient Near Eastern studies. But how important were the tablets for biblical studies? Early on during the interpretation of these texts, political disputes between Syria and Israel may have forced a retraction of connections that one translator had made with Israelite history. Even so, it appears that many of the initial claims of similarity to biblical names, the appearance of names of biblical sites (such as Sodom and Gomorrah), and affinities to the Hebrew language were premature assessments. The real significance of Ebla, for the Bible, may be one of comparing the Eblaite text with Hebrew poetic style and learning the traditions and religious background of a people who may have influenced subsequent civilizations including ancient Israel. It was in just this way that the texts from Ugarit helped scholars to understand biblical poetry and answer questions about biblical Hebrew word meanings and grammar. Whatever the case, Ebla has written a new chapter in the history of the Near East during the third millennium B.C.[7]

Drawing Closer to the Past

Digs have made a difference! They have recovered the knowledge of long-lost civilizations and long-dead languages. They have revealed the images of the past, not just in outline, but in many cases the very form of those whose names occupy space in the sacred text. There are a great many more examples that could have been cited, but the selections we've reviewed are sufficient to reveal how significant a contribution archaeology has made in drawing each of us closer to that world which was home to our fathers in the faith.

In the next dozen chapters, we will journey into this world of the Patriarchs to the prophets to explore how new discoveries in archaeology continue to inform our faith today and enrich our understanding of the beginnings of Bible history.

PART II

New Discoveries
in Archæology

5

THE PATRIARCHS

Living Legends or Legendary Lives?

Archaeology has shed considerable light on the stories of the Patriarchs in Genesis, Abraham, Isaac, and Jacob. Not that any records of these men have ever been found outside the Bible, but the veil which previously hid their times has been lifted. As a result, we now know more about the type of people they were, where they came from, how they lived, what they believed, where and how they are to be fitted into the histories of the great nations of ancient times than the later Israelites themselves.[1]

—G. Ernest Wright

The only history known to the Israelites during their bondage in Egypt was that bequeathed to them by their ancestors, the Patriarchs ("fathers who rule"). It was a history of covenant and promise between God and their fathers, which gave the people of Israel hope even in the midst of oppression. For this reason when God acted to deliver his people from the

Egyptians, He chose to identify himself with the Patriarchs—as "The God of Abraham, the God of Issac, and the God of Jacob" (Exodus 3:6,15-16; 4:5; Luke 20:37-38). By this they were to have assurance of their deliverance, for God had made a covenant with the Patriarchs, which He had sworn to fulfill (Exodus 6:3-8). In fact, the act of circumcision, which is still performed on Jewish males today, testifies to the Jewish community's continued identification with the biblical Patriarchs who lived 4,000 years ago. The Patriarchs remain the essential pillar of Jewish self-definition, and the Patriarchal covenant remains the historical basis for Israel's right to their ancient Land.

Playing Down the Patriarchs

It may seem a strange act of self-denial, then, that many critical Jewish scholars join their Gentile colleagues in the belief that the biblical accounts of the Patriarchs are not historical.[2] I can well remember the first time I became aware of this. I had completed my studies at Dallas Theological Seminary and was a graduate student at the Hebrew University in Jerusalem. At Dallas Seminary the Patriarchal narratives were taught as true history, and I had presumed the same at this leading Israeli academic institution. However, on my first day in a course on the history of early Israel, the teacher, who was one of Israel's foremost historical archaeologists, stated with complete conviction: "Abraham never existed, but his cousins did!" The professor went on to explain that the biblical stories about Abraham, Isaac, and Jacob were simply campfire accounts that had been passed down through the centuries and had grown into legends (he used the word *saga).* He said the Patriarchs were only a backward projection created by nationalist Jews during the mid-first millennium (600–400 B.C.). These nationalists were seeking to create a glorified though nonhistorical past. In support of his view, he stated that the archaeological evidence did not support the existence of a Patriarchal period. Archaeology aside, I remember pointing out, in my youthful reserve, that such a view for Israelis, whose territorial claims rested in part on the Abrahamic Covenant, and today are a matter of international contention, was tantamount to sawing off the limb on which they were sitting. Today, in my more mature judgment, I would say that it would rather fell the whole tree *(see* Romans 4:13; 11:28-29)!

Incidentally, Christians should also share a concern over this view because, in the New Testament, Abraham is called "the father of us all" (Romans 4:16), and believers in Christ are said to be Abraham's "sons" and "offspring, heirs according to promise" (Galatians 3:7,29). Furthermore, the historicity of the Patriarchs is accepted by Jesus and the New Testament authors (Matthew 1:1-2; 3:9; 8:11; Luke 13:28; 16:22-30; 20:37-38; John 8:39-58; Acts 3:13,25; 7:16-17,32; Hebrews 2:16; 7:1-9; 1 Peter 3:6) and used as a witness by them of God's pledge to perform His word (Romans 4:1-25; Galatians 3:6-29; Hebrews 6:13; James 2:21-23). The heart of Hebrews chapter 11 lists a "hall of Old Testament heroes" who demonstrated the reality of living by faith. As Ronald Youngblood points out:

> To the credit of the patriarchs, the author of Hebrews devoted more than half of those twenty-nine verses— fifteen, to be exact—to detailing the ways in which the patriarchs and their wives proved themselves to be men and women of faith.... [3]

Therefore, without the Patriarchs, whose faithfulness laid the foundation for our faith, neither Jews nor Gentiles have a promise! How can the prominence of the Patriarchs in Scripture—especially of Abraham as a central figure in both the Old and New Testaments—be dismissed as nothing more than a tradition? Does the archaeological record support or silence the hope of millions of faithful believers whose present faith and future blessings are based on a convenant with the fathers? Let's consider the archaeological evidence and decide for ourselves.

Verifying the Patriarchs

The old Albright school's conservative approach to the historicity of the Patriarchal narratives was no doubt initiated by the surprising archaeological verification of the Hittite empire. Now recognized as the third great Near Eastern empire of ancient history, scholars could not help but notice that references to the Hittites, the sons of Heth (Genesis 10:15), were abundantly sprinkled throughout the Patriarchal accounts (Genesis 11:27–50:26). For similar reasons, a modern reassessment of the archaeological evidence for the Patriarchs has returned some scholars to a more conservative view of the historicity of the Genesis accounts (Genesis 12–36). Why is this happening? Professor Nahum Sarna recently made this observation:

> As a whole, the Patriarchal narratives possess a distinctive flavor unparalleled in the rest of the Bible. They reflect a pattern of living and several socio-legal institutions that are peculiar to the period but often attested in Near Eastern documents. . . . the antiquity of the Genesis traditions is confirmed by several Patriarchal practices that directly contradict the social mores and norms of a later age. . . . [4]

The biblical account of the Patriarchs (including Joseph) in Genesis 12–50 indicates a Middle Bronze period date from the late third millennium to the mid-second millennium B.C. (2166–1805). Archaeological evidence for this period has emerged in the form of the Code of Hammurabi, Egyptian and Hittite texts, and thousands of clay tablets from the Amorite city of Mari (Tel Hariri), the Horite city of Nuzi, and the cities of Leilan and Alalakh. To these we can add the fabulous finds at the Syrian site of Ebla (Tel Mardikh), which though still controversial, have offered some comparative material. This evidence includes law codes, legal and social contracts, and religious and commercial texts.

A generation ago, the case that these artifacts made for the antiquity and historicity of the Patriarchs was accepted more

than it is today. In recent times, minimalist scholars have challenged these conclusions.[5] Their efforts, however, rather than
being destructive to the maximalist position, have aided it by
removing elements inconsistent with or unnecessary to the biblical portrayal of the Patriarchs.[6] In particular, Thompson's minimalist critical analysis of alleged parallels between the Nuzi
tablets and Patriarchal social customs have helped improve the
usage of these texts for a more accurate maximalist reconstruction of the Patriarchal age. Even so, the correction of parallels,
based on the Nuzi material, have proven to be far fewer than
Thompson originally proposed.[7] While there remains less
archaeological evidence for this time period than perhaps any
other, careful comparisons of the biblical accounts with the
available data have offered the following arguments in support
of Patriarchal historicity.

The World of the Patriarchs

The texts of numerous contracts from the ancient Near East
reveal that the social background portrayed in the Patriarchal
narratives is accurate and fits the time suggested by the biblical
chronology. One point of comparison between these texts and
the Bible involves the laws governing inheritances. In Genesis
49, Jacob blesses his 12 sons, apportioning to each son an *equal*
share of the inheritance. This, however, was changed at Sinai,
for the Mosaic Law stipulated that the firstborn son should
receive a *double* inheritance (Deuteronomy 21:15-17). This
apparent contradiction was formerly explained by the higher
critics according to Wellhausen's documentary hypothesis,
which held that different writers had composed conflicting
accounts of the Pentateuch at the same time late in Israel's post-
exilic history. But the extrabiblical texts from the ancient Near
East confirm that though this material may have been edited into
a final form at a later period, its original composition could have
taken place during the time of Moses.[8] In the case of the Patriarchal blessing in Genesis 49, an equal share in inheritance laws
is evident in the laws of Lipit-Ishtar (twentieth century B.C.).

However, 200 years later in Hammurabi's Code (eighteenth century B.C.), a distinction is made between the sons of a man's first wife—who get first choice—and the sons of his second wife. Then when we compare the texts from Mari and Nuzi (eighteenth-fifteenth centuries B.C.) we find that a natural firstborn son received a double share while an adopted son did not. First-millenium Neo-Babylonian laws reflect a similar progression, with the sons of a first wife getting a double portion and secondary sons only a single portion.

British Egyptologist Kenneth Kitchen suggests a number of other social comparisons from the archaeological record that offer correlation with a second-millennium date.[9] His list includes the price of slaves in silver shekels (as with Joseph, Genesis 37:28), the specific form of treaties and covenants (Genesis chapters 21, 26, 31), geopolitical conditions (Genesis 14), and references to Egypt (Genesis chapters 12, 45–47). Additional examples proposed by scholars have included the domestication of camels (Genesis 12:16), which has been attested in texts even earlier than the Patriarchs,[10] the adoption of sons through surrogates (Genesis 16:2-3; 30:1-3), attested to in Old Assyrian marriage contracts (nineteenth century B.C.),[11] and in Hammurabi's Code and at Nuzi, from Mesopotamian law guaranteeing the inheritance rights of an adopted son (such as with Eliezer in Genesis 15:2-4).[12] In each of these texts, the archaeological data seems to accord exactly with our information of conditions at the time. Therefore, according to the changing social customs reflected by these laws, only a second millennium context will fit the type of inheritance practice by the Patriarchs.[13]

The Names of the Patriarchs

One way of determining the chronological setting of historical characters is by considering their names. Names tend to reflect a unique cultural setting in time. Consider for a moment your grandparents' and parents' names. My grandmothers were named Tabitha and Jesse, and my grandfathers Peyton and

Ernest. My mother's name is Maurine and my father's name was Elmo. Because such names are time-bound they are rarely passed on (except as initials) to the next generation. Today in American culture it is more common to find a Brandon, Sabrina, or Meagan. The main exceptions are timeless names drawn from great persons of the past, most often biblical figures. For this reason we will always have Davids, Marys, Johns, and Pauls.

Let's begin by considering the names of Abram's closest relatives, such as his great-grandfather Serug, his grandfather Nahor, and his father Terah (and even Abram's own name). Researchers have confirmed that these names appear in Old Assyrian and Babylonian texts and that typographical references in Neo-Assyrian texts correspond with places in the Euphrates-Habur region of Syro-Mesopotamia. This geographical linkage with Abram and his lineage agree with the biblical accounts that his family came from Ur and settled in Haran (Genesis 11:28,31). In addition, if we try to place the names of the Patriarchs in a cultural setting, we find that they are most prominent with the Northwest Semitic language group of the Amorite population of the early second millennium B.C. (such as at Mari), and third millennium examples have also been attested at Ebla. Names with an *i/y-* prefix, such as *Yitzchak* ("Issac"), *Ya'akov* ("Jacob"), *Yoseph* ("Joseph"), and *Yishmael* ("Ishmael"), belong to this type of name, and the frequency of their appearance diminishes significantly in the first millennium and onward.[14] Thus the time during which men with these names would have lived would have been the pre-Israelite period—a fact that is in accord with the biblical text.

The Places of the Patriarchs

The places mentioned in the Patriarchal narratives also reveal a historical consistency when compared to the archaeological evidence from the ruins of Ur, Hebron, Beersheba, and Shechem. In particular, the city of Haran in upper Mesopotamia, which in the biblical text seems to have been a commercial center during the time of Abraham, was abandoned after the

17. *Excavation site at the 4,000-year-old Gate of Laish at Tel Dan.*

Patriarchal period and remained unoccupied from about 1800 B.C. to 800 B.C. Noting this point, Barry Beitzel, an archaeologist at Trinity Evangelical Divinity School, observes, "It's highly improbable [that someone inventing the story later] would have chosen Haran as a key location when the town hadn't existed for hundreds of years."

Did Abraham Pass Through This Gate?

The Israelite site of Tel Dan in the Golan Heights preserves the name of the ancient city of Dan, which many Bible readers recall from the geographical description in the Bible "From Dan to Beersheba." According to some Egyptian execration texts, Dan's earlier name was Laish (*see* also Judges 18:7,14).[15] This would have been the name of the city in the time of the Patriarchs. The archaeological excavations at this site have revealed a very large Canaanite city with a highly developed material culture, rich tombs, and massive fortifications of sloping ramparts. The great surprise in the excavation was to find in the midst of the ramparts a 4,000-year-old mud-brick gate built with an arch (an architectural achievement thought to have been invented by the Romans 2,000 years later!). Even more incredible is the fact that this mud-brick gate still stands today exactly as it was originally built, complete with all its courses to the very top.[16] This gate served as the main gate to Laish, and would have been used by all who visited the city. According to the gate's excavator, Avraham Biran, this may very well have included the Patriarchs:

> Abraham in the book of Genesis proceeded to defeat the kings of the north who took his nephew Lot prisoner, and the text says in Genesis 14 that, "Abraham came as far as Dan." Now, of course in those days the name of the city was Laish and not Dan. I imagine that the Biblical copyist who found the name Laish, said "who remembers Laish anymore, its been gone, forgotten," so he wrote Dan instead. But to my way of thinking, Abraham, no doubt, was invited to visit the city of Laish and for all I know had gone through the gate before it was blocked.[17]

18. *Reconstruction of the city gate of Laish as it appeared at the time of Abraham.*

Such a place as the gate of Laish provides confirmation that, as the biblical record states, there was indeed a city at Dan in the time of Abraham, thereby adding credibility to the Patriarchal narrative.

Proof for the Patriarchs at Fort Abram

Another place from the Israelite period has been proposed as incidental evidence for confirming the existence of the Patriarchs. Built in the Negev by David or Solomon in the early tenth century B.C. as part of a line of defenses against the Egyptians, the name of the place is listed in a hieroglyphic text on a wall relief in the Temple of Amun at Karnak (Luxor, Egypt). The name of this place is "The Fort of Abram" or "Fortified Town of Abram." Yohanan Aharoni believed that Fort Abram was the term used by the Egyptians for the Israelite city of Beersheba. That's because in the Egyptian list of cities in the Negev, Beersheba is not mentioned, yet it was a prominent site during that time. The most likely explanation for this is that the new defensive site at Beersheba had been given the name of Abram because he was the original founder of the city (Genesis 21:22-23). As Roland Hendel explains, "When a government builds fortifications, it is natural to name them for illustrious local or national heroes. Abram of biblical fame surely fits the bill."[18]

The Climate of the Patriarchs

Through the ages, changes in global and regional climate cycles have affected the movement of human populations. In Genesis we read of the Patriarchs moving from place to place because of regional disasters or famines. Today, the modern climate of the Near East is much drier and arid than it was in earlier periods of its history. Because current conditions do not reflect the ancient, when archaeologists want to correctly appraise the Patriarchal accounts of climatic conditions, they must compare the ancient documentary record of climate changes with the evidence revealed in excavations, core and pollen samples, and radiocarbon calibration.

According to archaeologist James Sauer, who has done extensive excavations and climateological surveys in Jordan and Syria, the material evidence accords with historical records to substantiate the biblical traditions of the Middle Bronze period.[19] He has found that during the time of the third millennium B.C. the entire region would have been much wetter. This would have made the Jordan Valley, especially around the present area of the Dead Sea (where the Patriarchal narratives place the Cities of the Plain), a fertile region—just as the Bible describes. Furthermore, the evidence for the arid cycles during this period correlate well with the famines documented in the archaeological records from Egypt, Canaan, and the surrounding regions. These, in turn, verify the settlement patterns of the Patriarchs, who sought relief from such conditions. This evidence led Sauer to agree with Albright's earlier conclusions concerning the antiquity of the Patriarchs and to suggest:

Since the memories of climatic change and of early geography seem so accurate, it would even be suggested that some of these traditions may not have been written down for the first time in the tenth century B.C.E. but were in fact written down much earlier.[20]

The Witness of Genesis Chapter 14

Yet another corroboration of the historicity and antiquity of the Patriarchal narratives is found in the account of an invasion of lower Canaan by a coalition of Mesopotamian kings *(see* Genesis 14). In the ensuing battle Abraham's nephew Lot, who was living in Sodom, was captured and carried away along with his household (Genesis 14:12). Abraham entered the fray and rescued his relative and after the victory met with Melchizedek, the priest of Salem (verses 18-24). So distinct is this account that the higher critics have been forced to either call it a fabrication or assign it to an isolated source (apart from the Higher Critical's school's alleged documentary sources used in the composition of the book of Genesis and based on the text's use of different names for God and supposedly priestly influence referred to as J=Jawehist, E=Elohist, and P=Priestly School). What makes this chapter so impressive is its detailed and precise listing of names and places (both foreign and local), often parenthetically explained by more contemporary names, such as "the valley of Siddim" for "the Salt Sea" (Dead Sea—verse 3), or "the valley of Shaveh" for "the King's Valley" (the lower Kidron Valley—verse 17). Such literary clarifications are among the traits that indicate this chapter has the mark of antiquity.

Despite the fact that the kings named in Genesis 14 have yet to appear in extrabiblical cuneiform accounts, we do know that the right names are connected with the right places. We know this because while the specific personages are not mentioned outside the Genesis narrative, such names do appear in various Mesopotamian texts of this period. To demonstrate this, let us consider the names of the four Eastern kings given in Genesis 14:1.

"Amraphel king of Shinar" is thought to be a typical West Semitic name from Lower Mesopotamia, found in both Akkadian and Amorite sources, and possibly connected with the Amorite name *Amud-pa-ila.*[21] "Shinar," in Egyptian texts, is used for Babylonia.[22] "Arioch king of Ellasar" appears as the *Arriyuk(ki)/Arriwuk(ki)* in texts from Mari (Amorite) and Nuzi (Hurrian).[23] At Mari this was the name of the fifth son of Zimri-Lim, Mari's king.[24] "Chedolaomer, king of Elam" is clearly an Elamite name, based on familiar Elamite terms: *kudur* ("servant") and *Lagamar,* a principal goddess in the Elamite pantheon.[25] It fits the type of Elamite royal names known as a *Kutur* type, and is known from at least three royal examples.[26] "Tidal king of Goiim" is well attested as an early form of the Hittite name *Tudkhalia,* which was the name of at least five Hittite rulers.[27] One is said to have served as a "king of peoples/groups," which reflects the political fragmentation that existed in the Hittite empire in Anatolia (Turkey) during the nineteenth and eighteenth centuries B.C. and permitted the kind of alliance pictured in Genesis 14.[28]

The political conditions depicted by the alliance in Genesis 14 and that of the Transjordanian coalition of kings in the Dead Sea basin were possible in only one period of history—the early second millennium B.C. Only at this time does the archaeological record reveal that the Elamites were aggressively involved in the affairs of the region (the Levant), and only in this period were Mesopotamian alliances so unstable as to permit such a confederation.[29] The term *"Goyim"* is a Hebrew translation of the Akkadian word *Umman,* a term used to characterize various peoples who came as invaders.[30] Thus, this king was most likely a vagabond ruler who assimilated various tribes and provinces into his army. Given this understanding and the shifting political situation, it is logical that an Elamite king would head a coalition of Mesopotamian city-states and launch a punitive raid on rebel Canaanite kings. After this time period, and especially during the first millennium B.C., the political map became completely incompatible with the conditions necessary for such formation.

To these time-bound indicators of historicity we may add 1) the accuracy of the invasion route taken by the Eastern kings, 2) the use of a Hebrew term for "trained men" in verse 14, which is attested outside this passage only in a nineteenth-century B.C. Egyptian text and a fifteenth-century B.C. letter from Ta'anak, and 3) the description of Melchizedek, which accurately depicts a second-millennium setting.[31] These details in Genesis 14, attested in extrabiblical documents of the time, could not have been invented and correctly assigned to their respective nations and geographical settings by a Hebrew writer living at a later time. Thus, the antiquity of this account, within the larger context of the Patriarchal narratives, indicates that there is substantial reason to regard the whole as historically accurate.

The Tombs of the Patriarchs

In the case of the Patriarchs of Israel, archaeology has preserved for us not merely their memories but also their memorials.

19. *Tomb of the Patriarchs at Hebron, over the Cave of Machpelah.*

We often say in a figurative way that people "bury their memories," but normally that phrase is not used in a literal sense. They do not often do so literally. However, when we come to the Patriarchs (and Matriarchs), the places of their burials are still with us today. What tales do these tombs tell?

The Burial Place of the Patriarchs

One of the best known and most controversial sites in the Land of Israel is the Tomb of the Patriarchs in the city of Hebron. The conflict that engulfs this town today between Jew and Arab over access to this sacred site is an ages-old testimony to the presence of the Patriarchs, from which both groups claim descent. In the Bible we read that after the death of Abraham's wife Sarah in Kiriath-arba (Hebron), Abraham bought from Ephron the Hittite a burial cave at Machpelah for his family (Genesis 23:17-20).[32] The Bible records that in the tombs at this cave were buried Abraham and Sarah, Isaac and his wife Rebecca, and Jacob and his wife Leah. Undoubtedly its character as the place of the Patriarchs made it God's choice for the country's capital under David (2 Samuel 2:1-4; 5:3-5). Standing over the area of the cave today is an archaeological wonder—a still-intact monumental building more than 2,000 years old. This building, which was built to commemorate and preserve the ancient burial site, is dated by most scholars to the time of Herod the Great. Other scholars, however, believe that the original construction is much older.

No one in recent history has explored inside the cave,[33] but there is evidence of the presence of several Middle Bronze Age I shaft tombs beneath the building. The only entrance into the cave during modern times was shortly after Israel regained access to the site during the Six-Day War of June 1967. The late Moshe Dayan had a very thin Israeli girl named Michael let down through the only available entrance to the cave, an 11-inch air shaft located within the upper level of the building.[34] While feeling her way along in complete darkness, she measured and photographed a long corridor (57 feet) and 16 steps leading to a large lower chamber. Other than the presence of several large stone slabs, which may be tombstones (one was inscribed in Arabic with words from the Koran), nothing beyond this point could be examined. Visitors to the Tomb of the Patriarchs today can enter only the upper level of the building, where centotaphs (commemorative tombs) of the Patriarchs and Matriarchs can be seen.

The Burial Place of Rachel

According to the Bible, two members of Abraham's family were not included in the family burial cave—Jacob's favorite wife, Rachel, and his esteemed son, Joseph. Joseph was buried in Shechem (modern-day Nablus), but the site of his grave is uncertain. Rachel, who died on the way to Bethlehem, was buried in this vicinity. A very late tradition places the site of her tomb where it is today along the Hebron road at the entrance to Bethlehem, but it doubtful that this is the actual place of burial based on a careful geographical comparison of the biblical descriptions in the books of Genesis, 1 Samuel, and Jeremiah. The Genesis account says that Rachel was buried on the road to "Ephrath (that is, Bethlehem)" (Genesis 48:7). Bethlehem today is located south of Jerusalem in the territory allotted to the tribe of Judah. However, Jeremiah, alluding to Rachel's death, says that it is "in [or near] Ramah" (Jeremiah 31:15), an area north of Jerusalem (modern-day A-Ram) in the tribal allotment of Benjamin. This placement close to Ramah or to Gibeah (just east of Ramah) seems supported by the statement in Samuel that "Rachel's tomb" was "in the territory of Benjamin at Zelzah" (1 Samuel 10:2). The original site of Ephrath has been identified with an ancient town built near the spring of Ein Prat, where the road from Bethel to the spring first passes between Ramah and Gibeah. Only a short walk from this site are located five huge stone structures that, from ancient times, the Arabs have

20. *Author with Megalithic structures called "The Graves of the Children of Israel" at Ephrah, identified with Rachel's Tomb.*

called *Kub'r B'nai Yisrael* ("the Graves of the Children of Israel"). The origin of these rectangular structures remains a mystery; they have tentatively been suggested to date from the megalithic era (2000–1500 B.C.), a time frame that includes the Patriarchs.[35] During the last century Clermont-Ganneau identified the site as that of Rachel's Tomb.[36] Further arguments in favor of the site was made recently by Israeli topographer and naturalist Nogah Hareuveni.[37]

So, while we may have only circumstantial evidence for the existence of the Patriarchs—based on the ancient Near Eastern documents that reflect their customs and practices—we can also add to this the witness of their tombs from antiquity.

Yet Another Challenge

We may conclude that, based on archaeology, we have a good case for drawing a reliable historical outline for the Patriarchs. Documentary parallels, places mentioned in the biblical account, the accuracy of historical details, and the continued

Proposed Dating for the Patriarchs

EARLY DATE 1 — LATE 3RD, EARLY 2ND MILLENNIUM B.C.

BIBLICAL PERSON / EVENT	PERIOD	DATE(S)	PROPONENTS	STANDARD	FIRST WRITTEN	EVIDENCE
Abraham Entrance into Canaan (Genesis 12:4)	Middle Bronze I / Middle Bronze I	2166–1991 / 2091	Archer Barker Waltke J. Davis (Fundamentalist/ Evangelical schools)	Internal Biblical Chronology	Moses	Antiquity of Accounts (Genesis 14) Nomadism-migration Personal names, places Excavations at Ur, Ebla Amorites (20th–18th centuries B.C.) Geopolitical conditions (MB IIA) Climate of region in MB I
Isaac Offered on Mt. Moriah (Genesis 22)	Middle Bronze I / Middle Bronze I	2066–1886 / 2051				
Jacob Entrance into Haran (Genesis 28:5)	Middle Bronze IA / Middle Bronze IA	2006–1859 / 1929				

EARLY DATE 2 — LATE 2ND MILLENNIUM B.C.

BIBLICAL PERSON / EVENT	PERIOD	DATE(S)	PROPONENTS	STANDARD	FIRST WRITTEN	EVIDENCE
Patriarchal Events	Middle Bronze IIA	2000–1800	Glueck Albright	Archaeology	Monarchy	Pottery in Negev Beni-Hasan mural (1890 B.C.)
Patriarchal Events	Middle Bronze IIA-B	1991–1786	Kitchen Milland	Egyptian Chronology	Moses	Egyptian backgrounds (Middle Kingdom) Geopolitical conditions (Genesis 14)
Patriarchal Events (remembered traditions)	Middle Bronze II B-C	1750–1550	A. Mazar	Archaeology	Court of David & Solomon	Mari/Nuzi archives Prosperous urban culture Hyksos Dynasty

LATE DATE — 1ST MILLENNIUM B.C.

BIBLICAL PERSON / EVENT	PERIOD	DATE(S)	PROPONENTS	STANDARD	FIRST WRITTEN	EVIDENCE
Patriarchal Events (remembered in monarchy)	Iron IA	1250–1150 (settlement period)	Aharoni Z. Herzog	Archaeology	United Monarchy	Excavations at Beersheeba (no MB) Anachronisms in Genesis accounts

EXTREME DATE — EXILIC-POST-MACCABEAN

BIBLICAL PERSON / EVENT	PERIOD	DATE(S)	PROPONENTS	STANDARD	FIRST WRITTEN	EVIDENCE
Patriarchal Traditions (created as religious history)	Persian/Greek	400–165	T.L. Thompson Van-Seters	Form Criticism Structural Analysis	Exilic/ Post-Exilic	Literary tradition/Oral tradition Use of folklore JEDP theory

existence of the tombs assigned to them from antiquity have helped to enlighten us about this era. However, one story from the Patriarchal period has been considered as so preposterous that critics have used it to color the form within this historical outline as fantasy. This is the story of the destruction of Sodom and Gomorrah and the Cities of the Plain (Genesis 18–19). Archaeology's answer to this challenge of historicity will be taken up in our next chapter, so read on!

6

SODOM AND GOMORRAH

Salty Story or Sinful Cities?

The Bible, unlike other religious literature of the world, is not centered in a series of moral, spiritual, and liturgical teachings, but in the story of a people who lived at a certain time and place.... Biblical faith is the knowledge of life's meaning in the light of what God did in a particular history. Thus the Bible cannot be understood unless the history it relates is taken seriously. Knowledge of biblical history is essential to the understanding of biblical faith.... If the nature of such periods is to be properly understood, and the biblical events fitted into their original context in ancient history as a whole, the original background to the biblical material must be recovered with the aid of archaeology.[1]

— G. Ernest Wright

The Bible records that in the time of Abraham, a pentapolis (a group of five cities) stretched along a well-watered plain in the southern portion of the Jordan Valley (Genesis 13:10-11).

In one of the Bible's most memorable accounts, we read that a cataclysmic destruction overthrew two of these cities—Sodom and Gomorrah (Genesis 19:24-29). According to the Bible, so wicked were the inhabitants (Genesis 18:20; 19:1-13) that a supernatural conflagration of "fire and brimstone" was sent by God in judgment. As a result, the cities' reputation as "sin cities" became a byword in the Bible; the prophets and Jesus often using the phrase "like Sodom and Gomorrah" in warnings of divine punishment. The infamy of these cities persists even through today as preserved in our English word *sodomy*.

Skepticism of the Scholars

For many Bible scholars and archaeologists the story of Sodom and Gomorrah is just that—a story. The most critical of Bible scholars, such as Theodor Gaster, called it a "purely mythical tale." To most critical scholars it is a "remarkable origin-story" created by late Israelite storytellers to communicate theological and social concerns, not to preserve the memory of historical places and events. Other scholars say there is a kernel of historicity within the larger substance of late literary tradition. It is not entirely fiction, but a "fragment of local recollection," taken over by the Israelites and embellished by imagination. Thus, the story incorporates a pre-Israelite, extrabiblical explanation from those in the region for its environmental degeneration and military disturbances.

Some scientific attempts to validate the historical event have been inconsistent in their treatment of the biblical and archaeological evidence. In one recent book[2] two geologists argue that a massive earthquake (more than 7.0 on the Richter scale) occurred along the strike-slip fault of the rift valley where the Dead Sea lies today. They conjecture that this earthquake, which ignited "light fractions of hydrocarbons escaping from underground reservoirs" (the "rain of fire and brimstone") destroyed Sodom, Gomorrah, and Jericho, and even stopped up the Jordan River for several days. These events are said to have all happened simultaneously around 2350 B.C.

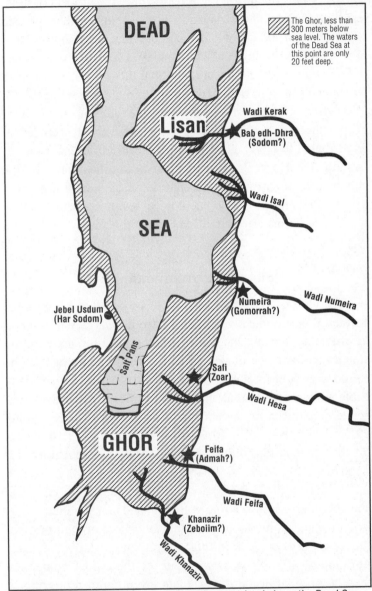

DEAD

The Ghor, less than 300 meters below sea level. The waters of the Dead Sea at this point are only 20 feet deep.

Lisan

Wadi Kerak

Bab edh-Dhra (Sodom?)

Wadi Isal

SEA

Wadi Numeira

Numeira (Gomorrah?)

Jebel Usdum (Har Sodom)

Salt Pans

Safi (Zoar)

Wadi Hesa

GHOR

Feifa (Admah?)

Wadi Feifa

Khanazir (Zeboiim?)

Wadi Khanazir

The Five Cities of the Plain, all at about the same level above the Dead Sea, and each one located beside a stream.

With this conclusion lumping together the biblical destinations of Sodom and Gomorrah and that of Jericho (which occurred over 900 years later), it is obvious that these authors' high regard for geology and climatology is not likewise extended to Scripture. Rather, they contend that these biblical accounts were the result of primitive recollections of these geological disasters, which were misremembered in the religious traditions of people through the ages. Consequently, these events were naïvely attributed to God and misconnected with different stories in Israelite historiography. Despite their "scientific approach," the authors offer no historical or archaeological evidence to support their theory, and, as one archaeological reviewer observed, they made "numerous errors in discussing archaeological sites and theories."[3]

Statements from Antiquity

The writers who penned the Bible, by contrast, believed the account was genuine history. They cited it as a reference of historical value, for of what worth would a fable be in seeking to convict an audience of the certainty of God's judgment? The mention of Sodom and Gomorrah's destruction by so many Bible authors to different audiences testifies to the event's universal recognition in the ancient Near East (see Deuteronomy 29:23; 32:32; Isaiah 1:9-10; 3-9; 13:19; Jeremiah 23:14; 49:18; 50:40; Lamentations 4:6; Ezekiel 16:46-49, 53-56; Amos 4:11; Zephaniah 2:9; Matthew 10:15; 11:23-24; Luke 10:12; 17:29; 2 Peter 2:6; Jude 7; Revelation 11:8). In addition, nonbiblical ancient historians also wrote of Sodom and Gomorrah in a realistic manner.[4] Some even stated that evidences of their destruction could still be seen in their day (*see* especially Philo, *De Abrahamo* 140f).[5] That is why, despite the critics' contention that the original account was a late invention or a misapplied memory, there have been repeated efforts by some archaeologists to locate the historical cities of Sodom and Gomorrah.

The Search for Sodom and Gomorrah

The search for Sodom and Gomorrah has generally concentrated on the Dead Sea region, although some scholars have argued that because of supposed volcanic activity (the fire and brimstone) the site should be sought in Arabia[6] or Iraq.[7] However, the biblical text specifies "the Valley of Siddim (that is the Salt Sea)" (Genesis 14:3), a known name for the Dead Sea.

In 1924, the renowned archaeologist W.F. Albright and the Reverend M. Kyle led an expedition to investigate the southern end of the Dead Sea.[8] Albright believed that the cities were beneath the waters south of the Lisan peninsula. He did not have equipment that would enable him to confirm his theory. In 1960 Ralph Baney explored the sea floor in this region using sonar and diving equipment. He found trees standing in a growth position at a depth of 23 feet, proving Albright's theory that the water of the Dead Sea had risen and submerged ancient land areas, but he did not locate any trace of ancient structures that might have been the remains of cities.[9] As a result, many scholars who held to the existence of Sodom and Gomorrah

21. *West wall of Bab edh-Dhra, looking north (biblical Sodom?).*

concluded that either the destruction was so total that no trace could have survived, or that the remains were beyond all hope of recovery.[10] Still, most Bible scholars felt that Sodom and Gomorrah had been located at a trough beneath the present sea basin at the southern end of the Dead Sea, or at a site known as Jebel Usdum, a salt dome on the southwestern shore of the Dead Sea. However, these theories were based on speculation, not archeological or geological support.

In the course of his search, Albright also discovered structures on land on the *eastern* shore of Transjordan across from the Lisan peninsula. At one site known in Arabic as Bab edh-Dhra, he found the remains of a heavily fortified and settled community with walled buildings, an extensive open-air settlement, houses, numerous cemeteries, and scattered artifacts—all signs that a large population had once lived there. Outside the ruins to the east was a group of large collapsed stone blocks (monoliths), averaging 13 feet in length. Albright interpreted these as part of a cult installation for religious rites. He dated the town to the third millennium B.C. (Early Bronze Age, 3150–2200 B.C.), and he believed the site had also ceased to be occupied within that period. He felt that there was a connection between this site and the Cities of the Plain, but because he failed to find an extensive layer of occupational debris, he theorized it had served only as a sacred pilgrimage center that was visited annually.

The Excavation of Bab edh-Dhra

In 1965 and 1967, excavations at the site of Bab edh-Dhra were carried out by Paul Lapp under the auspices of the American Schools of Oriental Research. These were later continued by Walter Rast and Thomas Schaub beginning in 1973.[11] The excavations revealed that the fortification wall surrounding the city was some 23 feet thick! It was uniquely segmented and the last segment had a gateway flanked by twin towers. Within this walled area was an interior city of mud-brick houses along the northwest side and a Canaanite temple with a semicircular altar and numerous cultic objects. Outside the townsite they found an enormous cemetery with thousands of buried people. One tomb alone held about 250 individuals along with a wealth of grave goods. It was obvious that the town had been a prominent settlement in the Early Bronze Age.

But something else caught the attention of the excavators: the evidence of extensive destruction by fire. The townsite was covered by a layer of ash many feet in thickness. The cemetery also revealed ash deposits, charred posts and roof beams, and

22. *Author next to seven-foot-thick ash deposits at Bab edh-Dhra (Sodom?).*

bricks that had turned red from the intense heat. What caused this fire? There could be many reasons why an ancient city was destroyed by fire, but at the site of Bab edh-Dhra, the northern-most of the sites, we have some very interesting evidence that readily fits with the biblical account of Sodom and Gomorrah. Archaeologist Bryant Wood, who has specialized in the search for Sodom, explains:

> The evidence would suggest that this site of Bab edh-Dhra is the biblical city of Sodom. Near that site, about a kilometer or

23. *Burial remains from cemetery at Bab edh-Dhra (biblical Sodom?).*

so away, archaeologists found a vast cemetery indicating that at one time there was a very large population living here at this place. As they began to excavate the cemetery, they found that in the final phase, just at the time the city was destroyed, there was a particular type of burial that was practiced at that time.... the dead were buried in a building right on the surface—a structure that archaeologists referred to as a charnel house. Prior to that last phase, they dug deep tombs and buried their dead beneath the surface of the earth. But during that last phase, they buried their dead in these buildings made of mud bricks built right on the surface of the ground. Some of those structures were rectangular, some of them were round, but they all had one common feature and that was that they had been burned—from the inside out.

Now, at first the archaeologists who excavated these buildings thought that perhaps this was some sort of hygienic practice in antiquity, that every so often because of the bodies that were placed in there, they would need to burn the interior of the structure to sort of clean it out for health purposes. But as they investigated exactly how this burning took place, they had to change their opinion on this. In one particular instance when they were excavating one of these charnel houses, they cut what we call a balk through that building as they were digging so that they had a vertical cross section of that house and the destruction, and what they discovered was that the fire did not begin inside the building but rather the fire started on the roof of the building, then the roof burned through, collapsed into the interior and then the fire spread inside the building. And this was the case in every single charnel house that they excavated.

Now, this is something that is quite difficult to explain naturally. You could explain the burning by some accident that took place and the fire spread to the town. You might explain it by an earthquake coming and causing a fire to spread. You might explain it by a conqueror coming and taking the city and setting it on fire. But how do you explain the burning of these charnel houses in a cemetery located some distance from the town? Archaeologists really have no explanation for that, but the Bible gives us the answer. The Bible talks about God's destruction on these cities because of their sin and it speaks of God raining fire and brimstone down on these cities from heaven and there in the cemetery, we have evidence that that is exactly what happened. The roofs of these buildings caught fire, collapsed, and caused the interior of the building to be burned. In the city, we did not have this kind of evidence because there had been so much erosion. We have evidence of the burning from the ash, but no collapsed roofs were found there. So in the cemetery we have evidence that supports exactly the biblical account.[12]

The severe burning of Bab edh-Dhra implies the presence of a mechanism capable of igniting and burning so vast an area. Geologist Frederick Clapp, who surveyed the shallow southern end of the Dead Sea (know as the Ghor) in the late 1920s and mid-1930s, noted its abundant deposits of asphalt, petroleum, and natural gas.[13] This reminds us of the statement in Genesis 14:10 that the Valley of Siddim was full of bitumen (tar) pits. Furthermore, there are unusual salt formations and the smell of sulphur, which also remind us of the references in Genesis 19:24-26 to a "pillar of salt" and "brimstone" (sulphur). Clapp conjectured that if these combustible materials had been forced from the earth by subterranean pressure brought about by an earthquake (earthquakes are common in this area), they could have been ignited by lightning or some other agency as they spewed from the earth. This accords with the Bible's description of this disaster as "brimstone and fire . . . out of heaven" with smoke ascending "like the smoke of a furnace" (Genesis 19:24, 28). Because all these factors favored the southern Dead Sea location, further surveys of this region were undertaken in the hopes of finding additional support for a connection with the biblical cities of Sodom and Gomorrah.

A More Extensive Survey

According to the biblical account, five cities—identified as Sodom, Gomorrah, Admah, Zoar, and Zeboiim—dominated the region and were known as "the Cities of the Plain." Sodom and Gomorrah were the two most prominent cities in the pentapolis. If we allow for the possibility that Bab edh-Dhra was indeed Sodom, then it would seem that we would be able to find traces of the other cities in that same general area.

That, in fact, has been the case. Along the shoreline south of Bab edh-Dhra is the site of es-Safi, identified from Byzantine times with Zoar. Rast and Schaub's investigations discovered three additional sites, one between Bab edh-Dhra and es-Safi known as Numeira, and two south of es-Safi known as Feifa and Khanazir. After surveys and excavations were done at these sites, it was determined that all of the sites had been destroyed or abandoned at about the same time (at the end of the Early Bronze III period, about 2450–2350 B.C.). What's more, the same ash deposits that were found at Bab edh-Dhra were also found at these sites. In fact at Numeira, a heavily fortified city, one layer was over seven feet thick! Beneath the ash layer excavators found remains in almost perfect condition, especially in houses where walls had been sealed by the ash.

At every one of these sites, the ash deposits had caused the soil to have the consistency of spongy charcoal, making it unfeasible for people to resettle in them after the destruction. The account of the destruction of these Cities of the Plain records that four of these cities were destroyed, but one—Zoar—was spared at Lot's request (Genesis 19:19-23). However, it is also recorded that though Lot fled to Zoar he was afraid to live there, choosing rather to live in the caves in the mountains outside the city (Genesis 19:30). It seems that because of the general destruction of the region, Zoar itself was also abandoned. This would then correlate the archaeological evidence with the biblical account. It is also significant that all five sites lie at the edge of the Ghor, directly along its eastern fault line. This makes possible a destruction of all the pentapolis from an earthquake-related disaster, as previously described.

Another factor that suggests the identification of these sites with the biblical cities is that the southeastern basin—beginning at the northern end of the Lisan peninsula and continuing south to the Wadi Hasa (Nahal Zered)—is known to have been prime territory for settlement. The alluvial fans (soil deposits from streams) and resources for irrigation encouraged heavy occupation.[14] In this regard it is significant that each of these five sites is alongside a wadi, which allowed each city to be fed by a freshwater spring. Albright had correctly theorized that each wadi in the Ghor could have only supported one township because of the paucity of water (in the wadis), and that they were politically unified because an upstream community could have diverted the water for its own use, depriving any settlements that were downstream.[15] In addition, an intensive study of the agriculture of the area determined that the ancient economy had been based on irrigation. This fits with the geographical description of the Cities of the Plain as "well-watered land like the land of Egypt" (Genesis 13:10). In addition, the southern third of the Lisan (literally "tongue") peninsula, where these sites are located, is very shallow—about 20 feet deep as compared with up to 1,300 feet deep in the northern two-thirds. This fact may indicate that the Lisan was once a plain that became flooded in later times.

These ruins are the only attested Early Bronze Age sites on the southeastern side of the Dead Sea. Because sites from this period are entirely absent on the western side, it seems that these sites should be identified with the lost Cities of the Plain. The only problem for some scholars is the assignment of an Early Bronze date for the time of Abraham and Lot. Thomas Thompson used a chronology that put the Patriarchs in a Middle Bronze I setting, which led him to reject a Patriarchal presence in the Cities of the Plains on the grounds that there was no supporting historical or archaeological evidence.[16] However, when we consider the reference to these sites in Genesis 14 (which best fits a third millennium B.C. date) and the probable reference to Sodom in one of the Ebla tablets (dated to Early Bronze III, 2650–2350 B.C.),[17] if a shift is made to an Early Bronze III date, Thompson's argument collapses. For with this shift an important assemblage of archaeological evidence suddenly

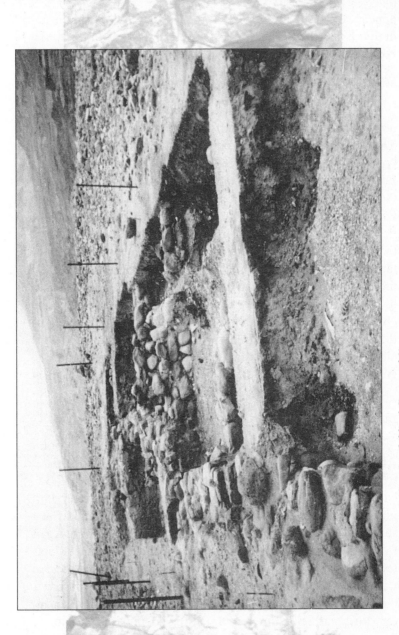

24. *Excavation area at Numeira (biblical Gomorrah?).*

appears for biblical correlation to a Patriarchal period, especially from these Dead Sea sites. This was, in fact, the
conclusion of one excavator who had explored these sites.[18]

Which City Goes with Which Site?

Identifying these sites as the Cities of the Plain encourages
us to attempt to further identify which site hosted which city.
The Bible pairs four of the cities as "Sodom *and* Gomorrah,"
"Admah *and* Zeboiim." Since Zoar was the nearby city to which
Lot begged to flee from Sodom, Zoar has to be near Sodom and
Gomorrah. Were, then, Sodom and Gomorrah to be identified
with the two sites north of Zoar or south of it? The Bible suggests that Sodom and Gomorrah were the most prominent of
the paired cities. They were singled out to represent the pentapolis in God's outpouring of judgment (Genesis 18:20-21). Of
these two cities, Sodom was the one Lot had chosen in his desire
to have what was best *(see* Genesis 13:11-12). It was also the
city whose king represented the other cities after the defeat of
the Mesopotamian kings (Genesis 14:17). In addition, it was the
city visited by the divine inquisitors in order to determine the
guilt of the rest (Genesis 18:22). Thus Sodom must have been at
the head of all the Cities of the Plain. If this was also a geographical headship, then the northernmost site is preferred, for
it is the site most visible from the hills of Bethel, where Lot had
first seen the city (Genesis 13:10-12), and from which point
Abraham later viewed its destruction (Genesis 18:27-28).

Of the five modern sites, clearly the northern site of Bab
edh-Dhra is the largest and most prominent, and therefore best
identified with Sodom. This would mean that Numeira, just
south of Bab edh-Dhra, should be identified as Gomorrah. Apart
from the argument of pairing, there is evidence that this is a correct interpretation. Linguistically, Numeira may be connected
with Gomorrah, for the modern Arabic designation preserves
the original biblical Hebrew name.[19] As for the site, the excavators Rast and Schaub reported that the southwestern sector of
the ruins revealed destruction by extensive burning: "This sector

of the town was destroyed by fire. The foundations of the buildings were buried under tons of burnt bricks."[20] Furthermore, in
one of the rooms sealed by ash debris, and thus with artifacts in
roughly the same state as when the city met its end, over 5,000
barley seeds were recovered. In ancient times barley was used to
make bread and manufacture beer. These foodstuffs may indicate the plentiful store of such grains in the city and could possibly reflect the statement in Ezekiel that one of Sodom's (and
its sister cities') sins was "fullness of bread" (Ezekiel 16:49 KJV).

When we employ the available data from the excavations
and the geographical pairing of these cities, we can identify Bab
edh-Dhra with Sodom, Numeira with Gomorrah, es-Safi with
Zoar, Feifa with Admah, and Khanazir with Zeboiim. Associates
for Biblical Research director Bryant Wood believes the evidence is compelling and therefore concludes:

> These sites from the Early Bronze age discovered in
> the country of Jordan just southeast of the Dead Sea
> form a north-south line right along the southern basin
> of the Dead Sea. They all date to the time of Abraham
> and it appears these are indeed the five "Cities of the
> Plain" mentioned in the Old Testament.[21]

A Message to Our Age

If the evidence for these sites continues to mount as future
excavators expect, then we finally have archaeological confirmation of the historicity of the sin cities of the Bible. This, of
course, is encouraging to those whose lives are lived in faith
and have nothing to fear from a God who once judged a group
of cities with fire from heaven. But to those who have lived sin-
fully in the sight of heaven, as the people of Sodom and
Gomorrah did, there can be little relief. These cities serve notice
that the God who punished sin in the past is scheduled for a
repeat performance. But this time He will not stop short with a
few cities; He will consume the whole world (2 Peter 3:10-12).
That is a prophecy not to be taken lightly, for Jesus warned that

it would be "more tolerable for the land of Sodom and Gomorrah in the day of judgment" than for those who knew these facts, but forgot their lesson for life (Matthew 10:15). In view of this, the archaeological document we call Scripture advises us to come to terms with God:

> Since all these things are to be destroyed in this way,
> what sort of people ought you to be in holy conduct
> and godliness, looking for and hastening the coming
> of the day of God (2 Peter 3:11-12a).

If these sites are indeed the sin cities of the Bible, they confront our culture afresh with their message that our present way of life ought to be lived in light of the prospect of future judgment. If we conform our own conduct by this timely warning, then even as the fact of Sodom and Gomorrah is forcing the world to remember, its lesson through us as believers will never be forgotten.

7

THE EXODUS

The First Passover Plot?

An Egyptian record of the exodus from Egypt is hardly to be expected. . . . [Nevertheless] the tradition is so vital an element in Israelite history as to make a denial of the event all but incredible.[1]

—Alan R. Millard

As these words are being written it is again Passover in the land. Throughout the world, Jews (and many Christians, *see* 1 Corinthians 5:7-8) are celebrating the redemption of the Jewish people from bondage in Egypt. In a ceremony that the Jewish community has celebrated in unbroken succession for almost 3,500 years, the Passover commemorates the signal event that began the Jewish nation—the Exodus. It is curious, then, that even as the *Seder* (the traditional meal) is set and the *Hagaddah* (the retelling of the scriptural story) is read, there are many Jewish and Christian scholars who believe the Exodus never happened! For example, Rabbi Sherwin Wine, founder of Humanistic Judaism, has contended that the Exodus was "created by priest scribes in Jerusalem" who used "a series of old legends and distorted memories which had no relationship to history."[2] Old Testament scholars N.P. Lemche and G.W. Ahlström consider the Exodus "fiction"[3] and "concerned with mythology rather than with a reporting of historical facts."[4] Years ago the Jewish scholar Hugh Schonfield wrote a book called *The Passover Plot,* in which he erroneously concluded that Jesus had staged His death and resurrection. But if the views of these scholars concerning the Exodus are correct, then *it* was the first Passover Plot!

Archaeology Explains a Difficult Text

The biblical narrative of the ten plagues is one of the most memorable and fundamental parts of the Exodus story. Who does not remember the river that turned to blood, the swarms of locusts, or my personal favorite as a kid—the piles of frogs! Is this just a superstitious tale or was there an accurate historical setting for these unusual plagues? Looking through archaeological lenses at the religion of Egypt we can understand the plagues as a divine polemic (attack) against the manifold gods of the Egyptians (the tomb of Seti I pictured at least 74). Associations between the individual plagues and specific gods whose control of the elements were disrupted or destroyed by the plagues can be made based on our information about these deities from the archaeological records.[5] However, there is one incident recorded in the Bible that runs through the whole of the plague narrative— the account of the hardening of Pharaoh's heart. Regardless of whether one argues that God or Pharaoh first hardened his heart, the reason for the act has often eluded biblical commentators. Yet, if we understand that this was also a polemical act, as the plagues that attend it, then we can look into the Egyptian archaeological record for clues as to its possible meaning.

The Egyptian Background

The Egyptian View of Pharaoh's Power

What we find is that the Pharaoh was considered to be an incarnation of the Sun god Ra and Horus-Osiris, the most important gods in Egypt.[6] Thus, he was viewed as the primary god of the world.[7] The Pharaoh's word was seen as a "creative force," the word of a god, which controlled history as well as the natural elements and could not be reversed or overruled by any other will. Therefore, by making the will of Pharaoh bow to the Divine Will, God demonstrated His sovereign power over the one who embodied the power of the Egyptian pantheon in the theology of Egypt.

The Hardening of Pharaoh's Heart

Egyptian discoveries provide us with a fascinating explanation as to why God may have chosen to "harden" Pharaoh's heart. In the theology of the ancient Egyptian death cult, as described in the Egyptian "Book of the Dead," after death the properly embalmed and entombed deceased had to go through a trial in the Hall of Judgment to determine his guilt or innocence. If judged guilty his fate was destruction; if innocent, then eternal life with its rewards. In order to pass through this judgment, the dead had to deny a long list of sins that were read against him

25. *Egyptian Book of the Dead mural on papyrus, entitled "The Weighing of the Heart."*

and successfully declare that he was pure. This act was called the "Negative Confession,"[8] and while it was being conducted the deceased's heart (depicted in a canopic jar) was being weighed in the scales of judgment against the standard of truth (represented by the hieroglyphic symbol of a feather). This judgment is vividly depicted in a mural painting known as "the weighing of the heart." Against the testimony of the deceased, his heart would confess the truth, showing his Negative Confession to be a lie. The heart, therefore, would tip the scales in favor of judgment and result in his destruction. Since all men sin and the natural inclination of the heart is to confess such sin, the ingenious Egyptians devised a means to keep the heart from contradicting the Negative Confession. They did this by writing magical incantations on a stone image of their sacred dung beetle, called a scarab, that was carved in the shape of a heart.[9] This stoneheart scarab was then placed in or on the chest cavity during mummification (a fact revealed by x-rays of Egyptian mummies).[10] Various incantations which ordered the heart "not to rebel against me" or "not witness against me" transferred the stony character of the scarab to the fleshly heart in the afterlife, making it "hard" and unable to speak.[11] This act of ritual "hardening of the heart" reversed the natural function of the unhardened heart and resulted in salvation since the deceased was now decreed sinless through silence.[12]

However, when God "hardened" Pharaoh's heart, who as a god himself represented the salvation of Egypt, He reversed the theological hope of all Egyptians. This hardening resulted in Pharaoh's inability to naturally respond to the fearsome plagues, and therefore stop them, by surrendering to Moses' request. Therefore, instead of the "hardening the heart" bringing salvation, it brought destruction.[13] Thus, archaeology has provided new insight into a difficult theological concept by giving us the proper background and setting of the Egyptian beliefs God through Moses wished to counter. In addition, in revealing the accuracy of the details in the biblical account it implies its historicity. Yet, finding historical backgrounds to the Exodus narrative does not necessarily mean that it reflects actual history. Therefore we must now turn to the difficult question of the historicity of the Exodus.

The Historicity of the Exodus

Establishing the historicity of the Exodus is one of the major problems remaining to biblical scholars. The biblical narrative of the Exodus has been notoriously difficult to confirm with archaeological evidence, thus causing serious doubt to be cast on the authenticity of the event.

One hindrance to accepting the Exodus as an actual event has been scholars' inability to reconcile the Exodus events to both a biblical *and* archaeological chronology. An early date in the fifteenth century B.C. (1446–1441 B.C.) for the Exodus is in greater harmony with the internal chronology of the Old Testament (*see* 1 Kings 6:1).[14]

The classic chronological study by Edwin Thiele[15] fixed an early date of 1447 B.C. for the Exodus.[16] According to this dating the pharaoh of the Oppression was either Thutmose I or Thutmose III and the pharaoh of the Exodus was Thutmose II or Amenhotep II. The ancient biography of an Egyptian naval officer named Amenemhab, who served under several pharaohs of this period, tells us that Thutmose III died at the time of the Passover in early March of 1447 or 1446 B.C.[17] Thus, his death occurred at exactly the right time to fit the biblical chronology and events of the Exodus. However, William Shea has recently argued in an unpublished paper[18] that Thutmose I and a recently installed co-regent son—a preliminary Thutmose II—died together in pursuit of the Israelite slaves (as perhaps implied in Exodus 15:4,19). He believes that their bodies were not recovered (hence the mummies ascribed to them in the Egyptian Museum in Cairo are misidentified). He bases his argument on new photographs by Oral Collins of the Wadi Nasb Sinaitic inscriptions, first discovered by Professor Gerster many decades ago, which purport to record the name of Thutmose I and depict images of both him and his son and events connected with the

Exodus. The problem for the early date is that despite its harmonization of biblical and extrabiblical sources, it lacks sufficient support in the archaeological record. A later date in the thirteenth century B.C. (1280–1200 B.C.) appears to offer more archaeological support (*see* Exodus 1:11),[19] but has significant chronological problems and cannot accommodate the events of the Conquest.

According to this date, the pharaoh of both the Oppression and the Exodus was Ramses II and his successor was Merneptah. The lack of consensus has generated other options which often require the revision of Egyptian chronology[20] or which take the biblical chronology as a rough estimate rather than a precise indicator.[21] This later revision moves the date back to 1470 B.C. Faulstich has arrived at incredibly precise dates for all of the Exodus events from his computerized correlations of known astronomical dating data, biblical information concerning astronomical events (star risings, moon phases, and eclipses), the Hebrew weekly day cycles, and specific dates given in the Bible.[22] Although no consensus has yet been reached, the continued search for archaeological evidence of the Exodus underscores the great importance of this event for students of the Bible.

The Importance of the Exodus

The importance of the Exodus has been emphasized by Eugene Merrill, professor of Old Testament at Dallas Seminary, who has called it "the most significant event in all of the Old Testament."[23] The Exodus is not simply one isolated event among many in the history of the Jewish people; it was *the* pivotal event upon which God's plan turns and both the Old and New Testaments are linked together. Professor John Durham explains:

> Both within the Book of Exodus and beyond it, the Exodus deliverance is depicted as the act by which Israel was brought into being as a people and thus as the beginning point in Israel's history. . . . with the

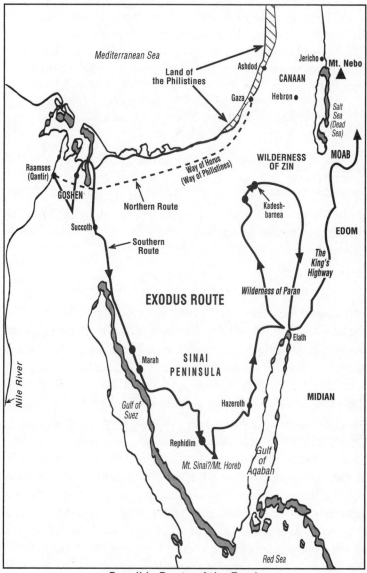

Possible Route of the Exodus

Exodus, he [God] revealed his presence to a whole
people and called them to nationhood and a special role
by relating himself to them in covenant. This special
role becomes a kind of lens through which Israel is
viewed throughout the rest of the Bible...one that
shapes much of the theology of the OT [Old Testa-
ment]. It is this special role, indeed, that weaves the
Book of Exodus so completely into the canonical
fabric begun with Genesis and ended only with Revelation.[24]

The Exodus ties together the testaments in such a way that
to deny it ever happened would unravel the theological threads
of both Judaism and Christianity. Thus it is natural that we
should seek the Exodus somewhere in the archaeological
record. But where do we look, and what should we expect to
find? Let's answer this last question first.

Should We Expect to Find the Exodus?

Should we expect to find any archaeological evidence for
the Exodus? Like the Patriarchs before them, the Israelites lived
a nomadic lifestyle during the Exodus. The demands of living in
the Sinai desert required that nothing be discarded, that every
item be used to its fullest capacity—and then recycled. Even
the bones of a finished meal would be completely reused in various industrial applications. The temporary tent encampments of
the Israelites would have left no traces, especially in the ever-
shifting sands of the desert. There may be traces of rock graffiti
in the Sinai[25] that suggest the Israelites' presence in this region,
but for the most part, because of the desert conditions, the
Israelites would have become "archaeologically invisible."

But what about the possibility of Egyptian records that confirm the occurrence of the Exodus plagues and the destruction of
the Egyptian army at the Red Sea? It is possible that some such
evidence may yet appear, but we should not expect the proudly
religious Egyptians to openly document disasters that defamed

their gods and memorialized their army's defeat at the hands of vagabond slaves. As Charles Aling notes:

> The peoples of the ancient Near East kept historical records to impress their gods and also potential enemies, and therefore rarely, if ever, mentioned defeats or catastrophes. Records of disasters would not enhance the reputation of the Egyptians in the eyes of their gods, nor make their enemies more afraid of their military might.[26]

This means that it is unlikely that we will find a record of the plagues, the drowning of the Egyptian army in the Red Sea, or Israelite footprints in the sands of the Sinai desert. If we cannot expect to find traces of an Exodus in these places, where can we look?

The Evidence for the Exodus

Historical Considerations

One way we can make a case for the occurrence of the Exodus is from what may be called "contextual plausibility." That is, even though we may not have direct historical evidence for any of the persons or events connected with the Exodus, or even be able to agree on specific dates, the general outline as presented in the biblical account is true to the times. Therefore the Exodus is far more likely to have occurred than not. The most plausible case at present has been made on the basis of the Egyptian evidence.[27] For instance, we can show that the details of Egyptian court life and certain peculiarities in the Hebrew language used to describe such activities indicate that the writer had firsthand knowledge of that particular Egyptian setting.[28] We have evidence that foreigners from Canaan entered Egypt,[29] lived there,[30] were sometimes considered troublemakers,[31] and that Egypt oppressed and enslaved a vast foreign workforce during several dynasties.[32] We also have records that slaves escaped,[33] and that Egypt suffered from plague-like conditions.[34] We can provide a computer model of a scientific mechanism for the parting of the waters at the Israelite crossing of the Red Sea.[35] We can prove the presence of people like the Israelites in the Sinai peninsula, at Kadesh-barnea, and at other places mentioned in the books of the Bible that record this history.[36] We can demonstrate from a comparison with ancient Near Eastern law codes that pre-dated the giving of the Law at Sinai that its form and structure fit the then-established standard for such texts.[37] Finally, we can provide archaeological data to support several dates for the Conquest and settlement periods, which followed the Exodus. This data comes from sites such as Jericho, Megiddo, and Hazor.[38]

Archaeological Considerations

At the commencement of the Exodus, when the Israelites left Egypt, the most sensible and direct route would have been to travel north along the present-day Gaza Strip in a direction that would take them to Canaan. However, the biblical account tells us that God forbade this route along the Mediterranean coastal plain. The biblical account reads:

> Now it came about when Pharaoh had let the people go, that God did not lead them by the way of the land of the Philistines, even though it was near; for God said, "Lest the people change their minds when they see war, and they return to Egypt" (Exodus 13:17).

Thus, the Israelites ended up taking a much longer southern route that went deeper into the Sinai. Not until the last decade did anyone know why God kept them away from the easier northern route. The cryptic reference to "war" in Exodus 13:17 was debatable because no one knew what people would have been at odds with the Israelites. The answer was discovered by Israeli archaeologist Trude Dothan, who specializes in the early period of the Philistine occupation of Canaan. At the site of Deir el-Balah along the ancient route called the "Ways of Horus," she uncovered the evidence that finally solved this Exodus riddle.[39] When I visited with her recently at the Hebrew Univer-

26. *Archaeologist Trude Dothan, who discovered an explanation for the Exodus route, with anthropoid coffins from Deir el-Balah.*

sity's Institute of Archaeology, I asked her to recount this discovery and explain its significance:

> I came to the site of Deir el-Balah in the Gaza Strip in search of the Philistines. What I found was a very fascinating and exciting Egyptian outpost from the period of the Exodus, the period in Egypt of Ramses II, who is considered to be the Pharaoh of the Exodus. The story of the site is intriguing, piecing together information from [grave] robbers and then from our professional archaeological dig. What the results are is that we found on the route from Egypt to Canaan an outpost which had been built [in the fourteenth century B.C.] as well as a fortress from the period of Seti I [and that of his son] Ramses II. Adjacent to the settlement itself was a cemetery full of large anthropoid (human shaped) coffins which are definitely in Egyptian style. Because I previously worked on the customs of the Philistines at Beth-Shean, a very important site in Israel and well-known from the Bible, I knew about coffin burials like these. [So I] tried to identify five of these

coffins with special head gear with portraits of the
Philistines known from the Egyptian reliefs in the
period of Ramses III.

The importance of this site is its geographical location
on the route from Egypt to Canaan. . . . a military route
of the Egyptians going up to Canaan. . . . When we
found the fortress [dated to] the end of the thirteenth
century, the idea came up that this was really one of
many fortresses dotting the way from Canaan to Gaza.
[Thus] the area was very well fortified, which is why
the Israelites did not want to go on the short way to
Canaan but chose the long way to the Sinai, because
they were afraid of the Egyptians and the fortification
that was on the short road.

We now know in light of the Deir el-Balah excavations that
"the Way of the Philistines" mentioned in the Bible is also "the
Way of Horus," mentioned in reliefs at the Egyptian temple at
Karnak. This relief also depicted some of the Egyptian fortresses along this route including the one Trude Dothan discovered. So, from this remarkable correlation between the Bible
and two archaeological sites, we can conclude that the Israelites
were warned to avoid this route because they would have run
into this line of northern defensive garrisons manned by Egyptian solders. The soldiers stationed there would have been prepared to fight to recapture and return to Egypt such runaway
slaves. Because the just-released Israelites were untrained in
battle, the desert wilderness was the safer option.

Considerations from Satellite Imagery

According to satellite image analyst George Stephen, the
route of the Exodus can still be seen today through the use of
infrared technology.[40] The satellites that employ this technology
for purposes such as intelligence gathering and mineral exploration can also isolate trails in the desert sands even though they
are thousands of years old. They do this by capturing heat patterns left in the earth. Such satellites have enabled archaeolo-

gists to recover information about ancient caravan routes, uncover traces of long-dried and buried riverbeds, and find lost cities beneath the sands. Stephens studied French SPOT satellite imagery of Egypt, the Gulf of Suez, Gulf of Aqaba, and portions of Saudi Arabia at a 530-mile altitude. He claims that he was able to see evidence of ancient tracks made by "a massive number of people" leading from the Nile Delta straight south along the east bank of the Gulf of Suez and around the tip of the Sinai peninsula. In addition, he says that he observed traces of "very large campsites" along the trail.

Of course it is not possible to determine whether these tracks were made by the Israelites themselves or by other caravaners down through the millennia. But it does demonstrate that large numbers of people could be sustained in the same region and on the same route as that taken by the Israelites in the Exodus.

Future Research

Clues from Volcanic Debris

With so many questions about the events of the Exodus still unanswered, it is certain that new proposals and archaeological projects will be forthcoming in the future. One recent project is a unique investigation of the site *Tell el-Dab'a*. This site in the eastern Nile Delta area has been identified with the biblical land of Goshen, where the Israelites lived prior to the Exodus.[41] An ongoing excavation has been conducted for years by the Smithsonian under the direction of Manfred Bietak. The new project has begun searching the site specifically for evidence of tephra (volcanic debris) deposits left by the eruptions of a volcano on the Mediterranean island of Santorini (Thera) during the Bronze Age.[42] According to the theory, this cataclysmic explosion, which left ash deposits in at least nine Aegean archaeological sites, may have also brought the plagues to the Egyptians, especially the plague of the "darkness that can be felt" (volcanic ash?—Exodus 10:21-23), and divided the waters at the sea crossing.

If these events can indeed be attributed to the Santorini eruption, then the Exodus could be established in Egyptian history and securely located within an Egyptian chronology (through linkage with an established Aegean chronology for the event) if the debate now raging over the date of the eruption itself can be resolved.[43] News from the field is that pumice from the eruption has now been found at Tell el-Dab'a in a level which can be securely dated to the early eighteenth Egyptian Dynasty, or about 1525 B.C. This offers both an answer to the eruption date controversy and perhaps a connection with the Exodus itself (which the biblical chronology indicates at around 1447/6 B.C.).

Clues from Grain Seeds

Following the same theory that geological evidence from the Santorini volcanic eruption can be used to date Exodus events, archaeologists Hendrik J. Bruins and Johannes van der Plicht have offered new evidence that they believe confirms the Exodus story.[44] The two compared new radiocarbon dates of cereal grains found among debris in the destruction of Jericho with their date of 1628 B.C. for the Santorini eruption (which was based on counting tree rings). Based on their findings, they concluded that the Santorini disaster predated the Jericho destruction by 45 years, a time span which they believe would fit the events of the Exodus and the 40-year wilderness wandering of the Israelites. This would make their date for the Jericho destruction at 1583 B.C. and the Exodus around 1543 B.C., much too early for even the traditional early date (at 1400 B.C.).

Bryant Wood, the director of the Associates for Biblical Research, defends an early date and takes exception with Bruins and van der Plicht's method of calibrating their dates:

> Not only my research at Jericho, but that of other scholars demonstrates that there is a gap of a century

and a half or so between C-14 dates and historically determined dates in the second millennium B.C. Currently there is a fierce scholarly debate going on concerning the date of the eruption of Thera. This is an extremely important date, because the eruption provides a benchmark in the histories of most Mediterranean cultures. Evidence for it has been found at a number of archaeological sites. Those who work from C-14 dates are convinced that it took place in ca. 1628 B.C., while those who work from archaeological dates are convinced that it took place around 1525 B.C. My work at Jericho provides another example of the discrepancy that exists between C-14 and historical dates in the second millennium B.C. It is evident that one of these methods is wrong, but which one?

Advocates of each, of course, claim the other is wrong. Historical dates are ultimately tied to astronomical observations recorded in antiquity. Presumably, astronomers can calculate backwards very accurately due to the precise movement of the universe. Proponents of C-14 dating, on the other hand, say that their corrected values are very precise because they are based on the counting of tree rings, year-by-year, back to 6,000 B.C. (dendrochronology). The Biblical date of 1400 B.C. is based on Assyrian chronology for the kingdom period, known very well from astronomical observations and Biblical data (480 years from the fourth year of Solomon to the Exodus, 1 Kings 6:1, and the 40 years in the wilderness). My dating of the destruction of Jericho is based on pottery, which is tied to eighteenth Dynasty Egyptian chronology, which is again tied to astronomical observations. . . . What about the possible connection between the eruption of Thera and the plague of darkness? In order for there to be a connection, the date of the event would have to be reduced to about 1450 B.C. before it could be correlated with biblical history.[45]

If the evidence of the Santorini eruption at Tell el-Dab'a confirms a 1525 B.C. date for the eruption, then the C-14 date must be adjusted. Even so, the research now in progress may eventually help resolve the unanswered questions that are still before us.

What Does the Evidence Prove?

Our survey of the Exodus question has attempted to present what can be known (at present) from the archaeological and historical record. What does our present data prove? Admittedly, direct archaeological evidence for the Exodus is still wanting. However, this lack of historical data does not mean that the Exodus didn't happen. Conclusive proof may yet appear in a future excavation but we do not need to wait for this in order to accept the historicity of the Exodus. Our case can be made from a comparison of the biblical context with what is already known from history and archaeology—a case that offers sufficient substance to resolve doubts over the reality of the event and makes probable greater archaeological confirmation in days to come. Therefore, those who celebrate the Passover this season—and every season to come—can do so with the assurance that its promise is not based on a plot, but on the proven performance of a God who has really redeemed!

8

THE CONQUEST

Did Joshua Really Conquer Jericho?

The conquest provides another example of the search for connections between biblical and historical-archaeological material. This concerns an event for which there is a considerable amount of archaeological evidence, a great amount of detailed description in the biblical sources, and volumes of diverse opinions and hypotheses produced by modern scholars.[1]

—Paul W. Lapp

According to the Bible, after 40 years of wandering in the wilderness of Sinai, Moses brought the Israelites to the Jordan River. At that boundary separating the chosen people from their chosen place, Moses ascended and remained on Mount Nebo, while Joshua, as his successor, led the people across the Jordan into the country of Canaan. In the scriptural story, this entrance into the Promised Land is accomplished by a series of military conquests in which the Israelites captured Canaanite fortifications. The best known of these conquests is the first city that

141

27. The excavations at Tel-Jericho, the first site of the Conquest.

fell—Jericho—whose walls, as every Sunday School teacher
has taught, "came tumbling down." Only a generation or so ago,
this account of conquest was accepted as historical by almost
everyone. In those days the report of Jericho's excavation by
the British archaeologists John and J.B.E. Garstang seemed to
have confirmed beyond doubt the biblical destruction of what
was known as the "Fourth City" at Jericho. Included in this
report was what was reported to be photographs of the very
walls that had collapsed when the Israelites blasted their trumpets. These photos were accompanied by Garstang's declaration that "there is no difficulty now in understanding the note of
confident faith which breathes in every line of the Bible narrative (Joshua vi)."[2]

From Confidence to Controversy

In the 1950s, however, Kathleen Kenyon excavated at
Jericho and concluded that Garstang was wrong. In fact, she
announced that her findings revealed that the city had been
destroyed around 1550 B.C., and therefore had long been unin-
habited when Joshua arrived on the scene. In addition, a generation of Israeli archaeologists digging at strategic sites
mentioned in the Conquest narrative have likewise found no
trace of destruction from Joshua's time. A dominant school of
thought in archaeological circles today believes that the events
recorded about the Conquest were written many hundreds of
years after the events they described took place. For this reason,
some scholars claim that these accounts do not contain accurate historical information, but only remembrances of traditions.
As Nadav Na'aman, professor of Jewish history at Tel Aviv University explains, "This enormous hiatus explains the many dis-
crepancies between the conquest stories and the archeological
evidence."[3]

In modern academic circles, the question of a historical conquest ("did Jericho's walls really fall down?") is no longer a
question at all. Israel Finkelstein, who serves as director of Tel
Aviv University's Institute of Archaeology and has excavated

some of the conquest sites, says, "It's not a possibility, it's over!" Finkelstein comes to this conclusion through an analysis of settlement patterns in the highlands of Israel. These, he says, indicate that the "real Israel," not the Israel of the biblical stories, emerged on the historical scene in the eighth or ninth century B.C. (300-400 years after the Bible places these events). Such modern conclusions alert us to the fact that many problems still remain for those whose quest is to confirm the Conquest.

The Problems for the Conquest

If we allow only the Sunday School story of Joshua and Jericho to form our notions of the Conquest, then the matter seems straightforward and simple. But beyond this, matters grow quite complicated. Amihai Mazar, director of the Hebrew University's Institute of Archaeology, explains the problem as scholars and archaeologists view it:

> The entire question of the Exodus and Conquest of the country by the Israelites remains very much enigmatic from the archaeological point of view, in spite of the fact that tons of papers and thousand of words were written on this subject by both historians and archaeologists who tried for dozens of years to illustrate this relationship. The period of the Judges, the settlement, is also a very difficult issue. Archaeological surveys in the country looking just on top soil, [that is just] looking for sites, found that during the time of the Judges (the twelfth–eleventh century B.C.) about 250 sites were founded in the hill country north and south of Jerusalem. This phenomenon of a new wave of settlements in the hill country can be related only to the appearance of Israel in this country. Now of course, we can ask ourselves, Where did they come from? Did they come from Egypt as the Bible tells us or were they local people who settled as many scholars believe? Or did they come from clans in Jordan? We have a debate concerning the interpretation of the finds. But the finds themselves remain a very important contribution to the

phenomenon to the emergence of Israel during that period.[4]

The debate over the interpretation of the finds is between those who accept the biblical account and those who rely on a strictly archaeological model. This dispute is about *when* (an early or late date) and *how* (the method of conquest) Israel entered Canaan.

The Problem of When

The Conquest date of 1400 B.C., based on the Bible's own internal chronology, was once assumed by most archaeologists. It was largely abandoned in favor of a later date following the archaeological patriarch W.F. Albright's own shift in thinking during his excavation of Beitin. Albright had identified Beitin as biblical Bethel, and when he discovered a destruction level datable to 1250 B.C., he felt compelled to revise the date of the Conquest. His evidence joined that from other archeological sites said to have been occupied by the invading Israelites. These all showed similar signs of massive destruction from 1250–1150 B.C. Who else could the destruction have been attributed to but the Israelites?

However, before we revise the biblical chronology in light of archaeology, we must examine the assumptions that have been made concerning this evidence. First, there were many other invaders coming into Israel during this time who could have been responsible for this destruction. In 1230 B.C. the Egyptian pharaoh Merneptah conducted some raids (mentioned specifically in his own record—the Stele of Merneptah), as well as the newly arrived Philistines,[5] who were aggressively seeking to expand their territory. There were also inter-tribal conflicts taking place in Canaan, and the biblical book of Judges records cycles of upheavals at some sites by oppressive Midianites and Canaanites.

Another important consideration that affects the question of "when" is how to interpret the biblical accounts concerning the extent of the destruction to be sought. The Bible does not

28. *The Stele of Merneptah, on which is found the first mention of Israel in an Egyptian text, indicating Israel was already in the Land by the thirteenth century B.C.*

support the assumption some archaeologists make about a massive destruction occurring at all the occupied sites. According to the biblical text, only two southern sites and one northern site were destroyed in such a way as to leave any evidence of destruction. Incidentally, Bethel (which forced Albright's revision of the Conquest chronology) was not one of these. According to the Bible, many sites were never conquered by the Israelites at all, but by the end of Joshua's life "very much of the Land remained to be possessed" (Joshua 13:1). This is a fact confirmed by the archaeological evidence. Bob Mullins, an area supervisor of the excavations at the biblical period (Iron Age) strata at Beth-Shean, makes this point when he says:

> In the terms of our own excavations at Beth-Shean we see the continuation of Egyptian presence from somewhere around 1450 B.C. all the way to around 1150 B.C. So this would lend weight to what the Bible says about [the cities of] Beth-Shean and even Megiddo not having been taken by Israel. What we see in terms of the archaeological evidence is that a shift in the population from Egyptian and Canaanite to Israelite exists at Beth-Shean and Megiddo [only] from the beginning of the time of Solomon. No biblical text clearly says who put an end to the cities of that time; we assume perhaps David. However, there is circumstantial evidence that would seem to indicate that Israel did in fact occupy parts of the hill country. We do know that in Judges 1:27 the Israelites did not conquer these valley regions which included such important cities as Megiddo and Beth-Shean.[6]

Consequently, the signs of widespread destruction at certain sites should not be considered as archaeological evidence against the biblical chronology and for a late date for the Conquest. These destructions better fit the period of the Judges, during which ongoing warfare was commonplace.

The Problem of How

Kenyon's excavations at Jericho convinced her that no one had occupied the city after 1550 B.C., thus making impossible a Conquest at either the early or late dates. This led many scholars to conclude that no Conquest had taken place at all! How, then, did the Israelites get into Canaan and occupy so much of the country? This question has been most intensively investigated by those who maintain a minimalist view of the Bible. The scholars have proposed revised models of Israelite "emergence" drawn from archaeological data or settlement patterns alone. Because the theories developed by these revisionist scholars have gained popularity and are undermining the historicity of the Bible among their readers, let's briefly survey their views.

One theory is known as the "Peaceful Infiltration" theory.[7] Based largely on Egyptian records, it argues that the Israelites gradually immigrated into Canaan, infiltrated the resident Canaanite population, and eventually overran and replaced (thus according to the biblical term "destroying") the Canaanite culture.

Another theory is called the "Peasant Revolt" theory.[8] Since proponents of this view see no evidence of Israel in the archaeological record, they radically revise Israelite history by identifying the Israelites as members of the lowest level of the Canaanite population. In a localized social phenomenon, these peasants revolted and overthrew their urban overlords.

Yet another theory, known as the "Transition Theory," has used the archaeological data from the transition between the end of the Late Bronze Age and the beginning of the Iron Age to argue that social and technological changes forced the emergence of the Israelites as a distinctive culture.[9]

Then there is the "Imagination Theory," which argues that climatic changes in the transition between archaeological periods provoked hill-country people (Israelites *and* Philistines!) to emerge in an attempt to form communities.[10]

Despite their dependence on the same archaeological evidence, each theory interprets the evidence differently, showing that the evidence itself is ambiguous. In the final analysis, none of these theories adequately answers how Canaanite culture ended and Israel managed to gain possession of so much of the land of Canaan. Finally, each view has to dismiss or reinterpret the biblical narratives in order to have it fit their revision of history.

Evidence for the Conquest

Is there any archaeological evidence that might support the traditional Conquest model? If such archaeological evidence can be found, it must be sought at the three sites said to have been burned by the Israelites: Hazor in the north, and Jericho and Ai in the south.

The Evidence from Hazor

The Bible notes that Joshua "utterly destroyed" all the cities of the kings of northern Israel, but it singles out Hazor as the one city which he burnt with fire (Joshua 11:11-13). The famous Israeli archaeologist Yigael Yadin began the excavations at the 175-acre site of Hazor in 1955, and his successor Amnon Ben-Tor is today continuing this work. Interpreting Israel's history primarily on the basis of the archaeological evidence, he nevertheless affirms the accuracy of the description in Joshua concerning Hazor's destruction:

> There is evidence of a massive destruction. I once called it the mother of all destruction. In Hazor, wherever you come down to the end of the Canaanite strata, you come upon this destruction. It is an unbelievable destruction . . . it left behind a thick debris of ashes. There was a terrible fire in the [Canaanite] palace. So much so, that the bricks vitrified and some of the clay vessels melted [and] some stones exploded because of the fire. . . . We can clearly say that the temperature was more than 1200 degrees centigrade. A normal fire is

half, about 600 or 700 degrees, [but in the afternoon] the wind is unbelievable. . . . put these . . . together and you'll get this kind of fire [with] very intense heat. So this fire destroyed a lot. . . . If you go back to the book of Joshua, you may remember that in the story of the destruction of Hazor, it says that after killing all the people, the Israelites set Hazor on fire and it was only Hazor that was destroyed by fire. . . . And in the case of Hazor, they were interested to tell how intensive the destruction of Hazor was . . . because Hazor was once the head of all those kingdoms; the most important of the Canaanite city-states (Joshua 11:10).[11]

Perhaps in the next few years Ben-Tor's excavation will confirm even more of the Joshua account. Recently his team unearthed ten palm-sized Akkadian cuneiform tablets that suggest that a Canaanite archive may have been at the site (one of the texts mentions a school for scribes that met at Hazor). These tablets also had multiplication tables and a list of items sent from Hazor to Mari. This later discovery was important because the name Hazor appeared in the text, confirming the biblical identification. Just this year (1997), the excavators revealed a Canaanite palace that Ben-Tor believes was destroyed by Joshua. Among the artifacts found within the palace were an altar and sacrificial remains, two unique figurines of deities, and what is thought to be a libation vessel the size of a bathtub with a now headless god sitting on one end holding a cup. Ben-Tor also believes that another, even earlier, palace exists below the present strata of excavation that may also contain archives. Ben-Tor has stated he thinks there is sufficient evidence (in addition to the tablets) to warrant the existence of these two Canaanite archives and will be working in the next few seasons to uncover them. If so, Hazor may soon make headlines with a monumental discovery rivaling that of the Dead Sea Scrolls!

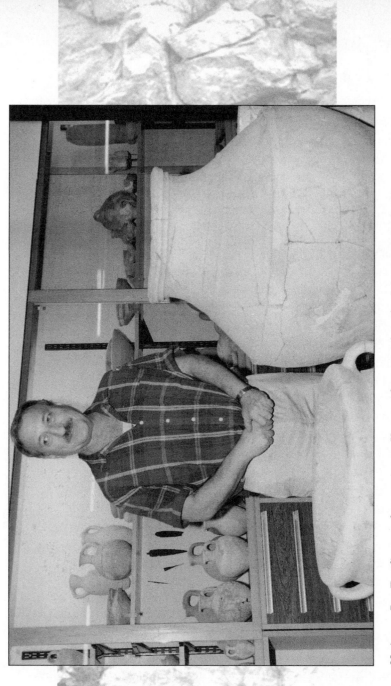

29. *Amnon Ben-Tor, director of excavations at Hazor, with remains from the Canaanite period at Hazor.*

The Evidence from Jericho

Because Jericho is the most famous of the Conquest sites it has been most often the subject of archaeological investigation. The latest excavation of the tell was by British archaeologist Kathleen Kenyon in the 1950s. She concluded that the ancient site had been destroyed and abandoned 150 years before the time the Bible says the Conquest occurred. Her evidence has been challenged by Bryant Wood.

Kenyon based her dating on what she did not find—that is, imported Cypriote pottery. Wood, on the other hand, has analyzed the local Canaanite pottery excavated by the various expeditions to Jericho.[12] His analysis indicates that Jericho was destroyed around 1400 B.C. (the end of the Late Bronze I period), rather than 1550 B.C. as claimed by Kenyon. What is more, Wood has shown that once the destruction is correctly dated, the archaeological evidence harmonizes perfectly with the biblical record:[13]

1. The city was strongly fortified in the Late Bronze I period, the time of the Conquest according to biblical chronology (Joshua 2:5,7,15; 6:5,20).

2. The city was massively destroyed by fire (Joshua 6:24).

3. The fortification walls collapsed at the time the city was destroyed, possibly by earthquake activity (Joshua 6:20).

4. The destruction occurred at harvest time in the spring, as indicated by the large quantities of grain stored in the city (Joshua 2:6; 3:15; 5:10).

5. The siege of Jericho was short, since the grain stored in the city was not consumed (Joshua 6:15,20).

6. The grain was not plundered, as was usually the case in antiquity, in accordance with the Divine injunction (Joshua 6:17-18).

7. The inhabitants had no opportunity to flee with their foodstuffs (Joshua 6:1).

8. Jericho lay abandoned for a period of time following the destruction, in accordance with Joshua's curse (Joshua 6:26).

Wood also offered as positive support: 1) Egyptian scarabs found in graves at the site form a continuous series from the eighteenth to the fourteenth centuries, showing that the cemetery was in use during the Late Bronze Age I period. 2) The stratigraphy of City IV (the site excavated by Garstang and Kenyon) further revealed 20 different architectural phases lasting for long periods of time and following 12 minor destructions. If, as Kenyon states, the city met its end at 1550 B.C. in Middle Bronze II, then all of these phases would have to be fitted into the previous Middle Bronze III period (1650–1550 B.C.), an impossibly short time for so much activity. 3) A radiocarbon sample taken from a piece of charcoal in the final destruction debris layer yielded a date of 1410 B.C. (plus or minus 40 years). Wood's analysis adds new archaeological support that City IV at Jericho should be dated with Garstang and the biblical chronology to 1400 B.C.

Evidence from Ai?

Ai was the second city conquered upon entrance to the Land and the last in our list of three burned with fire. According to the Bible, the site of Ai is "beside Bethel" (Joshua 12:9; cf. Genesis 12:8). Albright's identification of Beitin as Bethel led to the identification of the nearby site of et-Tell as Ai. However, excavations at the site by Joseph Callaway have produced no evidence of occupation between the Early Bronze Age (about 2400 B.C.) and the Iron Age (about 1200 B.C.). This meant that in a gap of more than 1,000 years, there were no Canaanites at the site to be conquered. Whether we accept the early or late date for the Conquest, Callaway's excavations leave us with the conclusion that either the biblical account is wrong or that the site has been misidentified. Thus two archaeologists who maintain a biblical priority are searching to see if the true sites of Ai and Bethel are actually elsewhere. Both believe that the proper site for Bethel is the modern-day village of el-Birah, and they have located nearby tels that offer some promise of meeting the biblical descriptions of these sites.

Archaeologist David Livingston believes that the site of Khirbet Nisya best fits the requirements of biblical Ai. His site well fits the topography and geography of the Bible, being in front of el-Birah (Bethel) and situated south of a broad valley with a wadi bearing the Arabic name of *Gai,* which seemingly has preserved the Hebrew equivalent of *Ai.* The Hebrew term *Ai* literally means "ruins," but if it has in mind the specific ruins known in the Bible as the fortified site Joshua conquered, Livingston may have a match. Although no Late Bronze walls or gates have yet been discovered, plenty of Late Bronze pottery has shown up, indicating that, like in similar sites,[14] later occupants had simply destroyed all earlier architectural structures.[15]

The other contender for Ai is the site of Tel el-Makater, which is currently being excavated by archaeologist Bryant Wood. He says of this site:

> Our organization, the Associates for Biblical Research, has been doing field work to locate what we believe should be the true site of Ai. . . . In 1996 we began work at Khirbet el-Makater, about 10 miles north of Jerusalem and east of el-Bira (Bethel). This new site offers a good possibility of being the site of Ai because it fits the topographical and geographical requirements of the biblical account. Our excavation so far shows promise of it being a fortified city from the time of Joshua. . . . We have discovered . . . a very large structure . . . walls which are about 6 feet wide . . . on the north side of the site . . . that is about 15 feet square. . . . In conjunction with the structure, we have found two very large . . . socket stones where the pivot for the door would have rotated. Very thick fortification walls and pottery from the Late Bronze I period (fifteenth century B.C.) have

also been found.... All of this evidence suggests that
we do indeed have a fortress that was from the time of
the Conquest. We have even found evidence for
fighting in the area of the large structure—a large
number of sling stones about the size of baseballs...
that were used in antiquity during warfare.... We also
have some evidence of fire.... So we feel that we have
with this site a good candidate for the Ai of the Conquest. We are only at the beginning of our work... as
we continue we hope we will find additional evidence
to support the truth of the biblical account.[16]

Both sites are still being excavated, and perhaps in the near
future we will have more solid evidence that can replace the
currently accepted problematic site of et-Tell and provide
greater confirmation of the Conquest.

Has Joshua's Altar Been Found?

Israeli archaeologist Adam Zertal is convinced that he found
the very altar Joshua erected on Mt. Ebal (described in Joshua
8:30-35). The popular magazine *Biblical Archaeology Review*
first published his article on the find,[17] and later, a book high-
lighting the discovery appeared.[18] If this identification is correct, direct verification for the historicity of (or at least this
feature of) the Conquest story is possible. However, Zertal's
interpretation that the structure was Joshua's altar was not
guided by a biblical chronology, nor even a conviction that there
was Conquest. Based on the great quantity of pottery shards
lying around it, the structure is dated to the early part of the Iron
Age (1220–1000 B.C.), too late a date for the biblical Conquest.[19]
Despite criticism that it is either an Iron Age farmhouse or
watchtower,[20] Zertal has continued to defend his position that it
is an altar. However, in light of its date, it is preferable to see it
as part of a cultic installation (high place) from the time of the
Judges.[21] If so, since sacred structures tend to be built and rebuilt
at sites that have a former cultic history, it is possible that this
altar could have replaced an earlier one from the time of Joshua.

The Problem of Evidence

Even with the kind of evidence Wood claims for Jericho and the possibility of a new identification for Ai, the archaeological evidence still is very limited and controversial. What it shows is that of the 17 sites listed in the Conquest account in the book of Joshua, 12 had some kind of settlement in the Late Bronze Age.[22] Of these, only two had evidence of a destruction during the Late Bronze I[23] and five during the Late Bronze II-Iron I.[24] Even though the identity of many of these sites is still disputed, accepting them for the sake of our statistics, they reveal that archaeology does not provide much information about these cities of the Conquest. Even the book of Joshua itself provides very little information. Apart from statements that tell us these cities were "taken," the text gives details only about the three that were burned (Jericho, Ai, Hazor). Unfortunately, some scholars assume this lack of evidence has somehow discredited the biblical account. Archaeologist David Merling explains:

> ... while archaeology has found nothing to discount any aspect of any story found in the book of Joshua, it is nonevidence that has produced the façade of disagreement between archaeology and the Bible. By not finding something, archaeologists consider that they have proved something. Nonevidence is not the same as evidence. Other conquests, whose histories have never been questioned, have been investigated for evidence of destructions. The lack of evidence among those sites should cause all archaeologists to question the use of nonevidence.[25]

Such assumptions, says Merling, have caused archaeologists to expect to find, at sites connected with Conquest, huge cities with major fortifications—but the Bible makes no such claims about these cities. It even appears that the account of the Conquest generally did not leave the kind of information that could be "proven" by archaeology.

Can the Conquest Be Found?

Why have attempts thus far to excavate indisputable evidence of the Conquest been largely without success? Keith Schoville, Professor Emeritus in the department of Hebrew and Semitic Studies at the University of Wisconsin (Madison), offers one explanation:

> These are matters that are very difficult to ascertain or to corroborate in terms of archaeological research. You just don't have . . . a tablet saying that the Israelites conquered such and such a place on such and such a date. That sort of thing doesn't exist.[26]

Another reason for this difficulty has been implied in our discussion about the nature of the Conquest itself. The facts, as the Bible presents them, indicate that there is relatively no evidence of conquest to find. Massive physical destruction of the whole of Canaan was neither the goal nor the outcome of the Conquest. The "ban" (sentence of destruction) under which Canaan was placed by God applied to the Canaanite populations *within* their cities, not the cities themselves *(see* Joshua 6:17,21), except for Jericho, Ai, and Hazor. In David Merling's estimation, the Conquest, as described in the Bible, was not likely to have left sufficient evidence of itself. In light of this understanding, if we *did* find evidence of a massive destruction along the Conquest route at the time that the Bible gives for the Conquest (1400 B.C.), it would actually cause a *greater* problem for the Bible!

Should we, then, be looking for such evidence at all? Eugene Merrill, Professor of Old Testament at Dallas Theological Seminary, is of the opinion that such efforts are pointless:

> . . . archaeological verifiability of the conquest is shown to be an exercise in irrelevance. All one could hope for is some indication that decimated occupants of the land were replaced by ethnically and culturally different settlers, a quest that is notoriously unfruitful.[27]

A reason such a quest was once deemed unfruitful was because while attempting to find evidence of occupational replacement the Israelites in their settlement period might simply have adopted the Canaanites' material culture (Deuteronomy 6:10-11). Not yet having developed their own distinctive material culture, the Israelites *looked like* Canaanites in the archaeological record. The Amarna letters, comprised of correspondence between Canaanite city-states and Egyptian officials at Amarna, indeed reveal that the Israelites were culturally inferior to the Canaanites. However, based on more extensive excavations and surveys, we now know that the Israelites did evidence a unique ceramic culture.[28] This repertoire of pottery enables the experts to distinguish the Israelites from their Canaanite neighbors. Although this culture is dated to Israelite immigration and settlement at the end of the thirteenth century B.C. (at least), others have also used it to argue an early date for the Exodus.[29] For instance, Manfred Bietaks's excavations at Tell el-Dab'a (Goshen) in Egypt have revealed a Canaanite-style pottery like that which appears in Canaan. This may be possible evidence that the Israelites were once in Goshen, or conversely, that Asiatics had simply entered into this Egyptian Delta region. At any rate, most critical scholars will dismiss this evidence because they presume a late date, and this pottery is dated early (from about 1650–1550 B.C.).

What, then, are we left with? Can evidence of the Conquest be found? Although the evidence is sketchy and certainly controversial, the answer to this is affirmative. However, we must look in the right places. We should not look for a Conquest stratum except in the three cities burned with fire, and even there, with subsequent destructions by other invaders, our expectations must be measured. Even when all of the ambiguous archaeological evidence is set aside we still have the witness of the most significant archaeological and historical document yet discovered by man—the Bible. Even if we decline to accept that Scripture was divinely inspired, as many scholars do, the Bible's realistic account of a partial Conquest clearly has the marks of historicity, not of an etiological embellishment. Extrabiblical data from the Amarna texts and socio-ethno-graphic and ecological-economic research have provided us a compatible outline within which the traditional details of the biblical narrative of the Conquest and settlement can be placed. Bruce K. Waltke tells us,

> In every way studied in which the textual tradition regarding the Conquest and the Settlement can be tested by archaeology, the two lines of evidence coincide. Furthermore, all the accredited Palestinian artifactual evidence supports the literary account that the Conquest occurred at the time specifically dated by the biblical historians. Therefore, from this data one has no reason to question the trustworthiness of the Bible. . . .[30]

So our quest for the Conquest has not been in vain. Whether it be the lack of sufficient evidence or the "irrelevance" of any such evidence, the search has forced a return to the biblical text. There, once our presuppositions about the Bible's historical uniqueness are corrected, we indeed find the historical Conquest after all.

2

KING DAVID

Mythical Figure or Famous Monarch?

...the greatest leaders of ancient Israel—
David and Solomon...we rarely view...in this
very real light. They are claimed as part of the
heritage of three major faiths. The age in which
they governed held profound consequences for
the future. Yet somehow they have been seen
unidimensionally within the restricted confines
of institutionalized "sacredness," which has
tended to strip them of whatever mortality and
humanity they surely possessed. David and
Solomon were real men—not myths or leg-
ends.... [1]

—Jerry M. Landay

The person of King David looms large on the pages of both the Old and New Testaments, being mentioned some 1,048 times. In the Old Testament he is the primary subject of 62 chapters and the author of 73 psalms. In the New Testament he figures prominently on both sides of Jesus' genealogy and in the place of His birth (Matthew 1:1,6,17,20; Luke 2:4,11; 3:31), for "the Christ is David's son" (Luke 20:41), who will inherit "the throne of His father David" (Luke 1:32). And recently, based on the historical conquests of King David, Jerusalem celebrated the 3,000th anniversary of his capture of their city from the Jebusites (2 Samuel 5:7-25).

With such an emphasis on David in the Scriptures, it may come as a surprise to many to learn that until recently all books dealing with the history of the Holy Land had to admit that no trace of David had ever appeared in the archaeological record. Typical was this statement from one of the leading authorities in biblical archaeology, Dame Kathleen Kenyon—words uttered just ten years ago:

> To many people it seems remarkable that David and Solomon still remain unknown outside the Old Testament or literary sources derived directly from it. No extra-Biblical inscription, either from Palestine or from a neighboring country, has yet been found to contain a reference to them.[2]

The Myth of King David

This lack of evidence led many critical scholars to doubt that a historical David had ever existed. Historical revisionists (or minimalists) argued that the "David Myth" had been a literary invention drawn from various heroic traditions to explain the formation of Israel's monarchy. In one development of this myth, according to the critics, a priestly school surrounding the Temple had sought a theological basis for their own concept of divine government. This was the concept of an ideal king (David) set against an imperfect king (Saul). According to the critics, Saul, of course, did not exist either, but served with David as contrasting theological models of man's choice (Saul) versus God's choice (David). Even so, David's frequent follies showed the superiority of a theocracy (rule by God) over a monarchy (rule by man). Without material evidence to help clothe these figures in flesh, they remained to many people nothing more than inspiring storybook characters.

Why Can't We Find More?

People are often puzzled as to why so little has been recovered from the earliest period of the monarchy—the times of Saul, David, and Solomon. One major reason for the lack of evidence may simply be that so little has actually been excavated in the areas related to their reigns. Israel is one gigantic tel, and in places like Hebron and Jerusalem, where the most evidence for this period would be expected, competing religious claims and political unrest make access to some of the most promising sites virtually impossible to archaeologists.

In those areas which have been excavated, there are other reasons for the scarcity of material remains. First, in terms of architecture, later buildings often have eclipsed earlier structures, leaving little of the original to be found. For instance, at the lowest level of the excavations at the southern wall of the Temple Mount, archaeologists have uncovered only a small section of a building that is datable to the time of Solomon. In general, thousands of years of later occupations cover most of the site. Second, in terms of finding monumental reliefs and sculptures, other cultures of this time period left such evidence, but the biblical command against the making of graven images generally eliminated this possibility in Israel.

But what about written records? We have the Bible; aren't there other writings from the biblical period? One reason few written records are found is because the Israelites, in contrast to their neighbors, wrote most of their court documents and other records on scrolls of perishable papyrus. Papyrus was both more efficient and less costly than other forms of writing material. In addition, it represented a more advanced way of communication for a literate society such as biblical Israel. In the Bible, we find evidence for the use of papyrus from the end of the Monarchy period; for example, we read that the prophet Jeremiah wrote his prophecies on papyrus scrolls (Jeremiah 36:2).

The Bible also notes how easily such writing could be destroyed; for example, King Jehoiakim took Jeremiah's scrolls and cut them up and burned them (Jeremiah 36:23).

Finds from the First Temple Period

Despite these considerations of the scarcity of material remains, on occasion exceptions to the rule are discovered. One exception to the law against graven images was an Iron Age ostracon from Ramat Rachel, which bore a painted figure sitting on a throne. Israeli archaeologist Gabriel Barkay has proposed that this might be a picture of the Judean king Hezekiah.

Also, while papyri documents are perishable, the seals which were once attached to these documents still remain. Excavations in the City of David have unearthed numbers of these clay seals (or bullae) in the ruins of houses that were burned by the invading Babylonian army at the close of the First Temple period. In addition, there are outstanding examples of more durable inscriptions from the beginning of the Monarchy and the First Temple period. The Bible notes that prophets of this era sometimes wrote on wood or metal (Isaiah 8:1; Ezekiel 37:16). At Deir Allah, located in the Jordan Valley, a mid-eighth century Aramaic inscription mentioning the biblical prophet Balaam (Numbers 22-24) was discovered written in red and black ink on plaster.[3] Hebrew inscriptions on stone include the Gezer Calendar (tenth century B.C.), and eighth century B.C. inscriptions such as the Siloam Tunnel Inscription, the Royal Steward Inscription, and the clay ostraca from Samaria, Arad, and Lachish. There are also significant finds inscribed on metal or ivory, such as the seventh-century B.C. silver scrolls from Ketef Hinnom and an ivory pomegranate scepter head. The silver scrolls preserve the earliest known biblical text (from the book of Numbers) and indicate that the biblical text was probably written down soon after the events it describes. According to the inscription on the scepter head, it most likely once belonged to a priest who officiated in the First Temple.

These discoveries, though scant, show the kinds of finds that may be expected and indicate that more is certainly there to be found. The most promising location for such evidence is a ridge south of the present-day Temple Mount in Jerusalem. On this nine-acre site, David's Jerusalem had its start alongside the already 2,000-year-old Canaanite/Jebusite city. Still called *'Ir David* ("David's City"), excavations by Kathleen Kenyon and Israeli archaeologist Yigael Shiloh have pinpointed structures probably mentioned by David, such as a 50-foot-high stack of rocks called the Stone-Stepped Structure, which might be the biblical Millo, upon which David may have built his Fortress of Zion (2 Samuel 5:9). The oldest known element at the site, a water system known as Warren's Shaft, is believed to have been used by David's general Joab to capture the Jebusite city (2 Samuel 5:6-9; 1 Chronicles 11:4-7).[4] And in the summer of 1997, Israeli archaeologist Ronny Reich uncovered in the southern area of David's City an immense stone structure thought to be a defensive tower. In addition, archaeologist Eilat Mazar, who directed excavations of the Ophel (an area between the Temple Mount and David's City), believes that David's royal palace lies waiting to be discovered just south of the Ophel (and north of the Stone-Stepped Structure).[5] The area, once off limits because of Arab orchards planted there, is now accessible to excavators. Perhaps in the near future direct evidence of David's presence will be unearthed here for all to see.

An Unexpected Find

A Key Inscription

Despite the excavations that have revealed an established Israelite presence in the Holy Land near the time of David— and have even uncovered structures in the City of David related to his time—critics continued to hold fast to the David Myth because no specific mention of David had ever surfaced in such excavations. However, these critics were forced to reconsider their opinions based on new evidence that was unearthed in

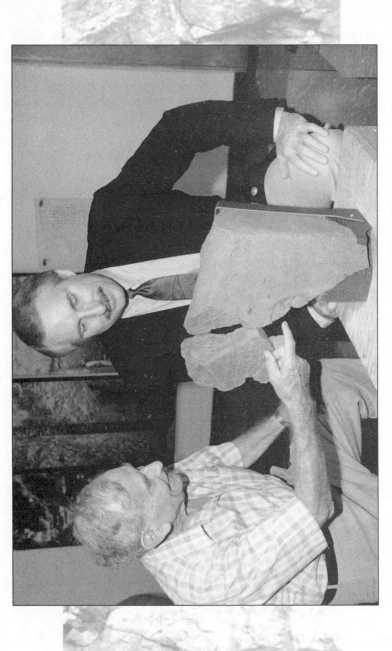

30. *The Tel Dan Stele, with excavator Avraham Biran pointing to the words "House of David" on a copy of the original.*

1993. The challenge to these revisionists came from a nearly 3,000-year-old monumental inscription (stele) written on black basalt by one of Israel's foreign enemies. Discovered at the northern Israelite site of Tel Dan, this startling inscription includes the words "House of David."

The archaeologist who made this discovery is Professor Avraham Biran, director of the Nelson Glueck School of Biblical Archaeology of the Hebrew Union College. The House of David Stele crowned 27 years of archaeological discoveries at Tel Dan, the site in northern Israel where the stele was found. When I visited Professor Biran recently at his office at the Jewish Institute of Religion in Jerusalem, we visited the Skirball Museum (located adjacent to his office), where many of his discoveries at Tel Dan are housed. Holding a replica of the House of David Stele, now enlarged with new pieces unearthed in 1994, he remarked on its contents and its contribution to biblical history:

> In a wall constructed somewhere around the end of the ninth to the beginning of the eighth century B.C. we

31. *The Tel Dan Stele. The words "House of David" are on the third line from the top, beginning with the second character (reading right to left).*

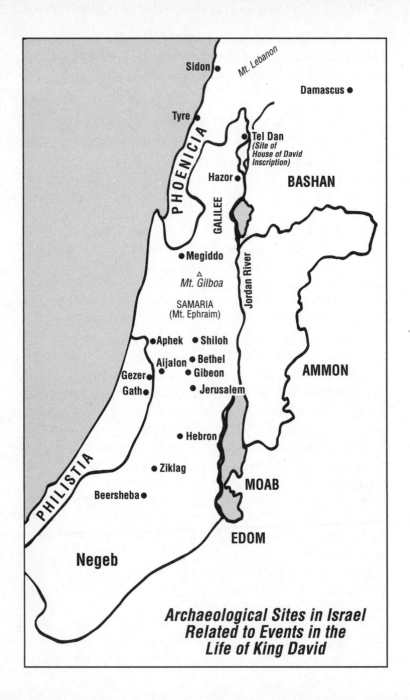

Sidon

Mt. Lebanon

Damascus

Tyre

PHOENICIA

Tel Dan
*(Site of
House of David
Inscription)*

Hazor

BASHAN

GALILEE

Jordan River

Megiddo

△
Mt. Gilboa

SAMARIA
(Mt. Ephraim)

Aphek   Shiloh

Aijalon   Bethel

Gezer   Gibeon

Gath   Jerusalem

AMMON

Hebron

Ziklag

PHILISTIA

Beersheba

MOAB

EDOM

Negeb

***Archaeological Sites in Israel
Related to Events in the
Life of King David***

found a fragment inscribed in Aramaic. Its lines speak of warfare between the Israelites and the Arameans, which from the Bible we know was constant between Israel and Damascus [during this period]. In this fragment a king of Damascus, Ben Hadad, is apparently victorious. He has killed someone and taken prisoners and horsemen. . . . But what was really thrilling was to find that he defeated a "king of Israel of the House of David"! So here you have the mention of the "House of David" in an Aramean inscription dated . . . about 150 years after the days of King David. The following year in another scene of excavation we found two more pieces and these two pieces link to the first one and give us the names of these kings. The king of Israel that is referred to is "Jehoram" . . . who is the son of Ahab. The king of the House of David [Judah] is "Ahaziahu" [Ahaziah], who is also mentioned in the Bible. . . . the exciting thing here is that you have a historical stele referring to historical events of which the Bible speaks at great lengths [2 Kings 8:7-15; 9:6-10].[6]

Professor Biran has more precisely dated the inscription to the time of the Aramean usurper Hazael, whom he believes authored the inscription. Hazael's entire reign was characterized by war with Israel, and he went down in biblical history as one of the Israelites' most brutal enemies (2 Kings 8:7-15). Told by the prophet Elisha that he would be king, he murdered the king of Aram, Hadad-'izr, and reigned between 842-800 B.C. After he ascended the throne, he immediately went to war against Israel, Judah, and Philistia. The biblical record indicates that he decimated Israel's army and turned both it and Philistia into vassal (subservient) states (2 Kings 10:32-33; 12:17). Judah also seems to have shared this same fate (2 Kings 12:17-18). Professor Biran thinks that the House of David Stele was erected as a memorial to these deeds, and was probably written in the latter part of Hazael's reign. The line that contains the reference to the House of David (line 9) is in the context of the slaying of the Israelite and Judean kings. These lines (7b-9), after reconstruction, read: "I killed Jehoram son of Ahab king of Israel and I killed Ahaziahu son of Jehoram king of the House of David."

What Does the Inscription Imply?

The term *House of David* is a dynastic title implying that if there was a "House of David" there must have been a David. As expected, biblical minimalists have countered that the discovery of the epithet *Beth-David* ("House of David") means nothing more than that a name was drawn out of Israelite story traditions and used as divine titles often were for places like Beth-el ("house of God"). In this sense, one historical revisionist contends that *Beth-David* is an "eponymic reference to Yahweh as Godfather." He writes:

> ... the place name *bytdwd* ["House of David"] hardly refers to a historical David, but much more likely to a temple dedicated to the divine epithet *dwd*, the historically known epithet of Yahweh, and the hero of biblical narratives seems to be rather derivative of the familial associations implicit in the form of this place name and its associations with the monarchy in Jerusalem."[7]

This view has been supported by the argument that a word divider (usually a dot written in between words to show they are separate) is absent in the letters *bytdwd*.

However, a number of epigraphists have defended the reference to a historical David,[8] including Anson Rainey of Israel and Alan Millard of England, both experts in ancient Aramaic inscriptions. They have demonstrated that there are examples of compound words or names where the word divider is absent.[9] In addition, Wheaton College archaeologist professor James Hoffmeier has pointed out that reading *bytdwd* as a place name is completely unattested in the Bible or any cognate literature from the ancient Near East.[10] On the other hand, the reading "House of David" as a title dependent on the historic founder of the line, the Judean King David, appears more than 20 times in

32. *The Mesha Inscription, which French scholar André LeMaire believes has the line "House of David."*

the Old Testament *(see,* for example, 1 Kings 12:19; 14:8; Isaiah 7:2; and so on).

Recently, the French scholar André LeMaire has added new support to an identification of the Tel Dan Inscription with the historic King David. He has identified the reading of the name *David* in a formerly unreadable line, "House of D...," on the Mesha Stele (or Moabite Stone). If this proves to be the case after scrutiny by other scholars, it will serve as a second example of the phrase "House of David."[11] However, even if the name of "David" were not on this ninth-century B.C. memorial inscription from Moab, like the Tel Dan Stele, it also contains other biblical names, such as Omri (1 Kings 16:28). In fact, scholars have not doubted the historicity of Omri simply because he is listed in the Mesha Inscription. If this is so, then why should the historicity of David be doubted if his name appears in an epithet in the Tel Dan Stele? Furthermore, the epithets "the land of Omri" and "the house of Omri" have been found in Assyrian texts.[12] If the Assyrians could specify states by the name of a dynasty's founder, regardless of who was currently in power, could not the Arameans? In this regard, the Aramean "House of David" Stele implies that the kingdoms of Israel and Judah during this period were, as the Bible describes, a formidable threat both politically and militarily to the surrounding nations. Revisionists, however, have thought that Israel and Judah were insignificant city-states. But would a dominant foreign power such as Syria have erected a monument commemorating the defeat of unimportant enemies?

In addition, we know that the Mesha Stele also has the term "son of Ahab." Why would the reference to Omri's son Ahab be considered factual while the line about David is thought to be fictional?[13] In other words, if there was a King Ahab as dynastic head, then why not a King David? The reason, of course, is that while extrabiblical evidence has existed for a King Ahab, none has previously existed for a King David. As Dr. Jack Sasson—professor of religious studies at the University of North Carolina at Chapel Hill—once noted, "No personality in the Bible has been confirmed by other sources until Ahab; not David or Abraham or Adam and Eve."[14]

If the Tel Dan Stele was accepted as having a legitimate reference to a historic King David, then the revisionist might have to revise his perspective and reconsider the presuppositions that prejudice his interpretation of the biblical text.

Was David Real?

Some scholars are willing to concede that the Tel Dan and Mesha Steles make it plausible that a real figure named David existed, yet they still insist that much of what is recorded in the Bible about David is totally fictional. But, the events ascribed to David in the Bible make more sense if David is assumed to be a real person. While a critic may claim that David's heroic conquest of a giant is mere fiction, there is nothing quite so contemporary as a politician caught in adultery and cover-up *(see 2 Samuel 11)!* Yet, both aspects of David's life are described with an equal sense of reality. There is, in fact, nothing about David that does not ring true to normal human experience. His devotion and his desires are portrayed in conflict, just as in the best of men. When his passion for God seems too saintly (for example, Psalm 23, 42), we are quickly reminded by his other passions that he is indeed a sinner (Psalms 32, 51). Lust, laziness, infidelity, murder, pride, fear, family feuds, marital failure—all of these are part of the history of this king. Such unidealistic elements are not usually painted into the portraits of myths and legends, and certainly not those intentionally designed to be national ideals and messianic progenitors. Therefore, the finding of a historical acknowledgment of the "House of David"—reported by an Israelite foe with no respect for Israelite traditions—adds material support to a literary account that already appears historically credible. Archaeologist Bryant Wood summarizes this proper understanding of the importance of the House of David Stele when he says:

> In our day, most scholars, archaeologists and biblical scholars would take a very critical view of the historical accuracy of many of the accounts in the Bible, particularly the early books of the Bible. Most scholars today would say that anything prior to the kingdom period is simply folk stories and myths, and here is where biblical archaeology can play a very important role because in the field of archaeology, we can come up with new evidence and new data to help us understand these biblical accounts. Many times the newer discoveries of archaeology have overturned older critical views of the Bible. Many scholars have said there never was a David or a Solomon, and now we have a stele that actually mentions David.[15]

At present more of the stele is still missing than has been found. Apparently the returning Israelite king who had reconquered Dan destroyed his enemy's "victory stele" and used the stone as building blocks. The majority of these stones may still remain buried somewhere at the entrance to the ancient city. Perhaps archaeologists will soon discover and bring together these lost pieces of the puzzle and complete for us the whole

picture. Until then, the small fragments we do have are sufficient to caution the historical revisionists against mythologizing
biblical characters such as David. Rather, the historical reality of
David encourages us to emulate the example set by this king of
old—who though imperfect always returned to a perfect God;
therefore, like him, we ought to live as those who are "after
[God's] own heart" (1 Samuel 13:14).

10

THE TEMPLE

Political Propaganda or Proven Place?

When one considers what Jerusalem, the spiritual center of the monotheistic religions, has represented to countless millions of people, and then tries to assess whether these people had, or even nowadays have, any idea of what the city was like originally, it is clear that there is a major gap between imagination and reality. . . . Although many scholars have in the past attempted to reconstruct the different phases of the Temple Mount . . . except for tantalizing clues in the ancient texts, they had mainly contradictory religious traditions, legends, and folk stories to guide them, and their reconstructions were distorted accordingly. . . . [But now our] excavations . . . centered around the ancient Temple Mount [have enabled us] to depict Jerusalem as it emerges anew from the insights we have gained.[1]

—Benjamin Mazar

The greatest architectural accomplishment in ancient Israel was its magnificent Temple in Jerusalem. Placed politically at the center of the country, it was also the religious focus of the nation, where God's glory was resident among His people. Consequently, it was destined to be at the center of religious and political conflicts. The Temple became the object of internal religious conflicts, with idolaters and reformers alternately desecrating or rededicating its holy places. External political conflicts brought Israel's enemies to repeatedly plunder its treasures and force the Judean kings to diminish and deface its structures in order to pay tribute. And twice, foreign powers destroyed the Temple completely.

Still at the Center of Conflict

Today, Jerusalem and its Temple Mount are again at the center of conflict, and Israel's new enemies have sought to wage a war on history by denying that the Temple ever existed. While archaeology is apolitical—as are most archaeologists in their archaeological aims—the archaeology of Jerusalem, especially near the ancient Temple Mount, has been continually attacked by Israel's modern enemies as Zionist political propaganda. And, as in the past, internal religious disputes continue to disturb the sacred site. In fact, archaeological excavations throughout Israel are regularly threatened by religious Jews who demand their closure, contending that these digs may be desecrating old Jewish cemeteries or contain ancient Jewish remains. Furthermore, any type of excavation on the Temple Mount itself is expressly forbidden both by Muslims and religious Jews. Islamic law allows only Muslims to worship on the Mount, and considers any penetration of the site for whatever archaeological purpose a veiled attempt by the Israeli government to remove an Islamic presence and rebuild the Jewish Temple. There have recently been Arab riots because of excavations that revealed a portion of the Herodian street along the southern end of the Western Wall[2] as well as the opening of an exit to the Hasmonean Tunnel that connects an archaeological excavation of an underground portion of the Western Wall and one of its gates.[3] By contrast, most religious Jews, who expect one day to rebuild their Temple, claim that only properly purified Jewish priests are permitted to enter the site, and say that the discovery of things pertaining to the Temple are the sole provenance of the coming Messiah.

As a result, most of the archaeological information available to us about the Temple Mount comes from explorations and excavations of the previous century. At that time, the area was under Turkish rule, and archaeologists were sometimes able to get permission to explore. But a small amount of new information has been gained in recent years from excavations that have taken place in the shadow of the ancient Temple. These new discoveries have enabled us to make significant new archaeological deductions concerning age-old questions about the Temple itself.

Counting the Temples Correctly

In our study of the Jerusalem Temple it's important to remember that in historical succession there were actually three Temples that stood on the Temple Mount between 960 B.C. and A.D. 70. The First Temple was begun in 967 B.C. and completed in 960 B.C. It was destroyed by the Babylonians in 586 B.C. (For information about the archaeological evidence of this destruction, *see* chapter 12.) The Temple was rebuilt under the leadership of a governor named Zerubbabel, with the foundations laid in 538 B.C. and the structure dedicated in 515 B.C. This Second Temple remained in its modest form of reconstruction for almost 500 years until the Roman period. Then the Roman-appointed Judean king, Herod the Great, completely restored it, beginning his work in 19 B.C. and dedicating it ten years later. This thorough restoration was from the ground up; Herod enlarged and refurbished the Temple and increased its platform to twice its former size.[4] Although historically and architecturally this was a third building, religiously it was still considered the Second Temple because the offering of sacrifices was

33. *Excavation of a camp of the Roman Tenth Legion, who destroyed the Second Temple in* A.D. *70 (Mount Herzl, Jerusalem).*

not interrupted during the transition between structures. It was in this newly restored Second Temple that Jesus was dedicated as an infant (about 6 B.C.). Though Herod had already dedicated the Temple, work on it continued for another 46 years (John 2:20). Then the Roman army destroyed the edifice in A.D. 70.[5] New evidence of this army's presence has been recently located outside Jerusalem in the excavation of a camp of the Tenth Legion (which destroyed the city and Temple). In addition, the Vespasian-Titus Inscription discovered in 1970 on a stone column near the Temple Mount commemorates the father emperor and son general of the Tenth Legion, as well as Silva, the Roman commander of the Tenth Legion. In A.D. 73, Silva attacked the Jews who had fled to Masada.[6]

Constructing the First Temple

The First Temple was built by King David's son Solomon according to God's plan (1 Chronicles 28:6). David provided for the Temple's construction during his last years through the royal treasury and a collection taken from the people of Israel (1 Chronicles 29:1-9). Following David's death, Solomon completed the Temple primarily through forced labor from the native Israelite population (1 Kings 5:13-16; 2 Chronicles 2:2). According to the Bible, the architectural pattern for the First Temple, like the Tabernacle before it, was divinely revealed (Exodus 25:9,40; 1 Chronicles 28:11-19). The construction itself took place on a high hill in the Moriah mountain range north of the City of David and the Ophel Ridge (the area where the city had been confined up to that point). Following the biblical trail of texts pointing toward the Temple from Genesis (22:2) and Exodus (15:17) through Samuel (2 Samuel 7:10), we believe that it occupied the highest point on this hill at the same place where Abraham had been stopped from slaying a son (Genesis 22:12-14) and the angel of the Lord from slaying a city (2 Samuel 24:16-25). Archaeological consensus locates this place today as the raised platform in East Jerusalem's Old City, known to Jews and Christians as the Temple Mount.

However, even though we have some details of its construction in the Bible, no one can be entirely certain what that First Temple actually looked like. I was reminded of this fact recently when I visited a special exhibit at the Bible Lands Museum in Jerusalem, entitled "Royal Cities of the Biblical World." In this exhibit made up of models of ancient cities and related artifacts was a superb model of the First Temple, accompanied by various computer visualizations of Solomon's Temple, done by three different designers. The text that described the model emphasized that every one of these models of the Solomonic Temple is theoretical because no actual remains of the First Temple survived the destruction that took place in 586 B.C. So how is it that model makers can construct such models? Archaeology supplies our answer, as Professor Amihai Mazar explains:

> We wanted very much to explore the Temple of Solomon. Unfortunately, we know that nothing remained, but the description of the Solomonic Temple in the scriptures is so exact that we can even draw the plan and can compare this plan to plans of other temples that were found in Syria and Canaan and Aramean sites in the Iron Age and the Bronze Age. [Furthermore,] this Temple of Solomon is based on a long tradition [of temples] which started about 1,000 years earlier and continued to 200 or 300 years later. So we can insert the biblical tradition concerning the Temple of Solomon in a much longer tradition [of ancient Near Eastern temples] which can be illustrated archaeologically.[7]

The Architecture of the First Temple

As Professor Mazar has noted, the picture archaeology draws for us of Solomon's Temple comes from studying and comparing the form of the temples among Israel's neighbors.[8] The style of the Jerusalem Temple appears to have been derived from the long-room type of temple common in Syria from the second millennium B.C.[9] The long-room temple was built with the entrance door on the short side (as opposed to a broad-room temple, which has the entrance on the long side). It is generally thought that the interior style was *tripartite* (three-part),[10] each division having a separate function with varying degrees of sanctity. The Temple at Jerusalem, in all of its constructions, adopted this form with its outside porch, inner holy place, and innermost Holy of Holies.

The best archaeological example of a Solomonic-type temple is an eighth-century long-room tripartite temple from Tel Tainat in the Amuq Valley at the northern Orontes in Syria. Excavated in the 1930s by the University of Chicago's Oriental Institute, this temple, which had an east-west orientation like the Jerusalem Temple, still had one set of a pair of lions that were made to support columns and guard the entrance. This temple was built next to the royal palace, as was Solomon's. Other good examples from northern Syria include four temples from two sites (Tel Munbaqa and Tel Emar), and a poorly preserved temple at En Dara. Also, of the three temples found in the excavations at Ebla, one is a long-room style, indicating a long history for this type of building. This same style of temple was imported into Canaan during the second millennium B.C. and appears (with variations) at Hazor and Tel Kitan (in the Jordan Valley). Two temples of this type from the Middle Bronze IIB Period (1750–1550 B.C.) also have been found at Shechem and Megiddo. The only known Israelite temple form is represented by a small temple within the Israelite fortress at Tel Arad (in the Negev).[11] Although originally erected in Solomon's time, and similar internally to the Jerusalem Temple, the style is that of the broad-room temple. This provides archaeological corroboration of the biblical account that Solomon's Temple was inspired by a non-Israelite source.

This foreign source, however, was not Syrian, but Phoenician. In keeping with the custom of his age, Solomon, when he constructed the Temple, relied upon the expertise of the Phoenician material supplier, Hiram (Huram), king of Tyre (2 Samuel 5:11; 1 Kings 5; 2 Chronicles 2:3-18). The biblical text adds that Hiram sent his Phoenician architects and craftsmen to advise their Israelite counterparts on building the Temple to contemporary specifications. One of these was a half-Jewish, half-Phoenician artisan named Huram-abi, who was given oversight of the Temple craftsmen.[12] Credit is given to him for the vast array of decorative, cast, and overlaid objects in the Temple (1 Kings 7:13-45; 2 Chronicles 2:13-14). The building of the Second Temple under Zerubbabel also involved Phoenician workmen (Ezra 3:7-10),[13] in harmony with the decree from the Persian king Darius to "rebuild" the Temple. Jews in captivity, and long removed from the original construction, could only rebuild (rather than replace) this Temple with the aid of Phoenicians skilled in following their own design.

While few examples of Phoenician temples exist (or have yet to be found) to confirm this design, it is certain that their constructions were descendants of the same long-room temple.[14] One Phoenician temple two centuries older than Solomon's was excavated in Hazor. It was 84 feet by 56 feet and tripartite. At each side of the entrance to the main hall was a round pillar, like those in Solomon's Temple. Also, ivory panels and sculptures in several Phoenician temples bear pattern decorations similar to the cherubim, palm trees, and open flowers carved in the paneling of the Jerusalem Temple (1 Kings 6:35).[15] In addition, the fourth-century A.D. Church Father Eusebius preserved in his writings the record of a Phoenician priest named Sanchuniathon, who gave details of how King Hiram of Tyre had supplied Solomon with supplies for the building of the Temple. Such archaeological information about comparative temples makes it possible to reconstruct a reasonably accurate portrait of the Solomonic Temple.[16]

A Trip Through the Temple

In appearance the First Temple was a modest building. It was about the size of a small church or synagogue: about 104 feet long x 35 feet wide x 52 feet high, covering 3,640 square feet, and situated on a platform approximately 10 feet high.[17] In

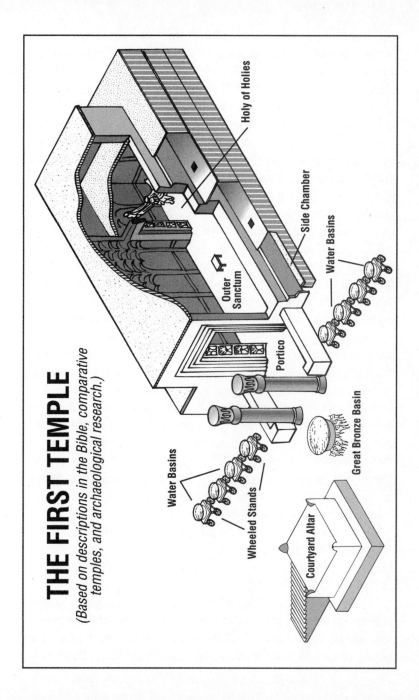

THE FIRST TEMPLE

(Based on descriptions in the Bible, comparative temples, and archaeological research.)

Holy of Holies

Side Chamber

Water Basins

Outer Sanctum

Portico

Water Basins

Wheeled Stands

Great Bronze Basin

Courtyard Altar

the front of the Temple to the east was an open courtyard in which stood the bronze altar. Not far away was located an immense basin called "the Bronze (or Molten) Sea." This basin, which held an estimated 15,000 gallons of water and rested on the backs of a dozen bronze bulls, was used for the ritual purification and cleansing of the priests engaged in offering sacrifices. Ten ornamented bronze rolling basins or lavers (called mekhonot), which were stationed nearby on both the north and south sides of the courtyard, transported the water to various places at the Temple. (An eleventh-century B.C. parallel to this rolling basin was discovered in Cyprus. Adorned with cherubim, this 13-inch, four-wheeled bronze cart supported a water basin.) At the westernmost end of the Temple complex was a belt of storerooms surrounding the holy places. Other objects made for use in the Temple, such as stone altars and iron incense shovels, have been found in many parts of Israel, most notably several eighth-century examples from Tel Dan in northern Galilee.

The holy places (the three rooms of the Temple) were first approached by ascending the Temple platform via ten steps leading up between the twin bronze pillars, which were named *Yakin* ("He [God] establishes") and *Boaz* ("in Him [God] is strength")—each about 40 feet high and 12 feet in circumference. Beyond the entrance porch lay the first and smallest room of the Temple, which led into the main room (the holy place). The door through which an individual entered probably had massive, interlocking doorframes similar to those discovered in the royal tombs at Tamassos, Cyprus, and an eighth-century B.C. ivory from Nimrud of a woman at a window.

This middle room was the largest in the Temple. Its interior walls were covered with elaborately carved cedar panels overlaid with gold, and the floors were covered with cypress boards so that no stonework remained visible. In addition, Solomon is said to have adorned this room with beautiful and precious stones. Housed within this awe-inspiring central chamber were the sacred objects from the Tabernacle: the Menorah (a golden seven-branched lampstand), the Table of Shewbread (the sacred presence bread), and the golden Altar of Incense. Specially made for this room (not originally in the Tabernacle) were ten tables (five on the north side and five on the south), which were accompanied by ten lamps on lampstands, as well as many implements made for use by the priests.

The innermost room was separated from the entrance by a large double veil (35 ˇ 70 feet) of fabric three fingers thick, and by a wall with only one door that was kept closed except on rare occasions. Access to this unlit, windowless room (the Holy of Holies) was forbidden to all except the High Priest, and to him only once a year at the high holy Yom Kippur (Day of Atonement). In this perfectly cube-shaped room (about 35 feet square), which was gilded throughout with an estimated 23 tons of gold, stood the most sacred object from the Tabernacle: the Ark of the Covenant (see next chapter). We can get an idea of what the gold-plated parts of the Temple must have been like based on similarly adorned temples in Egypt. The temple of Pharaoh Tutmose III (1450 B.C.) has inscriptions that record that the doorways, pillars, and shrines were all covered with gold. In the ruins of this building are slits in the stone columns and capitals, which most likely served to hold the gold sheets that covered them.[18]

Finds from the First Temple

After the First Temple was burned by the invading Babylonian army, Zerubbabel's Second Temple was rebuilt over the same spot. The builders even re-used some of the former stones, and thus eclipsed any remains from the First Temple. However, it is believed that some stones in the outer walls surrounding the Temple are Solomonic, and that parts of walls in the area of the Ophel are from the First Temple period. The only discovered item known to have been related to Solomon's Temple is a tiny ivory pomegranate that was once attached to the tip of a scepter. Dated to the eighth-century B.C., its relation to the Temple is indicated by an inscription on the scepter head: "Belonging to the hou[se of Y...]. A holy thing of the priests (or 'Holy to the

34. *Ivory pomegranate scepter head from staff of a priest who served in Solomon's Temple.*

priests')." The "house" mentioned in the inscription most likely is the "House of the Lord" or the Temple. A similar carved pomegranate (without an inscription) was found on the floor of a home dating to the sixth-century B.C. It may also have belonged to a scepter and been related to the Temple or used for decoration on a horse's bridle (such usage is depicted in Assyrian reliefs).[19]

Archaeology and the Second Temple

A Replica on Mount Gerizim?

From all indications, the Second Temple (of Zerubbabel) was built according to the same plan and dimensions as the First Temple. While the later reconstruction by Herod completely erased all traces of this Temple, an extraordinary find in Samaria has opened up the possibility of recovering an exact duplicate of Zerubbabel's Temple. The discovery was made on Mount Gerizim, a site sacred to the Samaritans because that's where

35. *Remains of the Samaritan Temple on Mount Gerizim.*

their ancient temple once stood. According to the first-century historian Flavius Josephus, the Samaritan temple was destroyed by John Hyrcanus in 113 B.C. It was this temple that the Samaritan woman referred to as the place where her "fathers worshiped" in her dialogue with Jesus (John 4:20). At the invitation of the excavation's director, Yitzhak Magen, I have twice visited the site on Mount Gerizim to view the discoveries. What has been found are the remains of the Samaritan temple, including its six-foot-thick walls, gates, and altars (on which they found sacrificial ashes and bones). In addition, two adjacent edifices, thought to be a royal residence and administrative building, were discovered and are presently being excavated. These buildings resemble the plan of the First Temple complex, which had a palace proper, throne room, House of Pharaoh's Daughter, Hall of Columns, and House of the Forest of Lebanon. The Samaritan temple was located beneath the floor of the fifth-century Byzantine church of Mary Theotokos, which had been uncovered in excavations during the 1920s. The temple's northern gate matches that of the temple described in the *Temple Scroll,* a Dead Sea Scroll document written when the Second Temple (of Zerubbabel) was still standing. That the Samaritan temple was most likely a replica of Zerubbabel's temple is implied by Josephus's account of its origin.

According to his record, Menachem, a priest in the Jerusalem Temple, fell in love with a woman named Nikaso, who was the daughter of the Samaritan's leader, Sanballat. Because she was a non-Jew, Menachem was told to choose between Nikaso and his priesthood. Choosing Nikaso and losing access to the Jerusalem Temple, Sanballat built his new son-in-law a rival temple on the sacred Mount Gerizim and made him its High Priest. Yitzhak Magen believes this account from Josephus is correct, noting that second-century B.C. inscriptions discovered at the site confirm that "the Samaritans adopted everything from the Jewish prayers to [their] sacrificial ritual."[20]

Excavation of the two adjacent buildings, in which the remains are more complete than those found in the temple, has taken priority. However, when all is finally excavated, our knowledge of this longest-lived phase of the Jerusalem Temple will be immensely improved.

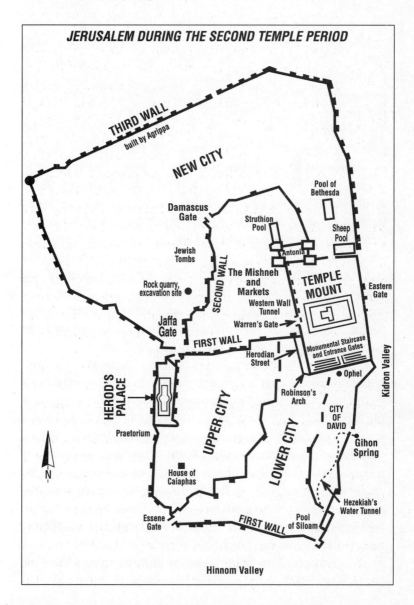

JERUSALEM DURING THE SECOND TEMPLE PERIOD

THIRD WALL
built by Agrippa

NEW CITY

Pool of Bethesda

Damascus Gate

Struthion Pool

Sheep Pool

Jewish Tombs

Antonia

SECOND WALL

The Mishneh and Markets

TEMPLE MOUNT

Eastern Gate

Rock quarry, excavation site

Western Wall Tunnel

Jaffa Gate

Warren's Gate

FIRST WALL

Herodian Street

Monumental Staircase and Entrance Gates

Kidron Valley

Ophel

HEROD'S PALACE

Robinson's Arch

CITY OF DAVID

Praetorium

UPPER CITY

LOWER CITY

Gihon Spring

N

House of Caiaphas

Hezekiah's Water Tunnel

Essene Gate

FIRST WALL

Pool of Siloam

Hinnom Valley

Revealing the Herodian Second Temple

Before Jewish access to the Temple Mount area was gained as a result of the Six-Day War in June 1967, our knowledge of the Herodian Second Temple was limited to a small section of a retaining wall (known as the "Wailing" or Western Wall) revered as the "only remnant" of the Temple that survived the Roman destruction in A.D. 70. This changed in 1968 when Israeli archaeologist Benjamin Mazar began extensive excavations at the southern end of the western and southern walls of the Temple Mount.[21] These excavations, which ended in 1978, revealed never-before-seen evidence of the Temple's ancient existence and glory. When I moved to Jerusalem in 1979 to begin archaeological studies, I was able to view many of the artifacts uncovered by these excavations exactly as they had been discovered before they were removed to museums. One item that impressed me was a large section of the upper balustrade, which had fallen just where the Roman army had toppled it 2,000 years before. One smaller section had broken off and lay against the corner of the wall. On it was an inscription that read, "To the Trumpeting Place." Here was the very place where the priests stood to blow the silver trumpets to summon the Israeli people to the sacred site.

Mazar's excavations revealed much more; some of the best-known finds are marvelled at by thousands of tourists every year. One of these is the remains of Robinson's Arch, part of the support for a great stairway connecting the upper and lower sections of the southwestern corner of the Temple Mount. Another is the monumental staircase at the southern wall and its gates (Double and Triple Gates), which served as the people's main entrance to the Temple. Jesus and His disciples climbed these stairs to enter and exit the Temple and discuss its buildings (Matthew 24:1-2; Mark 13:1-2; Luke 21:5-6). History records that Gamaliel taught his students on these stairs. One of those students was Saul, who later became the apostle Paul (Acts 5:34; 22:3).

36. *Temple balustrade inscription that reads "To the Trumpeting Place."*

37. *Author with fallen balustrade from Temple destroyed in* A.D. *70. Note broken portion at the top (right side), where the "Trumpeting Place" inscription originally was placed.*

Discoveries *Beneath* the Temple Mount

One of the most exciting—and most controversial—of the excavations at the western wall of the Temple Mount has been the dig that exposed an extensive course of the wall at the original ground level (52 feet below present ground level). This work began in conjunction with Mazar's excavation in 1968 and continued until 1982. It was renewed as the "Western Wall Tunnel" excavations in 1985 under the direction of Dan Bahat, former District Archaeologist for Jerusalem with the Israel Antiquities Authority.[22] Uncovered in the excavations was the exposed portion of the Herodian wall, which ran alongside a 900-foot-long tunnel that is three to four feet wide and six to eight feet high. Because it was believed that this tunnel was used by the priests who officiated in the Temple, it was given the popular name of "Rabbinic Tunnel." Features of the wall at the southern end of the exposed portion are truly amazing. Here, at a section dubbed the "Master Course," are four blocks bearing the unmistakable signs of Herodian craftsmanship (smoothed margins and bosses). These "foundation stones" are 11 feet high and range from 6 feet to 42 feet in length! The largest stone is estimated to be about 15 feet high, 42 feet long, and 14 feet deep, and weighs about 1,200,000 pounds! By contrast, the largest stone in the Great Pyramid of Egypt weighs only 22,000 pounds.

Along the Western Wall Tunnel was also discovered one of the ancient gates to the Temple Mount. First reported in the nineteenth century by Charles Warren, and thus named "Warren's Gate," it is a monumental gate that exited onto the Temple platform just south of the ancient Holy of Holies. Its interior looks much like the inside of present Wilson's Arch (although Wilson's Arch is dated to a later period). However, owing to a controversy with Muslim authorities in 1981, the gate was sealed and closed to further access. I first entered the tunnel and visited this gate in 1982, shortly after it was sealed. Since that time I have visited the site many more times, both with Dan Bahat and with the late Rabbi Yehuda Getz, who was involved

38. *Inside the 900-foot long Western Wall Tunnel. Along the right side is an exposed portion of the Herodian retaining wall of the Temple.*

with the gate's excavation. My interviews with these men and with the late former Chief Rabbi Shlomo Goren (whose clandestine dig beyond Warren's gate toward the Muslim Dome of the Rock provoked the riot which closed the gate) have been published in my book *In Search of Temple Treasures,*[23] and featured in the video by the same title.

Toward the northern end of the tunnel are signs that reveal where the stones were quarried (some of the stones are only partially cut). Just beyond the area where the original street ended is a water channel and aqueduct, called the Hasmonean Tunnel (although some would date it to a pre-Hasmonean era),[24] which emptied into the Struthion Pool just north of the ancient Antonia Fortress (where Jesus was scourged). The opening in September 1996, of a new exit to this Hasmonean Tunnel—an opening intended for public access—was protested by the Palestinians. In the ensuing riot, 53 people were killed.

A Walk on 2,000-Year-Old Streets

While excavations at the Western Wall Tunnel continue, excavations at the southern end of the Western Wall were renewed by Jerusalem archaeologist Ronny Reich in preparation for Jerusalem's 3000th anniversary (996 B.C.–A.D. 1996). Reich removed the debris at this site down to the original Herodian street level. In October 1996, as this work was being completed, I spoke with Reich at the site and he offered this summary of his team's work:

> We excavated outside the Temple Mount walls the main street of Jerusalem, which was paved between the Temple Mount and the Upper City and included the residential quarters of the city. . . . we have exposed here a sample of about 70 meters [230 feet] of street which was at least 500 meters [1,641 feet] long—the original length of the Temple Mount. . . . we exposed curbs of the street on both sides and the remains of traces of shops opening to the street from the west. On the east side were other shops in which people bought

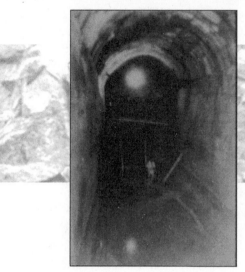

39. *Only known picture of the inside of Warren's Gate before it was sealed.*

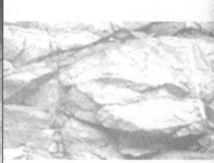

40. *Warren's Gate as it appears today after sealing.*

and sold all kinds of things which [will be determined] when we examine the finds found in the shops. I can already tell you that a large amount of stone weights to weigh commodities were found here and this is the first indication of commercial activity which took place here in the street. If you like, call it the mall of Jerusalem.... we have exposed outside the Temple Mount area—a secular place, although very close to the holy precinct of the Temple, yet still outside.[25]

It was thrilling to walk on this newly exposed street, knowing that I was one of the first to do so in 2,000 years. It was also interesting to stand within the entrances to these shops, realizing that similar shops had once spilled over into the sacred precinct of the Temple and had drawn condemnation from Jesus, prompting Him to drive out the money changers (Matthew 12:12-13; Mark 11:15-17; Luke 19:45-47; John 2:14-17). Today this ancient street is still littered with huge stones from the Temple Mount, left purposely to reveal the magnitude of the awful devastation suffered under the Romans. These stones themselves tell stories, as Ronny Reich describes:

We decided to clear the stones from half of the street and leave the stones on the other half just to commemorate the destruction of Jerusalem. These gigantic stones, on the average, weighed 2-4 tons each; some are larger... up to 15 tons.... As it seems, the Romans dismantled the walls stone by stone... simply pushing them from the upper parts of the wall down onto the street. In some places these fallen stones cracked the flagstones [the stones that paved the street], in other places the stones even sank into the street. Imagine, 10 tons of stone falling 25 meters [82 feet]. This is a very moving site for religious Jews who mourn every year on the ninth of the month of Ab [Tisha B'av] the [commemoration of the] destruction of the Temple. . . . We mourn the last 2,000 years every year, but here one can see it and touch it.[26]

41. *Shop entrances along the newly exposed Herodian-era street at the Western Wall showing portion of a pile of stones from Temple Mount's destruction in* A.D. 70 *(far right), and cracked flagstones of street (middle right).*

Discoveries like this make it impossible to believe the historical revisionists who deny that the Jewish Temple ever existed. Even more controversial—and threatening, to these revisionists—are the archaeological deductions that locate the Temple itself at the place of Islam's sacred structures.

Locating the Temple on the Temple Mount

The 25-acre platform that today dominates the Temple Mount has not been substantially disturbed since the Temple's last destruction, and archaeologists agree that the ancient Temples once occupied a spot on this platform. But the question is, Where? Because archaeological investigation of this area is prohibited, only deductions may be made based on nearby excavations and reports of excavations that took place on the Mount in the previous century. Over the years, a number of theories have been produced. One popular theory is that of Asher Kaufman, a physicist at the Hebrew University. Based on his reading of the Mishnah tractate *Middot* ("measurements") and physical computations, he puts the Temple in the northwest corner of the present platform, about 330 feet from the Muslim Dome of the Rock.

His theory of location is based on the alignment of the Eastern Gate with the entrance to the Temple proper, a supposed portion of the Temple's eastern wall (discovered by Ze'ev Yeivin in 1970), and foundation cuttings that seem to align with the modern site of a Muslim cupola known as the "Dome of the Tablets or Spirits." Problems with this location are the presence of an ancient dry moat (filled in by the Romans in A.D. 68) immediately to the north and the ancient Beth Zetha Valley to the northeast. These geographic features would have limited the construction of the Temple at this northern point. In addition, there is no evidence that the Eastern Gate of the Temple was in direct alignment with the Temple entrance nor that the present Golden Gate is the correct location of the ancient Eastern Gate.

Another theory in the opposite direction is that of Tel Aviv architect Tuvia Sagiv. He argues from architectural features and infrared surveys that the Temple was built about where the

42. *Former location of the Jewish Temple, according to Asher Kaufman—about 330 feet from the Dome of the Rock at the site of the small cupola (foreground).*

Muslim's Al-Aqsa mosque sits today, with its Holy of Holies at the spot of the al-Kas fountain.

However, among Israeli archaeologists, the consensus of location favors the traditional placement of the Temple just west and at the center of the platform at the present site of the Dome of the Rock. Archaeological evidence for this location was first put forward by Benjamin Mazar, director of the Temple Mount excavations, with the assistance of Leen Ritmeyer, who worked with the excavations for 18 years as chief architect.[27] Ritmeyer, who today heads his own archaeological design company in England, first deduced:[28]

> Josephus tells us that Herod made a Temple Mount twice as large as before. In the Mishnah tractate *Middot* we are told that the Temple Mount was measured at 500 cubits square. I investigated a particular step at the northwestern corner of the present-day Moslem platform, and using some early photographs, found that this was the remains of an earlier wall. Looking at the

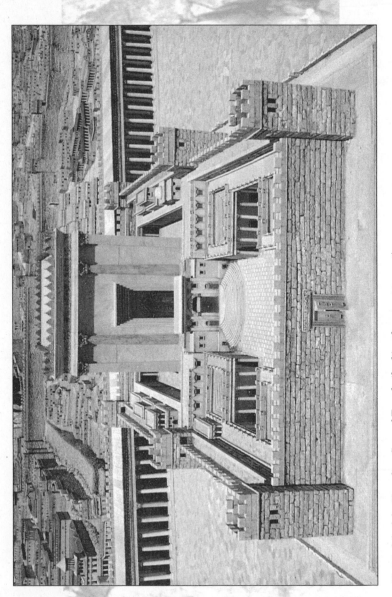

43. *Model of the Herodian Second Temple (looking from east to west).*

plans, I soon realized that this step was parallel with the eastern wall of the Temple Mount at a distance of 860 feet. If you divide that distance by 500, you come to the well-established [royal] cubit of just over 20 inches long going back to the early Egyptian period. So then I had two walls at a distance of 500 cubits.

Along the present-day edge of the northern platform, Brian Loren investigated cistern number 29, which Charles Warren in a previous century had recorded. He describes that on the inside he saw a well-cut rock scarp, which he identified as the northern boundary of this pre-Herodian Temple Mount. From this starting point at the western wall going along the northern wall a distance of 500 cubits we come to the eastern wall just north of the present Golden Gate. From that point you can project 500 cubits down to a bend, probably due to an earlier construction which was buried deep underground. Also on the west, Barclay's gate is L-shaped and the point where it bends is exactly 500 cubits from the eastern wall.

So once I had located three walls with their corners, it was relatively easy to complete the square and then take the measurements of this square and compare it with the present-day site. It came out exactly twice as large as before. [Additional] evidence that would support a location of this earlier Temple Mount are the underground tunnels which lead up from the Double and Triple Gates exactly opposite the pre-Herodian southern wall. On the west, the underground tunnels of Barclay and Loren are built up to the pre-Herodian western wall. So I believe I have found the location of the pre-Herodian Temple Mount.[29]

Drawing a diagram of these conclusions, Ritmeyer then artistically removed the later expansions made to this platform by the Hasmoneans and King Herod, which have been identified through archaeological excavations, and traced the dimensions of the various courts of the Temple as recorded in the Mishnah. That enabled him to pinpoint the Temple on the 500-cubit platform at the place of the present Dome of the Rock (for his diagram and precise identifications at this site, see the next chapter).[30]

In Anticipation of New Discoveries

Recent archaeological work, then, has made it impossible for people to deny the existence of the Jewish Temple in Jerusalem. Political propaganda and religious rivalries currently prevent us from finding additional evidence of the Temple that surely lies buried beneath the present platform, but there will come a day when all that is past and we can unearth the wonders dating from the glory days of the Temple. That prospect is made more special by the fact that this was the place where Jesus said the stones would shout. May we turn an ear of anticipation for that coming day!

11

ARCHÆOLOGY AND THE ARK

Sacred Superstition or Ancient Artifact?

Parallels to the Tabernacle have been drawn from archaeological and other sources.... Gold-plated wooded containers or portable shrines also boast a comparable degree of antiquity.... The concept was very close indeed to that of the Hebrew Ark of the Covenant, except that the latter was the most sacred object in preexilic Hebrew ritual and worship.[1]

—E.M. Blaiklock

The powerful presence of the Ark of the Covenant served to part the Jordan River, crumble the walls of Jericho, destroy Philistine cities, and kill irreverent Israelites. With that kind of history, the Ark was destined to become the centerpiece of scripts written for Hollywood movies. Unfortunately, this has left some people to assign this ancient artifact to the realm of sacred superstition. Then there are scholars who view the Ark as simply a literary creation, a piece of religious fiction designed for a theological drama. Others say that the armies of other ancient Near-Eastern cultures carried images of their gods into battle, and believe that the Israelites either borrowed or shared this regional mythology and carried their version of this pagan practice (the Ark) into difficult situations.

To the contrary, the biblical account demonstrates the theological uniqueness of the Ark with respect to other cultures. In addition, archaeologists have found artifacts that parallel the Ark, lending credibility to its existence. Archaeology has also been able to draw a description of the Ark that's compatible with the biblical data.

First let's consider the biblical description of the Ark, and then we'll look at archaeological examples that illustrate its design.

The Description of the Ark

The Ark of the Covenant (or Ark of the Testimony) was made in the form of a rectangular box approximately 4 feet in length and 2 feet in height and width.[2] This design is indicated in the Hebrew word *'aron,* which means "a box" or "chest."[3] Our English word ark comes to us through the Latin *arca,* which likewise means "chest." The lower portion of the Ark was constructed from acacia wood, which attests to its desert origin, for acacia trees are native to the Sinai region. This wood is so extremely durable that in the Greek version of the Old Testament, called the Septuagint, the word is translated as "incorruptible" or "non-decaying." Added to this imperishable wood was a layer of gold, applied for practical protection and religious symbolism. According to some, the wood was gilded (i.e., overlaid like gold leaf).[4] Others say the Hebrew text indicates that there were thin boxes of gold on both the inside and outside of the original wood repository, forming something like a "Chinese box."[5] Thus, the Ark may have actually been a three-layered container (a gold box + a wooden box + a gold box).

44. *Model of the Ark of the Covenant, prepared by Chaim Odem for the Temple Institute, Jerusalem.*

The upper portion of the Ark was a specially constructed slab of gold called "the Mercy Seat" (Hebrew *kapporet,* "covering"). This slab served as a flat lid for the box and fit into a rim or "crown" of gold that surrounded the top four corners of the outer box and helped hold the lid in place. This was to help keep the lid from accidentally falling off and exposing the contents of the Ark while in transport. The golden lid was topped by a pair of winged creatures called "cherubim." These were apparently formed out of one solid piece of gold. Is this a reliable description of a real object from antiquity? Comparison with similar relics unearthed in the ancient Near East will help to provide an answer.

Archaeological Parallels to the Ark

The Hebrew word for "ark" (*'aron*) was also used of Egyptian coffins (Genesis 50:26), and some of our best examples of ark-like objects come from Egypt. For example, in Luxor, in the

45. *Miniature replica of the Ark showing its construction as a three-layered box. Inside the first gold box are the tablets of the Ten Commandments.*

Valley of the Kings, archaeologists discovered the tomb of the young Egyptian pharaoh Tutankhamen (1343–1325 B.C.).[6] The objects from his tomb are on permanent display at the Cairo Museum in Cairo, Egypt. In this tomb was found an ark-like chest made of cedar some 32 inches long with transport poles that slid through bronze rings attached underneath. Also found was a larger shrine consisting of a rectangular wooden box overlaid with gold. The box had carrying poles, and there was an image of the god Anabis mounted on top. In addition, Egyptian sphinxes, usually appearing in pairs, adorned many of the ritual objects—in one case, another "ark." However, on this particular ark the sphinxes are engraved into the side.

Many Near-Eastern cultures adopted the Ark's cherubim concept of human and animal attributes to represent the powerful guardians of the gods. Examples of sphinxes, winged bulls, and griffins come from Assyria, Babylon, Greece, and Phoenicia as well as from Canaan. One especially beautiful ivory example from the eighth or ninth centuries B.C. was found in the palace of the Assyrian governor of Hadatu, at Arslan Tash in northern Syria.[7]

These symbols usually appear as combination creatures. For example, in Egypt the sphinx is a lion man, while in Babylon the primary figure is a bull man. In Israel, figures of ivory sphinx-like cherubim were discovered in the ruins which once were part of King Ahab's palace in Samaria. To what degree these later Israelite sphinxes represented an accurate depiction of the Ark's cherubim is difficult to determine. The images of winged creatures in comparative Near-Eastern cultures were influenced by their local pagan mythology, but the cherubim atop the Ark of the Covenant, according to Jewish tradition, were unique in form.[8]

Archaeology and the Concept of the Ark

In the Bible the Ark is depicted as the place where the God of heaven touches the earth of men. For example, we read of "... the Ark of the Covenant of the Lord of hosts *who sits above the cherubim*" (1 Samuel 4:4, emphasis added; *see also* 2 Samuel 6:2; 2 Kings 19:15; Psalm 80:1; 99:1; Isaiah 37:16). Therefore it is often referred to as "the *footstool* of ... God" (1 Chronicles 28:2, emphasis added; *see also* Psalm 132:7-8).

46. *An ark-like chest found in King Tutankhamen's tomb—circa 1334 B.C.*

This concept is illustrated in the ancient art of Israel's closest neighbors in Syria and surrounding Canaan.[9] In Assyrian and Babylonian reliefs a king is usually attended by a representation of the nation's deity, which was depicted by a winged solar disk hovering above his head (such as was done on the relief of King Darius on Mount Behistun). At Byblus, Hamath, and Megiddo archaeologists have found representations of a king seated on a throne flanked by winged creatures.[10] Similar images on the Megiddo ivories are of particular interest, because they reflect Phoenician craftsmanship, such as was employed in building both the First and Second Temples (1 Kings 5; Ezra 3:7). Thus they may give the nearest representation to what the Ark may have looked like. The purpose for this symbolism was to denote the divine status of the one enthroned, to show him as riding upon a heavenly chariot attended by a retinue of celestial beings.

Archaeology and the Contents of the Ark

The Ark contained sacred objects associated with God's presence with Israel in the desert. These objects were to serve as a witness of the Mosaic covenant to future generations of the Jewish people. The sacred shrines of other Near-Eastern religions held images of their gods, but because God forbade the Israelites to make physical representations of Him, the divine image was communicated through God's Law, which was contained within the Ark. This Law was comprised of ten words (Ten Commandments), which had been inscribed on a pair of stone tablets. These "tablets of the Law" remained a permanent fixture within the Ark (2 Chronicles 5:10).[11] The Hollywood version of these tablets is usually exaggerated. Whether intentionally or not, the cinemagraphic portrait of an 80-year-old man hefting huge stone slabs weighing hundreds of pounds down a rugged mountain makes the Bible seem more fantasy than reality.

Archaeology, however, offers a more accurate picture. Based on discoveries of similarly inscribed stone tablets, the

Ten Commandments were probably carved on stone flakes not much larger than the size of a man's hand.[12] This size is implied by the relatively small size of the Ark itself. The rabbinic sages Rabbi Meir and Rabbi Yehudah debated the contents of the Ark; the former said that the stone tablets and the Torah scrolls were placed side-by-side within the Ark. The latter contended that in the fortieth year of the desert sojourn, a shelf was attached to an exterior side of the Ark to hold the Torah scroll.[13] Either way, only small tablets could have fit within the Ark.

Archaeology also helps us to understand the reason why these tablets were deposited within the Ark. In the Near-Eastern cultures of Moses' time the custom was to put legal documents and agreements between rival kingdoms "at the feet" of their god in their sanctuary. This god acted as the guardian of treaties and supervised their implementation. Egyptian records provide an example of this in a pact between Rameses II and Hattusilis III. Their agreement was sealed by depositing a copy of the treaty both at the feet of the Hittite king's god Teshup and the pharaoh's god Ra. The tablets of the Law set within the Ark were likewise at the "feet" of God because the Ark was His footstool.[14] Another possible example of this custom may be seen in 1 Samuel 10:25, where the prophet Samuel recorded the ordinances of the kingdom and set them "before the LORD"— that is, at the foot of the Ark. King Hezekiah, too, may have been acting in accordance with this custom when he "spread out before the LORD" the threatening letter of the Assyrian Rab-shakeh (Isaiah 37:14).

A Brief History of the Ark

The Ark of the Covenant was constructed by the craftsman Bezalel ben Uri ("In the Shadow of God, the Son of my Light") under the supervision of Moses at Mount Sinai. It was transported from place to place with the Tabernacle through the long years of the Israelites' journey to the Promised Land and throughout the periods of the Conquest and settlement. It may be that the Ark served as a substitute for the Sinai experience of the Lord's presence when the Israelites entered Canaan. While the presence of God was visibly present in the desert, it was representively present with the Ark.[15] When King David conquered Jerusalem and made it the capital of the Jewish nation, he transported the Ark, with the Tabernacle, to Jerusalem. When David's son, Solomon, succeeded him on the throne, he built the First Temple and placed the sacred Ark within its innermost recesses in a room known as the Holy of Holies (1 Kings 6:19).

In the First Temple, the high priest would approach the Ark once a year, on the Day of Atonement, to bring before God the sacrificial blood that was to obtain another year of pardon for the sins of the Jewish nation. During the reign of the wicked Judean king Manasseh, the Ark was removed from the Temple and an idol put in its place (2 Kings 21:4-7). We don't know where the Ark was kept during this time, but it reappeared a generation later during the time of King Josiah and was returned to the Holy of Holies (2 Chronicles 35:3) after he brought about

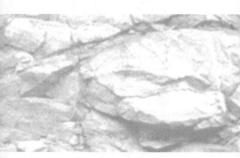

47. *One of the ivory cherubim (or sphinxes) from the palace of Ahab in Samaria.*

reform and effected extensive repairs to the Temple structure (2 Kings 22:1-7). About 38 years later, the First Temple was destroyed by the Babylonian commander Nebuzaradan (2 Kings 25:8-9), and though the Temple treasures were taken to Babylon and later returned (2 Kings 25:13-17; Ezra 1:7-11; Isaiah 52:11-12; Jeremiah 27:16-22; Daniel 5:2-4), the Ark was never mentioned among these items.

Has Archaeology Found the Place of the Ark?

Ever since the Babylonian captivity 2,500 years ago, the exact location of the Ark has been unknown. Although rumors persist that the Ark of the Covenant has been located here or there, no archaeological evidence has been produced to substantiate any of the claims. However, we may now be able to figure out where the Ark once rested within the ancient Holy of Holies. If, as we saw in the previous chapter, it is possible to deduce the location of the Temple building and its Holy of Holies, then it might be possible to locate where the Ark once was placed within this structure. According to ancient sources such as Josephus and the Mishnah tractate *Middot,* the Ark had rested on a bedrock platform. In Jewish tradition, this platform was called *'Even Ha-Shetiyah* ("the Foundation Stone"), and in Arabic, *es-Sakhra* ("the Rock"). According to research done by Leen Ritmeyer, former chief architect of the Temple Mount excavations and today director of Ritmeyer Archaeological Design in England, the huge rock within the present-day Islamic Dome of the Rock has to be the bedrock platform within the Holy of Holies. Ritmeyer explains how he came to this determination:

> It took me 20 years to figure it out. I was convinced that the Temple must have stood here somewhere. I started to look at the measurements of the Rock and the interior measurements of the Temple. We know that the interior measurements of the Temple were 20 cubits wide. The Holy [Place] was 40 cubits long and the Holy of Holies was 20 by 20 cubits. If you use the

> measurements of the 500 cubits measurements from the Mishnah it would measure 10.5 meters [34 feet] thereabouts. Comparing that with the size of the Rock, the Rock is larger than the Holy of Holies. Yet, the Mishnah [*Yoma* 5:2] says that this stone is called *'Even Ha-Shetiyah,* "the Foundation Stone." Why would they call it the Foundation Stone? Because if the Holy of Holies was smaller than the Rock, then the Rock would have served as a foundation for at least one of the Temples. With that information in mind, I started looking closer at the Rock for a foundation.[16]

Ritmeyer's look at the Rock began first by eliminating the signs of Crusader quarrying on the Rock, which in A.D. 1099 had been captured from the Muslims and converted into a Christian church called *Templum Domini* ("the Temple of the Lord"). He attributed cuts in the Rock on the north, south, and west sides to their actions. The Crusaders thought that the rock disfigured the Temple of the Lord and shaped it into what they believed was a more acceptable size, then built an altar on top of the Rock. In 1187, when the caliph Saladin recaptured the Dome of the Rock for the Muslims, they found it covered with marble slabs. Upon removing the slabs they found that the Rock had been mutilated. This mutilation included the enlarging of a cave and some deep tunnels dug beneath the Rock, which may indicate that the Crusaders were trying to locate the suspected hiding place of the Ark. The natural cave below the Rock was identified by them as the Holy of Holies, where they commemorated the angel's visit to Zacharias. They enlarged this cave in order to use it as a sanctuary, and because they burned candles and incense in the cave, it was necessary for them to cut a vertical shaft for ventilation (this formed the present hole in the Rock).

Thus, before the Crusaders disfigured the Rock, the upper level would have been larger and flatter. Ritmeyer then measured the flat areas in the southern part of the Rock, which he identified as foundation trenches. Their combined dimensions agreed perfectly with the known thickness of the walls of the

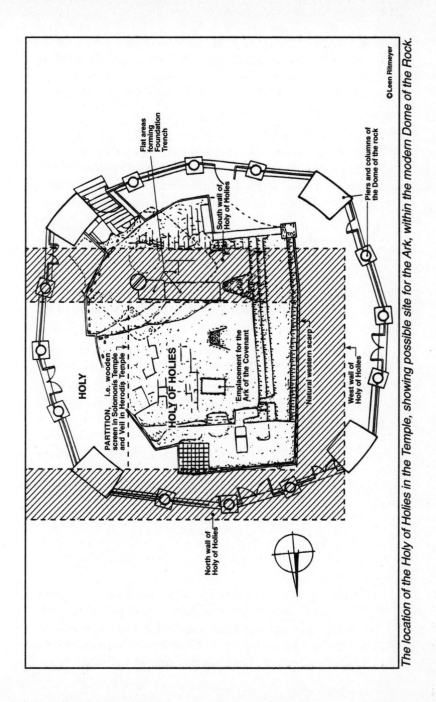

Flat areas forming Foundation Trench

South wall of Holy of Holies

Piers and columns of the Dome of the rock

HOLY

PARTITION, i.e. wooden screen in Solomon's Temple and Veil in Herod's Temple

HOLY OF HOLIES

Emplacement for the Ark of the Covenant

Natural western scarp

West wall of Holy of Holies

North wall of Holy of Holies

©Leen Ritmeyer

The location of the Holy of Holies in the Temple, showing possible site for the Ark, within the modern Dome of the Rock.

Second Temple (6 cubits or 10 feet and 4 inches). This foundation trench revealed the location of the southern wall of the Holy of Holies. The back wall would then have rested against the unchangeable natural rockscarp to the west. The northern wall would have been adjacent to the northern end of the Rock itself. This placement of the walls also agreed with Ritmeyer's earlier calculations about the placement of the original Temple platform. He found that the direction of the western scarp was virtually identical to that of the steps, which he had identified previously, and the eastern wall of the Temple Mount. So, the First and Second Temples would have had the same orientation—the longitudinal axis of the Temple at right angles with the eastern wall. This axis is also aligned with the highest point on the Mount of Olives, where the sacrifice of the red heifer (necessary for ritual purification—Numbers 19) took place. This became a further confirmation to Ritmeyer of his location of the Temple.

The Site of the Ark Discovered

Having identified these structures, Ritmeyer began looking for additional clues to position the Holy of Holies. He tells the story of how this identification was first realized:

> Once I began to research this problem in the Spring of 1994, the secrets of the *Sakhra* revealed themselves to me in such rapid succession that it was sometimes breathtaking. While flying to Israel, 30,000 feet high in the air, I got my first glimpse of the most spectacular of all the discoveries, namely that of the former location of the Ark of the Covenant! Averting my gaze from the in-flight video, I took out a large photograph of the *Sakhra* from my briefcase and tried to trace again those flat areas, which, of course, were familiar to me as foundation trenches.... I sketched over the flat areas on the photograph of the *Sakhra* the line of the southern wall of the Holy of Holies.... I drew the western edge of the Rock and the northern wall at the

northern end of the exposed rock.... I also drew a
dotted line where the veil, which separated the Holy of
Holies from the Holy [Place], would have hung. I did
not expect to find any remains as no wall had existed
there. I then suddenly noticed in the middle of this
square a dark rectangle! What could it be? The first
thing that came to mind was, of course, the [place of
the] Ark of the Covenant, which once stood in the
centre of the Holy of Holies in Solomon's Temple. But
that surely could not be true, I thought.... [However,]
according to my plan, it falls exactly in the centre of
the Holy of Holies. The dimensions of this level basin
agree with those of the Ark of the Covenant, which
were 1.5 x 2.5 cubits (2'7" ˘ 4'4" or 79 cm. ˘ 131 cm.),
with the longitudinal axis coinciding with that of the
Temple. Its location is rather unique, as it could only
have been the place where the Ark of the Covenant
once stood. It is clear that without such a flat area the
Ark would have wobbled about in an undignified
manner, which would not conceivably have been
allowed.[17]

According to Ritmeyer, then, this depression in the Rock
served as a base to secure the Ark within the Holy of Holies. It
could not have been created by the Crusaders because they covered the Rock with slabs to hide it, and would have placed a
statue (in such a base) in the middle of the Rock, not at the north
of the Rock (where the depression would have been at that
time).[18]

We can summarize Ritmeyer's research in the accompa-
nying diagram, which he drew. It depicts a north-south section
through the Herodian Temple Mount and its Courts in relation to
the present-day Dome of the Rock. One can see the original
bedrock designated "Sakhra," which was the highest point on
Mount Moriah—where Abraham had offered Isaac and the
Angel of the Lord had stood in the days of King David. Inside
is the natural cave from Solomon's time; the western scarp of
which is where the western wall would have been built. The

48. *The "Foundation Stone" (Sakhra) within the Muslim Dome of the Rock (viewed from northern scarp). Note the rectangular depression identified by Leen Ritmeyer as the setting place for the Ark of the Covenant during the First Temple period.*

floor of the Holy of Holies has an indented area where the Ark of the Covenant would have been placed in Solomon's Temple.

While it's impossible to archaeologically investigate the Rock to confirm Ritmeyer's conclusions, if he is correct, we now have for the first time identified the site of the Holy of Holies and of the former location of the Ark of the Covenant itself. In this case, the stone of stones has shouted with evidence that the Ark existed!

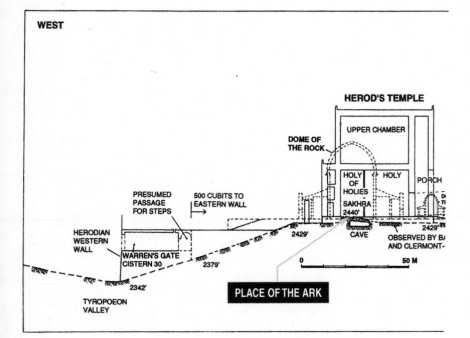

WEST

HEROD'S TEMPLE

UPPER CHAMBER

DOME OF
THE ROCK

HOLY
OF
HOLIES

HOLY

PORCH

PRESUMED
PASSAGE
FOR STEPS

500 CUBITS TO
EASTERN WALL

SAKHRA
2440'

HERODIAN
WESTERN
WALL

2429'

CAVE

2429'

WARREN'S GATE
CISTERN 30

2379'

OBSERVED BY B/
AND CLERMONT-

0

50 M

PLACE OF THE ARK

2342'

TYROPOEON
VALLEY

Placement of the Temple and the
Holy of Holies according to Leen
Ritmeyer. The Ark would have
rested to the left of the Sakhra in
the middle of the Holy of Holies
in this diagram.

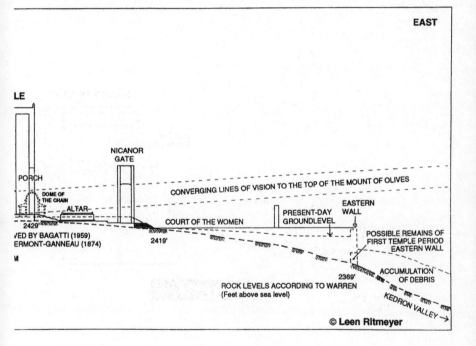

EAST

LE

NICANOR
GATE

PORCH

DOME OF
THE CHAIN

ALTAR

CONVERGING LINES OF VISION TO THE TOP OF THE MOUNT OF OLIVES

EASTERN
WALL

PRESENT-DAY
GROUNDLEVEL

2429'

/ED BY BAGATTI (1959)
ERMONT-GANNEAU (1874)

Μ

COURT OF THE WOMEN

2419'

POSSIBLE REMAINS OF
FIRST TEMPLE PERIOD
EASTERN WALL

2369'

ACCUMULATION
OF DEBRIS

ROCK LEVELS ACCORDING TO WARREN
(Feet above sea level)

KEDRON VALLEY →

© Leen Ritmeyer

12

KINGS AND PROPHETS

Sacred Signatures in Stone

Due to intensive archaeological research, Iron Age Judah is one of the best-known segments of the archaeology of Palestine.[1]

—Amihai Mazar

The late seventh century B.C.E. was a prosperous but tragic era. Biblical studies and archaeology together are revealing so much about this period as to make it one of the best known in ancient history.... Intensive archaeological field work, including both excavations and surveys, is responsible for making the late seventh and early sixth centuries B.C.E. so well known.[2]

—Philip J. King

One of the most cherished of modern Christian allegories is known as "Footprints in the Sand." The story reminds us that at the most difficult times of life, when it seems that we walk alone

221

and we see only one set of footprints in the sand, God has not been absent, but in fact has been carrying us!

There was also a time in Israel's history that it seemed that God had left the chosen people to survive on their own. The Israelites had chosen to be ruled by kings rather than the King, and so set their path in the course of all those nations that had gone before them. As a result, difficult times came. But in this time of national testing, God did not let His people walk alone. To guide them back to the proper path He sent prophets and priests, some of whom left their own "footprints," and as we shall see, even fingerprints, in the stones. Their "footprints" have left a firmer imprint than other events and people before this period of time—Iron Age II (1000–586 B.C.)—because the unearthed archaeological evidence improves vastly as we move forward from the end of Solomon's reign through Israel's Monarchy.

This evidence has improved our understanding of both the domestic and foreign context in which the people of Israel worked out their faith. One site that has greatly contributed to our knowledge of the foreign context is Tel Miqne, the site of biblical Ekron, which served as one of the main cities of the Philistines and the center of an important industry of the time. Recently a new and sensational discovery at the site has helped archaeologists to learn more about the Philistine presence.

Finding the Philistines

Identifying the Philistine People

In the Bible, one of the more prominent enemies of Israel was the Philistines. They emerged from a group of invading sea peoples from the Aegean during the twelfth century B.C. and became Israel's most formidable foe during the time of the Judges. They occupied a large place in the early history of Israel, crossing paths with such figures as Samson, Samuel, Saul, and David. And who does not know the Philistine names of the temptress Delilah or the giant Goliath?

The area inhabited by the Philistines was the Mediterranean coastal plain, and their access to this region, except during the brief reign of Solomon, prevented Israel from developing seafaring trade. It may have also prevented something else. One of the main trade and military routes, first called the "Way of Horus," and later the "Via Maris" ("Way of the Sea"), passed through their territory. Israel was called to be a witness of the true God to the nations—the very nations that regularly used this route. The Israelites' failure to possess this territory meant that this function of God's people was compromised during most of the Monarchy. Even though King David managed to bring the Philistine territory under Israelite control as a tributary (2 Samuel 8:11-12; 1 Kings 4:24), and Philistia was apparently forced to pay tribute as in the days of David's descendant Jehoshaphat, 873–848 B.C. (2 Chronicles 17:11), border conflicts still continued between the Philistines and Israel, as in the time of Ahaz, 731–715 B.C. (2 Chronicles 28:18).

Uncovering a Philistine City

One of these border towns, part of a pentapolis of Philistine cities mentioned both in Scripture and the Assyrian annals, was the town of Ekron. It was the earliest of the Philistine cities, built in the time of the Judges and totally destroyed—most likely during the wars of David—around 1000 B.C. This made it an important archaeological site for learning about the Philistines. Between 1983 and 1997 Israeli archaeologist Trude Dothan and American archaeologist Seymour Gittin worked to uncover the buried history of Tel Miqne, which they were certain was biblical Ekron. Summarizing Ekron's now-revealed history, Gittin says:

> Around 1000 B.C.E., we also know that the Philistines ran into lots of problems: the inland people, the Judeans of the United Monarchy, overran the coastal plain for about 250 years, as reflected in the gap at Tel Mikne-Ekron. [During this time] the Philistines were of relatively minor

importance, their cities had diminished in political and economic power. But around 700 B.C.E., with the coming of the Neo-Assyrian empire, everything changed. Ekron suddenly became re-urbanized, and a great olive oil industrial center was established. During this period of peace (the Paxis Syriaca), which lasted for about 100 years or well into the seventh century, Ekron prospered and became one of the great commercial centers in antiquity.[3]

At first the archaeologists could only play upon their hunches that this was the biblical site. The geographical situation at the junction of the coastal plain and the hill country of Judah was correct. The archaeological artifacts emerging from the tel appeared distinctively Philistine. Even so, after 14 years of excavation, nothing was unearthed that could definitively confirm this site as Ekron. Then at the close of the 1996 season, the last planned for the excavation, something unexpected happened. Seymour Gittin recounts the events of that day:

> We had been looking for years for inscribed and written material at Ekron. . . . Now when we began to excavate in the seventh century [strata] these huge monumental buildings, we were extra careful when we came across a stone that was shaped like a stele that would have had an inscription. Year after year, we carefully turned over these stones but we never found anything. But last summer the person in charge of Field 4, Steve Ortiz from the University of Arizona, approached me and said we have another candidate for a stele . . . please come and examine it, I think there is something scratched on this stone. I took a quick look and said, "No, it's just like the rest." After so many years of being disappointed, I thought this was another disappointment. Then, about 5 minutes later, he called me back and they had brushed away very carefully part of the upper segment of this stone and sure enough . . . there it was, wonderful incised lines—a foreign inscription. Although the stone was upside down and

49. *Archaeologists Seymour Gittin and Trude Dothan with the Ekron Inscription, Albright Institute, Jerusalem.*

covered by a lot of debris, one could make out letters
that clearly looked like old Hebrew or old Phoenician.[4]

What the searchers had found was a stone inscription that
finally confirmed they were digging at the biblical city of Ekron.
Remarkably, the stone identified not only the name of the city,
but also the names of two of its kings. Never before had such an
inscription been found in Israel in a historically identifiable context. Gittin describes this monumental find and its significance
for biblical studies:

> [This discovery is] one of the most exciting finds we
> have ever come across and no doubt will enter the
> annals of the archaeology of ancient Israel as one of
> the most significant epigraphic finds at least in this cen-
> tury. With the finding of this stone, we actually have
> the proof that this was indeed the ancient biblical site,
> the Philistine city of Ekron. Now the contents of the
> inscription, which is complete, contains 5 lines of 71
> letters. This stone marked the dedication of a sanctuary
> in a huge temple complex. The king at the time, prob-
> ably around 690 B.C.E., was Achish, the son of Padi, as
> the inscription tells us. He was the king of Ekron and
> built this sanctuary to his goddess. The information
> from this text, once it is published, will be extremely
> important for our understanding of this particular part
> of the biblical period. Of course this structure itself can
> be dated in terms of its last phase because we know
> that the Neo-Babylonian king Nebuchadnezzar in 603
> B.C.E. came to Philistia and destroyed Ekron . . . and
> with this destruction comes the end of Philistine mate-
> rial culture. What [this text] says among other things is
> that these kings that we knew about from the Assyrian
> annals were actually the kings of Ekron. This is another
> reason why this inscription is unique, because for the
> first time we have a monumental inscription with the
> name of a biblical site and its rulers in situ [in the place
> where it belonged] and in a destruction level that can
> be dated. Put all that together and one word comes to
> mind: unique! This is quite an unusual find.[5]

Another unusual find, which dates from the final Philistine phase of Ekron (ending 603 B.C.), was a golden cobra (known as a ureaus), which formed part of a statuette's headdress. The statuette was of an Egyptian deity (or royal figure) that was associated with its Neo-Assyrian-type palace. Such foreign religious influences were one of the factors that adversely affected the Israelites and made the Philistines such a threat to the Israelites in their land.

With the completion of the excavations at Tel Miqne-Ekron, we are now able to trace the influence of the Philistines from their beginning in Israel through their demise at the end of the Monarchy period.

The Most "Dangerous" Site in the Country

After the death of Solomon in 922 B.C., the United Kingdom over which he reigned was divided, and Jeroboam I assumed kingship over ten of the tribes of Israel, which became known as the Northern Kingdom (1 Kings 11:29-37). This weakening of the centralized government invited foreign attacks on both the Northern Kingdom and Judah, or the Southern Kingdom. One of the attacks on Judah that took place shortly after Solomon's death was by the Egyptian pharaoh Shishak, who plundered the Temple treasuries in Jerusalem (1 Kings 14:25-26). In 1994, an inscribed stele bearing his name was unearthed at Megiddo.[6]

After the division of the Kingdom, Jeroboam I of the north was afraid that the people of Israel would return to the House of David in the south (Jerusalem) because the Temple was there. So that his people could worship without making the required pilgrimage to Jerusalem, Jeroboam I established two rival cult centers in the northern cities of Dan and Bethel, located at the northern and southern extremities of his kingdom (1 Kings 12:26-29). His rival symbol for the two cherubim upon the Ark of the Covenant in Jerusalem were two golden calves or bulls. This cultic object had historically preceded the Ark at the time of the Exodus, and Jeroboam made much of this precedence when he called Israel to worship at these locations (1 Kings 12:28). Professor Amihai Mazar explains:

> We think that the cherubim in the Temple in Jerusalem were a kind of pedestal for the unseen God, so perhaps the bull was the parallel of the cherubim in the northern shrine. Of course they didn't have the Holy Ark itself, but perhaps it was kind of a religious symbol of an unseen god which perhaps was standing on, or carried by, these bulls [which] symbolized strength, power, fertility and so on.[7]

For God's prophets, these sites became the most dangerous in the country because they allowed for idolatrous enticements that would ultimately bring Israel to disaster. Hosea proclaimed God's indictment against the Northern Kingdom for this very reason:

> Through Ba'al [worship] he [Ephraim = Northern Kingdom] did wrong and died. And now they sin more and more, and make for themselves molten images, idols skillfully made from their silver, all of them the work of craftsmen. They say of them, "Let the men who sacrifice kiss the calves!" Therefore they will be like the morning cloud, and like dew which soon disappears (Hosea 13:1-3).

Archaeology has now made Hosea's words come alive by revealing some of the defiling influences that were described by the prophet.

The Evidences of Idolatry

Ancient Altars in High Places

Dan, the northernmost of Jeroboam's cultic sites, is situated at the foot of Mount Hermon in the Golan Heights and has been excavated over the past 31 years. Avraham Biran, who has directed these excavations, says, "We found the sanctuary which I am convinced is the sanctuary that Jeroboam built."[8] This identification was confirmed by Biran's discovery in 1976 of an

50. *Author with incense altar and shovel for removing ashes— discovered at Tel Dan.*

inscription at the site, which read, "To the god who is in Dan." This high place (in Hebrew, called a *bamah)* mentioned in 1 Kings 12:31, was a square platform (60 ˅ 62 feet) unearthed on the northwest side of the site. Mounted atop a flight of five ashlar steps, it was upon this platform that the golden calves were placed. In front of the platform was a large horned altar for burnt offerings. Evidently, this high place was completely destroyed in a violent conflagration (possibly under Ben-hadad), but some cult ritual objects were found, such as three large pithoi decorated with writhing snakes in relief, a clay bathtub and plastered installation that was probably used for libation ceremonies, a smaller horned altar, incense stands, an Astarte figurine, and several incense shovels.[9]

Cultic Calves

What about the golden calves? Biran conjectures: "The calves made of gold may have seen times of war. With all that happened in that part of the country those hundreds of years, they may have disappeared."[10] While the golden calves of Dan might never be discovered, archaeologists have found similar sacred bull figurines in other parts of the country. For example, in 1990 Lawrence Stager found a small bronze calf-idol (once burnished to resemble gold, along with parts of silver) in the remains of a Canaanite temple in Ashkelon, which was destroyed about 1550 B.C. Another bull-idol was discovered at a high place in Samaria, the ancient capital of the Northern Kingdom. Amihai Mazar, who recovered this figurine, recalls its discovery:

> I found it on a shelf in a small collection room in a kibbutz in northern Israel. A soldier, a member of this kibbutz, found it by chance during military training on a hill in the northern Samaria hills. When I saw it, I realized this was an important find. It is a bronze statue, quite heavy, about 9 inches long showing a young bull. This soldier took me to this hill and we excavated there for 2 days . . . and we found on this hill a large circle of stones, and a few pottery shards (twelfth century B.C.). . . . this was probably part of a [ritual] system [of which] more than 250 sites of this type are known, but very few excavated. This particular place probably was a kind of ritual place which the Bible calls a *bamah,* a high place on top of a hill surrounded by a standing stone, known as a *matsebah.* I interpreted this place as one of the earliest examples of such an open cult place which can be related to Israelites from the biblical period. . . . The Israelites imagined their unseen god standing on such a bull. So the golden calf in the temples of Dan and Bethel perhaps played this role and the fact that we find such a beautiful bull in a site which is perhaps related to the religious practice of Israelites in this early period is of great significance to the history of this religious symbol in Israel.[11]

The prophets record that the cult's contamination in the north was complete. All of its kings were corrupt and their social sins eventually brought the nation to condemnation. The last king to reign in the Northern Kingdom was Hoshea (732-722 B.C.). As if providing a last glimpse at the foreign influences that condemned the empire, archaeology has revealed the royal signet seal of the king. Inscribed in Hebrew with the words "belonging to Abdi, servant of Hoshea," the seal depicts an Egyptian figure standing above a solar disk (a symbol of the god Ra).[12] The Kingdom of Israel was destroyed in 701 B.C. by the Assyrians, who deported the population and replaced them with foreigners who would continue the religious conflict with Israel (as the Samaritans). Eventually the people in the Southern Kingdom would emulate the sins of their neighbors to the north, but because Judah had an irregular succession of godly kings, the people were spared from judgment for more than another century.

The Eradication of Idolatry

The last of the godly Judean kings was Josiah. He attempted to reverse the terrible apostasy brought by his ungodly grandfather Manasseh. He repaired the Temple, rid the sacred precincts of idols, reinstalled the Levites to service, and returned the Ark of the Covenant to the Holy of Holies (2 Chronicles 35:1-3). His reforms extended to all of Judah with the imperative to remove all traces of idolatry from the kingdom (2 Chronicles 34:33). Evidence of this reformation was recently unearthed at Ein Hatzeva, which is identified with the biblical site of Tamar (Ezekiel 47:19).[13] At this site on a hilltop near the southern bank of the Hatzeva spring in the desert region known as the Arabah (about 32 miles south of the Dead Sea), an Edomite shrine was discovered dating from the late First Temple period (time of Josiah). Set near the great trade circuit known as the "Spice Route," it had apparently served as a roadside cultic high place at which travelers could appeal to their gods for a safe journey.

The evidence of reform was seen in the more than 70 deliberately smashed pottery and stone cult objects lying beneath the piles of rocks that were used to destroy them. Some of these smashed relics included altars, statues, incense burners, libation vessels, chalices, and human-shaped incense stands. The intentional destruction of a shrine so far south shows the extent of Josiah's religious "clean up" operation. Such far-reaching action reminds us in our age of apostasy (1 Timothy 4:1-3; 2 Timothy 3:1-7) that if we are to see a revival in our day it must come without compromise, leaving no realm of business, trade, or entertainment untouched in our pursuit for purity (2 Corinthians 6:14-7:1).

Evidence of Jerusalem's Demise

The Babylonian Chronicles

Josiah's last-minute reforms were not enough to rescue the Southern Kingdom from the intoxication of idolatry. One of the surprising revelations from the extensive excavations in Jerusalem is that more idols have been discovered in this sacred city than anywhere else in the whole country. Many of these were fertility figurines, betraying the awful influence of a still-pervasive Canaanite culture. It's no wonder, then, that when the prophets pictured the ideal sanctity of a future restored Jerusalem, they described it as a day when "there will no longer be a Canaanite in the house of the LORD" (Zechariah 14:21). This fact underscores the magnitude of Judah's abominable acts, which the prophets predicted would lead to Jerusalem's fall to Nebuchadnezzar and the Babylonian army.

We have an archaeological testimony to some of the events surrounding this downfall in two tablets of a group known as the Babylonian Chronicles. These cuneiform tablets were bought by the British Museum late in the nineteenth century, but were not translated until 1956. Unlike other propagandistic inscriptions designed only to bolster the reputation of a conqueror, these tablets present a factual historical record written in a simple and straightforward manner. One entry in this chronicle records Nebuchadnezzar's first advance against Jerusalem:

The seventh year, the month of Kislev, the king of
Babylonia mustered his forces and marched to Syria
[Syria-Palestine]. He camped against the city of Judah
[Jerusalem] and on the second day of the month of
Adar he took the city and captured the king. He
appointed a king of his own choice there, took its
heavy tribute and brought them to Babylon.

Based on our knowledge of calendar systems from other
archaeological finds, the dates indicated in this report can be
translated precisely. The date Nebuchadnezzar gathered his
troops was December 598 B.C., and the date of his invasion of
Jerusalem was March 16, 597 B.C. The biblical text identifies
the Judean king as Jehoiakin (Jehoiachin), and Nebuchadnezzar's appointed replacement as Zedekiah (2 Kings 24:10-17).
This tablet ends with an entry in the year 594 B.C., which implies
that the next tablet in the series would record the crucial years
587-586 B.C., the dates of the final destruction of Jerusalem and
the Temple. Unfortunately, the next surviving tablet begins with
events that took place in 556 B.C. Perhaps the lost tablet that lies
in between will one day be found, but we do have other discoveries that record some of the events of those fateful days.

The Lachish Letters

One archaeological record that bears a grim testimony to
the actual siege and conquest of the city are some ostraca known
as the Lachish Letters (586 B.C.). These ostraca, recovered from
a room near the gate of the city of Lachish (Tel edh-Duweir), a
Judean city only 25 miles from Jerusalem, offer something of
the drama of those final hours. Even the emotional pathos of the
moment has been preserved for us. One ostracon depicts
Lachish's military commander Ya'osh's last-minute cry for help
as the lights were seen to go out at the nearby outpost of Azekah
in the wake of the dreaded Babylonian army. Though written in
the customary language of polite formality, we can still feel his
desperation when he writes, "May Yahweh cause my lord to
hear news of peace, even now, even now!" News of peace,

however, did not come, and the Babylonians marched right over Lachish and into Jerusalem, setting fire to the city when they captured it (2 Kings 25:8-10; Jeremiah 39:8).

The Israelite Tower

The terrible fall of Jerusalem to the Babylonians is still recorded in the stones of the city. In a deep pit (now housed within a school basement in the Old Jewish Quarter), often overlooked by tourists, are the remains of a structure that saw the invasion of those last days. Located just north of the Broad Wall, the Israelite Tower, excavated by Israeli archaeologists Nachman Avigad and Hillel Geva, is a remnant of the ancient city's defenses. Dramatic remains at this site show a thick deposit of burnt earth (a conflagration layer) and numerous fallen iron arrowheads, all evidence of the fierce battle that took place here at the northern perimeter as Babylonian battering rams broke through at this point and torched Jerusalem in 586 B.C.

51. *Israeli archaeologist Hillel Geva, excavator of Broad Wall and Israelite Tower—shown standing next to a portion of the Israelite Tower.*

Bullae, Bullae!

Two Significant Finds

Ironically, the very fire that destroyed the First Temple also uniquely preserved a part of her heritage. In 1982 in the Babylonian destruction level at David's City (Area G), on the lower terrace just east of the remains of an Israelite four-room house known as the House of Ahi'el, a cache of 51 small clay "buttons" were discovered.[14] Baked hard by the fire, these "buttons" were in fact ancient clay seals inscribed with the names of their owners. Although the fire destroyed the papyrus documents on which the seals had been placed, the fire had helped to preserve the seals against time. The technical name for such seals is "bullae," and so the place where they were found is called "The Bullae House." Seldom does archaeology reveal artifacts bearing the names of people mentioned in the Bible, but among these bullae was found the bulla of "Gemaryahu [Gemariah] the son of Shaphan." This name, which appears a few times in the book of Jeremiah, was the name of a scribe who served in the court of King Jehoiakim *(see* Jeremiah 36:10-12,25-26). He was one of those who advised Jehoiakim not to burn the scroll of Jeremiah, which contained Jeremiah's prophecies from 627–605 B.C. *(see* Jeremiah 36:25).

In addition, a hoard of over 250 inscribed bullae surfaced in 1975 through an Arab East Jerusalem antiquities dealer.[15] They, too, must have come from David's City, and most likely were removed in illegal digging and sold on the black market. Found among this collection was a seal bearing the name of Ishmael, who assassinated Gedaliah,[16] the inter-exilic governor of Judah appointed by the Babylonians after Jerusalem's destruction. Another seal had the name "Berekhyahu [Baruch] son of Neriyahu [Neriah] the scribe."[17] This Baruch was none other than the confidant and personal scribe of the prophet Jeremiah himself! He was a strategic part of the drama during the last days of the First Temple, and was once "hidden by the Lord" with Jeremiah when King Jehoiakim sought to arrest them (Jeremiah

52. *The site of a four-room house in David's City. The Bullae House, with its 51 seals, was discovered at a lower level in front of this structure.*

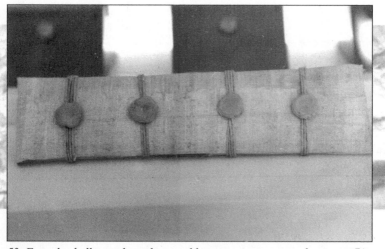

53. *Four clay bullae seals as they would appear on a papyrus document. Pictured from left to right are the seals of Gemaryahu ben Shaffan (Jeremiah 36:9-12), Berachyahu ben Neryahu the Scribe (Jeremiah 36:4), Azaryahu ben Hilkyahu (ancestor of Ezra), and Shefatyahu ben Tzafan.*

36:26). But an even more exciting revelation concerning this scribe was yet to come!

Bulla with a Fingerprint

Recently it was revealed that another bulla with the name of Baruch existed in a private collection in London.[18] This seal, however, has an incredible difference. Preserved in the now-hardened clay is the imprint of a finger. Since this bulla belonged to Baruch, he is the one who would have last touched it when sealing the papyrus scroll it secured. Therefore this is most likely the actual fingerprint of Baruch himself![19] Who knows what might have been written on the scroll sealed by this bulla? Could it have been a copy of the sealed deed of purchase mentioned in Jeremiah 32:14, or perhaps even a copy of Jeremiah's prophecies? Whatever it was, with this fingerprint we now may have an image of the very hand that helped pen a book of the Bible!

An Ancient Tomb with Treasure

Inscribed bullae are a kind of treasure from the past. Yet real treasure has also been found from the period of the Monarchy. Because Jerusalem has been repeatedly plundered (about 30 times), and for centuries had been combed by grave-robbers and Bedouin who sought antiquities for foreign buyers, no one expected to find any buried treasure left in the city. But in 1975, First-Temple burial caves were discovered underneath the rocky escarpment upon which St. Andrew's Church of Scotland presently stands. In 1979, excavations at this site (called Ketef-Hinnom and located across the Hinnom Valley from the western walls of the Old City) uncovered one of the richest finds ever discovered in Jerusalem. Among the treasures removed from a tomb at this site, known as repository chamber 25, were a vast assortment of jewelry and other items. Gabriel Barkay, who directed this excavation, reports:

> Inside this one chamber of the repository we discovered more than 1,000 objects, among them more than

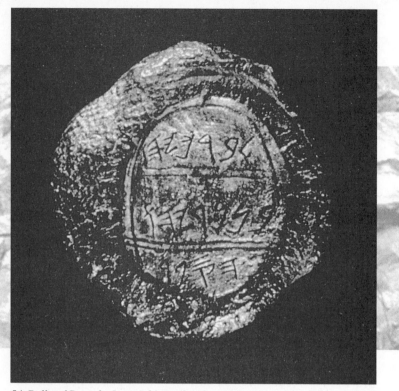

54. Bulla of Baruch, Jeremiah's scribe (fingerprint is at upper left portion of the seal).

360 intact pottery vessels, around 120 objects made of silver and several beautiful pieces of jewelry, earrings, finger rings, pendants, and around 150 beads of different colors and materials made mostly of semi-precious stones. . . . an inscribed seal used by one of Jerusalem's bureaucracy, probably a man in the service of one of the Judean kings. . . . [We also found] 40 arrowheads made of iron, some with the tip bent—which meant that they must have been shot at extremely stiff-necked Jerusalemites![20]

Changing the History Books

Barkay's humor aside, the excavation held more surprises for both his team and for biblical historians throughout the world:

> Inside this cave we also had some surprises. Inside the repository we had pottery finds which prove that the cave was still in use after the destruction of Solomon's Temple during the Babylonian's rule in Jerusalem. More than this, we also found a coin made of silver minted on the island of Kos in the Aegean in the sixth century B.C. This was shortly after the beginning of coinage and shows that the Jerusalemites had commercial contacts with the Aegean sea and the knowledge of this new means of exchange. This changes what is written in all history books about Jerusalem; these books have a gap following the destruction. In Jeremiah 40:41, we find a hint that people came from Samaria and the northern provinces to Jerusalem after the destruction of the Temple to offer incense and offerings at the site of the destroyed Temple. So cultic activity continued in Jerusalem after the destruction of the Temple, and [Jewish] people probably lived there. Here in this place we have the continuous use of a burial cave with pottery which dates to the sixth century B.C., the time of the Exilic period. This is a clue to the continuous existence of Jerusalem in a period in which we didn't think that Jerusalem existed.[21]

Another surprise that made a significant contribution to biblical understanding was a discovery made in another burial cave (Cave 20). Barkay explains:

> Cave 20 is a multi-chambered burial cave with a central hall with openings to burial chambers on all sides. The interesting thing about this cave is the fact that we have part of the original ceiling preserved. If we go to the biblical connections, we find this is a very important contribution because at the meeting point between the ceiling and the walls, there is an angular cornice. The

55. *Lamps and juglets* in situ *from Cave 25 at Ketef-Hinnom, the richest treasure trove ever discovered in Jerusalem.*

angular cornice measures exactly two palms in height and projects from the wall exactly one palm, or four fingers. Now in 1 Kings 7:9-11 it mentions that Solomon built his buildings in Jerusalem of ashlar blocks of well-hewn stones which were sawn, and he built the walls of his structures of these stones "from foundations to the coping." The Hebrew original has "from the foundations unto the *hand-breadths*." The hand-breadth is four fingers and is [equivalent to] 1/7 of a cubit. So they measured these cornices with hand-breadths and mathematically it fits exactly together with many other parallels in burial caves which preserve this element.[22]

This discovery provides us with a measurable example of the building practices that were employed in Solomonic building projects and probably those that followed during the Monarchy. It also gives us the accurate dimensions of a biblical cubit (which in this case followed the royal cubit of about 20 inches). But the greatest surprise of all was to come from Cave 25, as Barkay reveals:

Cave 25 was subdivided into smaller areas under the supervision of Gordon Franz from New Jersey. Inside also was a student of mine, Judith Hadley of Toledo, Ohio (today a teacher at Villanova University in Pennsylvania). She called me over and showed me an object still in the ground which looked like a cigarette butt. It was purplish grayish in color. . . . It was made of silver foil, 99 percent pure—something which has biblical connections because it mentions being purified seven times as silver [Psalm 12:6]. It was a silver plaque rolled up in order to form an amulet. . . . During the sifting of dirt from inside the repository after the excavations inside, we found another object of the same nature—rolled up to form a small cylinder. When these two objects were unrolled with enormous difficulties, over three years' [time], we found out that they were covered with delicately scratched characters in the ancient Hebrew script. The surprise was that the first word to be identified and deciphered was the name of the Lord, the tetragrammaton, the unpronounceable name which is sometimes Anglicized as "Jehovah." Now we discovered that on both amulets we have a text which is almost similar to the book of Numbers 6:24–26, known as the priestly benediction which is used in Jewish prayers and in Christian liturgy until this very day. . . . These are the earliest biblical verses that we own, and they predate the famous Dead Sea Scrolls by several centuries. And these are the only biblical verses we have that date back to the time of the Davidic dynasty, the time of the Judean monarchy, the time of the First Temple period. It's a sensation because we did not anticipate ever finding any written text which correlated with the biblical text from such an early period.[23]

Archaeology by Accident

The discovery of this most extraordinary unrobbed tomb is quite interesting. Barkay had not expected to find such treasure because when they first excavated the site it had almost been destroyed by quarrying. Most of the upper chamber of this tomb had been quarried away, and the roof and walls were missing. As they looked at the bare rock floor it appeared that everything that had once been contained in the room had been removed long ago. However, there was a local boy who hung around their excavation and kept bothering Barkay. So Barkay decided to put him to work at a dead-end job that would keep him out of the way—sweeping the bare rock floor of Cave 25! The boy, eager to please, did his job too well. He swept so hard that he swept right *through the floor!* And no one noticed until he started bringing out artifacts! It was then that the group realized the "floor" was not a floor at all, but the collapsed ceiling of the cave, which had long ago buried everything and hidden the fact from every grave robber till that day! So this bothersome boy instead became the biggest blessing in the history of the excavation!

What About the Message of the Prophets?

Archaeology has revealed the stage on which the kings and prophets of Israel acted out their roles in the divine drama. It has revealed their footprints and even fingerprints in the stones as physical evidence of their spiritual message. But is their message—especially the message of the prophets—trustworthy? Archaeology has revealed that the prophets did speak and that their message accurately fits the historical context. However, many modern scholars question the concept of predictive prophecy within the prophets' messages because it requires that a person believe in the supernatural. In the next chapter we will examine the issue of predictive prophecy and compare some of the prophets' messages with the archaeological record to see if there is corroboration or contradiction.

13

ARCHÆOLOGY AND PROPHECY

Can Stones Show the Supernatural?

The seeker after certainty in religion will be grateful for the multiplicity, as well as for the minuteness and distinctness of Scripural prophecy.[1]

—Thomas Urquhart

Archaeology has revealed a great deal of the social and political background in which the prophets issued their stirring prophecies. Understanding this background adds a new dimension to the reality and meaning of the biblical text. This sentiment was expressed by archaeologist William Dever, who in an interview, shared these words:

> For me, the great excitement about archaeology is that it enables you to read the Bible from a new perspective. When I read a description about daily life in one of the

Prophets, I am not thinking at that moment just about what the prophet is saying, I am thinking about the eighth century B.C.E., what it was actually like for the average Israelite. When I read the text, I read it with a sensitivity and an understanding that only a knowledge of archaeology can bring to the text. The text comes alive for me in a new way.[2]

Not everyone, however, shares Dever's enthusiasm. While Dever was less concerned about the prophets' word than their world, he nevertheless admits that archaeology reveals that word had a demonstrable historical context. To a Bible-believer, such a realization includes evidence of the supernatural revelation of God within history. To skeptics, however, our world is a closed system in which there exists no possibility of divine interventions contrary to the observable natural order. To them it seems unimaginable that anyone could believe that events could be foretold, much less fulfilled. But one cannot escape the fact that the pages of the Bible are filled with prophecy. From Genesis through Revelation, almost every book records some prediction of future events, hundreds already fulfilled, and many others still awaiting fulfillment. These prophecies are not painted with broad brush strokes, but with fine details. As such, the odds of only a few being fulfilled by chance are so astronomical[3] they must challenge the skeptic to consider the supernatural portrait they present. And as a part of history, the events prophesied, though stemming from the supernatural, may still reveal themselves in the stones.

The Period of the Prophets

The period in which the biblical prophets are said to have ministered to the Israelite nation is supported by numerous monumental and inscriptional evidences. Without respect of person the prophets equally called kings and commoners to account, turning them from idolatry when they heeded God's warnings, but suffering with them in exile when they resisted God's beckoning. Archaeology can show the practical reasons that provoked these prophetic indictments, reveal the places which were the subjects of the prophecies, and identify the people who turned a deaf ear to the predictions. In this way it may offer some evidence for the reality of prophecy itself.

The Purpose of Prophecy

In the ancient Near East, where the cultures surrounding Israel all had multiple deities, the context of Israel's faith was often a contest between national gods. In this battle for belief, the god whose crops flourished, or whose army was victorious, was considered the more powerful. Theologically, this was one of the greatest threats to God's people, and, unfortunately, it was a spiritual war they lost frequently (see Jeremiah 11:13). The prophets of Israel had to contend with nations that told the Israelites that their inability to resist the imposition of tribute payments or even exile by stronger powers proved that their God was inferior *(see* 2 Kings 18:32-35; Ezekiel 36:20). The prophets responded by explaining that Israel's God did not submit to pagan standards of sovereignty. They said that Israel's predicaments were actually proof of God's strength, for it was He who compelled foreigners to invade Israel to punish the people for their sins. The foreign powers that exiled Israel were simply the rods of God's anger (Isaiah 10:5-11; *see also* 2 Kings 24:2-3; Habakkuk 1:6-11). Therefore, Israel's God challenged the nations to put their gods to the test. His prophets announced the test that would unquestionably demonstrate who was truly sovereign:

> "Present your case," the LORD says, "Bring forward your strong arguments," the King of Jacob says. "Let them bring forth and declare to us what is going to take place . . . or announce to us what is coming. Declare the things that are going to come afterward, that we may know that you are god. . . . And let them declare to them the things that are coming, and the events that are going to take place" (Isaiah 41:21-23; 44:7).

According to the prophet Isaiah, this test of prophecy is designed both to cause "the omens of boasters to fail, [and make] fools out of diviners," and confirm "the word of His servant, and [perform] the purpose of His messengers" (Isaiah 44:25-26). Isaiah then offered evidence that God could meet His own challenge by presenting a remarkable prophecy that could be verified in later history.

A Proof of Prophecy

The proof that Isaiah puts forth is the edict of Cyrus, the Persian king who permitted the Jews to return to Judah and rebuild the Jerusalem Temple (2 Chronicles 36:22-23; Ezra 1:1-11):

> I have aroused one from the north, and he has come; from the rising of the sun he will call on My name; and he will come upon rulers as upon mortar, even as the potter treads clay (Isaiah 41:25).

This was a reference to Cyrus, who originated east ("the rising of the sun") of Babylon (from Persia), but came as an attacker from the north to exercise sovereignty over unresisting rulers (as symbolized by the potter's power over the "mortar" and "clay"). Yet, a much more definite reference is given at the end of chapter 44 and the beginning of chapter 45:[4]

> It is I who says of Cyrus, He is My shepherd! And he will perform all My desire. And he declares of Jerusalem, "She will be built," and of the Temple, "Your foundation will be laid." Thus says the LORD to Cyrus His anointed, whom I have taken by the right hand, to subdue nations before him . . . (Isaiah 44:28–45:1).

According to the internal chronology of the book of Isaiah, this prediction was given over 150 years *before* its fulfillment. It is unique in its precision—not only describing Cyrus' invasion of Babylon, but also providing such details as Cyrus' personal name (Isaiah 44:28; 45:1), actions with respect to the Temple (Isaiah 44:28) and the release of the Jewish exiles (Isaiah

45:13). This latter event fits exactly with Jeremiah's prophecy that Israel's captivity would end after 70 years (Jeremiah 25:12). In light of this remarkable proof of the divine control of history, Isaiah concludes with the divine declaration: "I am the LORD. . . . Behold, the former things have come to pass, now I declare new things; before they spring forth I proclaim them to you" (Isaiah 42:8-9). Not only did God pass His own test; it is understood that no one else ever will: "Who has declared this from the beginning, that we might know? Or from former times, that we may say, 'He is right!'? Surely there was *no one* who declared, surely there was no one who proclaimed" (Isaiah 41:26, emphasis added).

Pro-phecy or *Post*-phecy?

Non-conservative scholars argue that Isaiah did not write this prophecy prior to its fulfillment. They divide his book into a "First Isaiah" (chapters 1–39), which is dated to Isaiah's time (740–680 B.C.), and a "Second Isaiah" (chapters 40–66), which is dated much later than his time (after 536 B.C.). The reason this division was first proposed was because of a rationalistic assumption that the mention of the Persian Cyrus could have been made only by a writer who knew this event as past history. Thus, all such "prophecy" in the Bible was judged to be *vaticinium ex eventu* ("prophecy after the [fulfillment of the] event").

There is no literary or archaeological evidence in support of dividing Isaiah's messages, and I have defended its unity from the archaeological record in my book *Secrets of the Dead Sea Scrolls.* Yet, no matter how a person dates chapters 40–66, chapters 1–39 also contain predictive prophecy (7:16; 8:4,7; 9:1-2; 13:17-20; 37:33-35; 38:8). In addition, the specific naming of individuals in predictive prophecy is not restricted to this instance (see, for example, King Josiah named 300 years before his birth—in 1 Kings 13:2; cf. 2 Kings 23:15-17). Furthermore, the purpose of the Cyrus prediction was to encourage the Israelites who understood Isaiah's prophecy of the Babylonian destruction and captivity. There would be no comfort, much less assurance, of promised deliverance if the prophecy had been ambiguous, or proclaimed after the event itself![4] Some have even proposed that this encouragement extended to Cyrus himself. Although we cannot validate the tradition, the first-century historian Josephus wrote that what prompted Cyrus' decree to liberate the Jews was his being shown this very prophecy of Isaiah *(Antiquities of the Jews* xi. 1.2:5-6).

But the idea of *vaticinium ex eventu* simply cannot be harmonized with the biblical requirement that whatever prophecy is *not* fulfilled is not *true* prophecy (Deuteronomy 18:22).[6] If all Israelite prophecy was "after the fact," then how could the fulfillment of prophecy be held up as the decisive test that the God of Israel was distinct from the gods of the nations? Could not the prophets of other nations proclaim prophecy after the fact? In contrast, the ability to prophesy *before* the fact is consistently put forth as the authoritative proof of God's divine intervention and of Scripture's divine inspiration. In the New Testament, it continues as the authenticating mark of Jesus' messiahship, since one of the Messiah's functions was to fulfill the role of a prophet (Deuteronomy 18:15-19; Acts 3:22,26; cf. Matthew 21:11). If prophecies were not made in advance of the events they were said to predict, then anyone could qualify as a prophet. Yet it is predictive prophecy that served as the distinguishing qualification of the one who would speak for God.

Archaeology and Fulfilled Prophecies

The Prophecy About Cyrus

The person and career of Cyrus II are well-known from the historical records of Herodotus, *Persian Wars,*[7] *Xenophon,*[8] the *Nabonidus Chronicle,*[9] and the *Persian Verse Account.*[10] His first military campaign against the Lydian king Croesus in 546 B.C. was also implied by Isaiah's prediction (Isaiah 45:3). Then on October 12, 539 B.C., Cyrus launched an invasion against Nabonidus, king of Babylon. Both Herodotus and Xenophon describe how Cyrus had besieged the city but his action was mocked by the Babylonians, who had stored up years of reserves because they had long expected a Persian invasion. The arrogance of the well-stocked Babylonians is portrayed in the book of Daniel. He recorded that more than a thousand nobles engaged in a great feast even while Cyrus and his army camped outside the city's walls (Daniel 5:1), a fact also noted by Herodotus and Xenophon. Daniel does not here mention Nabonidus, but his son Belshazzar, whose role was confirmed by the archaeological discovery of a cylindrical inscription in one of the four corners of the ziggurat at Ur. In this inscription of Nabonidus from the sixth-century B.C., Belshazzar *(Bel-shar-usur)* is called Nabonidus' firstborn son and is included in the king's prayer, an act reserved only for royalty.[11] At Belshazzar's feast some of the sacred vessels from the Jerusalem Temple were put to use, perhaps to show that the Babylonian gods were superior in order to boost civic morale (Daniel 5:2-4). This action was itself predictive of future events, since Cyrus was prophesied as the one who would defeat Babylon and restore these vessels (Ezra 1:7-11; Isaiah 52:11-12). After Daniel interpreted the mysterious handwriting that appeared on a wall during the feast, he prophesied that Babylon would fall to Cyrus (Daniel 5:28). Daniel noted that this prophecy was fulfilled that "same night" as the Persian army invaded the city in a surprise attack. Herodotus and Xenophon affirm Daniel's statement of a swift and unexpected invasion in their description of how this took place. They record that the attack came after the Persian army diverted the water of the Euphrates River, which caused the river bed under the city walls to be empty and accessible to the troops. Thus Cyrus came to the throne and fulfilled the long-term prophecy of Isaiah and the near-term prophecy of Daniel.

The Decree of Cyrus

In the first year of his reign (538 B.C.), Cyrus issued the decree that allowed the captive Jews to return to Jerusalem and rebuild the Temple:

The LORD, the God of heaven, has given me all the kingdoms of the earth, and He has appointed me to build Him a house at Jerusalem, which is in Judah. Whoever there is among you of all his people, may his God be with him! Let him go up to Jerusalem, which is in Judah, and rebuild the house of the LORD, the God of Israel; He is the God who is in Jerusalem. And every survivor, at whatever place he may live, let the men of that place support him with silver and gold, with goods and cattle, together with a freewill offering for the house of God which is in Jerusalem (Ezra 1:2-4).

56. *The Cyrus Cylinder, which records the Persian king's edicts in language similar to those in the biblical books of Ezra and 2 Chronicles.*

Ancient documents reveal to us that the laws of the Medes and the Persians were unalterable and pervasive. As Alan Millard has observed, "wherever the Persian king was, there was the government, for everything depended upon his law. So when he made an announcement it had to be carried to every part of his empire that was affected."[12] Ezra gives an example of this by citing King Darius' law cursing those who would seek to alter Cyrus' law protecting the Jews who returned to rebuild the Temple (Ezra 6:1-12). In 1973 French archaeologists found a large Persian stele in a Greek temple at Xanthos, Turkey written in Aramaic, Greek, and Lycian that was very similar in structure to the decree recorded in Ezra.

Archaeologists have yet to uncover a copy of the Cyrus decree as preserved in the Old Testament. However, they have discovered a stone cylinder inscribed in cuneiform that provides significant Persian parallels to certain aspects of the biblical account.

The Cyrus Cylinder

This cuneiform record is known as the Cyrus Cylinder. Its text begins much like the biblical record, with Cyrus crediting his god Marduk with choosing him for a special task and exalting him to a position in order to perform it. It is also similar to Isaiah's prophecy in that Cyrus makes the point that his god "pronounced the name of Cyrus, king of Anshan, [and] pronounced his name to be the ruler of all the world."[13] In much the same way, God called Cyrus by name and pronounced him a ruler (Isaiah 45:1-2). Isaiah had said that Cyrus, as God's anointed (literally, "messiah"), would "perform all [God's] desire" (Isaiah 44:28). On the cylinder, Cyrus proclaims that the gods "Bel and Nebo love" his rule and want him as king "to please their hearts."[14]

Of even greater interest is the cylinder's statements concerning Persian policy toward captive peoples, such as the Israelites, and their looted sacred ritual objects:

> ... I returned to [these] sacred cities on the other side of the Tigris, the sanctuaries of which have been in ruins for a long time, the images which [used] to live therein and established for them permanent sanctuaries. I [also] gathered all their [former] inhabitants and returned [to them] their habitations. Furthermore, I resettled upon the command of Marduk the great lord,

all the gods of Sumer and Akkad whom Nabonidus has brought into Babylon to the anger of the lord of the gods, unharmed, in their [former] chapels, the places which made them happy. May all the gods whom I have resettled in their sacred cities ask daily Bel and Nebo for long life for me and may they recommend me ... to Marduk, my lord, may they say thus: Cyrus, the king who worships you, and Cambyses, his son, [...] all of them I settled in a peaceful place.[15]

The Babylonians captured the sacred vessels from the Jerusalem Temple and took them to Shinar, where their temple was located (Daniel 1:2). This was in keeping with the custom of conquerors carrying off statues of the conquered cities' gods in order to show the superior power of their own gods. The Babylonians also defiled these vessels in mockery of the God of Israel (Daniel 5:1-4). Cyrus, in keeping with the Persian policy reflected in the Cyrus Cylinder, respected the gods of foreign captives and returned all of the Temple vessels when he allowed the Jews to return to their homeland and rebuild the Temple (Ezra 1:7-11). This passage reveals that the Persians had kept an accurate inventory of these items (5,400, or 5,469 according to the Septuagint), and returned them to the Israelites. Both Isaiah and Jeremiah had prophesied that these vessels would be safely returned from Babylon (Isaiah 52:11-12; Jeremiah 27:16–28:6). When Cyrus transferred the vessels to Sheshbazzar of Judah (Ezra 1:7-11), he fulfilled these prophecies.

This isn't the only example in which archaeology has confirmed the fulfillment of Bible prophecy. The prophets of the Old Testament, and Jesus in the New, pronounced judgments that the archaeologist's spade has revealed were fulfilled quite literally.

The Prophecy About Nineveh

In the Bible, we read this prophecy against the city of Nineveh: " 'Behold, I am against you,' declares the LORD of hosts. 'I will burn up [your] chariots in smoke, a sword will devour your young lions, I will cut off your prey from the land, and no longer will the voice of your messengers be heard' " (Nahum 2:13). Zephaniah likewise predicted that Nineveh would become completely desolate, fit only as a habitation for the beasts of the field and fowls of the air (Zephaniah 2:13-15).[16]

Nahum's prophecy was given in 663 B.C. and Zephaniah's in 625 B.C.—at a time when the Assyrian empire was at the apex of its power. As impossible as their fulfillment might have seemed to their audiences, and as inexplicable as it has been to historians ever since, the glory of Assyria vanished into oblivion in the year 612 B.C. never to be heard from again—exactly as predicted! Excavations at the ruins of Sennacherib's palace at Nineveh by Sir Henry Layard in the 1850s confirmed that everything at the site was either burned, looted, or destroyed. He found Nineveh utterly deserted except for gazelles, jackals, and hyenas, which he noted made their dens in the sides of the barren mound that was once the ancient city.

The historical description of Nineveh's sudden demise has been left to us in the Babylonian Chronicles. One tablet, the record of the Babylonian king Nabopolassar, tells how he formed a coalition army of the Babylonians, Medes, and Scythians, and brought down the city after a short siege of only three months. Nahum had even predicted this coalition, specifically detailing the customary red-painted shields and tunics of the Medes and Babylonians, as well as the scythes attached to their chariot axles (Nahum 2:3). After these armies took Nineveh, a few of the officials and the king fled to another city but were later captured. Today, we still have remnants of a few of the ancient nations—such as Egypt, Greece, and Rome. But there is no nation of Assyria. Until the age of archaeology it was lost to history, a loss now regained as evidence of the fulfillment of predictions made by the prophets.

The Prophecy About Tyre

One of the most unusual prophecies has to do with the ancient Phoenician city-state of Tyre, which was located on the

Mediterranean coast near its modern-day namesake in Lebanon. Under King Hiram, (980–947 B.C.) Tyre had prospered to such a point that Solomon had imported both workmen and materials for the construction of David's palace and the Temple (2 Samuel 5:11-12; 2 Chronicles 2:3,7-16).

The prophet Ezekiel prophesied against Tyre between 592–570 B.C. As with the proclamations against Cyrus and Assyria, Ezekiel's prophecies concerning Tyre are equally detailed and specific:

> Thus says the Lord GOD, "Behold, I am against you, O Tyre, and I will bring up many nations against you ... and they will destroy the walls of Tyre and break down her towers; and I will scrape her debris from her and make her a bare rock. . . . Behold, I will bring upon Tyre from the north Nebuchadnezzar king of Babylon. . . . He will slay your daughters on the mainland with the sword; and he will make siege walls against you, cast up a mound against you, and raise up a large shield against you ... break down your walls and destroy your pleasant houses, and throw your stones and your timbers and your debris into the water. . . . And I will make you a bare rock; you will be a place for the spreading of nets. You will be built no more, for I the LORD have spoken" (Ezekiel 26:3-4,7-8,12,14).

Many nations were involved in the fulfillment of this prophecy. The destruction of Tyre began, as Ezekiel had predicted, with the Babylonian king Nebuchadnezzar (verse 7). He besieged the mainland city for 13 years (585–572 B.C.) and destroyed it. Then in 332 B.C. Alexander the Great set siege against the island city for a period of six months. He finally captured it by constructing a 200-foot wide causeway across the straits to the island, using the dirt and debris of the destroyed city on the mainland. As Ezekiel had predicted, Alexander threw the stones and timbers of its debris into the water (verse 12). Although the city recovered somewhat from these destructions, it never regained its former status.[17] It was again attacked and almost completely destroyed by the Muslims in A.D. 1291, finally fulfilling the prophecy that it would "be built no more" (verse 14).

Modern-day Tyre is a fishing town with a harbor, built down the coast from the ancient site. Ancient Tyre is now a barren rock that the local fishermen use to spread their nets to dry, just as Ezekiel had said (verses 4,14). Its once-imposing walls and gates are no more (verse 14), although the ancient causeway built by the Greek army still remains, like these other details, as a testimony to the specific fulfillment of Ezekiel's prophecy.

The same is true for prophecies made against many other ancient sites such as Babylon, Memphis, Thebes, Moab-Ammon, and Petra (Edom). Archaeologists have uncovered and are still uncovering dramatic ruins at many of these sites (such as the temples and tombs in Thebes and the altar and high place at Petra). In some cases modern cities have been built near these ancient sites, but their presence only serves to confirm the prophecies of the past. For example, stones from the ruins of Memphis were used to build the present city of Cairo. The site of Babylon is presently being rebuilt,[18] but still it, like the others, remains without habitation and is largely in ruins—in harmony with the ancient prophecies.

The Prophecy About the Temple Mount

In the Gospels we read that Jesus' disciples were awed by the beauty of the Temple, which was still under construction (Matthew 24:1-2; Mark 13:1-2; Luke 21:5-6). The rebuilding was begun by Herod the Great and his dynastic successors felt obligated to contribute as well to this project, which, on their part, was more politics than piety. As the disciples were pointing out newly set stones at the Temple, Jesus made an unexpected prophetic pronouncement: "Truly I say to you, not one stone here shall be left upon another, which will not be torn down." Jesus' words were fulfilled when the Roman army, under the command of the emperor Vespasian's son Titus, stormed the Temple precincts and burned the Temple in

57. *Excavations south of the Western Wall, showing rubble left from destruction of* A.D. 70 *on the Herodian street, broken by the impact of the stones pushed from the Temple area above.*

A.D. 70. The archaeological excavations at the foot of the Temple Mount, especially at the western and southern corners, have vividly revealed the massive destruction wrought by the Romans. On a section of the ancient Herodian street that lined the outside western wall of the Mount, heaps of the rubble pushed from the Temple area above were uncovered in excavations directed by Ronny Reich in 1995–1996. Despite this evidence, some people have wondered how the prophecy of "not one stone here shall be left upon another" can be considered fulfilled when many remains of the ancient Temple complex still remain (for example, the Western Wall and its tunnel, the monumental stairway at the southern wall and its double and triple gates). Leen Ritmeyer, who has conducted decades of research on the Temple Mount, answers this objection:

> If you read the text in Matthew, the site [the disciples] pointed out were the buildings of the Temple. Read the exact text—"the buildings of the Temple." The only buildings I know that belonged to the Temple were [those] built around it and the porticos. And all these buildings that stood on the Temple Mount were indeed left without one stone upon another.

Obviously Jesus was referring to those buildings (including the Temple itself) which were on the huge supporting platform. He would not have had in mind any other structures such as the retaining walls with their foundation stones at the platform's street level, nor even the platform itself (which also has remained intact). Archaeology has confirmed that no trace of these Temple buildings exists today, although some of their stones may have been put to secondary use in the walls and homes in the Old City of Jerusalem. Nevertheless, none remain in their original setting. In fact, after the destruction of the Second Temple, the Romans plowed under the Temple Mount and erected pagan structures upon it (which themselves were

58. *Western (Wailing) Wall, ancient remnant of a retaining wall for Herodian Temple platform.*

later destroyed). During the Byzantine period (fourth-seventh centuries A.D.) the entire site was deliberately left barren out of the belief that Jesus' prophecy was a curse against the site forbidding any future rebuilding.

Interestingly, historians have not yet been able to conclude exactly why the Temple was destroyed by the Romans. Conflicting accounts say that Titus gave specific orders not to destroy it, while others contend that the fire was accidentally started. This fire, it is believed, melted the gold that lined the inner walls of the buildings, causing it to flow into the cracks between the stones. This would have made it necessary for the soldiers to pull down the stones to retrieve the gold. However, I remember the answer my Orthodox professor of history of the Second Temple period at the Hebrew University in Jerusalem, Isaiah Gafni, gave when our class had reached an impasse concerning these theories. He said, "Well, maybe Jesus was right!" Indeed He was, for the ultimate explanation of this and every prophecy is that God both planned and performed it.

Archaeology from the Prophetic Perspective

The actors of history were usually unaware that they were part of a prophetic drama. Cyrus had no understanding that both his birth and role had been foretold by Isaiah the prophet when, as part of his foreign policy, he decreed the release and return of the Jews to Judah. Neither was there any consciousness of Jesus' prophecy concerning the Second Temple when the Roman Emperor Vespasian and his son Titus sent its stones hurling down one upon another. Yet, each was part of a fulfillment evidenced today by the archaeological remains that have documented their acts. Archaeology cannot in and of itself show the supernatural. This is the sole provenance of Scripture. However, when the prophetic statements are accepted and the stones are viewed from this perspective, their interpretation may offer further example and insight into the prophetic drama.

The Christian Reformed theologian B.B. Warfield once told his students that one could view their theological studies as one viewed a window.[19] One could see only the pane of glass, or they could look through it to the world which it revealed beyond. Many who study the stones see only the glassy side of the history. To see beyond to a world determined by the God of the Prophets, one must view each artifact through the lens of Scripture. Those who have done so have discovered a whole new world—a world that adds the excitement of expectation to every new archaeological discovery. No longer are these pieces of an impersonal history, but fragments of fulfillment of a supernatural story in which the conclusion bears a personal promise to the person who has faith.

14

ARCHÆOLOGY AND A MIRACLE

Reading Between the Cracks

The excessive skepticism of many liberal theologians stems not from a careful evaluation of the available data, but from an enormous predisposition against the supernatural.[1]

—Millar Burrows

I gained a new insight into biblical interpretation when I learned to read the "white spaces" in the Bible. Normally, of course, we would read the words on the page, but there is more there than meets the eye! The white spaces are what is not written, yet oftentimes there is a possibility that something occurred between those words of text on the page. This is what people call "reading between the lines."

An example of reading this way may be found in Genesis 4:17. There we read that "Cain had relations with his wife." Where did *she* come from? If we rely only on the words written on the page of this text, we would conclude that there were only four people alive on earth and the other three were Cain's parents [Adam and Eve] and his brother Abel. However, we read later in Genesis 5:4 that Cain's parents "had other sons and daughters" over an 800-year period. So by reading between the lines, we can understand that when Cain married it was to one of his sisters or cousins. Scripture is selective about what it says, so sometimes *we* have to fill in the gaps based on comparative texts or our knowledge of historical events. These are what fill the white spaces of our Bible.

When we turn to archaeology and deal with the stones, we must change the metaphor. Rather than reading between the lines, we must read between the cracks! One of the values of archaeology is that it can supply historical details that are lacking in the biblical text. By allowing us to "read between the cracks," archaeology helps us to coordinate biblical and historical facts about people, places, and events that would otherwise be unknown, and thereby certify uncertain passages.

Miracles in the Bible

Perhaps no passages are considered more "uncertain" in our skeptical age than those that concern the miraculous. In relation to archaeology and the miraculous, W.F. Albright once observed:

> Though archaeology can thus clarify the history and geography of ancient Palestine, it cannot explain the basic miracle of Israel's faith, which remains a unique factor in world history. But archaeology can help enormously in making the miracle rationally plausible to an intelligent person whose vision is not shortened by a materialistic world view.[2]

The Bible is not only a record of history but also of the miraculous in history. However, most archaeologists see miracles as an expression of religious faith, not something that can be validated in real history. But is it possible that in the realm of miracles, archaeology could also help us read between the lines and affirm what was thought to be impossible to certify in the realm of history? In order to answer this question, let's first consider the nature of miracles in the Bible.

The Nature of Miracles in the Bible

When people think of miracles related to the Bible, they usually think of the burning bush seen by Moses and the parting of the Red Sea. These would be classified as "first-class" miracles—that is, extraordinary events that manifest divine intervention in human or natural affairs. These should be kept separate from "second-class" miracles, which represent the common grace of God given for the daily living of our lives.

The Frequency of Miracles in the Bible

The frequency with which first-class miracles appear in the Bible also needs to be understood. Many people have the notion that the Bible is a collection of fairy tales because they assume that the miraculous appears on every page. But when we look for miracles in the Bible we find that they happen quite infrequently and only at certain designated periods of history. In fact, there are only four brief periods during which such activity occurred: 1) during the time of Moses and Joshua (1441–1370 B.C.) when God was establishing His nation; 2) during the time of Elijah and Elisha (870–785 B.C.) when God was establishing His prophets; 3) during the time of Daniel (605–538 B.C.) when God was establishing His people in exile; and 4) during the ministry of Jesus and His apostles (A.D. 28–90) when God was establishing His church.[3]

In each of these times, miracles occurred during pivotal periods of historical transition and national establishment. Miracles were given as a necessary sign to inaugurate each new era, to authenticate God's message and messengers, and to instruct those who observed the events. Given the thousands of years God has been dealing with man, it is surprising that He has been so restrained in His use of the miraculous. However, the sparsity of miracles is not meant to diminish the miraculous, but to emphasize that miracles have specific purposes. Many, if not most, of the miracles seen in three of the four transitional periods were associated with judgments on Israel's enemies (Egypt, idolatry, Babylon). Only during the fourth period, the time of Jesus and the apostles, were miracles primarily confirmatory.

Let's now take, as an example, a miracle that occurred during the reign of King Hezekiah, which took place during the second of our designated periods of miracles (the prophets). Does archaeology offer any historical support for the Bible's theological statement of the miraculous?

Examining a Miraculous Event

The Key Characters

Hezekiah—A Man of Construction

The reign of King Hezekiah itself was nothing less than miraculous. He came to the Judean throne in 715 B.C. as the godly son of one of history's most ungodly fathers, Ahaz. His legacy of godliness was that he was the greatest of the divided monarchy's reforming kings. He began his career of reform by returning Israel's worship to a centralized place as God had commanded—the Jerusalem Temple (2 Chronicles 29–31). To assure the religious revival Hezekiah wanted to bring about, he rooted out idolatrous practices throughout his realm, and even destroyed the last vestiges of Judean syncretism that had centered on the veneration of the ancient copper snake that Moses had made and had by now become a religious relic with the name "Nehushtan" (2 Kings 18:3-6). Snake cults were common in the ritualistic religions that influenced Israel,[4] as discovered at Tel-Miqne (Ekron), where a miniature golden snake from Hezekiah's time was discovered. Hezekiah knew that even though this sacred object had once been a symbol of salvation (Numbers 21:4-9; John 3:14), now it was a sign of sin.

Hezekiah's strengthening of Judah spiritually and politically led to the need for increased construction, particularly in the city of Jerusalem. During his reign he expanded the city onto the Western Hill, primarily to incorporate the refugees from the Northern Kingdom of Israel, which had been destroyed by the Assyrian king Sargon II (2 Chronicles 30:25). These ranks would swell even more as Sargon's successor Sennacherib attacked the Southern Kingdom and dispossessed its peoples. At first, however, Hezekiah's peaceful rule was unopposed. He had won a military victory over the Philistines, confining them to their old home along the Mediterranean coastal plain. With an even greater show of strength, he forged an alliance with Egypt and ended the payment of tribute to Assyria, which had begun with his fathers. For a time Hezekiah's resistance seemed successful. But then the Assyrian overlord Sennacherib came to reclaim his honor and the tribute owed by his vassal province.

Sennacherib—A Man of Conquest

At this time in history the ancient Near East had become a neighborhood ruled by might, and the mightiest and the baddest of the boys on the block were the Assyrians. One look at the graphic portrayals on archaeological reliefs that depicted their enemies' headless and handless corpses; their captives being blinded, impaled, or flayed alive; or the lucky ones being led off to exile with hooks through their jaws is convincing enough to conclude that the Assyrians were not an enemy one wanted to annoy. And Sennacherib, as their king, enforced this kind of brutality.[5] The Assyrian reliefs depicting the Lachish siege show Sennacherib enthroned and proudly surveying this scene of carnage, impalement, and capture. In addition, an Assyrian winged-bull inscription from Sennacherib's palace at Nineveh boasts, "I laid waste the large district of Judah..." while on the Lachish relief itself he proclaimed, "Sennacherib, king of the world...." Therefore, from the Assyrian perspective, Hezekiah's rebellion had pitted him against the world, and his plight was threatened to be earth-shattering!

The Plight

In 701 B.C. Sennacherib advanced against "all the fortified cities of Judah and took them" (2 Kings 18:13). Archaeological confirmation of this exists in the form of a monumental Assyrian relief made to commemorate his victory over one of these cities—Lachish. As previously mentioned, this relief was found preserved on Sennacherib's palace walls at Nineveh (see chapter 4). After Sennacherib took Lachish, nothing stood in the way of making the march against Judah's capital, Jerusalem. Hezekiah was not ignorant of the inevitable. At first Hezekiah tried to placate Sennacherib by paying his "back taxes" (2 Kings 18:14-16). However, failing to appease Sennacherib, Hezekiah adopted a more prudent plan to postpone his people's plight—the results of which have been revealed by archaeology.

When the Assyrian siege began, Hezekiah began an industrious program to secure Jerusalem's defenses. Two obvious problems faced Hezekiah: the need for better fortifications, and the need to prevent being cut off from the natural resources that sustained the city. The Assyrian "Rab-shakeh" (a high official)[6] addressed this latter fear when he said to the people of Jerusalem, "Is not Hezekiah misleading you to give yourselves over to die by hunger and by thirst...?" (2 Chronicles 32:11). Hezekiah addressed the latter need in an exceptional manner.

Hezekiah's Water Tunnel

Hezekiah was certain that Jerusalem would be cut off from its main water supply, the Gihon Spring, the source of which lay unprotected deep in the southern end of the Kidron Valley outside the old City of David. Hezekiah managed to divert its waters by stopping the upper outlet and directing its flow to the western side of the city (see 2 Chronicles 32:2-4,30). This was accomplished by an incredible feat of engineering that even modern engineers marvel at today. Hezekiah secretly carved through solid limestone a 1,750-foot tunnel underneath Jerusalem. This connected the Gihon Spring with the present-day Pool of Siloam, located within the walls at the city's southwestern

59. *Author's daughter Eleisha inside Hezekiah's Water Tunnel.*

corner. The Bible tells us about this feat (2 Kings 20:20), but not how it was accomplished. However, when a local exploration of the tunnel was made in 1880 (by boys swimming at the site) an inscription was discovered about 20 feet from the exit, where the tunnel is almost 15 feet high. Now called the "Siloam Inscription," this eighth-century account of the tunnel's construction fills in the "white spaces" of the biblical story.[7] It tells how two crews of workmen armed with picks completed their assigned task:

> ...And this was the account of the breakthrough. While the laborers were still working with their picks, each toward the other, and while there were still three cubits to be broken through, the voice of each was heard calling to the other, because there was a crack (or split or overlap) in the rock from the south to the north. And at the moment of the breakthrough, the laborers struck each toward the other, pick against pick. Then the water flowed from the spring to the pool for 1,200 cubits. And the height of the rock above the heads of the laborers was 100 cubits.

I have walked the length of this irregularly cut serpentine tunnel more than 30 times and it still amazes me. The pickmen did not go in a straight line but weaved in an S-shaped path, which increased the length of their route by more than 65 percent. Various attempts have been made to try and explain how the pickmen, without the aid of a compass or tools, could have perfectly met each other.[8] But for now it is still considered a mystery—and a miracle. Regardless of how his workmen did it, Hezekiah's tunnel was a lifesaver for Jerusalem. Now remained the job of securing his fortifications.

Hezekiah's "Broad Wall"

As the Assyrians approached Jerusalem, Hezekiah made last-hour preparations to resist Sennacherib's impending siege by fortifying the newly expanded, but weaker, western hill of the city. The Bible records these efforts of Hezekiah, noting that "he took courage and rebuilt all the wall that had been broken down, and erected towers on it, and built another outside wall" (2 Chronicles 32:5). Some of the fortification structures mentioned in this verse have been found in excavations in the Jewish Quarter.[9] One of the towers and a section of its rebuilt wall were discovered still preserved to a height of about six feet. The new "outside wall" that Hezekiah built was discovered by Israeli archaeologist Nahman Avigad during his excavations in the Jewish Quarter (1969–1982). Today this wall is called the "Broad Wall" because of its immense width (23 feet). This extreme thickness was necessary to withstand the terrible battering rams of the Assyrian army. This wall originally stood about 27 feet high and ran from the northern area of the Western Hill to the south, then westward toward the present Jaffa Gate. It then continued southward along the edge of the slope above the Hinnom Valley until it swung east to meet the southern tip of David's City at the place where Jerusalem's three main valleys met.[10] The construction of this massive wall reveals the people's desperation to ward off the Assyrian onslaught at all costs. And cost was a factor, for the Broad Wall was hastily built by using

60. *Standing on the Broad Wall, built by King Hezekiah and described by the prophet Isaiah.*

stones that came from people's houses. This fact is also recorded of Hezekiah in Scripture: "You saw that the breaches in the wall of the city of David were many . . . you counted the houses of Jerusalem, and you *tore down houses to fortify the wall*" (Isaiah 22:9-10, emphasis added). Here, then, is dramatic archaeological evidence of the great fear King Hezekiah and all the people felt when faced with the Assyrian advance. When I stood on this wall I reflected on how much pain these frightened people must have felt as they ripped apart their own homes in a desperate gamble to withstand a seemingly omnipotent power. What hope could they possibly have against a foe that had already captured or destroyed all the other cities they had gone against up to now? Yet, the biblical story reminds us that when our strength is gone, there is God. Realizing there was no other refuge than the God whose own covenant had sworn to preserve the penitent, the king abandoned his pursuit for greater protection and instead went (with the prophet Isaiah) to prayer (2 Chronicles 32:20).

Hezekiah's Miraculous Prayer

When Hezekiah prayed, he both repented for God's people and resorted to God's promise (in the Davidic covenant). God had spared Jerusalem once before when its sin had brought destruction (2 Samuel 24:16; 1 Chronicles 21:15), and Hezekiah believed that God could be entreated to do it again (see Isaiah 37:6-7,21-38). By contrast, the Rab-shakeh had told Jerusalem that there was no use in looking to God because He had been unable to save any of the other cities of the Northern or Southern kingdoms from Sennacherib (2 Chronicles 32:15; Isaiah 36:18-20). As a result, Isaiah the prophet brought this word from God: "I will defend this city to save it for My own sake and for My servant David's sake" (2 Kings 19:34; Isaiah 37:35). God promised that He would "put a spirit in [Sennacherib] so that he shall hear a rumor and return to his own land. And I will make him fall by the sword in his own land"(2 Kings 19:7). The familiar account of what happened next to fulfill this promised miracle is recorded in the parallel texts of Kings and Isaiah:[11]

> Then it happened that night that the angel of the LORD went out, and struck 185,000 in the camp of the Assyrians; and when the men rose early in the morning, behold, all of them were dead. So Sennacherib king of Assyria departed and returned home, and lived at Nineveh. And it came about as he was worshiping in the house of Nisroch his god, that Adrammelech and Sharezer killed him with the sword. . . .

The ancient Greek historian Herodotus (484–425 B.C.) told a similar story about Sethos, an Egyptian whose god was said to have sent field mice at night to eat the Assyrian army's quivers, bowstrings, and shield handles while they were camped at Pelusium. The result was that the next morning the army was unarmed and most of the soldiers were killed or retreated.[12] This account has led some scholars to suggest a confusion of traditions and that the biblical account may be reflecting a sudden outbreak of a virulent vermin-induced plague that slew the Assyrians. Other scholars believe Sennacherib reigned another 20 years after his failed attempt to conquer Jerusalem and engaged in other military exploits.[13] However one interprets the event, one thing is certain: After Hezekiah's prayer, Sennacherib was never again in Judah! Something happened which so shook this mighty monarch that he kept his distance until the day of his death. The historical details of his death by assassination in 681 B.C. are recorded in another archaeological discovery, the Babylonian Chronicle which states: "On the 20th of the month of Tebet, his son killed Sennacherib, king of Assyria, during a rebellion."[14] Although this Babylonian tablet generally confirms the biblical account, Jerusalem's salvation from the hands of Sennacherib is a fact confirmed by the Assyrians themselves.

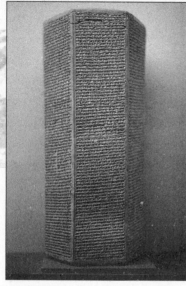

61. *The Taylor Prism, preserving Sennacherib's account of his seige against Jerusalem in the time of Hezekiah.*

Surveying the Evidence of the Miraculous

Today, five whole or fragmentary copies of Sennacherib's annals exist in which we can read his own report of the Assyrian assault against King Hezekiah. These annals were recorded on a six-sided clay prism inscribed in Assyrian cuneiform. Because it was discovered (at Sennacherib's palace in Nineveh in 1830) by the British Colonel R. Taylor, it is known as the "Taylor Prism," and other copies in other holdings are known as the "Nimrud Prism" and the "Oriental Institute Prism."[15] Although historians and scholars may dismiss the miraculous explanation given in the Bible, they cannot deny the witness of an enemy's testimony carved in stone. In leaving his record for those who would follow and preserve his memory, Sennacherib put his best face forward and inscribed the facts for all time:

> As for Hezekiah, the Judean who did not submit to my yoke, I surrounded and conquered forty-six of his strong-walled towns and innumerable small settle-

ments around them by means of earth ramps and siege-
engines and attack by infantry men.... I brought out
from them and counted 200,150 people of all ranks....
He himself I shut up in Jerusalem, his royal city, like a
bird in a cage.... Fear of my lordly splendor over-
whelmed that Hezekiah. The warriors and select troops
he had brought in to strengthen his royal city Jerusalem, did not fight.... He sent his messengers to pay
tribute and do obeisance.

An Archaeological Argument from Silence

What can we observe in Sennacherib's account of his siege
against Jerusalem? First, we find his affirmation that Jerusalem
was surrounded without any hope of rescue or escape. Sennacherib had exacted tribute from King Hezekiah and had militarily shut him up "like a bird in a cage." Second, we find his
confirmation that while he had surrounded Jerusalem, he could
not conquer the city. The best he could say was that he besieged
it—*nothing more!* And we can be sure that if he could have said
more he would have, for his list of conquests both precede and
follow his attack on Jerusalem. It was not the Assyrian way to
record a disaster, so in the typical fashion of a Near Eastern
monarch who could only boast for posterity but never admit a
failure, Sennacherib's silence speaks volumes.

The historical enigma of Sennacherib's only defeat in all of
Israel has not escaped the scholars. One writer attempting to
understand Jerusalem's successful escape from the Assyrian
siege could make only this observation: "... although we don't
know for sure what broke the siege, we do know that the
Israelites inside managed to hold out."[16] However, by reading
between the lines—or the cracks—we can set the stones side
by side with the Scriptures and receive an answer. In this case,
the archaeological record complements the Bible, and the Bible
supplements the archaeological record. The annals of Sennacherib reveal that the siege happened just as the Bible said. It
followed the devastation of Judah and put Hezekiah beyond the
means of all human hope. At this point the Bible supplies the

reason for Sennacherib's silence: God did a miracle. No better explanation has been offered, either by the Assyrians or the scholars!

A Tribute to the King of Miracles

King Hezekiah of Judah learned one of the most important lessons that any child of God can learn: "those who honor Me I will honor" (1 Samuel 2:30). Hezekiah had feared the truth of God rather than the taunts of the Rab-shakeh. By fleeing to God rather than fleeing from Sennacherib, Hezekiah gave honor to the God of Israel in whom he trusted. And God honored His covenant with His people (whom Hezekiah represented), and saved the nation. It seems that God also permitted Hezekiah to be honored as well. In his life he received special honor (2 Chronicles 32:23), as well as at his death. In a biblical epitath to the king we read, "So Hezekiah slept with his fathers, and they buried him in the upper section of the tombs of the sons of David; and all Judah and the inhabitants of Jerusalem *honored him at his death*" (2 Chronicles 32:33, emphasis added).

How was Hezekiah honored at his death? There may now be archaeological evidence to answer this question. In the region west of Jerusalem there exist strange earthen mounds known as *tumuli*. Tumuli are artificial hills of dirt and stone (shaped like small volcanoes) that were apparently erected as memorials to deceased kings or noblemen.[17] They were constructed following a special ceremony that occurred sometime between the death and final burial of the one honored. The memorial service involved having people meet around a fire in what was called a "burning" *(see* 2 Chronicles 16:14; 21:19). The people attending the ceremony brought vessels with spices and foods offered in honor of the deceased *(see* Jeremiah 34:5; 51:25).[18] The latest excavator of the tumuli, archaeologist Gabriel Barkay, illustrates for us what such a ceremony would have been like:

I could imagine the ancient people of the Kingdom of Judah one month after the burial of the king gathering together in thousands—the elderly, the women, the children, the warriors, the administration, everybody. They spread upon the hills in this vicinity and in the middle some of the priests organized the ceremony in which they burned a large fire in memory of the deceased monarch, chanted some laments, and gave a last word, as is mentioned in the Bible. At the end of the ceremony, each of the participants took a basket with some stones and dirt and poured it upon the place where the ceremony took place and piled up a whole mountain in memory of the deceased monarch.[19]

At the conclusion of the event the area would be covered over to form the tumulus. Outside of Jerusalem there are some 20 tumuli still extant,[20] and the largest of these contained remains which most likely connect it to the time of Hezekiah's reign, according to Barkay:

I excavated this one during a very cold winter in Jerusalem, working during snowy days with frozen fingers. We excavated only at the edges and to our amazement we took out of the ground several pottery pieces with seal impressions upon them inscribed *lamelek* ("belonging to the king"). These are well established and the date of them is well known—they belong to the time of King Hezekiah, to the late eighth century B.C. Now, of course the date of each of these tumuli is different, they are not all of the same date.[21]

Barkay has proposed that these tumuli are memorials to the 21 kings of Judah. If so, this largest of the individually dated tumuli (tumulus 4) should rightly belong to Hezekiah, the greatest of the Judean kings. Therefore, it may indeed explain the heretofore uncertain reference about giving honor to Hezekiah as stated in 2 Chronicles 32:33. If so, tumulus 4 was a tribute to Hezekiah's leadership by the people of Judah. This is the conclusion of Gordon Franz, who assisted in the excavation of the site: "This mound would be left for a memorial to a king who did great things for his God and people—a king who is truly worthy to be honored."[22] No doubt a part of this honor was in grateful remembrance for the miraculous deliverance that God had wrought through the prayers of His godly king—a miracle that the stones (reading between the cracks) still shout.

15

THE DEAD SEA SCROLLS

Archæology's Front-Page Story

[The Dead Sea Scrolls] have come to be recognized as among the most important archaeological finds of the twentieth century. Shrouded in mystery, surrounded by controversy, and steeped in the romantic tall tales of arcane scholarly research, this collection... illuminates one of the most significant eras in the history of Judaism, Christianity, and the Western world.... [1]

—Yadin Roman

   The American Dean of Biblical Archaeology, William Foxwell Albright, hailed the Dead Sea Scrolls as "the greatest manuscript discovery of modern times." And indeed that's the case. After the story of the discovery broke in 1948, the Scrolls became front-page news around the world. Even today, as the fiftieth anniversary of the Scrolls is being commemorated, their

•

mention can excite any conversation. Though the ancient authors of the Scrolls are yet unknown to us, the Scrolls themselves, hidden away by a community of pious Jews on the shores of the Dead Sea, continue to hold the fascination of the modern world. One of Israel's pioneer Scroll scholars, Yigael Yadin, wrote:

> [The scrolls] constitute a vital link—long lost and now regained—between those ancient times, so rich in civilized thought, and the present day. And just as a Christian reader must be moved by the knowledge that here he has a manuscript of a sect whom the early Christians may have known and by whom they were influenced, so an Israeli and a Jew can find nothing more deeply moving than the study of manuscripts written by the People of the Book in the Land of the Book more than two thousand years ago.[2]

What Are the Dead Sea Scrolls?

The Dead Sea Scrolls represent some 1,100 ancient documents which today consist of several intact Scrolls plus more than 100,000 fragments. The texts of the Scrolls were written in columns, primarily in Hebrew and Aramaic, but also with some Greek. Most were written on leather parchment (made from goat or sheep skins) and papyrus (a form of early paper), but one, the *Copper Scroll,* was written on pure copper. Between 223–233 of the total manuscripts are copies of books of the Bible. So far a representative of every book of the Old Testament has been found, with the exception of Esther.[3] This collection of biblical texts constitutes our oldest known copies of the Scriptures (although, as already discussed, archaeology has subsequently produced earlier portions of scriptural passages). The Scrolls also contain commentaries on the books of the Bible, apocryphal and pseudepigraphical works, and sectarian documents (some written by the sect's unknown leader, called in the Scrolls "The Teacher of Righteousness"). Other types of texts, such as targums, tefillin, and mezuzot, are also present. A *targum* is a translation of the Hebrew Bible into Aramaic. Its purpose was to give an understanding of the original text to contemporary readers who were no longer familiar with the older biblical Hebrew. *Tefillin* (also called phylacteries) are small, tightly rolled scrolls that contain passages from the Bible books of Exodus and Deuteronomy.[4] They were placed in boxes that were tied to the head or left arm. The *mezuzot* were placed in ornamental cases that were attached to the doorpost of a house. The tefillin and mezuzot fulfilled (in a mystical manner) the biblical commandment in Deuteronomy: "You shall bind them [God's commandments, according to the preceding context] as a sign on your hand and they shall be as frontals [emblems] on your forehead. And you shall write them on the doorposts of your house and on your gates" (Deuteronomy 6:8-9).

Because of this assortment of native and imported texts, many people refer to the Scrolls as a "library," with these various texts probably brought in by new members of the community and archived for collective study. As a whole, they represent the common heritage of Second Temple Judaism,[5] providing us our only window (outside of the New Testament and the writings of Josephus) into the diverse sects and beliefs of this period.

The Scrolls and the Bible

These documents are immensely helpful to students of this era, including students of Jesus and the New Testament, whose history intersected the latest period of the Dead Sea Community. They provide previously unknown information about legal practices and social customs only dimly echoed in the much later rabbinic writings (Talmud, Mishnah). They give new confirmation of and insights into the languages spoken by Jesus and His disciples and vividly reveal the cultural conditions and conflicts that produced respectively Jesus' parabolic method of teaching and His debates with so-called establishment Judaism. They are also particularly helpful for our understanding of the eschatological beliefs of Jews who lived during this period.

62. *The Aleppo Codex, the oldest version of the Hebrew Scripture text until the discovery of the Dead Sea Scrolls.*

They show us that the developed prophetic interpretations found in the New Testament were not the unique provenance of early Jewish-Christianity, but the shared interpretation of Jews whose expectations were centered on the Old Testament Messianic program. Furthermore, for those who seek to reconstruct an accurate biblical text, the Scroll's versions of the Old Testament permit us to see different textual traditions that predate the medieval Massoretic text, which served as the basis for modern Hebrew Bibles and for most translations from Hebrew into other languages.

The Scrolls also allow us to see how well the scribes who preserved these biblical texts for us did their job. Until the discovery of the Dead Sea Scrolls our oldest version of the Bible's Hebrew text was the Aleppo Codex (A.D. 935), which was only 1,000 years old. As old as that may seem, it was still more than 1,000 years removed from the originals from which the Bible was copied and passed on. How could we be sure that in the transmission of this text over that thousand-year period the scribes had not made mistakes that now appear in our Bible translations? But the biblical texts in the Scrolls closed this thousand-year gap and let us compare the Hebrew text behind our translations with those, in some cases, only a generation from the originals. This comparison revealed—amazingly— almost identical wording! So from our new knowledge of the text based on the Scrolls, we can approach our own Bible translations with greater confidence.

The Setting of the Dead Sea Scrolls

Twenty miles southwest of Jerusalem lies the Dead Sea at a record level of 1,300 feet below sea level. Coming down from bleak, rugged limestone cliffs, we meet the sun-parched desert. When we reach the Dead Sea itself we find a body of water 45 miles long and nine miles wide constituting a chemical stew of 26 percent solid matter in the form of dissolved salts. Into this harsh environment God's patriarchs and prophets came in times past, and it may have been this association that led an orthodox but breakaway community of Jews to settle at a site known today by its Arabic name Khirbet Qumran. These priestly families lived a ritually pure lifestyle atop a chalky plateau beside the Dead Sea. Surviving only because of a nearby spring of water they were able to channel to their retreat, they awaited the fulfillment of the biblical prophecies of the coming Messiah and the restoration of the Jewish nation to the divine ideal.

Not only did this area's geography draw the Dead Sea sect to Qumran, its environment also helped preserve the Scrolls. This was because of a combination of factors, including the hot and arid climate (often 125° Fahrenheit), the negative air flow within the caves in which the Scrolls were hidden, and the special sealed jars in which they were stored. Similar states of preservation have been observed in objects taken from the sealed tombs of the pharaohs in the dry sands of the Valley of the Kings in Luxor, Egypt.

Archaeologically, the settlement had a prior Jewish history, but at present we are uncertain how far back it went. The recent

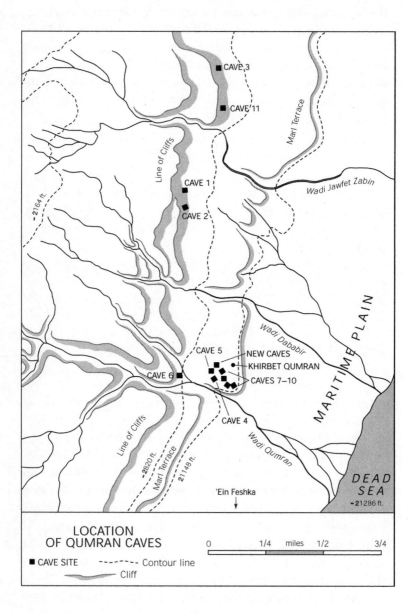

CAVE 3

CAVE 11

Marl Terrace

Line of Cliffs

CAVE 1

Wadi Jawfet Zabin

CAVE 2

2164 ft.

MARITIME PLAIN

Wadi Dababir

CAVE 5

NEW CAVES

KHIRBET QUMRAN

CAVE 6

CAVES 7–10

CAVE 4

Line of Cliffs

Wadi Qumran

2820 ft.

Marl Terrace

21148 ft.

DEAD
SEA
-21286 ft.

'Ein Feshka

LOCATION
OF QUMRAN CAVES

0   1/4   miles   1/2   3/4

■ CAVE SITE   -------- Contour line
                          Cliff

discovery of Persian period (sixth–fifth century B.C.) materials (pottery shards and an almost complete perfume bottle) during a clean-up at the conclusion of the spring 1996 excavation season on the Qumran plateau may suggest that a returning post-exilic company made the site their home rather than Jerusalem. Identifying it with one of the early biblical cities in the region, possibly Secacah or one of King Uzziah's "towers in the wilderness" *(see* 2 Chronicles 26:10), they may have decided it would be the proper place to figure out the prophetic puzzle left to them by the prophets of the pre-Exilic and Exilic periods.

The People of the Dead Sea Scrolls

The Jewish sect that retreated into the wilderness has still not been conclusively identified by scholars. Theories range from Essenes to Sadducees to Zealots to a blend of these with the Pharisees, to an altogether separate group. What we learn from their own documents is that they identified themselves with biblical Israel in its sin in the wilderness *(Damascus Document* 5:17-20).[6] By doing so, they hoped to fulfill the prophet Isaiah's prophecy of a voice crying in the wilderness for Israel's repentance, which would bring the Messiah, end the period of Gentile domination, and finally restore Israel to a place of glory *(see 4QpPsalm^a* 3:1; *1QSamuel* 8:12-16; 9:19-20). They saw themselves as an eschatological fulfillment of the historical exodus, whose ultimate conquest was of Jerusalem and the Land of Israel (cf. Joshua 11:16–12:24). The period of transition in which they lived awaited the days of the eschatological wars and the climax of re-taking all the Land as part of the Final Redemption.[7] Because the prophet Ezekiel had predicted that eschatological blessings would flow from the final Temple to the desert and the Dead Sea ("western sea"), making it fresh (see Ezekiel 47:1-2,12; Zechariah 14:8), they felt they lived in the area where the Redemption would first be realized. Therefore, those at Qumran saw themselves as the vanguard for a new era, chosen by God to herald the Messianic Age.

In the 1950s, excavations by the original excavator Roland de Vaux (the official report is yet unpublished) uncovered walls around the settlement, courtyards, a watchtower, a dining hall, a meeting room, a scrollery (where scrolls were prepared), an aqueduct, many cisterns and ritual immersion pools *(miqvaot)*, pottery workshops, kilns, stables, and several cemeteries. The latest excavations took place at the end of 1993 as part of Operation Scroll. The area of Qumran was resurveyed for the third time and dozens of caves in the limestone cliffs and in the marl terrace were checked. Emil Goldie and Yitzhak Magen conducted the excavation in the community center and found new silos, a factory of date presses, and other buildings previously unrecorded. So what we have at this site is a community dating back as far as 300 years B.C. and extending up until A.D. 68, when the Romans attacked the settlement and turned it into an army garrison.

The Discovery of the Dead Sea Scrolls

The Scrolls were first discovered by semi-nomadic shepherds of the Ta'amireh Bedouin tribe; these shepherds had settled between Bethlehem and the Dead Sea. For generations they had kept their flocks and herds in the Judean Desert, which was honeycombed with ancient caves. One of these shepherds, a teenager by the name of Muhammed edh-Dhib, which means "Muhammed the wolf" (because he killed wolves which attacked the sheep), claims responsibility for the original discovery.[8] As his story goes, he and his friends were tending their goat herds when he found that one of his goats had wandered away. After roaming far from his companions in search of the missing goat, he came upon a cave with a small opening at its top (now designated Cave 1). Thinking that the goat had fallen inside, he threw a stone into the cave's opening to scare it out. Instead of the sound of a startled goat, he heard the sound of breaking pottery. Curiosity made him lower himself into the cave, and upon seeing ancient jars, the hope of hidden treasure made him stay. But to his disappointment all that was inside were leather scrolls, thought to be useless to the Bedouin except for making sandal straps. After collecting the best of the Scrolls (seven in all) and letting them hang in his tent for almost two years, they were sold to the Bethlehem merchant Khalil Iskander Sahin (Khando), who in turn sold some of them to the Syrian Orthodox Archbishop Mar Athanasius Samuel, who made their presence known to the world. Eventually the Scrolls came into the possession of the State of Israel when Hebrew University professor Eleazar Sukenik bought three of them through the Armenian Anton Kiraz. Some years later, Sukenik's son, Yigael Yadin, bought the remaining four Scrolls from the Archbishop himself. This latter purchase involved a bit of drama. The Archbishop did not want to get involved in Middle Eastern politics; he did not want to sell the Scrolls directly to Israel because such a sale would be contested by Jordan. So the Archbishop tried to sell the Scrolls in the United States, offering them through an ad in the *Wall Street Journal*. Learning of the ad, Yadin had Hebrew Union College (Cincinnati, Ohio) pro-

63. *Bedouin who identifies himself as Muhammed edh-Dibh, who as a young shepherd boy discovered the Dead Sea Scrolls, in one of the early-discovered caves.*

fessor Harry Orlinsky, one of the few men who could authenticate the Scrolls, clandestinely pose as "Mr. Green," and purchase the Scrolls for Israel for $250,000, a paltry sum, since the *Isaiah Scroll* alone is worth over $20 million today.

More Caves, More Scrolls

After the initial discovery, both Bedouin and archaeologists began looking for additional caves, finding ten more with manuscripts between 1952–1956. The sites of discovery span the hills along the western shore of the Dead Sea ('Ain Feshkha, Qumran, Jericho, Ein Gedi, Masada, Murabba'at, Nahal Hever, Nahal Se'elim, Nahal Mishmar, and Khirbet Mird). The richest of these caves was Cave 4, discovered in 1952. This single cave yielded over 40,000 Scroll fragments that amounted to some 400 documents (100 of them biblical). Just a year earlier excavation work had begun at the site of the nearby Qumran settlement. When Cave 4 was discovered just across the wadi from the plateau, the settlement was linked for the first time with the Scrolls.

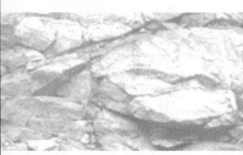

64. *Section of the* Copper Scroll, *which lists 64 locations of hidden treasure.*

The Secret Scrolls of Cave 4

Incidentally, it was these extremely fragmentary texts from Cave 4 that, a few years ago, were the source of a controversy claiming deliberate suppression, scandal, and cover-up. Since 1990, when all the photographs of these fragments were finally released to scholars, these rumors have been put to rest. More recently the excitement has focused on the publication of some of these Cave 4 texts relating to the Dead Sea sect's view of the Messiah. Newly released documents such as *4Q246* (Aramaic "Son of God"), which speaks of a messianic (or anti-messianic) figure as "Son of God and Son of the Most High"; *4Q541 (4QAaron A),* which depicts a priestly Messiah who atones for Israel; *4Q285 (Serekh Milhamah),* which describes the Messiah as the Prince of the Community, the Branch of David, and portrays him slaying his enemies in an end-time battle; and *4Q521 (Messianic Apocalypse),* which says the Messiah will heal the sick and resurrect the dead. Such texts raise new questions about the harmony of this pre-Christian Jewish concept of the Messiah with that seen in early Jewish-Christianity in the New Testament.

Additional Famous Finds

Among some of the additional famous documents found in the caves north of Qumran were *1QIsaA (Great Isaiah Scroll,* a complete copy of Isaiah) in Cave 1; *1QM (War Scroll),* a sort of apocalyptic preparation manual, also from Cave 1; *11Q19 (Temple Scroll),* from Cave 11, which for the most part gives plans for building a new Temple in restored Jerusalem. It also helps resolve a legal question concerning the Sadducees' purpose for handing Jesus over for crucifixion, revealing that the Sanhedrin justified their action from a text in Deuteronomy that mandated the death penalty for one who betrayed his nation. According to John 11:49, the High Priest Caiaphas, the leader of the Sanhedrin, considered Jesus guilty of treason. In addition, there is the mysterious *3Q15 (Copper Scroll)* from Cave 3, which lists 64 hiding places throughout the Judean Desert, Jerusalem, and a few other spots where immense amounts of Temple treasure in the form of gold, silver, and precious objects supposedly were buried 2,000 years ago! For a complete survey and study of many more of these famous finds, see my book *Secrets of the Dead Sea Scrolls.*[9]

New Discoveries at Qumran

A common misconception is that all the Dead Sea Scrolls have been found. Many people are not aware that hundreds more may still be hidden in caves in the Judean Desert and that the search for these continues today, although at a much slower pace than in the past. To highlight this fact, I have chosen several yet unpublished examples of new discoveries at Qumran. The first of these describes nine new caves discovered near the Qumran site. These caves have trails connecting them to the caves to the north where the first seven scrolls, the *Temple Scroll,* and the *Copper Scroll* were all found. The second reports a new inscription discovered at Qumran. And the third showcases a mysterious object discovered in 1954 but identified only recently. In order to make these contemporary finds feel as fresh as they are, I will allow those most closely associated with them to speak for themselves.

The Discovery of Nine New Caves

National newspapers and prime-time television news reports in the fall of 1995 tempted their audiences with the story of four new caves discovered at Qumran whose exact whereabouts had to remain secret. At the same time (before the dig) and then in 1996 (after the dig), I visited with Hanan Eshel and Magen Broshi, who discovered and excavated these caves, and asked them about their findings. The caves were not four as reported, but nine, and while no written scrolls were discovered within them, they were nonetheless instrumental in helping establish an accepted theory about the caves and the Qumran

settlement. Hanan Eshel, professor at Bar-Ilan University in Tel
Aviv, recounts for us this excavation:

> During September 1995 through February 1996, six
> weeks of excavations were directed by Magen Broshi
> and myself north of Qumran. In the beginning of 1993
> I found a network of paths north of Qumran.... trails
> leading to caves that were never recorded in any of the
> publications about Qumran.... [On these trails] we
> found there three coins [two were Hasmonean] and 60
> [Roman boot] nails. Now after finding a nail and after
> locating this trail, we decided that we wanted to check
> if this trail was really used in the Second Temple period.
> So with a metal detector we walked on 210 feet. On this
> trail we found those nails which came from sandals of
> the Roman period.... So I believe that on this area a lot
> of people walked. Those paths led to a series of artificial
> collapsed caves which have never been mentioned in
> scholarly publications.... There is a great difference
> between caves in the limestone cliffs, like caves 3, 11, 1,
> 2, and 6, where living conditions are inconvenient, and
> the marl caves, which can be used for comfortable
> dwelling. The caves in the marl are easy to carve and
> shape.... In our excavation nine caves north of the
> aqueducts were excavated.... in only two caves,
> labeled Caves C and F, did we find evidence for human
> habitation in the end of the Second Temple period....
> on the floor of Cave C we found 280 shards that came
> from cooking pots, bowls, four jars; and I think that is
> enough evidence that this cave was used for dwelling.[10]

This evidence appears to confirm once and for all that the
Qumran community was indeed responsible for storing the
Scrolls in the caves a short distance from their settlement. Furthermore, it is now clear that a larger population lived adjacent
to the site, and that the population of Qumran should no longer
be limited to those 200 men who could fit within the meeting
room at the site.

A New Qumran "Inscription"

In February 1996, two uninscribed ostraca (pottery shards written with ink) were discovered at the site of Qumran while cleaning up from a dig on the Qumran plateau, which had been directed by James Strange of the University of South Florida. These represent the first such inscriptions ever found at this site. One had evidence of scribal practice on it, while the other contained 16 lines of text. This latter ostracon was assigned to two scholars for study and translation—Hanan Eshel's wife, Esther Eshel, and Frank M. Cross of Harvard. Esther Eshel gives her analysis of the contents of this inscription:

> The lines written in Hebrew start with the words: "In the year two," probably referring to the freedom of Israel. This text describes a transaction done in Jericho in which goods were given to a man named Elazar. It seems that the ostracon gives us a list of supplies brought to Qumran from Jericho.[11]

65. *The newly excavated Cave C, among nine new caves found at Qumran in 1996.*

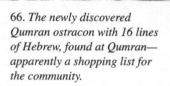

66. *The newly discovered Qumran ostracon with 16 lines of Hebrew, found at Qumran— apparently a shopping list for the community.*

One significance of this discovery is that, like the previous finds of footpaths and cave dwellings, this helps establish an accepted theory about the Qumran community. Some people had previously argued that no Jewish religious sect had lived at Qumran, but rather Jewish Zealots had manned a military outpost there. This was argued, in part, because of the absence of "mundane" documents that indicated a settled community. But the inscribed ostracon shows the existence of mundane documents at Qumran, confirming that a community had lived here.

A Qumran Mystery Solved

In 1954 Qumran site excavation director Roland de Vaux and his crew unearthed an odd-looking object that could only be described as a "stone disk." He consigned it to the storerooms beneath the Rockefeller Museum as a numbered enigma. A Christian scholar living in Jerusalem and currently working on de Vaux's original excavation reports for the purpose of publication is Stephen Pfann. He identifies the mysterious object as a Dead Sea sundial and describes its purpose in the Qumran community:

We have [now] come to understand that this was actually a sundial which was used not just for the purposes
of telling the time of the day. There are [also] various
lines on the dial that were used for different parts of the
year.... [the Qumran community] had a 364-day calendar, which is a solar calendar, as opposed to the lunar
calendar used at the Temple.... [to use this sundial, the]
sun cast its shadow across ... a pin (that was actually
found here).... The calendar itself seems to have been
made in Babylon because the markings on it match the
types of marks for the day that would be at that latitude
and longitude, and so originally marked the Assyrian
year.... This sundial also was used for marking off the
rising of the moon and the stars in their plane as it goes
over. The Assyrians considered the sun and the moon
in its rising to be something that was a blessing from
God, that was a creation of His every day. [The Qumran
community] felt that they were very much a part of that
as they stood here in the morning not speaking a word
to their neighbor. They would stand before the sun in
its rising and say prayers such as the Psalms, which
speak of awakening the dawn. This was an important
part of their life. They believed just as the sun and moon
were established within their courses and had borders,
God also had established borders for them to live within
as far as their role within the community and also in the
way they were to live out their life in the Torah.[12]

Sundials like this were used in the Second Temple to regu-
late the times of daily worship. Their use at Qumran may have
been similar, since its priestly community regarded itself as a
symbolic temple aligned with the heavenly Temple and believed
that its times of appointed rituals (such as immersion, prayer,
worshiping, eating meals) were actually ordained by God. As
Pfann explains:

For them, being on time was extremely important
because up in heaven was already set in course the
meetings and worship of the liturgical year that God
had with His angels. Unless the people of God remained

67. *"Sundial" found by excavators at the Qumran community near the Dead Sea.*

on time and faithful to the calendar and the times which He had set in the heavens, they would be out of sync with what was going on in heaven.[13]

Pfann further believes that the sundial may have also had a part in the community's messianic expectations, since they expected to welcome the Messiah at a messianic banquet at Qumran, an event to be calculated by the sundial.

Such archaeological artifacts, when finally understood, can help open up new doors of discovery related not only to the Qumran sect, but also to other Jewish sects of their day with whom they compared or contrasted. Indeed, with recent new finds and even more on the archaeological horizon, the greatest of all archaeological discoveries—the Dead Sea Scrolls—may in days to come grow yet greater.

New Excavations Promise Greater Revelations

The Qumran plateau that extends out from the present-day remains of the ancient settlement is believed to yet hold more discoveries. The 1996 seasons of excavation under James Strange were unable to verify a subterranean anomaly indicated by the use of seismic and ground-penetrating radar. The belief is that a man-made paleochamber may exist beneath the plateau with a hidden entrance also buried nearby. Within this chamber may be stored treasures of the community, including a cache of previously unknown scrolls. New electromagnetic instrumentation conducted by the Geophysical Institute of Israel has now revealed that the main paleochamber was missed by only 9 feet. Therefore, new explorations will begin again in the Spring of 1998. I will be directing the excavation of the paleochamber at this promising location. Through the means of sub-surface drilling and the use of a remote camera we will seek to confirm the new readings. We do not yet know what will be uncovered, but we are certain that much more lies on the archaeological horizon of Qumran. Perhaps you and I will awake some morning soon to find reports in our newspapers of a great new discovery, announcing to the world that the Dead Sea Scrolls are once again archaeology's front-page story!

68. *Author sitting on cliff above Qumran settlement and overlooking Cave 4 (middle of picture), where Dead Sea Scrolls were discovered.*

ARCHÆOLOGY AND JESUS

Theological Fiction or Trustworthy Facts?

_____

The archaeological discoveries [concerning Jesus] are not known outside sophisticated circles; yet, few areas of scholarly research prick the imagination and stir the excitement of scholars and students so much as new archaeological discoveries. In the past three decades, spectacular discoveries are proving significant for research on the historical Jesus.[1]

—James M. Charlesworth

_____

Let's begin our look at the archaeological evidence for Jesus' historical presence by considering the following statement by Marcus Borg:

> The truth of Easter does not depend on whether there really was an empty tomb.... It is because Jesus is known as a living reality that we take Easter stories

seriously, not the other way around. And taking them
seriously need not mean taking them literally.

If the above statement seems reasonable to you, count your-
self among the ranks of modern critical scholarship who find
faith in Jesus to be of greater reality than the facts about Him.
This position does not necessarily question that a historic Jesus
did exist, but whether the Jesus of the New Testament actually
existed. Promoting this view in a previous generation was
Rudolph Bultmann, whose works have become textbooks in
many Christian seminaries. He proclaimed, "All that remains of
Jesus is an eschatological call to decision; the picture of his
person and work has disappeared."[2]

With the present-day advent of the Jesus Seminar, a forum
of New Testament scholars whose quest to discover the actual
words of Jesus in the Gospels is based on separating the "Christ
of faith" from the "Christ of fact,"[3] many Christians have begun
questioning whether what they were taught about Jesus in
Sunday school was trustworthy fact or theological fiction. At
issue in this debate is whether the Gospels, which present the

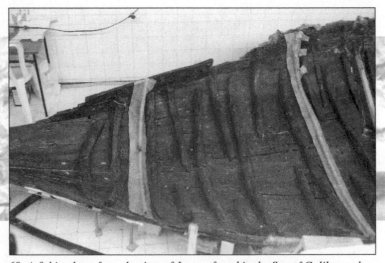

69. *A fishing boat from the time of Jesus—found in the Sea of Galilee and
recently restored using a chemical preservation technique.*

claims of Jesus through the records of His disciples, are accurate records. If they can be shown to compare favorably with the inscriptional and artifactual evidence from archaeology, should they not be reckoned as carefully composed history rather than theological creations of a later Christian community, contrived to address the problems of their day?

A first-century date for the Gospels (if not all of the New Testament) has now been confirmed by comparison with such discoveries as the Dead Sea Scrolls and the Nag Hammadi Gnostic codices. This has launched the new field of Jesus research, in which scholarship seeks to return to the Jewish roots of Jesus through a proper archaeological and historical investigation.[4] This approach was commended by the German theologian Leonhard Goppelt, who, rejecting Bultmann's pessimistic conclusion, held that the "Christ of faith" must be found by searching for, not separating from, the "Christ of history." He states:

> Of primary importance for the gospel tradition is the integration of the earthly ministry of Jesus and the kerygma so that the former becomes the supportive base for the latter. This "recollection" about Jesus remains, especially in the large Gospels, the primary intention. . . . If we desire to represent New Testament theology in keeping with its intrinsic structure, then we must begin with the question of the earthly Jesus.[5]

In this chapter our goal is to consider several primary pieces of archaeological evidence for the earthly Jesus. These corroborate various persons and events in the Gospels, revealing the accuracy of the Gospel writers and the trustworthiness of the historic message they confessed. After all, if Jesus is called by some the "Rock of Ages," should not the stones of the centuries also speak of Him?

The First Christmas

Some recent archaeological evidence has provided new insights into the time and place of the birth of Jesus. The Gospel

70. *Inside Herodium.*

of Luke gives the time of birth with a specific reference to a census decreed by Quirinius, the governor of Syria (Luke 2:2). While inscriptional evidence reveals that there was more than one ruler with this name, a Quirinius within the time frame of Jesus' birth has been found on a coin placing him as proconsul of Syria and Cilicia from 11 B.C. until after 4 B.C.[6] Quirinius' census, mentioned also by Luke in Acts 5:37, has numerous parallels in papyrus census forms dating from the first century B.C.–first century A.D. For example, both the Oxyrhynchus papyrus 255 (A.D. 48) and British Museum papyrus 904 (A.D. 104) order compulsory returns to birthplaces for census-taking, just as Luke records (Luke 2:3-5).

In addition, the traditional place of Jesus' birth—in a cave in Bethlehem—has had a long history at the site of the Church of the Nativity. The Church Father Jerome, who moved to Bethlehem in A.D. 385, already referred to it then as "the most venerable spot in the world."[7] Paulinus of Nola said that the Roman emperor Hadrian (A.D. 117–138) had planted a grove for the worship of Adonis (a Roman mythical figure) on the site to profane the Christian faith.[8] Eusebius in the fourth century described how Helena, the mother of Constantine (who sought to preserve traditional Holy Land sites connected to Jesus), covered the cave and manger with a church. Excavations have revealed the remains of the cave, which was defaced by various opponents of Christianity in early times. Similar excavations by the Franciscans in Nazareth have found, beneath the floor of the present-day Church of the Annunciation, remains of a third-century Jewish-Christian synagogue (possibly the one referred to in Luke 4:16).[9]

The Late Herod the Great

Herod the Great was the Roman-appointed king over Judea from 37 B.C. until his death in 4 B.C. Under His reign, Jesus was born and His family threatened. Herod's fame lay in his great building activities, and remains of some of his projects still command prominent positions on the landscape of modern

Israel and Jordan. One of these, known as the Herodium, stands imposingly on the horizon in the vicinity of Bethlehem and is about a three- to four-hour walk from Jerusalem. The Herodium was a hideaway for Herod, whose life was frequented by enemy attacks and assassination attempts. Originally there stood twin hills in the area, but Herod had his builders remove part of one of the hills and then raise the other hill so that his retreat would have no rivals. He constructed a crown around the hill comprised of two circular walls (one inside the other), then sloped the hill to meet these walls and formed a hollow, volcano-like structure in which he built his villa-palace-fortress. The first-century Jewish historian Flavius Josephus records that the king was buried at the Herodium borne by a parade of his kinsmen, a Thracian company, Germans and Gauls in full battle order, and 500 slaves and freedmen carrying hundreds of pounds of burial spices.[10]

Israeli archaeologist Ehud Netzer of the Hebrew University's Institute of Archaeology has been excavating at the site

71. *Author at suspected burial place of King Herod—monumental building, lower Herodium.*

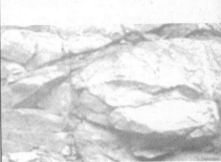

72. *Archaeologist Ehud Netzer with inscription on which is written the full title of King Herod.*

since 1973, and he believes that he has finally located this long-sought Herodian burial chamber:

> The Herodium was not just a palace but a memorial for the king. It was the only site named after King Herod and the site where he planned to be buried. We are trying to locate this burial place [at the Herodium]. In the course of our excavations we found a very impressive building, [which] we thought might be the mausoleum. Gradually we located some other objects across the street, [for example] a miqve (ritual bath), which have to do with burial tombs in the Second Temple period, and also wonderful stones which were the facade of the tomb. This same architectural style [appears] in monumental tombs in Jerusalem and elsewhere. We hoped to find the tomb itself in the shape of a cave or underground burial room. Unfortunately, the [Palestinian] Intafada which started in 1987 stopped our work, but I'm looking for peaceful times to continue the work in the near future.[11]

The suspected entrance of the mausoleum lies not within the artificial mound but near one of the lower pools at a site called the monumental structure. It resembles royal architecture with a colonnaded facade, and a long level course on the hill above it may have served as the place for the parade of Herod's burial bearers. Netzer assumes that the tomb, when found, will be empty, having been robbed in antiquity—but who knows? Netzer was able to excavate at the Herodium during the summer of 1997, but a new wave of terrorism in this West Bank area has again threatened the dig. So for now, we will have to wait to see! Even so, the site itself bears ample testimony to the vanity of a king whose handmade hill overshadowed a humble stable in which was born the King of kings!

In the Name of the King

Meanwhile, Netzer and Guy Stiebel (of the Hebrew University Institute of Archaeology) have also renewed the excavations at Masada, which were last directed by the late Yigael Yadin in the 1960s. Masada was a mountain fortress next to the Dead Sea built by Herod the Great as a last refuge for troubled times. Designed with Herod's particular needs in mind, it included northern and southern palaces, a swimming pool, a richly decorated reception hall, a Roman-style bathhouse, ritual baths, and a synagogue. Masada is best known for its use during the period of the Great Revolt (A.D. 66–73) as a last stand for the Jewish resistance known as the Sicarii. Overrun by the Roman army, the Jewish inhabitants committed suicide rather than be devastated and desecrated by the half-crazed Romans who had spent years trying to scale the fortress walls.

This past season, Netzer and Stiebel uncovered at Masada the first inscription ever found with the full title of the infamous Herod. Its discovery adds the "flesh-and-blood" of historical reality to this king and his dynasty, who figure prominently in the career of Jesus. The discovery occurred last year while clearing rubble from a cave near the site of the synagogue from a roof that had collapsed in antiquity, burying several large storage vessels (known as amphorae) and numerous artifacts.[12] Among the broken fragments from the amphorae a number of ostraca with Greek and Latin inscriptions were found. One of the ostraca, which came from an amphora that had contained wine, bore the now-famous inscription. Netzer describes it as follows:

> The inscription is three lines, a standard form found in such inscriptions. The first line is a date and gives the year this [wine] was made. The second line gives the place and the [specific] type of the wine, and in the last line we have the name: "Herod, King of Judea."[13]

Here was the name and title of the New Testament tyrant who lavishly added to the Temple in Jerusalem, met the wise men searching for the infant Jesus, but whose own search for Jesus ended with the order to slaughter the infants in Bethlehem (Matthew 2:1-18).

Where Jesus Liked to Preach

According to the Gospel accounts, the center of Jesus' ministry was the town of Capernaum, the former home of the prophet Nahum (*Caper* = "village" of Nahum), located beside the Sea of Galilee. The black basalt walls of the very synagogue where He often preached have been uncovered beneath all four corners of the polished white limestone synagogue dated from the Byzantine period.[14] A first-century date for these walls has been confirmed from pottery finds beneath the floor of a cobblestone pavement dating from the same time as the basalt walls under the nave of the synagogue.[15] The Bible records that Jesus here performed a notable miracle for the Roman centurion proselyte who built the synagogue (Matthew 8:5-13; Luke 7:1-10). Recently the Roman presence was confirmed through the excavation at Capernaum of a number of Roman-style buildings, including a Roman bathhouse.[16] Even the house of Peter, where Jesus often stayed and where He healed Peter's mother-in-law of a fever (Matthew 8:14-15; Mark 1:30-31; Luke 4:38-39) appears to have been discovered just 84 feet south of the synagogue.[17] Made of the same native basalt rock, it lay beneath an octagonal building from the Byzantine period, which was used to venerate holy places. Its presence confirms that this site had an early tradition as a place connected to Jesus. The house's narrow walls would not have supported a masonry roof, so it probably had a roof of wooden branches covered with beaten earth.[18] This would have made its roof similar to that of another house in Capernaum in which a hole was dug to let down a paralytic man for Jesus to heal (Mark 2:4).

Where Jesus Performed Miracles

Not far from Capernaum has been discovered the ancient site of Bethsaida, the hometown of Simon Peter, Philip, and Andrew (John 1:44; 12:21). Excavated since 1989 under the direction of Israeli archaeologist Rami Arav,[19] the site has recently yielded impressive remains from the earlier Iron Age fortifications of Geshur, including the royal palace where Absalom would have resided for three years (2 Samuel 13:38), a Roman-period stele of a minotaur, a pre-Christian pottery shard bearing an image of a cross, and a golden earring.[20] From the period of the New Testament there has been uncovered the evidence of the fishing industry (anchors, fishhooks), which employed these disciples of Jesus, as well as a street and houses certainly used by them on occasion. In one of these houses was discovered a grinding stone that reminds us of the bread that was made in this place, not only by women, but also by Jesus when He performed the miracle of the multiplication of the fish and the loaves at this site to feed the 5,000 (Matthew 14:1-21; Mark 6:30-44; Luke 9:10-17). From this site Jesus also went to meet the disciples walking on the water of the Sea of Galilee (Matthew 14:22-33; Mark 6:45-51; John 6:15-21). Having witnessed such miracles, and yet rejecting the Messiahship of Jesus, Bethsaida was condemned along with the nearby cities of Chorazin and Capernaum (Matthew 11:21-23; Luke 10:13-15).

Caiaphas Comes to Light

Moving from the Galilean ministry of Jesus we come to His ministry in Jerusalem. One of the most prominent figures in all the Gospel accounts that describe Jesus' final week of conflict in the Holy City is the high priest Caiaphas. Caiaphas, who served as the leader of the Sanhedrin from A.D. 18–36, is known in the Gospel accounts as the one who prophesied that Jesus would die for the nation, set in motion the plan to kill Him (John 11:49-53; 18:14), and then presided over the late-night trial at which Jesus confessed Himself to be the Messiah and was subsequently condemned (Matthew 26:57-68). It was in the courtyard of Caiaphas's house that Peter waited for word about Jesus, but instead betrayed Him three times before the cock crowed (Matthew 26:69-75).

Whether or not the place identified as Caiaphas's house today in Jerusalem is the actual site, we now have discovered the actual remains of the high priest in his ossuary within his family tomb. The find occurred by accident in November of 1990 when workers were building a water park in Jerusalem's Peace Forest, which is south of the Temple Mount.[21] The discovery was made when the roof of the burial chamber collapsed and revealed 12 limestone ossuaries. One of the ossuaries was exquisitely ornate and decorated with incised rosettes. Obviously it had belonged to a wealthy or high-ranking patron who could afford such a box. On this box was an inscription. It read in two places *Qafa* and *Yehosef bar Qayafa* ("Caiaphas," "Joseph, son of Caiaphas").[22] The New Testament refers to him only as Caiaphas, but Josephus gives his full name as "Joseph who was called Caiaphas of the high priesthood." Inside were the bones of six different people, including a 60-year-old man (most likely Caiaphas).[23] At the time of the discovery Steven Feldman, associate editor of *Biblical Archaeology Review,* observed that "the find should be particularly exciting to some believing Christians because to them it may bolster the Bible's accuracy. . . ."[24] Indeed it does, especially when we add together

73. *The richly ornamented ossuary of Joseph Caiaphas, the high priest who presided over the trial of Jesus (the inscription bearing his name is on the smaller side).*

74. *Author with ossuaries from the first century discovered in a burial cave on Jerusalem's Mount of Olives.*

the facts that Caiaphas handed Jesus over to Pontius Pilate, whose existence archaeology can also attest to.

Pontius Pilate Appears

For ten years, from A.D. 26–36, Pontius Pilate was the Roman officer in charge of Judea. During this time he had one of the most unforgettable confrontations of his life—with Jesus of Nazareth. Pilate has the distinction of being the only person that Jesus chose to talk with during His trials. He refused to answer the Judean king Herod Antipas and only under oath did so for Caiaphas. Pilate alone seems to have been singled out for an explanation for Jesus' unique purpose in ministry (John 18:36-37). It was Pilate who uttered the immortal words "What is truth?" and who would have apparently released Jesus had it not been for the Sanhedrin applying political pressure (John 19:12-15). Perhaps it was for this reason that Pilate placed a *titulus* (sentence inscription) above Jesus on the cross, which read in Hebrew, Latin, and Greek, "Jesus the Nazarene, the King of the Jews" (John 19:19). We only know that Pilate himself ordered it written, and refused to change it when the Sanhedrin protested its public display (verses 21-22).

Pilate's official residence was the Mediterranean seaboard city of Caesarea Maritima. It was fitting that in 1961, during Italian-sponsored excavations at Caesarea's Roman theater, a stone plaque bearing Pilate's name was discovered. The two-foot by three-foot slab, now known as the Pilate Inscription, was found re-used as a building block in a fourth-century remodeling project, but it was an authentic first-century monument, apparently written to commemorate Pilate's erection and dedication of a Tiberium, a temple for the worship of Tiberias Caesar, the Roman emperor during Pilate's term over Judea. The Latin inscription of four lines gives his title as "Pontius Pilate, Prefect of Judea," a title very similar to that used of him in the Gospels (see Luke 3:1). This was the first archaeological find to mention Pilate, and again testified to the accuracy of the

75. *Inscription from Caesarea bearing Pontius Pilate's name.*

Gospel writers. Their understanding of such official terms indicates they lived during the time of their use and not a century or two thereafter, when such terms would have been forgotten.

A Witness to Crucifixion

Archaeology reveals that crucifixion probably began with the Phoenicians (around the tenth century B.C.), was adopted by the Assyrians as a form of torture known as impaling (see the Lachish relief), but was most perfected by the Romans, who chose it as a method of execution for state criminals. Both the army of Spartacus, as well as some 800 Pharisees, were recorded put to death in Jerusalem by crucifixion. Yet despite widespread references to its practice in ancient literature such as the Dead Sea Scrolls,[25] the writings of Josephus,[26] the Talmud,[27] various Roman annals,[28] and the New Testament, no material evidence of a crucified victim had ever been found in the Holy Land until 1968. It was then that the remains of a crucified man from Giv'at ha-Mivtar, a northern suburb of Jerusalem, were discovered in an ossuary from near the time of Jesus.[29] The name of the man, based on an Aramaic inscription on the ossuary, was Yohanan ben Ha'galgol,[30] and from an analysis of the skeletal remains we can determine that he died in his thirties, about the same age as Jesus when He was crucified.[31] The significant evidence of crucifixion was an ankle bone still pierced with a seven-inch-long crucifixion nail and attached to a piece of wood from a cross. When the man was crucified, the nail had apparently hit a knot in the olive wood *patibulum* (upright stake) and become so lodged that the victim could not be removed without retaining both the nail and a fragment of the cross. This rare find has proved to be one of the most important archaeological witnesses to Jesus' crucifixion as recorded in the Gospels.

First, it reveals afresh the horrors of the Roman punishment. A study of the remains appears to indicate the position the body assumed on the cross. According to proposed reconstructions, this was either with the legs bent and turned adjacent to the body or nailed on either side of the upright stake (this latter position

76. *Right heel bone of a first-century man from Giv'at ha-Mivtar (a suburb of Jerusalem) showing evidence of crucifixion. Several fragments of olive wood were found between the nail head and the bone.*

is currently favored). Therefore, this method of execution forced the weight of the body to be placed on the nails, causing terribly painful muscle spasms and eventually death by the excruciating process of asphyxiation. This particular position may have been used along with the breaking of the legs, which Yohanan's bones indicate, to hasten death. When Jesus and the two criminals were crucified it was on both the afternoon of the greatest festival in Judaism (Passover) and the Sabbath. The Jewish rulers demanded a quick crucifixion so as to not desecrate the approaching holy day (John 19:31-32). Such details of the horrors of crucifixion, as attested by archaeology, reveal that the Gospel writers really had been historical eyewitnesses of the crucifixion, just as they said (John 19:35).

Second, it was once claimed that the Gospel's description of the method of crucifixion was historically inaccurate. Scholars once argued that nails could not have been used to fasten a crucified victim to a cross because nail-fastened hands and feet would not have been able to support their bodies. The victims were rather bound by ropes.[32] Yet after the resurrection Jesus revealed His crucified body to His disciples and said, "See My hands and My feet" (Luke 24:39). The scars He revealed were not from rope burns but "nails." In like manner, scholars contended that Jesus' body, as the bodies of most criminals and insurrectionists, would not have received a proper burial, but instead would have been dumped into a common grave set aside for the corpses of those defiled by crucifixion. According to them, the narrative concerning Jesus' burial in the tomb of Joseph of Arimathea (Luke 23:51-56), from which He was resurrected, was a fictitious tale.

The discovery of the nail-pierced ankle bone refutes those who say nails could not have been used. The most recent examination of Yohanan's other bones by anthropological analysts has not revealed a nailing of the wrists. This may have been because of Roman economy in crucifixion, in which both the horizontal and vertical parts of the cross were re-used. Ancient sources reveal that wood was scarce in Jerusalem, for Josephus

(*War* 5:522-23) notes that Roman soldiers were forced to travel ten miles outside of the city to find timber for their siege machinery. The fact that Yohanan's bones were found in secondary burial within a tomb also disproves the second scholarly hypothesis. This crucified victim, like Jesus, had received a proper Jewish burial.[33]

An interesting testimony to the later veneration of Jesus as a crucified victim has come by way of a crude piece of graffiti found in 1856 in one of the guardrooms of the Palatine in Rome, the site of the imperial palace. Drawn by a pagan mocking Christian worship, the graffiti dates to the first half of the third century A.D., and depicts a crucified figure with an ass's head and a kneeling worshiper beside. The Latin inscription reads, "Alexamenos worshiping his god." To such a pagan, elevating a crucified felon to the place of divinity was absurd. Yet, such faith makes no sense unless there is a historical reality behind it. Some of this reality can be felt as we are able to literally touch, through archaeology, the places of the events associated with Christ's death, burial, and resurrection.

Touching the Tomb of Jesus

Archaeology has revealed numerous tombs in Jerusalem with similarities to the New Testament's description of the tomb of Jesus. One is "Herod's Family Tomb," located today on the grounds of the famous King David Hotel. It presents a Herodian-period tomb of the wealthy class with a rolling stone still in place beside the entrance. However, when tourists in Jerusalem are taken to visit the tomb of Jesus, they are regularly shown two sites that guides say vie for the title of the burial place of Jesus. One is the Protestant site known as Gordon's Calvary, named after its discoverer in 1883, Charles Gordon. The other is the traditional site of the Church of the Holy Sepulchre, which has a history going back at least to the fourth century A.D. (based on the existence of columns still in use today from the church of Constantine[34] and its description in Byzantine sources). While most evangelical Christians prefer the serene and undisturbed

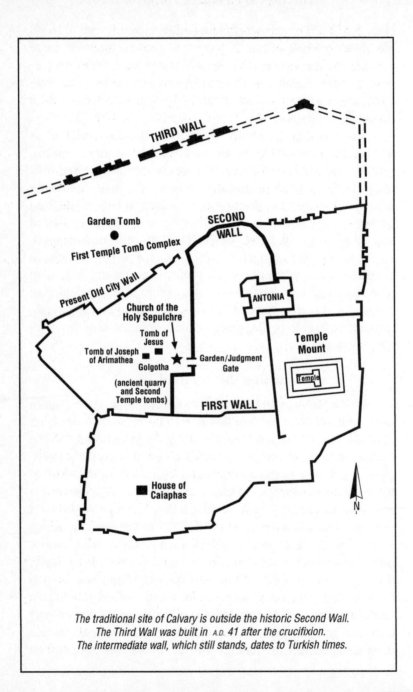

THIRD WALL

Garden Tomb

First Temple Tomb Complex

SECOND WALL

Present Old City Wall

ANTONIA

Church of the Holy Sepulchre

Tomb of Jesus

Tomb of Joseph of Arimathea

Golgotha

Garden/Judgment Gate

Temple Mount

Temple

(ancient quarry and Second Temple tombs)

FIRST WALL

House of Caiaphas

N

The traditional site of Calvary is outside the historic Second Wall.
The Third Wall was built in A.D. 41 after the crucifixion.
The intermediate wall, which still stands, dates to Turkish times.

setting of the Garden Tomb situated next to the hill Gordon identified as Skull Hill or Golgotha, there is no archaeological evidence to support this site. Previously its main support came from the fact that it was outside the present walls of the Old City, whereas the Church of the Holy Sepulchre was within them. Since the New Testament made it clear that Jesus was crucified "outside the walls" (John 19:20; Hebrews 13:11-12), and it was assumed that the modern walls followed the ancient course, the support for the Church of the Holy Sepulchre depended primarily on tradition. However, in the late 1960s Kathleen Kenyon found proof that the wall now enclosing the traditional site was a "Third Wall" constructed after the time of Jesus (about A.D. 41);[35] therefore, when Jesus was crucified, it would have been outside the *earlier* "Second Wall." In addition, in 1976, Magen Broshi uncovered a portion of a Herodian wall in the northeast section of the church. This means that when Jesus was crucified the area upon which the church is built was just outside the western wall of the city on the line of the First Wall. Others have found that a "Garden Gate" was on this wall, which agrees with references to a garden in this area (John 19:41; 20:15).[36]

Furthermore, Jerusalem archaeologists Gabriel Barkay and Amos Kloner have shown that the Garden Tomb is undeniably part of a system of tombs in the area, the most prominent of which are next door to the Garden Tomb on the property of the French School of Archaeology, the Ecole Biblique.[37] All the tombs in this complex of tombs date from First Temple times or Iron Age II (eighth-seventh centuries B.C.).[38] Because the New Testament says that Jesus was buried in "a new tomb, in which no one had yet been laid" (John 19:41), the Garden Tomb must be excluded from consideration. By contrast, the tombs in the vicinity of the Church of the Holy Sepulchre are late Second Temple tombs (first century A.D.). In the late 1970s excavations at the site revealed the foundations of Hadrian's Roman Forum, in which the Temple of Aphrodite had been built (about A.D. 135). Just as he had done at the site of the Jewish Temple,

Hadrian had built pagan temples and shrines here to supercede earlier religious structures. If this site were the one venerated by early Christians as the tomb of Jesus, it would explain this location for the building. The fourth-century church historian Eusebius says that Hadrian built a huge rectangular platform over this quarry, "concealing the holy cave beneath this massive mound."

The rock upon which the Church was built can still be seen in part today through a section preserved for viewing. This rock bears evidence of earthquake activity, a fact that accords with the Gospel story (Matthew 27:51). Excavations intended to expose more of this rock have revealed that it was a rejected portion of a pre-Exilic white stone quarry, as evidenced by Iron Age II pottery at the site. In this light, it has been suggested that Peter's citation of Psalm 118:22, "The stone which the builders rejected . . . ," may have a double meaning *(see* Acts 4:11; 1 Peter 2:7).[39] By the first century B.C. this rejected quarry had gone from being a refuse dump to a burial site. This site was also located near a public road in Jesus' time *(see* Matthew 27:39), which helps to qualify it as the authentic site because it fits both the Jewish and Roman requirements as an execution site *(see* Leviticus 24:14).[40] For this reason the rock may have been called "the place of the skull" because it was a place of death.

There is yet another consideration in favor of the Church of the Holy Sepulchre: the type of tomb in which Jesus was laid. In the first century, two types of tombs were in use. One was the more common *kokim,* which are long narrow niches cut into the chamber of the burial cave walls at right angles. The other, called *arcosolia,* were shallow benches cut parallel to the wall of the chamber with an arch-shaped top over the recess. These types of tombs were reserved for those of wealth and high rank. This seems to be the type of tomb in which Jesus was laid because Jesus' tomb was said to be a wealthy man's tomb (Matthew 27:57-60; cf. Isaiah 53:9), the body could be seen by the disciples when it was laid out (possible only with a bench-cut tomb—John 20:5,11), and the angels were seen sitting

77. *An arcasolium-type tomb, like the tomb of Jesus (Kidron Valley, Jerusalem).*

where both Jesus' head and feet had been (John 20:12). The badly eroded tomb in the Garden Tomb has neither of these characteristics,[41] whereas the so-called Tomb of Jesus at the traditional site, though deformed by centuries of devoted pilgrims, is clearly composed of an antechamber and a rock-cut arcosolium.[42]

Determining a Verdict

When the disciples first came to Jesus' tomb, we read that "they did not find the body of the Lord Jesus" (Luke 24:3). In the same manner down through the ages skeptics and critics have also come, whether literally or figuratively, and the verdict of history has remained the same as in ancient times: "They did not find the body of the Lord Jesus." In the final analysis, archaeology may bring us to the tomb, but only faith—informed by the facts—can bring us to Christ. Yet because archaeology has shown us that the facts that support faith are accurate—an identifiable tomb attesting to literal events—faith in the Christ of history *does* depend upon a historically empty tomb for its

Significant New Testament Archaeological Discoveries

NAME	LANGUAGES	DISCOVERER	LOCATION FOUND	DATE FOUND	SUBJECT	DATE OF ORIGIN	BIBLICAL SIGNIFICANCE
Dead Sea Scrolls	Hebrew Aramaic Greek	Bedouin shepherds	Judean Desert caves (Qumran)	1947–1993	Biblical manuscripts (OT), commentaries, documents	225 B.C.–A.D. 68	Extrabiblical sources for Jewish sects of New Testament period, Messianic concept, parallels to doctrines and practices in New Testament, prophecy
John Rylands Papyrus	Greek	Grenfell	Fayum, Egypt	1920	John 18:31-33, 37-38	A.D. 125	Oldest fragment of New Testament manuscript
Oxyrhynchus Papyri	Greek	Grenfell, A.S. Hunt	Oxyrhynchus, Egypt	1897–1900	Papyri documents, census	A.D. 6–104	Showed Koine Greek of New Testament was common language of people, parallels to census in Luke and Acts
Pontius Pilate Inscription	Latin	A. Frova	Caesarea Theatre	1961	Commemorative stele to Tiberias Caesar	26–36	Mentions name and title of Roman prefect who sentenced Jesus
Arch of Titus	Latin	⸻	Southern entrance to Roman Forum	⸻	Victory of Titus over Jews	A.D. 81	Depicts destruction of Temple predicted by Jesus, which occurred in A.D. 70
Vespasian-Titus Inscription	Latin	B. Mazar	South of Temple Mount	1970	Column of Tenth Legion	A.D. 79	Names of Vespasian, Titus, Silva who fulfilled prophecy of Jerusalem's destruction
Remains of Crucifixion	⸻	Tzaferis	Givat Ha-mivtar tomb	1968	Heel bone pierced with nail and wood from cross	2nd Century B.C.–A.D. 70	First physical evidence of crucifixion during time of Jesus
Caiaphas Ossuary	Hebrew	Z. Greenhut	Peace Forest, Jerusalem	1990	Burial bone box of priestly family	A.D. 42–43	First evidence of high priest who presided over trial of Jesus

Herod the Great Ostraca	Latin	E. Netzer	Masada	1996	Wine label	A.D. 73	Name and title of King Herod of the Gospels
Church of Holy Sepulchre excavations	—	Corbo, Kenyon, Broshi	East Jerusalem	4th Century A.D.	Limestone quarry, garden, excavation site, tombs	Second Temple Period	Place of crucifixion and burial tomb of Jesus
Pool of Siloam	—	Bliss, Dickie	Kidron Valley, Jerusalem	1897	Pool at southern end of Hezekiah's tunnel	Second Temple Period	Place of healing miracle in John 9:1-41
Pool of Bethesda	—	White, Fathers	East Jerusalem	1903	Ritual healing site	3rd Century B.C.	Place of healing miracle in John 5:1-15
Erastus Inscription	Latin	American School of Classical Studies (Cadbury)	Corinthian Theatre	1929, 1947	Commemorative monument in pavement	A.D. 50–100	Name and title of city treasurer of Corinth mentioned by Paul in Romans 16:23
Bema Seat (Tribunal)	Latin	Broneer	Corinth	1935, 1937	Speaker's platform	c. A.D. 50	Place where Paul stood before Gallio in Acts 18:12-17
Codex Sinaiticus	Greek	Constantine von Tischendorf	St. Catherine Monastery, Mt. Sinai	1844	Most of Old Testament and all of New Testament	4th Century A.D.	Earliest complete New Testament, important for textual criticism
Nag Hammadi Papyri	Coptic	Two brothers from al-Qasr	North of Luxor, Egypt	1945	Sectarian library of 13 codices	4th–5th Century A.D.	Gnostic texts, Gospel of Thomas with apocryphal Jesus sayings
Soreg Inscription	Greek	Clermont-Ganneau	East Jerusalem	1871, 1935	Warning sign to Gentiles at Temple area	19 B.C.–A.D. 70	Barrier to forbidden area mentioned in accusation against Paul (Acts 21:27-31)
Kinneret Boat	—	Members of Kibbutz Ginosar	Sea of Galilee (Kinneret)	1986	First-century A.D. fishing boat	A.D. 30–70	Background to Gospel accounts describing fishing vessels and practices

reality. While archaeology can only reveal the tomb, the persons and events attending to its historic purpose (Herod, Pilate, Caiaphas, crucifixion, and so on), the resurrection is interwoven with these facts so as to command the same consideration. The first generation of Jewish Christians who were bequeathed the Gospels no doubt had firsthand experience with the history and places they describe. Archaeology has restored for us much of what they experienced, and many of the questions modern scholars have concerning the authenticity of the Gospels might be answered if such archaeology was more carefully considered. As Bargil Pixner, Prior of the Dormition Abbey on Mount Zion, has advised,

> Five gospels record the life of Jesus. Four you will find
> in books and one you will find in the Land they call
> holy. Read the fifth gospel and the world of the four
> will open to you.[43]

When we read the four Gospels in light of the fifth, the Jesus of history and the Christ of the Gospels are found to be one and the same. Whether or not such an affirmation can be drawn from archaeology calls into question the nature and limits of archaeological proof—an issue that we will address next.

PART III

Listening to the
Stones Today

17

WHAT CAN ARCHÆOLOGY PROVE?

Perspectives on Archæology and the Bible

The relationship between archaeology and the Bible has often been misunderstood. The most dangerous error—albeit one often committed in innocence by religious persons—is to suppose that the task of archaeology is to "prove the Bible..." That claim is simply not open to archaeological investigation. We may be able to show the likelihood of certain events described in the Bible happening in such a way as to make the claim possible. But acceptance of the claim itself is a matter of faith, since it cannot be proved—nor for that matter disproved—by archaeology.[1]

—Shalom Paul and Bill Dever

Archaeology has frequently been used in efforts to prove that the Bible is a divine document, or at least a reliable and trustworthy one. Not long ago the man on the street believed that what is known as *biblical* archaeology was archaeology that demonstrated the Bible's stories to be true. This impression has been fostered by the secular press, which often overstates the relationship of new discoveries to the Bible. In just the past year discoveries in the lands of the Bible have propelled biblical archaeology onto the front pages of newspapers and news magazines. For example, the April 1995 issue of *U.S. News & World Report* featured the cover story: "Solving the Mysteries of the Bible: Archaeology's Amazing Finds in the Holy Land." It was followed that December by *Time* with a cover story entitled: "Are the Bible's Stories True? Archaeology Sheds New Light on Moses, King David, the Exodus and Whether Joshua Really Fought the Battle of Jericho." Such story lines imply that archaeology can be used to prove (or disprove) the Bible. But what *can* archaeology prove?

The View Has Changed

Before we venture to answer what archaeology can prove, we need to understand something about the current trend in biblical archaeology. News headlines like those above, which treat archaeology in a sensational manner, cause the majority of biblical archaeologists today to cringe. The reason for this, which is largely unperceived by biblically literate people, is because the aim of archaeology has changed. The current majority view is voiced by Thomas W. Davis when he states: " 'Can archaeology prove the Bible true?' is no longer a question field archaeologists in the ancient Near East even ask."[2]

As University of Maryland archaeologist Kenneth Holum explains, "The point of our work is no longer to try to prove or disprove the Bible. It is to help scientists understand the ancient cultures."[3] Today, biblical minimalists (those who limit the historicity of biblical accounts) often regard biblical maximalists (those who do not limit the historicity of biblical accounts) as nonobjective and unprofessional. The minimalists even prefer to discard the term *biblical* archaeology and replace it with a term like *Syro-Palestinian* archaeology. The intention in this change is to remove archaeology from an identification with the Bible and render it simply a regional branch of archaeology in general. This was not the case before 1970. Just two decades ago it was the Bible that determined the questions that archaeologists asked. The Bible was accepted as a reliable guide for archaeological excavation and archaeological excavation in turn served to confirm the historical reliability of the Bible. Representatives of this school of archaeology were regularly quoted by defenders of the faith as "the experts" who agreed with the Bible.

The Experts Agree

One of the most-often quoted of these experts was Rabbi Nelson Glueck. Famous for his archaeological excavations in the Negev, he became equally famous for one of his statements about the relationship of the Bible to archaeology:

> As a matter of fact, however, it may be stated categorically that no archaeological discovery has ever controverted a biblical reference. Scores of archaeological findings have been made which confirm in clear outline or in exact detail historical statements in the Bible. And, by the same token, proper evaluation of biblical descriptions has often led to amazing discoveries. They form tesserae in the vast mosaic of the Bible's almost incredibly correct historical memory.[4]

Glueck put his conviction into practice when he sought to locate King Solomon's long-lost port city of Ezion-geber. Memory of its location had been, in Glueck's words, "snuffed out like the flame of a gutted candle." How then could the archaeologist begin his search? By consulting the one book of the Bible that documented this site. Glueck later said this:

> Assuming, however, as we did, that the biblical statement was literally correct, it was not too difficult to rediscover it. ... the biblical statement [was] that it was located "beside Eloth, on the shore of the Red Sea, in

78. *William Foxwell Albright, the Dean of American Biblical Archaeology (on location at Tel Hazor).*

the land of Edom" (1 Kings 9:26; 10:22). And that is exactly where we found it, in the form of the small, sanded-over mound of Tell el-Kheleifeh on the north shore of the Gulf of Aqabah, which is the eastern arm of the Red Sea.[5]

Another biblical supporter of a past generation was the American Dean of Biblical Archaeology, William Foxwell Albright. Albright used archaeology to challenge aspects of the then-popular view of Julius Wellhausen, a German higher critic whose Documentary Hypothesis taught that there was no real history in the Bible until the time known as the post-Exilic period. This meant that people such as Noah, the Patriarchs, Moses, Joshua, David, Solomon, Elijah and Elisha, and Daniel and events such as the Flood, Exodus, Conquest, Monarchy, the Babylonian destruction, and exile either had no historical basis or were historically unreliable. Albright countered, especially in the case of the patriarchal narratives in the Pentateuch, that the facts of archaeology were on the side of the Bible. To this end he wrote:

Discovery after discovery has established the accuracy of innumerable details, and has brought increased recognition of the Bible as a source of history.[6]

A Clearer Understanding

Glueck and Albright represented the older conservative school of thought. Yet even though their statements were positive of biblical confirmation through archaeological discovery, not every member of this school believed that the Bible was without error nor that all of what it records as history literally happened. As an example, consider Albright. Although branded by reviewers as a "closet fundamentalist" for having made the above statement, it is clear that he was not in the fundamentalist [or evangelical] camp. This was evident by his statement (made on the exact same page as the aforementioned quote!) that "the theory of verbal inspiration [a basic tenet of fundamentalist and evangelical camps]—sometimes mis-called a doctrine—has been proved erroneous."[7] While a biblical conservative (compared to his colleagues) and, as one scholarly acquaintance has reported, probably a Christian believer,[8] Albright used archaeology to interpret the Bible, and not vice versa.

Many popular books written to defend the historical accuracy of the Bible—in quoting the conclusions of men such as Glueck and Albright—have unfortunately left the impression with their audiences that these men shared their high views of biblical inspiration. Because many of these readers are not trained in archaeology, they may unintentionally misuse "archaeological evidences" to confirm "biblical facts" when in reality the finds do not support their (or their research assistants') claims. Of course, all archaeological evidence is subject to interpretation, and when offered as a "proof" of something theological, will always be rejected by some scholars. Nevertheless, those who attempt to use archaeology with an apologetic purpose need to exercise proper caution so that they will not "turn off" by inaccuracies or overstatements those they would wish to persuade.

What Happened to *"Biblical* Archaeologists"?

The older generation of biblical archaeologists were classically trained and generally were considered scholars in the field of biblical studies. As an example of how such training makes a difference, compare two archaeologists in the same family, F.G. Kenyon and his daughter Kathleen Kenyon. Both served the British Empire as archaeologists. But the father was educated as a classical scholar and an expert in New Testament Greek textual criticism, while the daughter was trained as a modern historian and had her expertise in field archaeology. As a result, they approached their archaeological endeavors and their writings with a different focus. In F.G. Kenyon's book *The Bible and Archaeology* (1940), the focus was on biblical scholarship and the reconstruction of ancient Near Eastern history in corroboration of it. In Kathleen Kenyon's book *Archaeology in the Holy Land* (1960), evidence was seldom taken from the biblical and literary texts; rather, all the emphasis was placed on the mute evidence of the excavations.

The Pendulum Swings

One reason for this shift has been the critical school's assessment that biblical archaeology is still perceived by the public as having a "fundamentalist agenda." By this they mean that archaeology is conducted only to validate the historicity of the biblical text. They object to attempts to demonstrate the historicity of the patriarchal or Exodus-Conquest narratives through archaeological methodology because, as they view these accounts, they are theological, not historical, in nature. Thus most modern archaeologists have abandoned the Albright and Glueck schools, which began with the biblical text and correlated archaeological data with it, and instead have adopted T.L. Thompson's dictum (1974) that "archaeological materials should not be dated or evaluated on the basis of written texts which are independent of these materials; so also written documents should not be interpreted on the basis of archaeological hypotheses."

This approach has produced, as Kenyon observed, "a pessimistic assessment of the role of archaeological information in establishing the value of the earlier parts of the Old Testament as historical sources."[9] In addition, the ideals of this humanistic new-world archaeology eschew the thought that archaeological projects might neglect strata from other periods (for example, the Islamic period) in preference for the "more important" Israelite strata beneath. This is because, as one author explains:

> ... the Bible, like all literary sources, is a secondary source for archaeologists. The primary data are the artifacts which are uncovered in the process of excavation.... While the Bible can be used to clarify some of the data, it has little or no relevance for some periods which are studied by Syro-Palestinian archaeology. The goal of this discipline then is not the clarification of the Bible but the recovery of the material culture of antiquity....[10]

The worldviews of the biblical maximalist and minimalist are opposite and cannot be reconciled. For the archaeologist concerned with material evidence relevant to the biblical text, it is impossible to not prioritize the Israelite strata.[11] There are also differences in the interpretation of the same archaeological data. Rationalistic higher-critical and evolutionary assumptions will produce a varied interpretation of evidence even when a shared scientific approach is followed. Such interpretation in mainstream archaeology follows the pendulum swing. Take for example, the historicity of the books of 1 and 2 Chronicles. Because some of the geographical and historical details on occasion appear at variance with information in the books of 1 and 2 Kings, questions have been asked about the historicity of the chronicler's sources. Just two decades ago, however, even critical scholars felt that the historical accuracy of 1 and 2 Chronicles had already been established. In 1965 Professor Jacob

Myers concluded this in his commentary on 1 Chronicles in the Anchor Bible series: "Archaeological and historical studies have now rendered [Chronicles] more respectable and have shown it to be at times more accurate than some of its parallel sources."[12] Modern scholars, however, have again doubted the historical reliability of the chronicler's sources, arguing that they have not been corroborated by the archaeological evidence. Instead, they propose that the most likely source for his information must have been the chronicler's own theological inferences.[13]

A New Golden Age?

Just as the pendulum in recent years swung away from biblical confirmation, new discoveries with clear references to biblical places and persons have once again prompted the pendulum to begin its swing back toward a validation of scriptural integrity. This renewed optimism has been heralded in the popular press:

> Now the sands of the Middle East are yielding secrets hidden for thousands of years that shed surprising new light on the historical veracity of those sacred writings. . . . Some have even hailed the discoveries as the beginning of a new 'golden age' of biblical archaeology."[14]

These new discoveries, many of which have been surveyed in this book, have excited the public, startled the skeptics, and helped to begin returning archaeology to a place where it may once again be used to support the biblical text. Therefore, in the remainder of this chapter and in the next, let's consider the legitimate role of archaeology in its relationship to the Bible and faith.

Proving the Bible

Those who seek to use archaeology to "prove the Bible" have already assumed an improper premise. The Bible describes itself as the "Word of God," and therefore its word cannot be proved or disproved by archaeology any more than God Himself is subject to the limited evidence of this world. Roland de Vaux, who excavated the ruins of Qumran, the community of the Dead Sea Scrolls, firmly stated:

> It must be understood that archaeology cannot "prove" the Bible. The truth of the Bible is of a religious order; it speaks of God and man and their mutual relations. This spiritual truth can neither be proven nor contradicted, nor can it be confirmed nor invalidated by the material discoveries of archaeology.[15]

The stage of the Bible is historical and geographical, but its drama is divine. Theological statements include historical or scientific data, but to use history or science to establish theology is wrong, since God cannot be confined to the realm of history and science. God does work within history, however, and to the degree that we can properly interpret history in light of Providence we can sometimes witness His working. Therefore, it is not circular reasoning to use the Bible to interpret the evidence of archaeology, as if the Bible were only proving itself, for no absolute interpretation of archaeological data is possible apart from an absolute standard. On the other hand, if archaeology is used to interpret the Bible, then archaeology has assumed an imposition on Scripture outside of its realm of evaluation. In this case, such a comparison should be expected to produce chronological inconsistencies and historical inaccuracies because a fallible and incomplete standard (archaeology) is being applied to an infallible and complete one (the Bible).

Therefore, while it is better not to speak of "proving" the Bible through archaeology, archaeology nevertheless has great value in relation to validating the history of the Bible.

The Bible and History

From what has just been said about the theological nature of the Bible a person might conclude that everything in the Bible must be outside the realm of objective corroboration. Many theologians and archaeologists today have concluded just this. Recently I discussed this issue with several of Israel's leading archaeologists. They could not understand why there was a problem in acknowledging much of the Bible's history as wrong while still believing the Bible itself was right! They kept insisting that the Bible could still be true even if it contained much that was false.

These men had been taught that truth in religion is independent of facts. In the post-modernist way of thinking, stories that communicate "truth" do not need to be true. From this perspective the religious ideals of the story transcend history and science, and though the biblical authors were quite wrong about such matters, their principles were still right, and that is what really matters. In other words, who cares if the Bible presents its theological truths in a context that is chronologically contradictory, historically corrupt, and culturally confused? It is the message, not the medium, that is important!

In response to this view, we must recognize that the historical and scientific statements of those who penned the Bible are in context inseparable from their theological statements. For example, the miracle of the parting of the Red Sea (Exodus 14:13-31) occurred historically at the time of a certain pharaoh (verse 10), geographically at a specified place (Pi-hahiroth in front of Baal-zephon, verse 9), and is described in scientific terms appropriate to the day: "swept the sea back by a strong east wind all night and turned the sea into dry land . . . and the waters were like a wall . . ." (verses 21-22). If the biblical authors erred in the history and science upon which their theological truths were formed, how could they escape from error in their theology itself? Some people, not wanting to be "absolutists," argue that the Bible is "inspired" and even "infallible," but that this extends only to the "words of God" contained within the Bible. For them, although the Bible may be unreliable in matters historical and scientific, it is reliable in matters theological. But how can we know which parts of the Bible are really the "words of God"? In the biblical accounts of the Creation, Flood,

Exodus, and Conquest, how do we distinguish the infallible "words of God" from the fallible words of science and history, especially when both in context are ascribed to God? Why should we trust theology from a source that cannot get its facts straight? If the biblical text can be shown to have erred in factual knowledge and is the product of cultural conditioning, should not its religious content be regarded as equally suspect?

Fiction or Facts?

When we consider the relationship of the Bible to history, we are faced with two options: 1) All the Bible's statements are to be regarded from a theological rather than factual perspective, or 2) all the Bible's statements are to be regarded as factual even though a theological perspective is adopted. The first option fails, as archaeology itself has shown, because many aspects of the history of the Bible *have already been* demonstrated to be factual. The discoveries of the places, the people, the wars, the cultural contacts, the forms of treaties, and more—down to the smallest details—have verified the accuracy of the text. These details, used in context in support of the theological statements, argue for the second option. The Bible's authors never imply that the historical or scientific events they reported are anything less than fact. If it is objected that they may have only *thought* that they were factual, we still must contend with museums filled with archaeological evidence that many events *were indeed* factual. With respect to the paucity of archaeological evidence for early biblical history, judgment should at least be tempered by the fact that archaeology has shown, in later periods, that the historical statements are reliable.

Among Israeli archaeologists, an encouraging sign of accepting the Bible as usable history at a period many have declared non-historical was recently offered by Eilat Mazar, granddaughter of the famous excavator at the Temple Mount, Benjamin Mazar. Her proposal for the location of King David's buried palace is based primarily upon a passage of Scripture:

> A careful examination of the biblical text combined
> with sometimes unnoticed results of modern archaeo-
> logical excavations in Jerusalem enable us, I believe, to
> locate the site of King David's palace.[16]

Her "careful examination of the biblical text" involved
simply taking directional statements in 2 Samuel as both historical and reliable. Based on these she concluded that an area
barely excavated by Kathleen Kenyon in the 1960s, which had
some scant remains, strongly indicated the possible presence of
the palace.

What Has the Final Word?

In conclusion, I would argue that we cannot separate the
Scriptures. The God who gave His Law at Sinai (a theological
statement) gave it in a law code (historical statement) that
archaeology has shown was common to the ancient Near East of
Moses' day. If archaeology does not seem to support biblical
history in every case, the limitation is not from the Bible but
from archaeology. It must be remembered in archaeology that
the absence of evidence is not evidence of absence. As the history of archaeology has demonstrated, given time, the evidence
will eventually be supportive of the biblical text. Because of the
randomness of both the absence and presence of evidence, the
pendulum continues to swing in archaeology between minimalists and maximalists. As a friend of mine who works as a curator
at the Rockefeller Museum in Jerusalem put it: "Absolute truth
in archaeology lasts about 20 years!" Even so, if we are to
advance our knowledge of the biblical text to any degree, the
source for that understanding must come from archaeology. As
University of Wisconsin professor Keith Schoville reminds us:

> All of us who love the Bible . . . sometimes fail to realize
> is that despite all the work that scholars do in inter-
> preting the Bible, the only real new light that we have
> coming into our study of the Bible is what archaeology
> provides. So, archaeology and the interface between
> archaeology and biblical text is an important consider-

ation for everyone who is a biblical scholar, whether
they be a professor in seminary or a lay person going to
a Sunday school class.[17]

Therefore, even if the *interpretation* of the facts may
change, the evidence has established that what we are dealing
with in the Bible is not fiction. In the next chapter we will move
beyond these shifting pendulum swings to consider the relationship between archaeology and faith to determine if there is
a still point in the midst of changing interpretations that can help
us better hear what the stones are saying.

18

WHERE DO THE STONES LEAD YOU?

Faith and Archæology

To one who believes in the historical mission of Palestine, its archaeology possesses a value which raises it far above the level of the artifacts with which it must constantly deal, into a region where history and theology share a common faith in the eternal realities of existence.[1]

—W.F. Albright

There are facts that develop faith, and then there are "facts" that depend on faith. For an example of the latter, consider the tabloid headline that read, "Adam and Eve's Tomb Found in Israel."[2] The article went on to tell of the discovery of a pair of 300,000-year-old skeletons near Jerusalem. Identifying them as the first couple was a scroll found beside the bodies. According to the article, the French archaeologists who made the amazing find confirmed that the male skeleton had lost a rib while the female had an extra one! This, of course, is nonsense journalism, designed to entertain rather than educate. With every archaeological report we hear we should exercise some restraint until we examine the facts.

Facing the Facts

For example, in 1980 a family tomb was excavated in East Talpiot, a suburb of Jerusalem. Ossuaries with inscriptions bearing the names of Joseph, Mary, and Jesus were discovered. Many Christians jumped to the conclusion that this was the "holy family," including a BBC film crew in 1992. But this could not be the family of Jesus, and of course, not Jesus Himself. For one, the Jesus in this tomb had a son! (This, by the way, was not the first ossuary to be discovered with the name Jesus on it.) For another, Joseph's tomb has been traditionally located in Nazareth, where the family lived through Jesus' lifetime. The names Joseph, Mary, and Jesus were all quite common names for their time (as in fact they still are today). Thus we cannot jump to a conclusion about the family tomb in East Talpiot because the names on the ossuaries were the same as that of a well-known family in the Bible.

Then there is the matter of faith and interpretation. The Shroud of Turin is a prime example. Despite all the extraordinary claims and tests, there is not yet a definitive evaluation on the shroud. Some scholars claim it is genuine and evidence of the resurrection. Others of equal caliber and faith commitment claim it is a forgery or at best an actual ancient burial cloth that became identified with Jesus and revered as a religious relic. How do we decide? We might never be able to make a determination based on scientific analysis, and all the faith in the world will not make it Jesus' cloth if in fact it is not. In this case it is better to reserve our judgment. After all, the resurrection of Jesus does not depend on the authenticity of the Shroud of Turin!

The Facts of Faith

Yet well educated people often *do* believe unfounded reports. This may be simply because they want to, or they lack specific knowledge or the ability to confirm a claim, or because an authority figure has related it to them. Even so, such faith is not real faith; biblical faith always has a believable basis, for a person is able to accept as truth only something that can be true. This, of course, assumes that we have an objective (absolute standard of truth) rather than subjective (you have your truth and I have mine) view of truth. Theologians who say that facts don't matter are leading people to have faith in their faith. But it is not faith itself that makes the difference; rather, it's the object of faith. If the thing in which we believe is trustworthy, if it can perform what it promises, then our faith rests in something that is worthwhile. Yet two problems exist in the modern mindset that prevent the possibility of faith: one is the assumption of a non-faith perspective, and the other is the assumption of errors in the only source for faith—the Bible.

The Assumption of a Non-Faith Perspective

One of the problems facing today's generation—as well as upcoming generations—is that they generally have not inherited a biblical worldview from their society or culture. In its place has been taught, or assumed, in every field of thought, an evolutionary process. To be sure, this evolutionary worldview is completely incompatible with a biblical worldview. But it is also incompatible with the world as known by the ancients and revealed by the modern spade. How did primitive society evolve so quickly from Neolithic Neanderthals scribbling on cave walls to Bronze Age civilizations with architectural structures and literary compositions rivaling those of our modern age? From the earliest archaeological records, civilization erupts into history fully able to achieve and communicate in an advanced manner. The evolutionary worldview as espoused by Darwin did two things: 1) it showed that evolution was a fact contradicting literal interpretations of scriptural legends of creation, and 2) it showed that its cause, natural selection, was automatic—with no room for divine guidance or design.[3] Evolutionists themselves understand this fact, as noted recently by a newspaper reporter:

> Religious conservatives see evolution as a symbol, the cornerstone of a society increasingly indifferent to human life and right and wrong.... It has to do with Jesus, not with Genesis. Evolution tends to make the Adam and Eve story irrelevant. If there's no Adam and Eve and no fall from grace, and no original sin, then there's no reason for Jesus Christ to make things right again by dying on the cross.[4]

If we are to find facts that are indeed in harmony with faith, we must approach the Bible on its own terms, without the imposition of an evolutionary presupposition. We must come to the Bible as inerrant, not subject to our "superior" judgment as to what truth it contains.

The Assumption of Errors in the Bible

The concept of an inerrant Scripture is alien to the contemporary theological scene. Many archaeologists tend to focus on the yet unsolved problems between archaeology and the biblical text: The early history of a patriarchial period appears to be largely missing thus far from the archaeological record. Neither Joseph nor Moses appear in the Egyptian hieroglyphic texts, nor do finds in the ancient land of Canaan reveal anything of the Exodus. Silence from all sources except the Bible has led many biblical archaeologists and scholars to conclude that they never existed. The model of a military conquest has been challenged in light of the settlement patterns revealed in the archaeological excavations, and evidence for the glory of the Solomonic empire has faded faster than it has been found. Yet the problem here is not what is *not* seen, but what is not *yet* seen. To illustrate, let's consider an experience a young man named William Dembski had with his father. His father challenged him to solve the problem of joining, in a continuous fashion, nine dots arranged in three parallel rows in the form of a square. He was allowed to draw only four continuous line segments:

• • •

• • •

• • •

Although William tried every possible combination, he needed five lines, from his point of view, to correctly complete the puzzle. After a while he began to doubt that it could be done. Finally, he concluded that five was the only possible answer and four was an erroneous answer. He figured either his dad was trying to trick him or else had himself committed an error in thinking that he could solve the problem with only four lines. Then his dad showed him the straightforward solution:

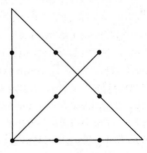

The problem for young Dembski was that he had assumed that his continuous line segments could not go outside the dots. This limited perspective prevented him from reaching the proper solution. In later thinking about this attitude toward the problem he drew this conclusion:

> Given my assumption, I was perfectly correct in attributing error to my dad. But my assumption was itself ill-conceived. I myself was in error for holding an assumption that was not required, and that prevented me from solving the problem in the way my dad had set out.... only when I became willing to relinquish this faulty assumption could I understand the solution my dad had intended. Error is thus a two-edged sword. In attributing it we may be committing it ourselves.[5]

In applying this conclusion to the question of error in Scripture, if we likewise make the assumption of error simply because we cannot at present understand the solution to a perplexing problem in Scripture, or because we cannot resolve it according to our method, we may find that we or our methods are in error, and that our lack of trust in the Father who works "outside the lines" of our limited understanding will forever prevent us from solving it. The answer, as young Dembski learned, was to ask his father. This is the essence of faith—a trust in One who is trustworthy whether or not we fully understand, and an acceptance that there is a solution beyond our limited perspective. With this we can live life confidently, looking for an answer to our puzzles, yet not being puzzled without one.

Faith versus Facts

Even when we discard our old presuppositions and take the Bible on its own terms, we must be careful when viewing it within an archaeological context to not let "facts" become the opponent of faith. We do so when we expect too much from archaeology and too little from the Bible. Viewing archaeology as history and the Bible as theology, some people have been able to stay at a safe distance from those convicting parts of Scripture by saying to themselves, "After all, they are just stories!" To an extent this is true. Although the Bible is historical, its history has been selected to fit a theological agenda.

Archaeology, on the other hand, is even more selective, revealing only the history of a particular part of a specific place chosen by a single archaeologist. The general direction of information from the Bible and archaeology is parallel, not perpendicular. It is more complementary rather than confirmatory. Therefore, the intersection of the Bible and archaeology should not be expected often. However, some rare intersections do occur (as this book illustrates), and when they do, "safe" skeptics may find themselves caught against the light in the traffic of convictions. If some people want to believe the Bible holds truth yet is a cracked vessel, they may do so. But by adopting such a view, they can never be certain whether or not some measure of truth has leaked out or if some contamination has seeped in. We should instead recognize that archaeology is a handmaiden to the Bible and must be kept in its proper place, as Keith Schoville advises:

> I think, at least for myself, my approach is to treat the Bible as historically accurate and to give it its due. We must leave open the possibility when there seems to be some conflict between archaeological information and biblical information that all the information is not yet in. We cannot yet make a definitive statement about these problems and that in time more information may come that will help us resolve them. So, I think we have to realize that archaeology does not always have final and specific answers to the questions that we would like to have answered.[6]

With this kind of understanding, we are able to accept the changes that frequent archaeological interpretation and to use it to an advantage in the exposition of the unchanging truths of the Bible.

The Shifting Sands of Archaeology

The shifting sands of scholarship toward the Bible in relation to archaeology concerns the interpretation of the archaeological data and not the data itself. For this reason, one

generation may find that archaeological data weighs conclusively in favor of the Bible, while the next may find that the
same data is inconclusive at best or contradictory at worst. We
can hope that what we are seeing on the horizon at the present
time is a shift toward a positive integration of archaeology and
the Bible. There is a renewed popular interest in how archaeology reveals the Bible, and some scholars are again catching
the vision of what archaeology can offer to biblical studies. For
example, consider the recent enthusiastic words of James
Charlesworth, one of the leading New Testament scholars of
today:

> Now thanks to archaeology, we can hold a coin sim-
> ilar to the one Jesus used when He said, "Render unto
> Caesar the things that are Caesar's and to God the
> things that are God's." And the face on the coin in our
> hands is that of Caesar, a man now dead and gone. We
> can also now hold in our hands a Herodian lamp and
> comprehend more deeply Jesus' story of the foolish
> virgins who did not bring enough oil to refill their tiny
> lamps. Moreover, through various other additional
> archaeological finds from first-century Palestinian
> Jews, we can begin to imagine what the man Jesus
> must have been like. Then we are freed from the peren-
> nial temptation to make him a model man in our own
> image. Most excitingly, we are freed from the cancer of
> Docetism and the false belief that Jesus only appeared
> to be human. If that is the only service archaeology can
> help render to faith, it will have been one that saves the
> body of faith. In brief, archaeology cannot form faith,
> but it can help inform faith.[7]

Faith Before Facts

The early Church Father Tertullian correctly observed the
proper order between faith and facts when he stated, "I do not
understand in order to believe, I believe in order to understand."
As we have seen in the previous chapter, archaeology can take

us only so far in arriving at the facts of a matter, and much less in helping us toward faith. Bryant Wood, the executive director of the Associates for Biblical Research, puts well the priority of faith when he says:

> Many people have the idea that archaeology can prove the Bible. Well, that is true to a certain extent. Archaeology can help to verify certain historical events that have taken place in the past but archaeology can only go so far in that archaeology can perhaps demonstrate the truth of some historical event, but it certainly cannot verify the truth of the miraculous. So we get to a point where we have to accept the message of the Bible on faith and we can't depend upon archaeology for that. So archaeology is a wonderful tool for helping us to understand our Bible, the world of the Bible, the antiquity, and so on, but when it comes to the spiritual message of the Bible, that is a matter of personal faith.[8]

Therefore, such a use of archaeology poses a threat for the person who has safely maintained a distance from God or has felt comfortable in his denial of the Bible's integrity. For while archaeology can lessen the doubt of the unbeliever in the historicity and trustworthiness of the Bible, it can conversely increase his doubt in his ability to meet the demands of righteousness revealed. For this one must come by faith alone, but not with a faith that is alone—it is a faith informed by facts.

Facts Catch Up to Faith

When I lived in Jerusalem as an archaeology student, I was firmly told that there was no archaeological evidence to support the existence of Jesus. But in the two decades that have followed, so much incidental evidence has been discovered throughout the Land—and especially in Jerusalem—that such statements are no longer voiced by anyone in the archaeological community. Gordon Franz, an archaeologist and teacher of historical geography in the Holy Land, states the proper perspective to adopt in spite of evidence that still remains outstanding:

> When *all* of the evidence is in, and has been *properly*
> understood, archaeology will confirm what the Bible
> has already stated to be true.[9]

The important words in this statement are *"all* of the evidence" and *"properly* understood." As we know, not all the evidence is in. As Edwin Yamauchi has said, "It may take 8,000 more years of excavation, but eventually archaeology will prove the Bible to be true." This is a faith position based on the facts that have already been confirmed as an indicator of those yet to be confirmed. However, for many people, facts have not been confirmed because they have not been *properly* understood. For this reason the person who desires to understand must make an effort to study the available resources in order to know what can be known. There are many avenues for such self-education (see appendix), and the next best thing to knowing is knowing where to find out. A good place to begin is your local library!

In the final analysis, if your faith is in archaeology, it is in the wrong place. If you wait for archaeological proof of the Bible before you're willing to begin considering the Bible as trustworthy, you will wait beyond your lifetime. There are indeed a number of unsolved biblical issues between archaeology and theology, but in the end, the facts finally will catch up with faith.

Where the Search Leads

Though archaeology is more than a century old, compared with the history it has yet to uncover, it is still very much in its beginnings. But what a propitious start it has had, for to it applies the motto on the Great Seal of the United States (printed on the back of a dollar bill): *annuit coeptis*—"He [God] smiles on our beginnings." Archaeology has had a good beginning and it promises a great future. But that future depends much on whether or not we who live in the present truly value the past. The world was shocked on October 22, 1996 when the headlines of the *London Times* announced: "Lost Forever: A Nation's

Heritage Looted by Its Own People." On that day in war-torn Afghanistan, the country's National Museum in Kabul was reduced to rubble by Mujahidin rebels as they forced their way into what was once one of the world's foremost collections of multicultural antiquities. As one commentator on the incident reported:

> Rebels blasted into vaults and shattered display cases, looted the relics, and sold them here and there around the world for quick cash. Rockets slammed into the museum's roof, burying ancient bronzes under tons of debris. Pottery from prehistory was thrown into bags like cheap china. The Bagram collection, one of the greatest archaeological finds of the 20th century, disappeared. Nearly 40,000 coins, some of the world's oldest, vanished. The museum, once a repository for Afghan history, became a military post, and the storied past has now been ruined by the unbridled present.[10]

As a result, the Afghan nation lost its history, but more than this, it also lost its birthright for coming generations, for without a heritage from the past there can be no legacy for the future. This tragedy of our modern day may be repeated on a lesser scale if we devalue our past. While not physically destructive, neglect of these treasures bequeathed to us by time severs us from knowledge vital to who we are and where we have been. Such an abandonment is socially destructive, consigning us to generations whose only frame of reference will be themselves.

Archaeology, then, is for all of us. It is our means of connecting with a forgotten past so that we can build upon its triumphs and tragedies and make better memories for the future. The past of biblical archaeology, however, is not forgotten, but enshrined within a greater history that points to the most promising future of all within the purpose of God.

So our journey with biblical archaeology down the ancient path of remains and relics ultimately brings us back full circle to where it all begins—the Bible, whose truth the stones will always shout. Within these pages you have heard the stones;

where do they lead you? In this book I have attempted to pass on part of the heritage of the past to you. Such material confirmation of long-recorded but unseen events calls us to confirm its ancient message in our modern lives. The reality of these rocks, which touch upon the divine drama, challenges us to add a new reality to our present faith. As a result, we will ourselves find that timeless legacy that is the foundation for our future (*see* 1 Timothy 6:17-19). It is my prayer that in your own search you will follow the stone-lined trail that leads always to Him whose Word is truth.

> *We search the world for truth. We cull*
> *The good, the true, the beautiful*
> *From graven stone and written scroll,*
> *And all old flower-beds of the soul;*
> *And, weary seekers of the best,*
> *We come back laden from our quest,*
> *To find all the sages said*
> *Is in the Book our mothers read.*[11]

Study Aids, Notes, and Indices

Archæological Sites in Israel

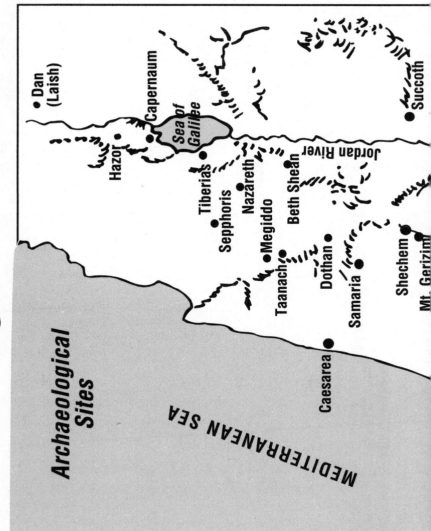

Archaeological
Sites

MEDITERRANEAN SEA

- Dan (Laish)
- Capernaum
- Hazor
- Sea of Galilee
- Tiberias
- Sepphoris
- Nazareth
- Megiddo
- Taanach
- Beth Shean
- Jordan River
- Succoth
- Dothan
- Shechem
- Samaria
- Mt. Gerizim
- Caesarea

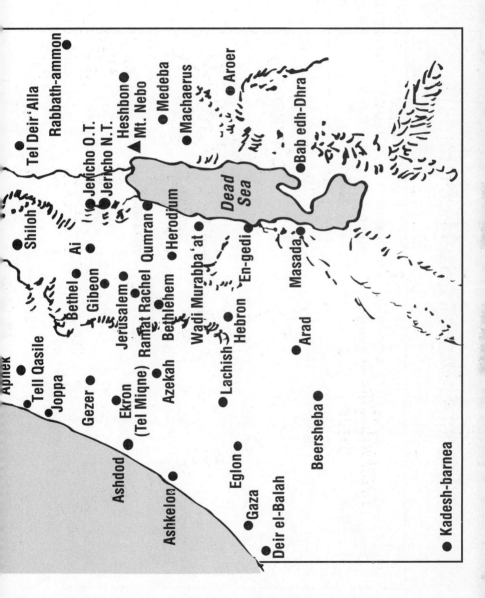

Archæological Periods

ARCHAEOLOGICAL PERIODS IN PALESTINE	APPROXIMATE DATES B.C.	EGYPTIAN DYNASTIES	APPROXIMATE DATES B.C.	BIBLICAL CORRELATIONS	APPROXIMATE DATES B.C. (early chronology)
Neolithic Pre-pottery Neolithic Pottery	8000–5000 5000–4300				
Chalcolithic	4300–3300	Badarian, Nagada	3900–3300		
Early Bronze I Early Bronze II Early Bronze III Early Bronze IV	3300–2900 2900–2600 2600–2300 2300–2100	I and II III to V (Pyramid Age) First Intermediate Period (VII–X)	3100–2686 2686–2340 2175–2040	Post-Flood	
Middle Bronze I Middle Bronze IIA	2100–1900 1900–1700	XII Second	1991–1786	Patriarchs	2150–1850 1876–1446

Archaeological Period	Dates	Egyptian Period	Dates	Biblical Period	Dates
Middle Bronze IIB	1700–1600	Intermediate Period	1786–1580	Sojourn in Egypt	
Middle Bronze IIC	1600–1550	Hyksos	1730–1580		
Late Bronze I	1550–1400	New Kingdom XVIII	1580–1314	Conquest	1406–1400
Late Bronze IIA	1400–1300	Empire Age XIX	1314–1194	Judges	1400–1050
Late Bronze IIB	1300–1200				
Iron IA	1200–1150	XXI	1085–950	United Monarchy	1050–930
Iron IB	1150–1000				
Iron IC	1000–918				
Iron IIA	918–800	XXII	950–730	Divided Monarchy	930–586
Iron IIB	800–586	XXVI	656–525		
Iron III	586–332			Captivity	586–539

Timeline of Israel's History

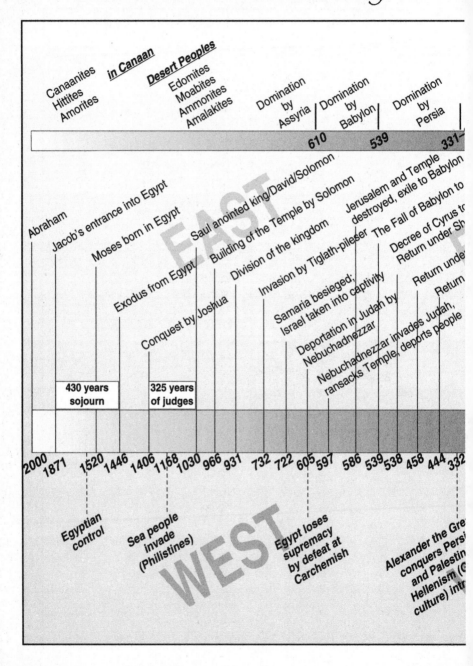

in Canaan

Canaanites
Hittites
Amorites

Desert Peoples
Edomites
Moabites
Ammonites
Amalakites

Domination by Assyria — 610
Domination by Babylon — 539
Domination by Persia — 331

EAST

Abraham

Jacob's entrance into Egypt

Moses born in Egypt

Exodus from Egypt

Conquest by Joshua

Saul anointed king/David/Solomon

Building of the Temple by Solomon

Division of the kingdom

Invasion by Tiglath-pileser

Samaria besieged; Israel taken into captivity

Deportation in Judah by Nebuchadnezzar

Jerusalem and Temple destroyed, exile to Babylon

The Fall of Babylon to

Decree of Cyrus to Return under Sh

Nebuchadnezzar invades Judah, ransacks Temple, deports people

Return under

Return

| 430 years sojourn | | 325 years of judges |

2000 1871 1520 1446 1406 1168 1030 966 931 732 722 605 597 586 539 538 458 444 332

Egyptian control

Sea people invade (Philistines)

WEST

Egypt loses supremacy by defeat at Carchemish

Alexander the Gre conquers Pers and Palestine Hellenism (G culture) intr

Timeline of Israel's History

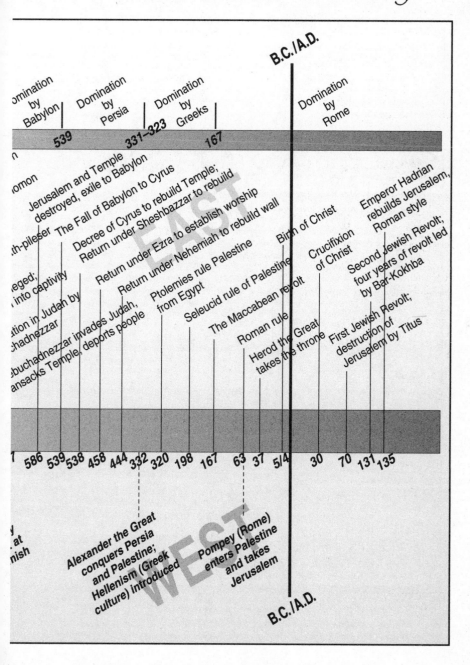

B.C./A.D.

Domination by Babylon | Domination by Persia | Domination by Greeks | Domination by Rome

539   331–323   167

...omination by Babylon

...omon

...th-pileser

Jerusalem and Temple destroyed, exile to Babylon

The Fall of Babylon to Cyrus

Decree of Cyrus to rebuild Temple; Return under Sheshbazzar to rebuild

Return under Ezra to establish worship

Return under Nehemiah to rebuild wall

Ptolemies rule Palestine from Egypt

Seleucid rule of Palestine

The Maccabean revolt

Roman rule

Birth of Christ

Herod the Great takes the throne

Crucifixion of Christ

First Jewish Revolt; destruction of Jerusalem by Titus

Second Jewish Revolt; four years of revolt led by Bar-Kokhba

Emperor Hadrian rebuilds Jerusalem, Roman style

...eged;
...into captivity

...tion in Judah by
...chadnezzar

...buchadnezzar invades Judah,
...ansacks Temple, deports people

EAST

WEST

586 539 538 458 444 332 320 198 167 63 37 5/4 30 70 131 135

Alexander the Great conquers Persia and Palestine; Hellenism (Greek culture) introduced

Pompey (Rome) enters Palestine and takes Jerusalem

...at
...nish

B.C./A.D.

Chronology of Historical Figures

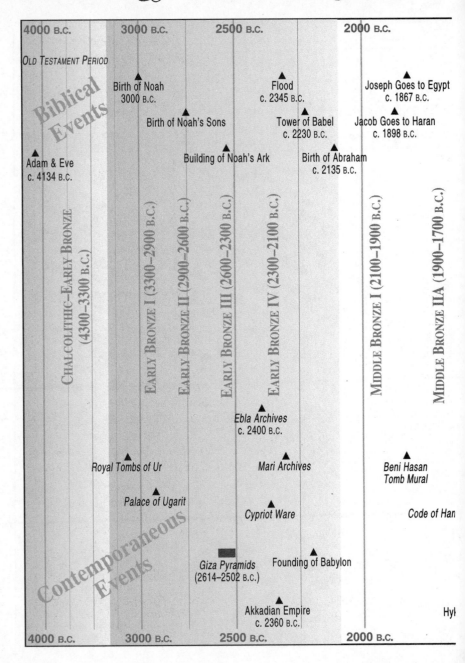

| | 4000 B.C. | 3000 B.C. | 2500 B.C. | 2000 B.C. |

Old Testament Period

Biblical Events

Birth of Noah
3000 B.C.

Flood
c. 2345 B.C.

Joseph Goes to Egypt
c. 1867 B.C.

Birth of Noah's Sons

Tower of Babel
c. 2230 B.C.

Jacob Goes to Haran
c. 1898 B.C.

Adam & Eve
c. 4134 B.C.

Building of Noah's Ark

Birth of Abraham
c. 2135 B.C.

CHALCOLITHIC–EARLY BRONZE (4300–3300 B.C.)

EARLY BRONZE I (3300–2900 B.C.)

EARLY BRONZE II (2900–2600 B.C.)

EARLY BRONZE III (2600–2300 B.C.)

EARLY BRONZE IV (2300–2100 B.C.)

MIDDLE BRONZE I (2100–1900 B.C.)

MIDDLE BRONZE IIA (1900–1700 B.C.)

Ebla Archives
c. 2400 B.C.

Royal Tombs of Ur

Mari Archives

Beni Hasan
Tomb Mural

Palace of Ugarit

Cypriot Ware

Code of Han

Contemporaneous Events

Giza Pyramids
(2614–2502 B.C.)

Founding of Babylon

Akkadian Empire
c. 2360 B.C.

Hyl

| 4000 B.C. | 3000 B.C. | 2500 B.C. | 2000 B.C. |

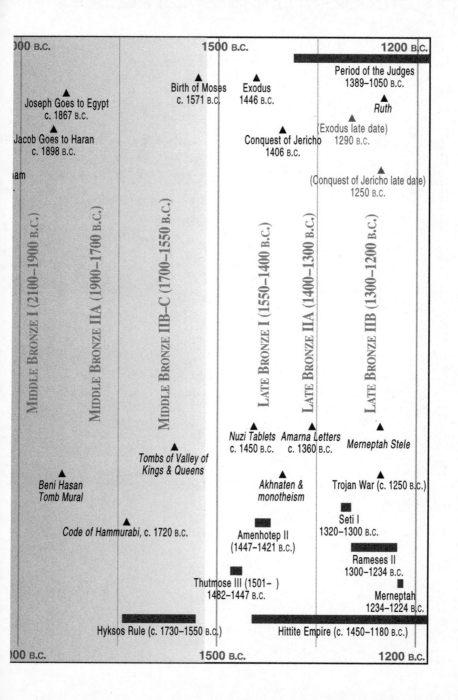

2000 B.C.   1500 B.C.   1200 B.C.

Joseph Goes to Egypt
c. 1867 B.C.

Jacob Goes to Haran
c. 1898 B.C.

Abraham

Birth of Moses
c. 1571 B.C.

Exodus
1446 B.C.

Period of the Judges
1389–1050 B.C.

Ruth

(Exodus late date)
1290 B.C.

Conquest of Jericho
1406 B.C.

(Conquest of Jericho late date)
1250 B.C.

MIDDLE BRONZE I (2100–1900 B.C.)

MIDDLE BRONZE IIA (1900–1700 B.C.)

MIDDLE BRONZE IIB–C (1700–1550 B.C.)

LATE BRONZE I (1550–1400 B.C.)

LATE BRONZE IIA (1400–1300 B.C.)

LATE BRONZE IIB (1300–1200 B.C.)

Nuzi Tablets
c. 1450 B.C.

Amarna Letters
c. 1360 B.C.

Merneptah Stele

Tombs of Valley of
Kings & Queens

Akhnaten &
monotheism

Trojan War (c. 1250 B.C.)

Beni Hasan
Tomb Mural

Seti I
1320–1300 B.C.

Code of Hammurabi, c. 1720 B.C.

Amenhotep II
(1447–1421 B.C.)

Rameses II
1300–1234 B.C.

Thutmose III (1501–)
1482–1447 B.C.

Merneptah
1234–1224 B.C.

Hyksos Rule (c. 1730–1550 B.C.)

Hittite Empire (c. 1450–1180 B.C.)

2000 B.C.   1500 B.C.   1200 B.C.

Chronology of Historical Figures

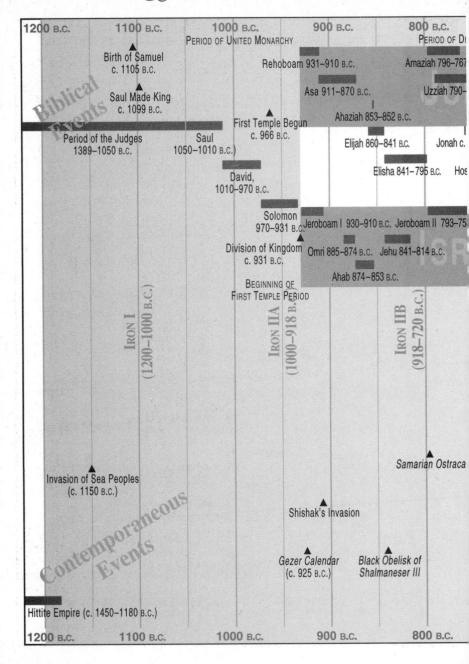

| 1200 B.C. | 1100 B.C. | 1000 B.C. | 900 B.C. | 800 B.C. |

PERIOD OF UNITED MONARCHY

PERIOD OF DI

▲ Birth of Samuel
c. 1105 B.C.

Rehoboam 931–910 B.C.

Amaziah 796–767

Biblical Events

▲ Saul Made King
c. 1099 B.C.

Asa 911–870 B.C.

Uzziah 790–

▲ First Temple Begun
c. 966 B.C.

Ahaziah 853–852 B.C.

Period of the Judges
1389–1050 B.C.

Saul
1050–1010 B.C.)

Elijah 860–841 B.C.

Jonah c.

David,
1010–970 B.C.

Elisha 841–795 B.C.

Hos

Solomon
970–931 B.C.

Jeroboam I 930–910 B.C.   Jeroboam II 793–75

Division of Kingdom
c. 931 B.C.

Omri 885–874 B.C.   Jehu 841–814 B.C.

BEGINNING OF
FIRST TEMPLE PERIOD

Ahab 874–853 B.C.

ISR

IRON I
(1200–1000 B.C.)

IRON IIA
(1000–918 B.C.)

IRON IIB
(918–720 B.C.)

▲ Samarian Ostraca

▲ Invasion of Sea Peoples
(c. 1150 B.C.)

Contemporaneous Events

▲ Shishak's Invasion

▲ Gezer Calendar
(c. 925 B.C.)

▲ Black Obelisk of
Shalmaneser III

Hittite Empire (c. 1450–1180 B.C.)

| 1200 B.C. | 1100 B.C. | 1000 B.C. | 900 B.C. | 800 B.C. |

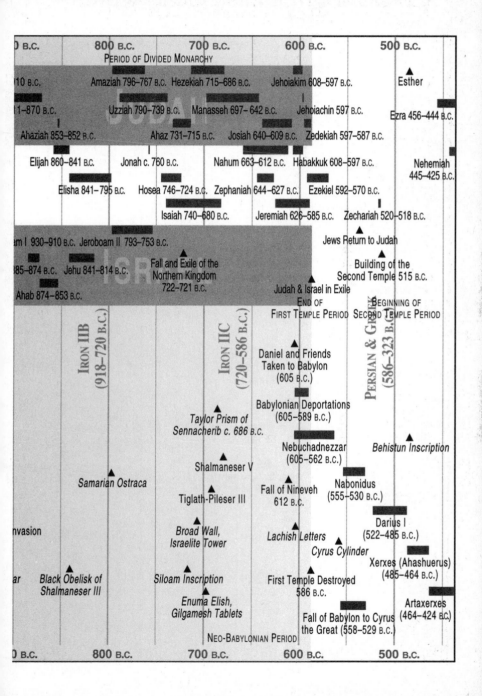

0 B.C.   800 B.C.   700 B.C.   600 B.C.   500 B.C.

PERIOD OF DIVIDED MONARCHY

Amaziah 796–767 B.C.   Hezekiah 715–686 B.C.   Jehoiakim 608–597 B.C.   Esther

10 B.C.

1–870 B.C.   Uzziah 790–739 B.C.   Manasseh 697– 642 B.C.   Jehoiachin 597 B.C.   Ezra 456–444 B.C.

Ahaziah 853–852 B.C.   Ahaz 731–715 B.C.   Josiah 640–609 B.C.   Zedekiah 597–587 B.C.

Elijah 860–841 B.C.   Jonah c. 760 B.C.   Nahum 663–612 B.C.   Habakkuk 608–597 B.C.   Nehemiah 445–425 B.C.

Elisha 841– 795 B.C.   Hosea 746–724 B.C.   Zephaniah 644–627 B.C.   Ezekiel 592–570 B.C.

Isaiah 740–680 B.C.   Jeremiah 626–585 B.C.   Zechariah 520–518 B.C.

am I 930–910 B.C.   Jeroboam II 793–753 B.C.   Jews Return to Judah

85–874 B.C.   Jehu 841–814 B.C.   Fall and Exile of the Northern Kingdom 722–721 B.C.   Building of the Second Temple 515 B.C.

Ahab 874–853 B.C.   Judah & Israel in Exile

END OF FIRST TEMPLE PERIOD   BEGINNING OF SECOND TEMPLE PERIOD

IRON IIB (918–720 B.C.)

IRON IIC (720–586 B.C.)

PERSIAN & GREEK (586–323 B.C.)

Daniel and Friends Taken to Babylon (605 B.C.)

Babylonian Deportations (605–589 B.C.)

Taylor Prism of Sennacherib c. 686 B.C.

Nebuchadnezzar (605–562 B.C.)   Behistun Inscription

Shalmaneser V

Samarian Ostraca   Fall of Nineveh 612 B.C.   Nabonidus (555–530 B.C.)

Tiglath-Pileser III

Darius I (522–485 B.C.)

nvasion   Broad Wall, Israelite Tower   Lachish Letters   Cyrus Cylinder

Xerxes (Ahashuerus) (485–464 B.C.)

ar   Black Obelisk of Shalmaneser III   Siloam Inscription   First Temple Destroyed 586 B.C.

Enuma Elish, Gilgamesh Tablets   Artaxerxes (464–424 B.C.)

Fall of Babylon to Cyrus the Great (558–529 B.C.)

NEO-BABYLONIAN PERIOD

0 B.C.   800 B.C.   700 B.C.   600 B.C.   500 B.C.

Chronology of Historical Figures

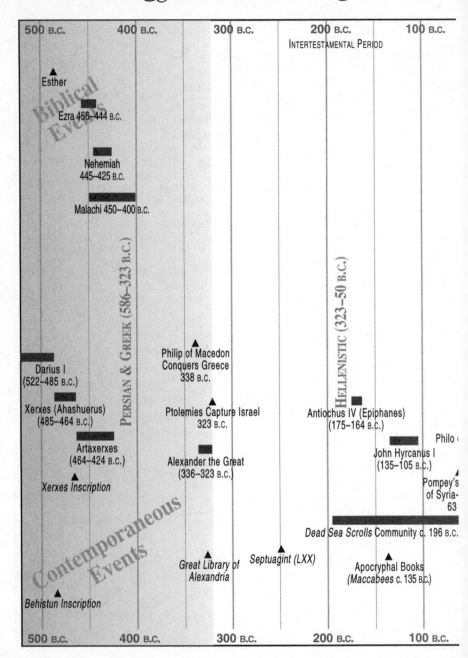

500 B.C.   400 B.C.   300 B.C.   200 B.C.   100 B.C.

INTERTESTAMENTAL PERIOD

Esther

Ezra 456–444 B.C.

Nehemiah
445–425 B.C.

Malachi 450–400 B.C.

PERSIAN & GREEK (586–323 B.C.)

HELLENISTIC (323–50 B.C.)

Biblical Events

Philip of Macedon
Conquers Greece
338 B.C.

Darius I
(522–485 B.C.)

Xerxes (Ahashuerus)
(485–464 B.C.)

Artaxerxes
(464–424 B.C.)

Xerxes Inscription

Ptolemies Capture Israel
323 B.C.

Alexander the Great
(336–323 B.C.)

Antiochus IV (Epiphanes)
(175–164 B.C.)

Philo

John Hyrcanus I
(135–105 B.C.)

Pompey's
of Syria-
63

Contemporaneous Events

Dead Sea Scrolls Community c. 196 B.C.

Great Library of
Alexandria

Septuagint (LXX)

Apocryphal Books
(Maccabees c. 135 B.C.)

Behistun Inscription

500 B.C.   400 B.C.   300 B.C.   200 B.C.   100 B.C.

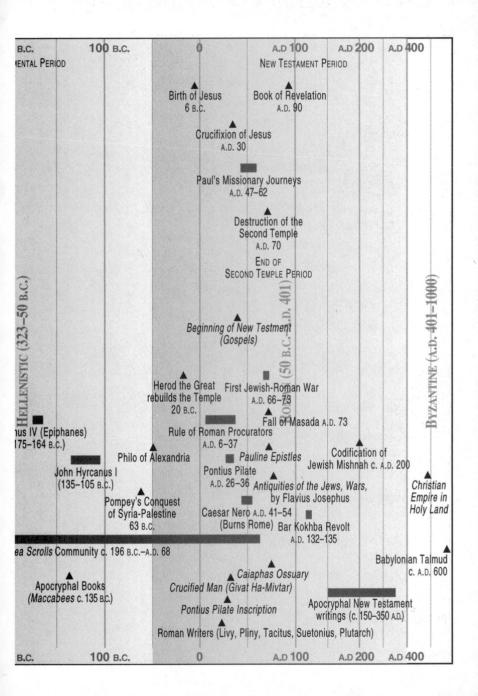

MUSEUMS

with Biblical Archæological Exhibits

The following list represents only a few of the major museums with archaeological collections with reference to the world of the Bible. These museums are included so that more people can experience the fruits of archaeology "firsthand" in their travels at home and abroad. Many of these museums could also be included as part of organized tours and should be suggested to tour organizers. Local university museums, as well as Bible colleges and seminaries, may also have significant items of interest and should be contacted for information on their holdings. Contact the museums of your choice directly for opening and closing times. In the addresses below, where two telephone numbers are listed, the second is usually a fax number.

MIDDLE EAST

Israel

Citadel Museum of the History of Israel
Near Jaffa Gate, Old City
P.O. Box 14005
91140 Jerusalem
(02) 283273/283394

Four thousand years of the history of Jerusalem are displayed through dioramas, holograms, and models based on archaeological research and excavation.

361

The Samuel Bronfman Biblical and Archaeological Museum
Israel Museum
Ruppin Boulevard
P.O. Box 1299
Jerusalem 91012
(02) 698211

An archaeological wing within Israel's national museum featuring some of the most famous artifacts from the biblical (Israelite) and Christian periods.

Shrine of the Book
Israel Museum
Ruppin Boulevard
P.O. Box 71117
Jerusalem 91710
(02) 666754/631833

The museum of the Dead Sea Scrolls located at the beginning of the Israel Museum complex, but with separate opening and closing times.

The Bible Lands Museum
Granot Street
P.O. Box 4670
Jerusalem 91046
(02) 611066/638228

Displays hundreds of artifacts from the world-famous private Browosky collection depicting the nations outside Israel that were influential in biblical history. Located adjacent to the Israel Museum.

Rockefeller Museum
Suleiman Street
P.O. Box 586
91004 Jerusalem
(02) 282251

Important collections of biblical artifacts excavated during the British Mandate period. Also repository for Dead Sea Scroll jars and hundreds of fragments, many still unpublished.

Skirball Museum

Hebrew Union College-Jewish Institute of Religion
13 King David Street
Jerusalem 94101
(02) 203333

Collection of artifacts from excavations of the biblical cities of Laish (Dan), Gezer, and Aroer.

The Burnt House

13 Tifereth Israel Street
Jewish Quarter, Old City
Jerusalem
(02) 287211

Recreation of the destruction of Second Temple Jerusalem at the site of the excavation of a Judean home destroyed in A.D. 70.

Wohl Archaeological Museum

Hurvah Square, corner of HaKaraim Street
Jewish Quarter, Old City
Jerusalem
(02) 283448

Display of Second Temple period artifacts within the remains of an excavated Herodian mansion of a priestly family.

Ariel Museum

The Center for the Study of Jerusalem in the First Temple Period
The Jewish Quarter
Shoeni Halachot Street
Jerusalem 97500
(02) 286288/274352

Includes replicas of artifacts from the First Temple period, model of the First Temple archaeological sites. Located nearby and included in the center's tour are the archaeological sites of the Broad Wall and Israelite Tower.

Franciscan Biblical Museum
Church of the Flagellation
Second Station, Via Dolorosa
Christian Quarter
Jerusalem
(02) 280271

Collection of particularly Herodian period artifacts excavated by Franciscan archaeologists in Jerusalem, Nazareth, Capernaum, and Bethlehem with special reference to early Christianity.

Reuben and Edith Hecht Museum
University of Haifa
Mount Carmel
Haifa 31999
04-240577/25773

Special emphasis on religious practices in Israel from the biblical period, including artifacts related to cultic practices.

Eretz Israel Museum (Land of Israel Museum)
2 University Street
Ramat Aviv
Tel Aviv
(03) 414244

Recreations of the customs and technologies of the ancient biblical world as well as reconstructions of Philistine city and religious buildings. The excavation of Tel Qasile, a major Philistine site, can also be visited on its grounds.

Hazor Museum
Kibbutz Ayelet Hashahar
Galilee
(06) 934855

Collection of artifacts from the excavations of Tel Hazor. Located next to the ancient tel.

Golan Archaeological Museum
P.O. Box 30
129000 Qatzrin
(06) 961350

Exhibits of artifacts depicting life in the Golan Heights during the biblical period. Located next to ancient Qatzrin where reconstructions of Jewish daily life during the Byzantine period are featured within the archaeological site.

Jordan

Jordan Archaeological Museum (Citadel Museum)
Department of Antiquities
P.O. Box 88
Citadel Hill
Amman
6-38795

National museum of Jordan, including artifacts from Israel (West Bank). Most notable are the famous *Copper Scroll* from the Dead Sea caves and items from a Middle Bronze Jericho tomb. Located on the site of Jebel Qal'a (biblical Rabath Ammon).

Turkey

Anadolu Medenyitleri Muzesi (Museum of Anatolian Civilizations)
Ankara Kalesi
Ankara
4-324-3160

Collections inclide cultic items, Hittite artifacts, clay tablets from state archives, and royal seals.

Eski Sark Eserler Muzesi (Museum of the Ancient Orient)
(Archaeological Museum)
Osman Hamdi Yokusa
Sultanahmet
Instanbul
1-520-7740

Located in the Archaeological Museum complex near the Hagia Sophia Church is this collection of Egyptian, Assyrian, and Hittite artifacts, including the Siloam Inscription from Hezekiah's Water Tunnel in Jerusalem.

Arkeolojii Muzesi (Archaeological Museum)
Turgutreis Park
Izmir

Located at the site of New Testament Smyrna, this collection has items from the Aegean, including various statues and statuettes.

EUROPEAN MUSEUMS

Austria

Kunsthistorisches Museum (Museum of Cultural History)
Ägyptische-Orientalische Sammlung (Egyptian-Oriental Collection)
Burgring 5
A-1010 Vienna
222-934-541

Features artifacts related to daily life of ancient Egyptians and ancient Near East (Yemen, South Arabia).

Germany

Ägyptisches Museum (Egyptian Museum)
Karl-Marx-Universitat (Karl Marx University)
Schillerstrasse 6
701 Leipzig
28 21 66

Egyptian collection including Middle and New Kingdom artifacts, mummies, as well as Greek-Roman and Christian period remains.

Ägyptisches Museum (Egyptian Museum)
Schloss-Strasse 70
D-1000 Berlin 19
030-32091-261

Biblical period Egyptian artifacts including the Amarna period and the famous bust of Queen Nefertiti.

Staatslische Museen zu Berlin (Berlin State Museum)/ Pergamon Museum
Bodestrasse 1-3
Berlin, 1020
2 20 03 81

One of the world's most important ancient Near Eastern collections including the Babylonian Ishtar Gate and restored altar from Pergamum as well as Sumerian and Assyrian artifacts.

France

Musée du Louvre (The Louvre)
34-36 Quai du Louvre
75058 Paris Cedex 01
(1) 40 20 50 50

One of the world's greatest collection of ancient Near Eastern antiquities including the famous Code of Hammurabi, Squatting (Egyptian) Scribe, and the Ugaritic inscriptions from Ras-Shama.

Netherlands

Bijbels Museum (Biblical Museum)
Herengracht 366
1016 CH Amsterdam
(020) 6242436/6247949

Artifacts from ancient Egypt and Middle East, including inscribed tablets, reconstructed house from biblical period, and replicas of the Ark of the Covenant and Dead Sea Scrolls.

Great Britain

British Museum
Great Russell Street
London WC1B 3DG
(01) 636 1555

One of the world's greatest collections of antiquities from the ancient Near East, Greece and Rome, including the Rosetta Stone, Siege of Lachish Relief,

Black Obelisk of Shalmaneser III, monumental relief sculptures from Nineveh and Nimrud, Amarna Letters, Enuma Elish, Gilgamesh Epic, and the frieze sculptures from the Greek Parthenon.

National Museums and Galleries on Merseyside (Liverpool Museum)
William Brown Street
Liverpool L3 8EN
051-207-0001

One of England's largest collections of ancient Near Eastern, Egyptian, and Mediterranean antiquities. Exceptional exhibits from Ur, Jericho, and the Middle Kingdom period from Beni-Hasan.

Fitzwilliam Museum
University of Cambridge
Trumpington Street
Cambridge CB2 1RB
(0223) 332900

Collections of ancient Near Eastern and Egyptian artifacts including the huge sarcophagus lid of Ramesses III, reliefs and ivories from the Assyrian palace at Nimrud, and a Samaritan inscription.

Ashmolean Museum
University of Oxford
Beaumont Street
Oxford OX1 2PH
(0865) 278000

Britian's oldest museum with exquisite collections of Mesopotamian, Egyptian and Palestinian antiquities including the only completely restored Egyptian shrine in the country.

Greece

National Archaeological Museum
1, Tositsa Street
Athens
 (301) 6513744

Collections include sculptures and artifacts with reference to daily life and culture during biblical and Roman period Greece.

Museum of Ancient Corinth
Ancient Cornith

Artifacts from the excavations at ancient Corinth illustrating cultic and daily life during early Jewish-Christian period, including synagogue inscriptions, a statue of Augustus and bust of Nero. Especially useful to New Testament students.

NORTH AMERICA

Canada

Royal Ontario Museum
100 Queenís Park
Toronto, Ontario M5S2C6
(416) 586-5549

Rich exhibits covering the rise of civilizations in Mesopotamia and Egypt, and historical overviews with artifacts from Israel, Jordan, and Syria.

United States

East

Harvard Semitic Museum
6 Divinity Avenue
Cambridge, MA 02138
(617) 495-4631

Exhibits include items from excavations at Nuzi, Samaria, Ashkelon, and Carthage.

University Museum of Archaeology/Anthropology
University of Pennsylvania
33rd and Spruce Streets
Philadelphia, PA 19104
(215) 898-4000

Collections from excavations sponsored by the University in the ancient Near East and Israel; also hosts temporary exhibits related to the Bible.

Yale University Art Gallery
1111 Chapel Street
New Haven, CT 06520
(203) 432-0600

Holdings include large collection of artifacts from Dura-Europos synagogue in Syria, Jerash in Jordan, Assyrian reliefs, and over 900 ceramic vessels from the Levant.

Dumbarton Oaks
1703 32nd Street, NW
Washington, DC 20007
(202) 338-8278

Houses the Byzantine Collection Galleries with extensive Early Christian and Byzantine period manuscripts and art objects.

National Museum of Natural History
Smithsonian Institution
10th and Constitution Streets, NW
Washington, DC 20007
(202) 357-1300

Houses an exhibit called: "Western Civilization: Origins and Traditions," which includes artifacts from the ancient Near and Middle East including Bab-edh Dhra (Sodom?) and a seal from Tell el-Kheleifeh inscribed with the name of Jotham, King of Judah (750–731 B.C.).

Walters Art Gallery
600 North Charles Street
Baltimore, MD 21201
(301) 547-9000

Collection of ancient Near Eastern, Egyptian, Etruscan, Greek, and Roman art and artifacts including Egyptian mummies and large Roman relief scupltures.

Museum of Fine Arts
465 Huntington Avenue
Boston, MA 02115
(617) 267-9300

Fine ancient Near Eastern collection including reliefs from the Assyrian palaces at Nineveh, and Nimrud, glazed brick from Nebuchadnezzar's Babylon, and over 500 seals and pieces of jewelry.

Brooklyn Museum
200 Eastern Parkway
Brooklyn, NY 11238
(718) 638-5000

Ancient Near Eastern collection with 12 colossal reliefs of the Assyrian monarch Ashurnasirpal II (883–859 B.C.), and extensive assemblege of Egyptian art from 4000 B.C.– A.D. 638.

Metropolitan Museum of Art
Fifth Avenue at 82nd Street
New York, NY 10028
(212) 879-5500

One of the world's leading museums, items of interest include reliefs, ceramics, and ivories from Assyria and Sumeria, an Egyptian temple of Isis (27 B.C.–A.D. 14), and Greek and Roman artifacts.

South

Emory University Museum of Art and Archaeology
Michael C. Carlos Hall
Emory University
Atlanta, GA 30322
(404) 727-7522

Significant collection including artifacts from Jericho, Caesarea, Mesopotamian cuneiform tablets and cylinder seals, Egyptian mummies, papyrus fragment of the Book of the Dead, and large exhibit of ancient Greek art.

Eisenberg and Nicol Museums
Southern Baptist Theological Seminary
Boyce Library, Third Floor
2825 Lexington Road

Louisville, KY 40280
(502) 897-4011

Special exhibits of items from Jericho and Ai (et-Tell), cuneiform tablets, Roman and Byzantine period manuscripts (A.D. 300–1000), and replicas of famous inscribed objects such as Rosetta Stone and the Black Obelisk of Shalmaneser III.

Midwest

Field Museum of Natural History
Roosevelt Road at Lake Shore Drive
Chicago, IL 60605
(312) 922-9410

Highlight of this museum is the fabulous exhibit "Inside Ancient Egypt" which provides the opportunity to explore a life-sized tomb complex imported from Saqqara, 23 mummies, and a burial boat.

Oriental Institute
University of Chicago
1155 East 58th Street
Chicago, IL 60637
(312) 702-9520

One of North America's best biblical period collections housed in five separate galleries for Palestine, Mesopotamia, Assyria, Egypt, and Persia.

Spertus Museum of Judaica
618 S. Michigan Avenue
Chicago, IL 60605
(312) 922-9012

Designed to educate and entertain younger children concerning biblical archaeology, includes life-size archaeological tel that can be excavated to discover replica artifacts, an open marketplace with demonstrations of ancient crafts, and an ancient Israelite house.

Kelsey Museum of Archaeology
University of Michigan
434 South State Street
Ann Arbor, MI 48109

(313) 764-9304

Large collection of art and artifacts from the ancient Near East and Egypt (including a mummy room with interactive displays), Greece, and Rome.

Horn Archaeological Museum

Andrews University
Berrien Springs, MI 49104
(616) 471-3273

A collection of 8,000 artifacts from the Early Bronze Age to Byzantine emphasizes the University's excavations at Tell Hesban and Tell el Umieri. Also has an large collection of cuneiform tablets.

Detriot Institute of Arts

5200 Woodward Avenue
Detriot, MI 48202
(313) 833-7900

Important Egyptian antiquities, Assyrian relief of Tiglath-pileser III (744–727 B.C.) and tile relief from Ishtar Gate at Babylon (the only example in North America).

Museum of Art and Archaeology

University of Missouri-Columbia
1 Pickard Hall
Columbia, MO 65211
(314) 882-3591

Numerous artifacts from Israel from 3100–586 B.C., including biblical period ossuaries, pottery, lamps, figurines, and jewelry, as well as Mesopotamian, Egyptian, Roman and Greek artifacts.

Cleveland Museum of Art

11150 East Boulevard at University Circle
Cleveland, OH 44106
(216) 421-7340

Over 1,100 pieces of ancient Egyptian, Greek, Etruscan, and Roman art, including sculptures, vases, jewelry, and coins.

Toledo Museum of Art
2445 Monroe Street at Scottwood Avenue
Toledo, OH 43697
(419) 255-8000

Collection includes items from Sumer, Syrian, the Assyrian palace at Nimrud (883–859 B.C.), numerous Egyptian reliefs and sculptures, and an extensive assemblege of ancient glass.

Cincinnati Art Museum
Eden Park
Cincinnati, OH 45202
(513) 721-5204

Good collection includes ancient Near Eastern, Egyptian, and Classical antiquities, including Nabatean sculptures from Jordan.

Skirball Museum, Cincinnati Branch
Hebrew Union College
3101 Clifton Avenue
Cincinnati, OH 45220
(513) 221-1875

More than 100 objects, including seals, tablets, jewelry, pottery, figurines, lamps, and coins. A special item of interest is a jar and lid from one of the Dead Sea caves.

West

Badè Institute of Biblical Archaeology
Pacific School of Religion
1798 Scenic Avenue
Berkeley, CA 94709
(415) 848-0528, ext. 242

Collection of artifacts from biblical Mizpah (Tell en-Nasbeh), and special display showing how archaeologists work.

Skirball Museum, Hebrew Union College
3077 University Avenue
Los Angeles, CA 90007
(213) 749-3424

Over 1,300 artifacts from Israel, Egypt, Mesopotamia, and Phoenicia (donated mostly by archaeologist Nelson Glueck), including cuneiform tablets, lamps, pottery vessels, amulets, figurines, weapons, and jewelry.

Los Angeles County Museum of Art
5905 Wilshire Boulevard
Los Angeles, CA 90036
(213) 857-6111

Fine Near Eastern gallery including Assyrian and Egyptian artifacts and an outstanding collection of ancient Iranian items (3000 B.C.).

Stanford University Museum of Art
Lomita Drive and Museum Way
Stanford, CA 94305
(415) 723-4177

Smaller collection of ancient Egyptian artifacts including reliefs, statuettes, mummy portrait, and busts.

GLOSSARY

This list includes terms that appear in the book, as well as other terms related to archaeology (Note: Terms in parentheses indicate the plural form of a word.)

ACROPOLIS: Citadel or highest elevation of a city. Often the setting for the city's most striking temples and other public structures.

AGORA: In Greek cities, an open market or square for public affairs, corresponding to the Roman forum.

AKKADIAN: Semitic language that was spoken in Babylonia and Assyria, and written in cuneiform.

EL-AMARNA LETTERS: Akkadian cuneiform clay tablets discovered mainly at el-Amarna in Egypt; correspondence between Amenhotep III and Amenhotep IV and kings in Canaan and other kingdoms in the region (fourteenth century B.C.).

AMPHITHEATER: Oval-shaped structure surrounding an arena for gladiatorial spectacles.

AMPHORA: Greek word for a two-handled storage jar.

APOCRYPHA: Books included in the Septuagint (Greek) and Vulgate (Latin) versions of the Hebrew Bible but excluded from the Jewish and Protestant canons.

APSE: A semicircular section projecting from the side of a church or monumental building, often vaulted.

ARABAH: Desert region in the Rift Valley between the Dead Sea and the Gulf of Elath/'Aqaba; in the biblical period, also denoted the valley north of the Dead Sea (Jericho).

ARAD LETTERS: Seventh-sixth centuries B.C. Hebrew ostraca discovered at Arad, mostly belonging to the archive of Eliashib, commander of the Arad citadel, dealing mainly with food distribution and military matters.

ARCH: A distinctly Roman architectural device in which wedge-shaped blocks were arranged in a semicircular covering for an opening so that pressure from a building's weight is exerted laterally instead of downward.

ARCOSOLIUM (ARCOSOLIA): A Hellenistic-to-Byzantine-period burial niche, designed to hold a sarcophagus. It was cut into the stone wall of a cave, with a ledge below and an arch above. Suggested to be the type of tomb in which Jesus' body was laid.

ARTIFACT: Any material object altered by human intervention for some purpose; a stone or metal knife, clay formed and fired to a figurine, coin, and so on.

ASHERAH: Canaanite goddess, consort of El and mother of the gods. At Ugarit, called "Lady Asherah of the Sea."

ASHLAR MASONRY: Square or rectangular cut stones, uniform in size and shape and laid in horizontal courses; laid regularly either as a wall in itself or as facing for a rubble wall.

ASHTORETH: Hebrew form of the name of the Semitic goddess of love and fertility *(see* Astarte).

ASSEMBLAGE: The sum total of objects found in a specific archaeological context (e.g., pottery, stone implements), perhaps a building or a stratum *(see* stratigraphy).

ASSYRIOLOGISTS: Those who study the ancient literary and non-literary remains of the Assyrian empire.

ASTARTE: Canaanite/Phoenician fertility and love goddess; identified with the Greek goddess Aphrodite (equivalent of biblical Ashtoreth).

AUTOGRAPHA: The original (but now lost) copies of the books of the Bible. The doctrine of verbal plenary inspiration is usually said to extend only to the autographa, not the variant copies that came from it. The science of textual criticism is an attempt to work backward from our present copies of the Scriptures to determine the reading of the autographa.

BA'AL: A generic term meaning "lord" or "master"; any of numerous Canaanite/Phoenician chief local male deities (e.g., Ba'al Hamon, Ba'al Zaphon); Semitic god of rain and fertility, known at Ugarit as "the Rider of Clouds."

BABYLONIAN EXILE: Dispersion of the residents of Judah to Babylonia, in Mesopotamia, following the conquest by King Nebuchadnezzar and the destruction of the First Temple in Jerusalem in 586 B.C.

BALK (BAULK): The vertical face of the wall of soil left around a trench, or square; the 3-foot-wide walkway left around the sides of a square; an unexcavated strip left standing in an excavation (usually 0.5-1 m. wide) to provide visual evidence for the sequence of debris (stratification) when surrounding areas have been removed by digging. The face of a balk is known as a "section," and drawings of it as "section drawings."

BAMAH (BAMOT): Hebrew word used by archaeologists to describe a place of worship in a natural setting outside towns, or the artificial mound or platform within a town thought to simulate it, misleadingly rendered "high place" in English.

BAR-KOKHBA: Leader of the Second Jewish Revolt against Rome (A.D. 132–135).

BASALT: A kind of dense, greenish, dark gray or brownish-black igneous volcanic rock. Much basalt is found in the mountains of Galilee.

BASILICA: An elongated rectangular building with a central nave and side aisles. Roman basilicas served as business and legal buildings.

BEDOUIN: Tribal nomadic Arabs that inhabit desert regions in the Near and Middle East. Members of the Ta'amireh tribe were responsible for discovering many of the Dead Sea Scrolls as well as other archaeological artifacts from tombs in the West Bank and Jordan.

BEMA: A speaker's raised platform, often used as a place of judgment. It is used in this way in the New Testament for the place of the believer's final judgment (Greek, "the bema-seat of Christ"—2 Corinthians 5:10).

BES: Ancient Egyptian dwarf god of music and dancing and the protector of women in childbirth.

BICHROME WARE (MB IIC/LB I): Middle Bronze Age IIC and Late Bronze Age I pottery group, characterized by geometric and faunal designs in black and red, of both Cypriot and Syro/Canaanite traits and provenance.

BICHROME WARE (IRON AGE): Phoenician pottery group in vogue mainly from the eleventh-ninth century B.C.; most globular flasks, jugs, and bowls decorated with black, red, and sometimes white concentric circles.

BOSS: The untrimmed, projecting face of a stone after its edges or margins have been trimmed square of draft cut.

BULLA (BULLAE): Seal impression stamped on a lump of clay or other plastic material, used in antiquity to seal documents.

BYZANTINE EMPIRE: Eastern Roman Empire, fourth–seventh centuries.

CALDARIUM (CALDRIA): Hot room in a Roman bath.

CANDELABRUM (CANDELABRA): An ornamental candlestick.

CANON: The authoritative list of books regarded as Scripture; in this text, referring primarily to the New Testament canon.

CAPITAL: The topmost section or member of a classical column or pilaster.

CARBON-14 DATING: Technique in which the degree of disintegration of the carbon-14 content (one of the essential elements of all organic matter) is measured to determine the date of an artifact.

CARDO (CARDINES): One of two main streets in a Roman city plan, running north-south and intersecting at right angles with the east-west streets.

CASEMATE: A room built within a defensive wall. A casemate wall is a double wall with a row of casemates between its outer and inner faces; a double wall with partitioned compartments, sometimes used for storage or dwellings.

CATACOMB: An underground place for burying the dead, consisting of galleries or passages with recesses for tombs.

CENOTAPH: Empty (commemorative) tomb or monument erected in honor of someone buried elsewhere.

CERAMIC TYPOLOGY: The observation of changing patterns or forms in ancient ceramic pottery, used to establish chronological sequence in dating.

CHARNEL HOUSE: Above-ground burial site composed of a small house built of field stones as used in the Early Bronze site of Bab-edh Dhra.

CHEMOSH: God of the people of Moab in Transjordan.

CODEX (CODICES): Ancient manuscript(s) bound in the form of a book (especially a Bible) rather than a scroll; book of laws in the Byzantine period.

COLLARED-RIM JAR/PITHOS: Large jar of the Late Bronze Age, mainly Iron Age I (at some sites also early Iron Age II), with ridge under the neck, once thought to be indicative of Israelite settlements only.

COSMOGONY: The study of the perceived origin and operation of the universe.

COURSE: Each horizontal row of bricks or stones.

CUNEIFORM SCRIPT: The wedge-shaped writing originally developed from about 3000 B.C. by the Sumerians in southern Iraq to write on clay tablets. It was later adapted for writing a number of other languages (Sumerian, Hurrian, Urartian, Hittite, Elamite, Ugaritic, and most notably Akkadian), spoken by the earliest Semitic inhabitants of Iraq, and then used as the international diplomatic language until superseded by Aramaic under the Persian Empire. At Ras Shamra (Ugarit) it was specially modified to write the local language in a wedge-shaped alphabet. Cuneiform was written by pressing the end of a flat stylus, or stick, into moist clay tablets. This produced wedge-shaped impressions, since the writer tended to press his stylus harder on one side.

CURSIVE: Rapid, handwritten form of a script.

CYLINDER SEAL: Cylinder (usually of stone) carved with figures, designs, or writing; when the seal is rolled onto a soft substance, a continuous band of relief is imprinted; a typical Mesopotamian object, usually pierced for suspension.

DAGON: Semitic god of grain: at Ugarit, the father of Baal; in Philistia, the god of Ashdod.

DECAPOLIS: Loose confederation of ten commerce-oriented Hellenized cities in north Transjordan, north Palestine, and south Syria, second century B.C.

DEIR: Arabic word meaning "monastery."

DEMOTIC SCRIPT: Earliest form of Egyptian cursive script used for common purposes.

DENDROCHRONOLOGY: The study of annual ring growth patterns in trees to determine climateological changes and associate them with historical events.

DOCUMENTARY HYPOTHESIS: In its classic form, particularly associated with the German biblical scholar Julius Wellhausen (1844-1918), this hypothesis proposed four literary sources as the primary elements in the Pentateuch or Hexateuch, which, in chronological order are *J* (Jehovist or Yahwist), *E* (Elohist), *D* (Deuteronomist), and *P* (Priestly Code). *J*, the oldest, has been assigned to the tenth or ninth century B.C.

EL: Chief of the Canaanite pantheon, called "King Father Shunem" and "Bull El" at Ugarit.

ENLIL: Babylonian wind- and storm-god, responsible for the Flood.

EPIGRAPHY: Study of ancient writing or inscriptions.

EPIGRAPHIST: One who by profession or training is employed in the decipherment and analysis of ancient forms of writing.

ESSENES: Jewish sect mentioned by first-century Jewish historian Flavius Josephus and Roman author Pliny. Essene communities are said to have been located near Ein-Gedi at the Dead Sea and Jerusalem. The Essenes are the chief candidates for identity of the community that produced the Dead Sea Scrolls.

EUSEBIUS' ONOMASTICON: *See* onomasticon.

EXECRATION TEXTS: Egyptian texts (twentieth and nineteenth century B.C.) inscribed with the names of rulers of towns and ethnic groups in Palestine and Syria, accompanied by execrations and curses; constitutes an important source concerning these regions in the Middle Bronze Age II.

EVEN HA-SHETIYAH **(Hebrew: "Foundation Stone"):** *see* Foundation Stone.

EXEMPLAR: An archetype from which another manuscript is copied.

FAÇADE: The vertical face of a building, usually its front.

FAIENCE: An artificial material consisting basically of powdered quartz or sandy body with lime and either natron or ash, covered by a vitreous alkaline glaze varying in color. It was widely used for the manufacture of beads, amulets, and small vessels, especially in Egypt.

FILL: Rubbish, gravel, sand, or soil brought in to level uneven ground or raise a floor or other structure; natural accumulation.

FIRST INTERMEDIATE PERIOD: Period in Egypt from c. 2180 to 2133 B.C., between the end of the Old Kingdom and beginning of the Middle Kingdom.

FIRST JEWISH REVOLT: Great revolt by the Jews of Palestine (A.D. 67-70) against Rome, culminating in the destruction of the Temple in Jerusalem in A.D. 70.

FIRST TEMPLE PERIOD: Period from the building of the Temple in Jerusalem by King Solomon in the tenth century B.C. to its destruction by King Nebuchadnezzar of Babylon in 586 B.C.

FISSION-TRACK DATING: A method of determining age by measuring traces of split uranium-238 atoms present in obsidian and other glassy volcanic minerals.

FLAGSTONE: Flat, evenly shaped paving stone.

FORM CRITICISM: The type of biblical criticism pioneered by the German scholar Hermann Gunkel (1862-1932), who investigated the history of different forms of literature and their relationships to their social setting (*Sitz im Leben*).

FORUM (FORA): In Roman cities, an open square for public affairs; marketplace. In Greek cities it was known as the *agora*.

FOUNDATION STONE: The highest point of Mount Moriah, which was said to have protruded through the platform supporting the Temple within the Holy of Holies. In this way it served as the foundation for the Ark of the Covenant, which is said to have been placed upon it.

FOUNDATION TRENCH: Long, narrow trench dug for a wall's founding courses.

FOUR-ROOM HOUSE: Characteristic Iron Age structure sometimes attributed to the Israelites, consisting of three rooms or pillared spaces around a rectangular fourth space, possibly a courtyard open to the sky.

FRESCO: Decorative painting made with pigments on freshly spread, moist lime plaster.

FRIEZE: The middle member of an entablature, between the cornice and the architrave. Often enriched with relief carving.

FRIGIDARIUM: The cold room of a Roman bath.

GENIZAH: Repository in a synagogue for discarded sacred books and objects.

GLACIS: A sloping bank, usually plastered, at the external foot of a fortification wall for construction purposes and to make attack more difficult; constructed of stone, compact earth, bricks, and so on.

GREAT REVOLT: The Jewish war against Rome, which began in A.D. 66 and ended at the fall of Masada in A.D. 73.

HABIRU: Unsettled people in Late Bronze Age Canaan having no property rights; mentioned in the el-Amarna letters and identified by some scholars with the ancient Hebrews, but also from cuneiform texts as being with mercenary bands.

HAGGADAH (Hebrew: "telling"): The term used for a written text that contains the story of the exodus from Egypt as well as an order of service *(Seder)* for the Passover.

HAR: The Hebrew word for "mountain," as in *Har Ha-Bayit*, "The Temple Mount" *(see* Arabic word *Jebel).*

HARAM: The Arabic word for a sacred enclosure or sanctuary, for example, Haram es-Sharif ("Noble Enclosure") for the Temple Mount.

HEADERS: Ashlar rectangular stones positioned in wall construction so that the ends, rather than the sides, face outward. Headers and stretchers alternate in each course.

HELLENISTIC: The period following the conquest of Alexander the Great.

HENOTHEISM (Greek *heno,* "one" + *theos,* "gods"): The worship of one god among many. One god received primary worship, usually the chief of the gods.

HERODIAN: A term describing any period or architectural structure connected with Herod the Great or the Herodian Dynasty.

HERODOTUS: Greek writer born in 484 B.C. who was known as "the Father of History." His historical writings concerning biblical places such as Babylon and personalities such as Darius were once doubted as to their accuracy, but have now been shown to be more reliable than not on the basis of archaeological excavation.

HEXAPLA TEXT: Edition of the Hebrew Bible compiled in the third century A.D. by Origen; consists of the Hebrew text, Greek translation, and four Greek versions, including the Septuagint.

HIERATIC SCRIPT: Later Egyptian cursive script used mainly for everyday purposes, mostly written on papyri or ostraca.

HIEROGLYPHIC SCRIPT (Egyptian): Script invented in c. 3000 B.C., composed of phonograms and semograms used mainly in monumental inscriptions and decorations.

HIERON: Greek term for a temple or sacred enclosure.

HIGHER CRITICISM: A term introduced into biblical studies in the late eighteenth century. It does not describe an exaggerated form of ordinary criticism but rather a particular type, distinct from Lower Criticism *(see* later). Its purpose is to determine the date, literary structure (if composite), and origin of the books of the Old Testament with the assistance of all relevant evidence. Strictly speaking, though much obscured in fact, historical problems fall outside its traditional range.

HIGH PLACES: *See* Bamat.

HOLE-MOUTH JAR: Type of jar with a wide mouth and no neck, used for storage and food preparation.

HOLY ARK: The wooden box containing the Tablets of the Law, kept in the Holy of Holies in the Temple at Jerusalem. Since the destruction of the Temple by the Romans, the Holy Ark in synagogues has contained scrolls of the first five books of the Old Testament. The Ark is often used as a symbol in Jewish art.

HOLY OF HOLIES: Inner chamber of cultic sanctuary; innermost chamber of a temple.

HORVAH (HORVAT): The Hebrew word for an ancient ruin; used interchangeably with the Arabic *Khirbeh* (*Khirbet*).

ICONOGRAPHY: Imagery or symbolism in art.

INFRARED TECHNOLOGY: A photographic technique by which even the most blurred writing is made clear and legible.

IN SITU (Literally, "at the site," "in place"): Used to designate the precise position in which artifacts and architectural fragments were originally found.

JEBEL: Arabic word for "mountain" as in *Jebel Musa* for "Mount Moses" (i.e., Mt. Sinai).

JESUS SEMINAR: An international group of higher critical scholars who convene in order to apply various methods of form criticism to the Gospels in order to distinguish the original words of Jesus from theological statements about Him.

KHIRBEH (KHIRBET): Arabic word used to describe an ancient site with remains visible on the surface. When used as part of a place-name, the final *h* changes to a *t*, as in Khirbet Qumran.

KING'S HIGHWAY: One of the two most important highways that connected Egypt with Mesopotamia, crossing Transjordan from north to south, close to the desert's edge (*see* also Way of the Sea).

KOINE: The Greek dialect in which the Septuagint, The New Testament, and other commercial contracts and correspondence on papyrus were written.

KOKH (-IM): Recessed niches for holding sarcophagi or bones in an ancient Roman-period tomb.

KRATER: Large bowl; mixing bowl.

LACHISH LETTERS: Ostraca inscribed in Hebrew, found at Lachish, and dated to the last days of Judah. The ostraca contain important information about this period.

LACUNA: A gap in the text of a manuscript.

LAMELEKH SEALS (Hebrew) seal impressions: Literally, "(belonging) to the king," seal impressions on Judahite jar handles of the late eighth century B.C. depicting a four-winged beetle or a two-winged object and one of four place names: Hebron, Socoh, Ziph, or Mmst; their exact administrative function is under debate.

LAYER: A level of build-up in a mound *(see also* stratigraphy).

LEVANT: Countries of the eastern Mediterranean: Israel, Jordan, Lebanon, and Syria.

LEVELS: The various layers of debris recognized in an excavation are conventionally called *levels* or *strata (see also* stratigraphy).

LIME PLASTER: Plaster made of ground shells or limestone.

LITERARY DEPENDENCE: The use of a text as the primary source document for historical or factual statements.

LOCUS (LOCI): Any three-dimensional feature in a square, such as a layer of earth, a wall, pit, bin, and so on, primarily used to describe the smallest coherent unit in an excavation; but loosely used to mean a room or other large architectural unit. This definition varies from excavation to excavation.

LOWER CRITICISM: The study of manuscripts and variant readings *(see also* Higher Criticism).

MADABA MAP: Mosaic pavement in a Byzantine church at Madaba, Jordan, representing a map of the Holy Land, dated to the second half of the sixth century.

MARDUK: God of Babylon, and head of the pantheon during the time of the Babylonian empire.

MARI DOCUMENTS: Akkadian cuneiform letters and administrative records excavated at Mari on the Euphrates, dating to the eighteenth century B.C.; some of them mention cities in Canaan.

MASORETIC: Accepted text of the Hebrew Bible.

MASSEBAH (MASSEBOTH): A Hebrew word used by archaeologists to describe vertical stones, usually monoliths, thought to have been set up as memorials or objects of worship.

MASSORETIC: A system of vowels and critical apparatus in our present Hebrew text of the Bible; while written down in the seventh century A.D., the system follows a tradition of pronunciation established by Jewish scribes in the first century A.D.

MASTABA: The earliest form of Egyptian pyramid-building, in which each section of the structure was built as a separate platform in a step fashion.

MAXIMALIST (BIBLICAL): A biblical scholar who gives maximum authority to the biblical text as a source for historical and factual information about the past.

MENORAH: Seven-branched candelabrum (candlestick) used in Jewish rituals.

MINARET: Tower from which the Muslim call to prayer is made.

MINIMALIST (BIBLICAL): A biblical scholar who minimalizes the biblical text as an authoritative source for reliable historical and factual information about the past.

MIQVEH (MIQVAOT): (Hebrew "ritual bath"): Facility for Jewish ritual bathing, either public or in a private home.

MISHNAH: Collection of oral Jewish law and traditions, compiled c. A.D. 200; the basic part of the Talmud.

MONOLITH: From the Greek *mono* (one) and *lithos* (stone). A single block of stone, especially a large one, shaped into a pillar or a monument.

MONOTHEISM: (Greek *mono*, "one" + *theos*, "god"): The belief in or worship of only one God.

MOSAIC: A picture or inscription made by piecing together small cut stones of different shapes and colors.

MOTIF: An object (or a group of objects) that forms a distinct part of a design.

MUMMIFICATION: A process of preserving the mortal remains of a corpse through a complex procedure involving the removal of bodily fluids and organs and the application of various spices and wrappings. This process is thought to have originated with the Egyptians.

NAOS: (Greek "shrine"): In the Greek east the cella or innermost sanctuary of a temple.

NAVE: The central aisle of a building or the central and side aisles of a cruciform church. The area designated for the laity in worship.

NECROPOLIS: Greek for *cemetery* (literally, "city of the dead"); used mainly to denote large and important cemeteries.

NICHE: Hollowed recess in a wall to hold, for example, a Torah ark (in a synagogue), a statue, an interment (in a tomb), or for decorative purposes.

NUMISMATICS: The collection, study, and dating of coins.

OBELISK: Upright, four-sided pillar (usually monolithic) that tapers toward the top to form a pyramid shape.

ONOMASTICON: Alphabetical list of place names mentioned in the Bible and identified by the author with contemporary sites; most generally used is the one written (in Greek) by Eusebius, bishop of Caesarea, in the early fourth century and translated and annotated (in Latin) by Jerome in the late fourth century.

ORTHOSTAT: Upright stone slab, used mainly for lining walls and pilasters, sometimes shaped like an animal or other forms.

OSSIGARIUM: *See* Secondary Burial.

OSSUARY: A box, urn, or other receptacle for the bones of the dead after the flesh has decayed (secondary burial).

OSTRACON (OSTRACA): Greek for "potsherd"; used by archaeologists to describe any fragment of pottery, bone, or wood that has writing on it.

Because papyrus was expensive, ostraca were commonly used in Egypt and Palestine for everyday writing purposes in the local cursive scripts, but not the cuneiform script.

PALEOETHNOBOTANY: The study of plant life in ancient cultures.

PALEOGRAPHY: Study of ancient alphabets, writing styles, and inscriptions (*see also* epigraphy).

PAPYRUS (PAPYRI): A writing material or paper made from the papyrus reed growing in the Nile River. Widely used in ancient times.

PARCHMENT: Refers to writing paper that, in ancient times, was made from animal skins or vellum.

PASSOVER: The name of the celebration commemorated in memory of the Jewish exodus from Egypt, during which God's wrath "passed over" the Israelites but fell upon their oppressors (Exodus 12).

PENTATEUCH: The first five books of the Old Testament: Genesis, Exodus, Leviticus, Numbers, and Deuteronomy taken together.

PHARISEE: Member of the traditional party of Jews in the Second Temple period noted for their strict observance of the law (cf. Sadducee).

PHASE: A stage within an occupational level defined by excavation; a reuse or rebuilding of a structure or smaller feature, such as a repair of a wall or floor.

PHILISTINE POTTERY: Pottery characteristic of sites in Philistia in the twelfth-early tenth century B.C.; decorated mainly with geometric patterns, fish, and bird motifs in black and red, often on a white slip, featuring a mixture of Mycenean, Cypriot, Canaanite, and Egyptian traits.

PHOTOGRAMMETRY: The science of measuring archaeological sites for maps or drawings by the use of aerial and surface photography.

PILASTER: Vertical pier or support beam, usually square or rectangular in shape, which is built into a wall with only a little of its thickness projecting. Architecturally it is treated as a column.

PITHOS (PITHOI): Large storage jar.

POLYTHEISM: (from Greek *poly*, "many" + *theos*, "gods"): The belief in or worship of more than one god.

POTASSIUM-ARGON DATING: Determination of the age of an object on the basis of the half-life of the radioactive isotope of potassium as it decays to form argon.

POTSHERDS: Broken pieces of ceramic pottery found in excavations. It's typically the most abundantly preserved evidence in archaeological remains.

PROTO-AEOLIC CAPITAL: Stone capital decorated with volutes (stylized palmettes) typical mainly of Israelite/Judean monumental architecture.

RADIOCARBON DATING: Radiometric dating method for determining the age of organic objects based on measuring the predictable rate of decay of the radioactive isotope of carbon 14 (C-14) in comparison to the rate of an ordinary isotope of carbon (C-12).

RAMPART: Raised earth mound or embankment used as a fortification or fortification wall.

RED HEIFER: A pure red cow that, according to the purification ritual recorded in Numbers 19, was burnt to ashes and then mixed with water to be sprinkled on everything connected with the sanctuary and its services. The ceremony of the red heifer was conducted on the Mount of Olives and continued until the destruction of the Temple in A.D. 70. Orthodox Jews believe that the ceremony's reinstatement is essential to the revival of a priesthood and the rebuilding of the Temple.

RESISTIVITY DETECTOR: Instrument used in subsurface detection. It measures slight variations in how objects below the ground level conduct electrical current.

REVETMENT: Superficial facing applied to a wall built of some other material.

ROSETTE: An ornament resembling a rose.

SADDUCEE: Member of the priestly Jewish aristocracy (second century B.C. to first century A.D.); opposed the Pharisees' literal interpretation of the law.

SAKHRA: Arabic term for the rock within the Muslim Dome of the Rock, where, according to the Koran, Abraham offered Ishmael *(see* Foundation Stone).

SAMARIA OSTRACA: Sixty-three ninth- or eighth-century B.C. ostraca uncovered at Samaria, which record dispatches of wine and oil and contain important linguistic, topographical, and economic data relating to the kingdom of Israel.

SANHEDRIN: Highest court of justice and supreme council of the Jewish people (first century B.C. to sixth century A.D.).

SARCOPHAGUS (SARCOPHAGI): Stone coffin.

SATELLITE TECHNOLOGY: Remote sensing technology whereby orbiting satellites with ground-penetrating radar can retrieve images of objects buried beneath the surface at depths as great as 200 feet.

SCARAB: Beetle-shaped stamp seal, mainly Egyptian.

SCRIPTORIUM: Place where books were written or copied.

SECOND TEMPLE PERIOD: Period in Israel beginning with the return of the Babylonian exiles in 536 B.C. and ending with the destruction of Jerusalem and the Temple in A.D. 70.

SECONDARY BURIAL: The reburial of bones after the flesh has decomposed *(see also* ossuary).

SECTION: A vertical cut—normally the side of an excavation trench—which reveals the structure (or stratigraphy) of a mound. It is recorded in drawings, properly made on site, confusingly also referred to as "sections" (e.g., section drawings).

SEDER (Hebrew: "order"): The term used for the "order" of the Passover service, during which the account of the Israelite exodus from Egypt is recounted *(magid)* and a ritual meal is consumed.

SEPTUAGINT: Pre-Christian third-century B.C. Greek translation of the Hebrew Bible, written, according to legend, by 70 scholars in 70 days; the first vernacular translation.

SHEKEL: An ancient unit of weight used by the Babylonians, Phoenicians, Jews, and other peoples of the Ancient Near East. Also a coin of this weight, especially the main silver coin of the Jews; used between the second century B.C. and second century A.D. in Syria-Palestine.

SHEPHELAH: Literally, "lowland"; the hilly region between Israel's southern coastal plain and the Judean foothills.

SIX-DAY WAR: A war between the Israelites and surrounding Arab countries that occurred from June 5-10, 1967, during which East Jerusalem and the Temple Mount were taken by Israel as part of the territory captured.

SQUEEZE: A facsimile of an inscription or other carving made by pressing it with a plastic substance.

STELE (STELAI): An upright slab or stone pillar used for inscriptions, reliefs, and tombstones. Stelai served a variety of purposes in the ancient world: as funerary monuments, as monuments commemorating royal victories, and for dedications to gods.

STOA: A long, covered walk or hall with columns in front; a colonnade or portico; Greek freestanding building, usually one story high, consisting of a long rear wall and a row of columns in front bearing a sloping roof.

STRATIFICATION: The layers of a mound created by successive destructions; superimposed occupational layers as they are uncovered in excavation.

STRATIGRAPHY: The process of observing, interpreting, and recording the layers of a mound created by successive destructions. This is one of the major interpretative principles of field archaeology borrowed from geology. It depends on the fact that where one deposit of debris overlies another, the upper must have accumulated after the lower, since the latter could not have been inserted beneath it. In practice there are numerous modifications to this general rule, for many acts of nature, from earthquakes to burrowing animals, will disturb any orderly sequence of deposits as will interference by man (pits, graves, fills, foundation trenches, and so on). It is the modern archaeologist's main purpose to distinguish one deposit from another by its texture, color, or contents (which may of course include intruders from other levels), and to draw diagrams (sections) of a site's stratigraphy so that others may check the interpretation. The various layers of debris so recognized are conventionally called either *levels* or *strata*.

STRATUM (STRATA): A layer of soil containing artifacts and debris representing a particular time and culture at a site; the combination of all loci belonging to one construction, habitation, and destruction cycle, representing one historical and cultural period of habitation at a site; usually distinguished from one another by differences in soil makeup, architecture, artifacts, and so on.

STRETCHERS: Ashlar rectangular stones laid in wall construction so that the side faces outward. Headers and stretchers alternate in each course.

SUBSURFACE INTERFACE RADAR: Instrument used to find tombs and buildings by measuring masses of density beneath the earth's surface.

SYNCRETISM: The attempt to harmoniously adopt and merge elements of more than one religious system.

TALENT: Ancient weight and money unit; heaviest unit of weight system and highest value of monetary system.

TALMUD: Interpretation of the Mishnah and the Gemarah (c. A.D. 200-500).

TARGUM: Any of several Aramaic translations or paraphrases of the Hebrew Bible.

TELL (TEL): The Arabic word (with one *l* in Hebrew) used in reference to the unnatural mounds created by the repeated destruction and rebuilding of ancient cities and villages on the same site. The word is now used in most languages for such mounds throughout the Near East. This same word appears in the Hebrew text of Joshua 11:13: "cities that stood on their tells."

TEMENOS: A sacred enclosure (sanctuary) containing one or more temples, encircled by a wall.

TERRA COTTA: Typically reddish, unglazed ceramic (earthenware) material.

TETRARCH: Governor of the fourth part of a country or province within the Roman Empire (instituted by Diocletian in A.D. 292).

THEOCRACY (Greek: *theos* = "God," and *cratos* = "rule"): The period in Israel's history during which a divine administration was mediated by priests and prophets on the basis of the Mosaic Covenant.

THEOTOKOS: "Mother of God," epithet of Mary, mother of Jesus.

TRICLINIUM (TRICLINIA): A dining room; the name arose from the Roman practice of installing three banqueting couches together in a "U" shape around a table.

TUMULUS (TUMULI): Small mound or stone heap, often covering a tomb.

TYPOLOGY: The study and grouping/taxonomy/classification of man-made objects (which may include texts) through shared characteristics (form, decoration, surface technique, manufacturing technique, and so on), to achieve various research goals such as dating and location of production centers.

UGARITIC: Canaanite language of ancient Ugarit in Syria.

UMAYYAD DYNASTY: Caliphs who ruled the Muslim Empire from 661 to 750.

UNITED MONARCHY: Political unification of the Israelite tribes by David in the tenth century B.C. until the division between the (northern) Israelite kingdom and the (southern) Judahite kingdom after Solomon's reign, c. 928 B.C.

VATICINIUM EX EVENTU: Latin term designating the concept that (biblical) prophecy was written after the events it describes had occurred, in contrast to predictive prophecy, which bears the supernatural element of divine determination.

VELLUM: A fine-grained unsplit lambskin or calfskin prepared for the copying of (biblical) manuscripts.

VOTIVES: Objects offered or dedicated for a specifically religious purpose; often carefully buried later to avoid their use for profane purposes.

VULGATE: Latin version of the Bible authorized and used by the Roman Catholic Church.

WADI: Arabic term for a rocky watercourse or valley that carries water only during the rainy season; the watercourse is dry for most of the year.

WAQF: Muslim endowment fund and supervisory council.

WAY OF THE SEA: One of the two most important highways that connected Egypt and Mesopotamia, crossing Canaan/Israel along the Mediterranean coastline and then branching north and northeast; the Via Marisi of later periods *(see also* King's Highway).

ZIGGURAT: Stepped Mesopotamian temple.

ZOOMORPHIC (Greek: "animal-shaped"): Refers to either literary descriptions or graven or sculptured images of deities or of creatures associated with deities whose form or aspects of that form are depicted as animal-like.

SUGGESTED RESOURCES

in Biblical Archaeology

Whether just researching or building a basic library in archaeology or biblical studies, these titles should be among the first consulted or acquired. Most are recent works, which usually have an advantage over older works in this field because of the ever-growing body of data coming from ongoing excavations.

General Biblical Archaeology

There are many books on biblical archaeology in print. Many are reprints of older works that have now been superceded by more recent works; others are either quite academic or narrow in focus. Those listed here represent a mix of popular and scholarly works (mostly conservative in viewpoint) that provide useful and reliable information of a general nature.

Gary K. Brantley, *Digging for Answers: Has Archaeology Disproved the Bible?* (Alabama: Apologetics Press, Inc., 1995). Christian maximalist response to minimalist arguments.

Gaalyah Cornfeld, *Archaeology of the Bible: Book by Book* (New York: Harper & Row, 1976). As the title states, this book provides information with photographs for every book in the Old and New Testament. Written by a popular Jewish researcher.

Kenneth A. Kitchen, *The Bible in Its World: The Bible and Archaeology Today* (Downers Grove, IL: InterVarsity Press, 1977). Christian maximalist arguments by a well-known British Egyptologist.

Amahai Mazar, *Archaeology of the Land of the Bible: 10,000–586 B.C.E.* (New York: Doubleday, 1990). This volume in the *Anchor Bible Reference Library* is one of the most current textbook treatments of biblical archaeology. The Israeli author is director of the Hebrew University of Jerusalem's Institute of Archaeology.

Alan Millard, *Treasures from Bible Times* (Michigan: Lion Publishing Corporation, 1985). Leading British evangelical maximalist presents selected archaeological discoveries related to the Bible in full-color format.

Keith Schoville, *Biblical Archaeology in Focus* (Grand Rapids: Baker Book House, 1978). Textbook treatment of biblical archaeology by a leading American evangelical maximalist scholar.

J.A. Thompson, *The Bible and Archaeology,* rev. ed. (Grand Rapids: Wm. B. Eerdmans Publishing Co., 1972). A standard maximalist survey of biblical archaeology and history by Australian scholar (a bit dated, but useful).

Clifford A. Wilson, *Rocks, Relics and Biblical Reliability* (Grand Rapids: Zondervan Publishing House, 1977). A brief and useful treatment of archaeology's contribution to the Bible by a leading Australian maximalist scholar. Great for students.

Donald J. Wiseman and Edwin Yamauchi, *Archaeology and the Bible: An Introductory Study* (Grand Rapids: Zondervan Publishing House, 1979). A British and American maximalist present a brief (non-pictorial) survey of the subject. Good for students.

Edwin Yamauchi, *The Stones and the Scriptures: An Introduction to Biblical Archaeology* (New York: J.B. Lippincott Co., 1972). Christian maximalist presentation by a leading evangelical biblical scholar.

Biblical Archaeology of Jerusalem

Because of the prominence of Jerusalem in the Bible and the extensive archaeological work done in the city, a number of books devoted especially to its excavation are available.

Ancient Jerusalem Revealed, ed. Hillel Geva (Jerusalem: Israel Exploration Society, 1994). Contributions by Israeli archaeologists concerning excavations in Jeruslaem from 1968-1993.

Dan Bahat with Chaim Rubinstein, *The Illustrated Atlas of Jerusalem* (Jerusalem: Carta, 1990). A major work that illustrates biblical Jerusalem as well as the Jerusalem of other periods based on the latest archaeological discoveries.

W. Harold Mare, *The Archaeology of the Jerusalem Area* (Grand Rapids: Baker Book House, 1987). An excellent popular survey by an evangelical seminary professor and past president of the Near East Archaeological Society.

Hershel Shanks, *Jerusalem: An Archaeological Biography* (New York: Random House, 1995). A beautifully illustrated volume by the editor of the popular magazine *Biblical Archaeology Review*.

Archaeology and the Old Testament

These books are designed for specific areas of biblical studies, primarily in the area of the Old Testament, and provide details that multisubject volumes often overlook.

Charles F. Aling, *Egypt and Bible History: From Earliest Times to 1,000 B.C.* (Grand Rapids: Baker Book House, 1981). Evangelical maximalist treatment of Egyptian history related to the Bible (defends early date).

Trude Dothan and Moshe Dothan, *People of the Sea: The Search for the Philistines* (New York: Macmillan Publishing Company, 1992). A popularly written and well-illustrated archaeological study of the ancient Philistines by Israel's leading authorities on the subject.

Exodus: The Egyptian Evidence, eds. Ernest S. Frerichs and Leonard H. Lasko (Winona Lake, IN: Eisenbrauns, 1997). Presents latest discussion by archaeologists of what evidence can be deduced from the discoveries made in Egypt for the historicity of the Exodus.

Alfred J. Hoerth, *Archaeology and the Old Testament* (Grand Rapids: Baker Book House, 1997). An up-to-date treatment of archaeological discoveries as they relate to the Old Testament. Helpful.

Jack P. Lewis, *Archaeological Backgrounds to Bible People* (Grand Rapids: Baker Book House, 1971). Provides the archaeological evidence supporting and informing significant personalities in the Bible by a leading American evangelical maximalist scholar.

P. Kyle McCarter, Jr., *Ancient Inscriptions: Voices from the Biblical World* (Washington, D.C.: Biblical Archaeology Society). Provides a thorough listing of important inscriptions related to the Bible. Designed to be used with a slide set available from the publisher.

T.C. Mitchell, *The Bible in the British Museum: Interpreting the Evidence* (London: British Museum Publications, 1990). Helpful survey of the most significant discoveries related to the Bible, looking specifically at artifacts housed in the British Museum.

Archaeology of the New Testament

Archaeological information of the New Testament period has increased dramatically in the past decades, yet few biblical students have accessed this vital research. The following works present the latest discoveries from the field and their contribution to New Testament studies.

E.M. Blaiklock, *The Archaeology of the New Testament* (Grand Rapids: Zondervan Publishing House, 1974). A brief evangelical maximalist survey written in popular style.

Jack Finegan, *The Archaeology of the New Testament: The Life of Jesus and the Beginning of the Early Church,* rev. ed. (New Jersey: Princeton University Press, 1978). A site-by-site study of archaeological discoveries pertinent to the New Testament by a leading nonevangelical scholar.

John McRay, *Archaeology and the New Testament* (Grand Rapids: Baker Book House, 1991). Up-to-date, thorough presentation of archaeological discoveries related to the New Testament by one of America's leading evangelical maximalist scholars.

William Stephens, *The New Testament World in Pictures* (Nashville: Broadman Press, 1987). A large collection of black-and-white archaeological and site photographs compiled by the past editor of the *Biblical Illustrator.*

Archaeology and the Historical Jesus

These books represent some of the best recent works that present archaeological discoveries in relation to putting together a more accurate portrayal of Jesus within the context of first-century Judaism.

James H. Charlesworth, *Jesus Within Judaism: New Light from Exciting Archaeological Discoveries,* The Anchor Bible Reference Library (New York: Doubleday, 1988).

Eschatology, Messianism and the Dead Sea Scrolls, eds. Craig Evans and Peter Flint (Grand Rapids: Wm. B. Eerdmans Publishing Co., 1997). This first volume in the new series *Studies in the Dead Sea Scrolls and Related Literature* presents a collection of scholarly articles for popular readers.

Jesus and the Dead Sea Scrolls, ed. James H. Charlesworth (New York: Doubleday, 1992). This volume in the Anchor Bible Reference Library presents evidence for the historical Jesus, aids to the interpretation of parables, and discusses the background of social and religious controversies related to the research on the Dead Sea literature.

J. Randall Price, *Secrets of the Dead Sea Scrolls* (Eugene, OR: Harvest House, 1996). Up-to-date survey of the story, reputed scandal, and most recent excavations related to the Dead Sea Scrolls. Sections deal with the New Testament, Jesus, perceptions about the Messiah and other related theological concepts, and the Temple.

John J. Rosseau and Rami Arav, *Jesus and His World: An Archaeological and Cultural Dictionary* (Minneapolis: Fortress Press, 1995). Most up-to-date treatment of the New Testament world by an American and Israeli archaeologists of the minimalist viewpoint.

John Wilkinson, *The Jerusalem Jesus Knew: An Archaeological Guide to the Gospels* (Nashville: Thomas Nelson Publishers, 1978). A very useful presentation of the biblical archaeology of Jerusalem in the New Testament period by the director of the British School of Archaeology in Jerusalem.

Biblical Archaeology References

These resources represent the most complete source for information about archaeological excavations and assist Bible students in interpreting the important facts as they relate to biblical issues.

Gonzalo Báez-Camargo, *Archaeological Commentary on the Bible* (New York: Doubleday & Co., 1984). Archaeological discoveries in relation to the Bible are given selectively book by book and verse by verse.

Craig S. Keener, *The IVP Bible Background Commentary* (Downers Grove, IL: InterVarsity Press, 1993, 1999). Results of archaeological research are applied in providing cultural background to every verse of the Bible. New Testament complete (1993); complete Old Testament being released (1999).

The New Encyclopedia of Archaeological Discoveries in the Holy Land, ed. Ephraim Stern, 4 volumes (Jerusalem: Carta / The Israel Exploration Society, 1993). The most up-to-date and complete account of excavations in Israel and Jordan, usually by the site excavators themselves.

The New International Dictionary of Biblical Archaeology, eds. E.M. Blaiklock, R.K. Harrison (Grand Rapids: Zondervan Publishing

House, 1983). Articles by leading scholars who support the maximalist viewpoint.

The Oxford Encyclopedia of Archaeology in the Near East, ed. Eric M. Meyers (Oxford: University Press, 1996). Prepared under the auspices of the American Schools of Oriental Research, this five-volume work includes 1,125 articles written by 550 international scholars. The advantage of this set is that it covers sites and regions outside the Holy Land, and therefore not covered in the encyclopedia listed above.

Biblical Archaeology Magazines

Keep the latest in archaeological research and excavation coming to you at home with a subscription to one of these magazines. Very few local libraries carry these titles, but might if requested. There are specialized journals on various fields of biblical archaeology from the Dead Sea Scrolls to Ebla. Check with a major university library or seminary for titles.

Archaeology in the Biblical World (annually). Published by the Near East Archaeological Society. Evangelical-Christian maximalist orientation to biblical archaeology by field archaeologists and teachers of biblical studies. For subscription, contact: NEAS, 29528 Madera Ave., Shafter, CA 93263.

Bible and Spade (quarterly). Evangelical-Christian maximalist orientation to biblical archaeology published by Associates for Biblical Research. For subscription, contact: P.O. Box 125, Ephrata, PA 17522.

Bible Review (bi-monthly). A sister publication to *Biblical Archaeology Review*, popular—focuses on biblical studies as informed by archaeology. Order from same address as *Biblical Archaeology Review*.

Biblical Archaeologist (quarterly). Popular publication published by the American Schools of Oriental Research for more serious students of archaeology. For subscription, contact: ASOR, 126 Inman St., Cambridge, MA 02139

Biblical Archaeology Review (bi-monthly). Best popular full-color biblical archaeology magazine. Order from: P.O. Box 7026, Red Oak, IA 51591-2026. For subscription information in the U.S. call: 1-800-678-5555.

Biblical Illustrator (Southern Baptist Convention). Helpful and colorfully illustrated articles on Bible characters, events, and customs based on archaeological discoveries. For subscription, contact: Customer Service, 127 Ninth Ave. North, Nashville, TN 37234-0113, 1-800-458-2772.

Internet Sites

Biblical archaeology is flourishing on the web. Check out these sites, as well as posted archaeological link sites. Some excavations in progress maintain a website (see for example: Hazor) and many of the museums we have listed have a website offering a virtual tour of their exhibits. You will also find a website for the archaeological magazines we have listed as well as for publishers of biblical archaeological resources, such as Eisenbrauns.

http://averbury.arch.soton.ac.uk/Journal/journal.html—Electronic journal of archaeology that features section on biblical archaeology.

kps1@cornell.edu—Source of information for opportunities in archaeological fieldwork.

http://www.bridgesforpeace.com/bfpfood.htm—Website of Bridges for Peace, located in Jerusalem, featuring the latest reports of archaeology in Israel.

http://www.christiananswers.net/abr/abrhome.html—Website of Associates for Biblical Research, featuring biblical archaeology and the organization's report on its own archaeological excavations.

http://www.eden.rutgers.edu/~stiegld/links.html—Virtual archaeology library on the web; excellent resource.

http://www.indiana.edu/~librcsd/resource/humanities/religion/bibl e.html—Indiana University professor Jack Abercrombie presents a database from excavations that depicts the material culture of the ancient Canaanites and Israelites and related peoples.

http://www.lpl.arizona.edu/kmeyers/archaeol/bib arch.html—A collection of resources pertaining to biblical archaeology.

http://www.plu.edu/~oakmande/context/ptj.html—Kenneth Hanson and Douglas Oakman present archaeological data informing the theme "Palestine in the Time of Jesus: Social Institutions and Social Conflicts."

Videos

The Archaeology of Jerusalem: From David to Jesus (Biblical Archaeology Society).

Biblical Archaeology from the Ground Down (Biblical Archaeology Society).

Secrets of the Dead Sea Scrolls (Harvest House Publishers).

The Stones Cry Out (Harvest House Publishers).

NOTES

Preface

1. Benjamin Disraeli, *Letters* (1832).

2. Interview with William Dever by Hershel Shanks, "Is the Bible Right After All?" Interview with William Dever (Part 2), *Biblical Archaeology Review* 22:5 (September/October 1996): 74.

3. This, of course, is not entirely the case. Better-known examples which continue to have either departments of or offer regular courses in "biblical" archaeology include Wheaton College as an example of a Christian school. Some historic secular universities such as the University of Chicago, Harvard, Princeton, and the University of Wisconsin (Madison) also continue to have departments that teach biblical archaeology. Jewish schools, such as Hebrew Union College and the Hebrew University, of course maintain Institutes of Archaeology and are primary training facilities for such.

4. This experience includes a brief student involvement with the City of David excavations directed by Yigael Shiloh (1979); work at the Shrine of the Book, the Museum of the Dead Sea Scrolls (1979-1980); field work and ceramic analysis with the University of Texas at Austin's excavations at Tel-Yin'am, directed by Harold Liebowitz (1990-1991); and as assistant to James Strange as director of excavation on the Qumran Plateau (1997). Most of my involvement, however, has been with the archaeologists themselves by way of my own research and writing, although I have also taught courses on biblical archaeology at various Bible colleges.

Introduction: An Invitation to Hear the Stones

1. As cited in *Bible and Spade* (1972), © 1959 by the Rodeheaver Company.

Chapter 1—*The Adventure of Archaeology*

1. As cited in E.M. Blaiklock, *Out of the Earth: The Witness of Archaeology to the New Testament* (London: Paternoster Press, 1957), p. 10.

2. John Daniszewski, "Undersea world of Cleopatra revealed: Submerged ancient Alexandria gradually is uncovered by archaeologists," *Austin American Statesman*, March 16, 1997, A25.

3. "Archaeologists find ruins of Cleopatra's palace," Associated Press report, *San Antonio Express & News*, November 3, 1996.

4. For more details on these discoveries, see "Alexander's Lighthouse Found, But Will Its Library Disappear?: Ancient Wonders of the World Rediscovered," *Biblical Archaeology Review* 23:3 (May/June 1997): 14.

5. "Tunip-Tessup of Tikunai: A 3,500 Year-Old Cuneiform Inscription from a Syrian Kingdom May Tell Us Who the Habiru Were," *Biblical Archaeology Review* 22:6 (November/December 1996): 22.

6. Personal correspondence, March 1997.

7. "Snakes didn't always slither," *U.S. News & World Report*, April 28, 1997, p. 14.

8. Bonnie Rochman, "The Missing Link?: Rare Tombs Could Provide Evidence of Jerusalem Essenes," *Biblical Archaeological Review* 23:4 (July/August 1997): 20-21.

9. Cited by M. Larsen in "Orientalism and the Ancient Near East," *Culture and History 2* (1987), p. 96.

10. W.F. Albright, *The Archaeology of Palestine,* rev. ed. (Harmondsworth, Middlesex: Pelican Books, 1960), p. 128.

11. Donald J. Wiseman, *Illustrations from Biblical Archaeology* (London: The Tyndale Press, 1958), p. 5.

12. Writers such as Zuallart, Footwyck, and Rauwolf in the sixteenth century left notices of the topography and monuments of the Holy Land. In the seventeenth century, Pietro della Valle preserved some valuable archaeological information. In 1714 the Dutch scholar, Adrian Reland, published the most important archaeological work till his time: *Palestine Illustrated by Ancient Monuments;* and in 1743 Bishop Pocoke first published systematic plans of sites and inscriptions.

13. Interview with Bryant Wood, New Orleans, Louisiana, November 25, 1996.

Chapter 2—*Digging for Answers*

1. *Benchmarks in Time and Culture: An Introduction to Palestinian Archaeology, Essays in Honor of Joseph A. Callaway* (Atlanta, GA: 1988), p. 3.

2. This concept was preserved in mystical Judaism and continues in the hassidic movement of today. At the time of this writing (1997) a mystical phrase coined by a splinter group of Bratslav hassidim has appeared on bumper stickers, building graffiti, roadside signs—almost everywhere. The ubiquitous phrase is "Na-Nah-Nahma-Nahman me Uman," which has no translation but is believed by members of this group to be a "mantra of divine origin. . .endowed with great spiritual power." Jeremy Shere, "A Rebbe Nahman Story," *Jerusalem Post* international edition (February 22, 1997), p. 18.

3. Interview with Amihai Mazar, Institute of Archaeology, Jerusalem, October 1996.

4. Interview with Amihai Mazar, October 1996.

5. Interview with Bryant Wood, New Orleans, November 1996.

6. Interview with Bryant Wood, November 1996.

7. Gonzalo Báez-Camargo, *Archaeological Commentary on the Bible* (New York: Doubleday & Company, Inc., 1984), p. xxii.

8. Interview with Amihai Mazar, Institute of Archaeology, Jerusalem, October 1996.

9. For a full discussion of this practice and the Gospel passages, *see* Bryon McCane, "Let the Dead Bury Their Own Dead": Secondary Burial and Matthew 8:21-22," *Harvard Theological Review* 83 (1990): 31-43.

10. For a complete explanation of this concept and practice *see* Eric Meyers, *Jewish Ossuaries: Rebural and Rebirth* (Rome: Pontifical Biblical Institute, 1971), and "The Theological Implications of Ancient Jewish Burial Custom," *Jewish Quarterly Review* 62 (1971-72): 95-119.

11. This is a modified version of that given by Gordon Franz, "Let the Dead Bury Their Own Dead (Matthew 8:22; Luke 9:60)," *Archaeology and Biblical Research* 5:2 (Spring 1992): 57.

12. A. Momigliano, "Biblical Studies and Classical Studies: Simple Reflections about Historical Methods," *Biblical Archaeologist* 45 (1982): 224.

13. Interview with Amihai Mazar, Institute of Archaeology, Jerusalem, October 1996.

14. Edwin Yamauchi, *The Stones and the Scriptures* (Grand Rapids: Baker Books, 1981).

Chapter 3—*Digs That Made a Difference*

1. Nelson Glueck, *Rivers in the Desert: A History of the Negev* (New York: Farrar, Straus and Cudahy, 1959), p. ix.

2. As cited in E.M. Blaiklock, *The Archaeology of the New Testament* (Grand Rapids: Zondervan Publishing House, 1970), p. vi.

3. Two excellent sources for further study on hieroglyphics are: W. Vivian Davies, *Egyptian Hieroglyphics,* Reading the Past Series, volume 6 (Berkeley: University of California Press, 1987), and Karl-Theodor Zauzich, *Hieroglyphs Without Mystery,* translated and adapted by Ann Macy Roth (Austin: University of Texas Press, 1992).

4. For more information on the Rosetta Stone see the booklet *The Rosetta Stone* (London: Department of Assyrian and Egyptian Antiquities of the British Museum) and P. Kyle McCarter, Jr., *Ancient Inscriptions* (Washington: Biblical Archaeology Society, 1997), pp. 35-39.

5. For more information on the Behistun monument see George G. Cameron, "Darius Carved History on Ageless Rock," *National Geographic* 98:6 (December 1950), pp. 825-44.

6. For details on this discovery and its content, see W.G. Lambert and A.R. Millard, *Altra-Hasis: The Babylonian Story of the Flood* (Oxford University Press, 1969); and A.R. Millard, "A New Babylonian 'Genesis' Story," *Tyndale Bulletin* 18 (1967): 3-18. For the translation with commentary of the Enuma Elish see Alexander Heidel, *The Babylonian Genesis: The Story of Creation* (Chicago: the University of Chicago Press, 1951).

7. For a thorough treatment of the ancient Near Eastern parallels from an evangelical perspective see John H. Walton, *Ancient Israelite Literature in Its Cultural Setting: A Survey of Parallels Between Biblical and Ancient Near Eastern Texts* (Grand Rapids: Zondervan Publishing House, 1989).

8. *See* Tikva Frymer-Kensky, "What the Babylonian Flood Stories Can and Cannot Teach Us About the Genesis Flood," *Biblical Archaeology Review* (November/December 1978).

9. Even if the structure of these Mesopotamian narratives are similar to that displayed in Genesis 1–11, this simply could be the result of using an accepted literary convention of the times.

10. A.R. Millard, "A New Babylonian 'Genesis' Story," *Tyndale Bulletin* 18 (1967): 17-18.

11. *See* P.J. Wiseman, *Clues to Creation in Genesis,* ed. D.J. Wiseman (London: Marshall, Morgan & Scott, 1977), pp. 143-52.

Chapter 4—*More Digs That Made a Difference*

1. *Archaeology and Old Testament Study*, ed. by Winton Thomas (Oxford: Clarendon Press, 1967), p. xxiii.

2. For examples there is a wall painting of a tribute-bearing delegation for a Thebean tomb dating to the reign of Amenhotep III (fifteenth century B.C.). In the painting, high-ranking and wealthy Canaanites are portrayed wearing varigated robes with unusually long sleeves (*see also* 2 Samuel 13:18). By giving Joseph such a garment, Jacob was possibly identifying him with the great kings of the land over which Joseph's dream told him he would one day rule.

3. Jehu is here called "the son of Omri." Was the Assyrian account or the Bible wrong? There are two possible solutions: 1) Because of Omri's prominence, the Assyrians used his dynastic eponymn for Israel and her rulers. Some Assyrian texts indicate that the term "son of Omri" was only a shorter way of writing "son of the house of Omri" or "Israelite." 2) Jehu was really a descendant of the "house of Omri" from a different branch than Ahab. The Bible is careful to note that Jehu is called upon to destroy "the house of Ahab" rather than the "house of Omri" of which he himself was a member. *See* Tammy Schneider, "Did King Jehu Kill His Own Family?: New Interpretation Reconciles Biblical Text with Famous Assyrian Inscription," *Biblical Archaeology Review* 21:1 (January/February 1995): 26-33, 80,82).

4. It should be noted that some scholars contend that the figure is an emissary of Jehu since the Assyrian text speaks only of the tribute of Jehu, and the king himself would not have been required unless there was compelling reason.

5. *See* David Ussishkin, "Answers at Lachish," *Biblical Archaeology Review* 5:6 (November/December 1979): 16:39.

6. For additional information on this discovery see Johannes Lehman, *The Hittites: People of a Thousand Gods* (New York: The Viking Press, 1975), and A. Kempinski, "Hittites in the Bible: What Does Archaeology Say?" *Biblical Review* 5 (1979): 21-45.

7. For further study on the history and significance of Ebla, see Chaim Bermant and Michael Weitzman, *Ebla: A Revelation in Archaeology* (New York: Times Books, 1979), and Giovanni Pettinato, *The Archives of Ebla: An Empire Inscribed in Clay* (New York: Doubleday & Co., 1981).

Chapter 5—*The Patriarchs*

1. G. Ernest Wright, *Biblical Archaeology*, abridged ed. (Philadelphia: Westminster Press, 1960), p. 21.

2. While Albright had sought to defend the historicity of the Patriarchs, two American scholars—Thomas L. Thompson and J. Van Seters—who had followed Wellhausen's theory led the attack on Albright's methods and of historicity. Not all critical theory scholars have rejected all historicity, but, like British archaeologists Kathleen Kenyon and Ronald Hendel, some accept the preservation of historical memories in aspects of the Patriarchal stories while denying there was ever a "Patriarchal period." Most critical scholars would agree that the biblical text includes authentic details from the second millennium (1200–1000 B.C.) which were transmitted orally and recorded much later. (*See* Kathleen Kenyon, *The Bible and Recent Archaeology*, p. 20; Ronald S. Hendel, "Finding Historical Memories in the Patriarchal Narratives," *Biblical Archaeology Review* (July/August 1995): 52-59, 70-71. Conservative scholars, as well as some critical scholars, such as Noel David Freedman and James Sauer, however, believe that a third-millennium date for the Patriarchs is valid.

3. Ronald F. Youngblood, *The Book of Genesis: An Introductory Commentary*, 2d ed. (Grand Rapids: Baker Book House, 1991), pp. 285-86.

4. Nahum N. Sarna, "The Patriarchs," *Genesis: World of Myths and Patriarchs*, ed. Ada Feyerick (New York: University Press, 1996).

5. Two reappraisals of patriarchal historicity which advanced the minimalist position were Thomas L. Thompson, *Historicity of the Patriarchal Narratives: The Quest for the Historical Abraham* (Berlin: de Gruyter, 1974), and John Van Seters, *Abraham in History and Tradition* (New Haven, CT: Yale University Press, 1975).

6. For an analysis of the minimalists' criticism of the Nuzi materials that supports this conclusion *see* Duane Garrett, *Rethinking Genesis: The Sources and Authorship of the First Book of the Pentateuch* (Grand Rapids: Baker Book House, 1991), pp. 70-79.

7. For example, Kenneth Barker, in examining the Nuzi parallels available to him, found only one completely wrong in agreement with Thompson. *See* Kenneth Barker, "The Antiquity of the Patriarchal Narratives," *A Tribute to Gleason Archer: Essays on the Old Testament*, eds. W.C. Kaiser, R. F. Youngblood (Chicago: Moody Press, 1986), p. 135.

8. For a defense of this position *see* Duane Garrett, *Rethinking Genesis: The Sources and Authorship of the First Book of the Pentateuch* (Grand Rapids: Baker Book House, 1991), pp. 83-86.

9. Kenneth A. Kitchen, "The Patriarchal Age: Myth or History?" *Biblical Archaeology Review* 21:2 (March/April 1995) 48-57, 88-95.

10. *See* James A. Sauer, "Holocene Climate Change and the Domestication of Beasts of Burden," *Fifth International Conference on the History and Archaeology of Jordan*, Irbid, Jordan (Spring 1992), John J. Davis, "The Camel in Biblical Narratives," *A Tribute to Gleason Archer: Essays on the Old Testament* (Chicago: Moody Press, 1986), pp. 141-15; A.R. Millard, "Methods of Studying the Patriarchal Narratives as Ancient Texts," *Essays on the Patriarchal Narratives*, ed. A.R. Millard, D.J. Wiseman (Leichester: InterVarsity Press, 1980), pp. 49-50.

11. *See* James B. Pritchard, ed., *Ancient Near Eastern Texts*, 3d ed. (Chicago: University Press, 1976), p. 543; for discussion *see* M.J. Selman, "Comparative Customs and the Patriarchal Age," *Essays on the Patriarchal Narratives*, eds. A.R. Millard, D.J. Wiseman (Leicester: InterVarsity Press, 1980), p. 107.

12. *See* James B. Pritchard, ed., *Ancient Near Eastern Texts*, 3d ed. (Chicago: University Press, 1976), p. 545; for discussion see Kenneth A. Kitchen, *The Bible in Its World* (Downers Grove, IL: InterVarsity Press, 1977), p. 70.

13. *See* M.J. Selman, "The Social Environment of the Patriarchs," *Tyndale Bulletin* 27 (1976): 114-36; "Comparative Customs and the Patriarchal Narratives," *Themelios* 3 (1962): 239-48.

14 *See* Kenneth A. Kitchen, "The Patriarchal Age: Myth or History?" *Biblical Archaeology Review* 21:2 (March/April 1995): 90, 92. Ronald Hendel argues against Kitchen that this type of name is perfectly normal through all periods of Northwest Semitic—see "Finding Historical Memories in the Patriarchal Narratives," *Biblical Archaeology Review* 21:4 (July/August 1995): 57.

15. According to Joshua 91:47, it was also known as Leshem.

16. According to it excavator, Avraham Biran, the reason it was preserved "was not because of anything that we did, it appears that the people in antiquity, for some reason or the other, the people of Laish, the Canaanites who lived in Laish, had decided that the gate was of no use so they blocked it and filled it with earth and then they covered it. So all the steps that led into the city were covered with the natural soil of the area so all that we did was simply to remove the earth and to uncover the construction both of the steps and here's another stone construction which was probably an embarkment holding, protecting the gate. Maybe there was something wrong in the structure. We found a crack in the tower and maybe that was reason they decided to abolish the gate and to open up another gate somewhere else" (Interview at Hebrew Union College Skirball Museum, Jerusalem, October 12, 1996).

17. Interview with Avraham Biran, Skirball Museum, Jerusalem (October 12, 1996).

18. Roland Hendel, "Finding Historical Memories in the Patriarchal Narratives," *Biblical Archaeology Review* 21:4 (July/August 1995): 58.

19. James A. Sauer, "A Climatic and Archaeological View of the Early Biblical Traditions," *Scripture and Other Artifacts: Essays on the Bible and Archaeology in Honor of Philip J. King*, eds. M.D. Coogan, J.C. Exum, L. Stage (Louisville, KY: Westminster John Knox Press, 1994), pp. 366-98.

20. Ibid., p. 391.

21. *See* H.B. Huffmon, *Amorite Personal Names in the Mari Texts* (Chicago: University of Chicago Press, 1965), pp. 128-29.

22. Gerhard von Rad, *Genesis: A Commentary,* trans. John H. Marks (Philadelphia: Westminster Press, 1961), p. 171.

23. *See* Kenneth A. Kitchen, "The Patriarchal Age: Myth or History?" *Biblical Archaeology Review* 21:2 (March/April 1995): 56.

24. *See The International Standard Bible Encyclopedia*, s.v. "Arioch," by R.K. Harrison (Grand Rapids, Wm. B. Eerdmans Publishing Co., 1982): 290. Gerhard von Rad, *Genesis: A Commentary*, trans. John H. Marks (Philadelphia: Westminster Press, 1961), p. 171, believes that this is the same person!

25. Kenneth A. Kitchen, *Ancient Orient and the Old Testament* (Chicago: InterVarsity Press, 1966), pp. 44.

26. For these examples see *Cambridge Ancient History*, eds. J. Boardman, I.E.S. Edwards, et al., 3d ed. (Cambridge University Press, 1973), pp. 272, 820-821; II/2 (1975), p. 1041; and III/2 (1991), p. 748.

27. Gerhard von Rad, *Genesis: A Commentary*, trans. John H. Marks (Philadelphia: Westminister Press, 1961), p. 171.

28. *See* John C. Studenroth, "Archaeology and the higher Criticism of Genesis 14," *Evidence for Faith: Deciding the God Question*, ed. John Warwick Montgomery (Dallas: Probe Books, 1991), pp. 159, 162.

29. *See* Kitchen, *Ancient Orient and the Old Testament*, pp. 46, 73; "The Patriarchal Age: Myth or History?" *Biblical Archaeology Review* 21:2 (March/April 1995): 57.

30. *See* Bruce Vawter, *On Genesis: A New Reading* (Garden City, NY: Doubleday, 1997), p. 188. A.E. Speiser, *Genesis, Anchor Bible* (Garden City, NY: Doubleday, 1983), pp. 107-08.

31. For the details supporting these conclusions, *see* Gordon J. Wenham, *Genesis 1-15, Word Biblical Commentary* (Waco, TX: Word Books, 1987), pp. 318-20.

32. The ancient name indicates that the town was originally divided into four (arba) quarters or districts, although Joshua 14:15 states that the name Arba was given to the town because of a renown member of the Anakim. It was also called Mamre. Some of the various locations identified with the city were known as Elonei ("oaks of") Mamre, the Eschol, and the (Cave of) Machpelah (facing Mamre).

33 Several entrances into the cave were reported from medieval times: Ali of Herat in 1192, Ishak al Khalil in 1351, and Mujir ad-Din in 1496, although their information is somewhat different than what the modern exploration revealed.

34. *See* Nancy Miller, "Patriarchal Burial Site Explored for the First Time in 700 Years," *Biblical Archaeology Review* 11:3 (May/June 1985) 26-43.

35. Another theory on the origin of the structures was expressed to me by Hillel Geva, who would date them as late as the Byzantine period.

36. *See* Cleremont-Ganneau, *Archaeological Researches in Palestine* 2 (1873-74): 278.

37. Nogah Hareuveni, *Desert and Shepherd in Our Biblical Heritage*, trans. Helen Frenkley (Tel Aviv: Neot Kedumim—The Biblical Landscape Reserve in Israel, 1991), pp. 64-73.

Chapter 6—*Sodom and Gomorrah*

1. G. Ernest Wright, *Biblical Archaeology*, abridged ed. (Philadelphia: Westminister Press, 1960), p. ix.

2. David Neev and K.O. Emery, *The Destruction of Sodom, Gomorrah, and Jericho: Geological, Climatological, and Archaeological Background* (New York: Oxford University Press, 1995).

3. Ronald S. Hendel, "Reviews," *Biblical Archaeology Review* 23:1 (January/February 1997): 70.

4. The first-century historian Flavius Josephus wrote extensively about Sodom and Gomorrah (*Ant.* 1:170-206) as did Philo (*Somn.* 2:192; *Abr.* 227, 228; *Congr.* 92; 109). Extrabiblical Jewish literature also include frequent references to the cities, such as the Dead Sea Scrolls (*1QapGen* 21:5ff.; 21:23-22:25), *3 Macc.* 2:5; *Sir.* 16:7; *Ab.* 6:13; *Apoc. Ezra* 2:19; 7:12; *T. Levi* 14:6; *T. Naph.* 3:4; 4:1; *T. Ash.* 7:1; *T. Benj.* 9:1; *Targ. Pseudo-Jonathan* on Genesis 18:20-21; TB *Sanh.* 109a,b).

5. *See also* for geographic references: Strabo, *Geographia* 16.2.44; *Eusebius Onomasticon* 42.1-5; Josephus, *Antiquities* 1:174; 4:85; 9:7; Diodorus, *Biblical History* 19:98; Tacitus, *History* 5.7; Pliny *HN* 5.71ff.

6. E. Meyer, *Die Israliten und ihre Nachbarstämme* (Halle: Max Niemeyer, 1906).

7. Charles Pellegrino, *Return to Sodom and Gomorrah: Bible Stories from Archaeologists* (New York: Random House, 1994), p. 180.

8. *See* W.F. Albright, "The Jordan Valley in the Bronze Age," *Annual of the American Schools of Oriental Research* 6:13-74.

9. *See* R.E. Baney, *The Search for Sodom and Gomorrah* (Kansas City, MO: CAM, 1962).

10. W.F. Albright, T*he Archaeology of Palestine and the Bible*, 3d ed. (New York: Fleming H. Revell, 1935): 135-36; D. Neev and K.O. Emery, "The Dead Sea: Depositional Processes and Environments of Evaporites," *Ministry of Development-Geological Survey*, Bulletin 41 (Jerusalem: Geological Survey of Israel, 1967): 30.

11. For the published reports of these excavations, see W.E. Rast and R.T. Schaub, "Survey of the Southeastern Plain of the Dead Sea," *Annual of the Department of Antiquities of Jordan* (Hashemite Kingdom of Jordan, Department of Antiquities, 1973), 19:5-54, 175-85. For a more popular review see the articles based on these reports in *Bible and Spade* (Summer 1974, Winter 1977, Summer/Autumn 1980, Winter/Spring 1983, and Autumn 1988).

12. Interview with Bryant Wood, New Orleans, November, 1996.

13 F.G. Clapp, "The Site of Sodom and Gomorrah," *American Journal of Archaeology* 40 (1936): 323-44.

14. *See* J. Donahue, "Geological Investigations at Early Bronze Sites," *Annual of the American Schools of Oriental Research* 46 (1981): 140-41; and J.R. Harlan, "Natural Resources of the Southern Ghor," *Annual of the American Schools of Oriental Research* 46 (1981): 155-59.

15. As noted by Willem C. van Hattem in his article, "Once Again: Sodom and Gomorrah," *Biblical Archaeologist* 44:2 (Spring 1981): 89.

16. Thomas L. Thompson, *The Historicity of the Patriarchal Narratives*, Beihefte zur Zeitschrift für die Alttestamentliche Wissenschaft 133 (Berlin: De Gruyter, 1974), p. 328.

17. *See* Alfonso Archi, "The Epigraphic Evidence from Ebla and the Old Testament," *Biblica* 60 (1979): 555-66, "Further concerning Ebla and the Bible," *Biblical Archaeologist* 44:3 (Summer

1981): 151-52; Mitchell Dahood, "Ebla, Ugarit and the Bible," *The Archives of Ebla: An Empire Inscribed in Clay*, ed. G. Pettinato (New York: Doubleday, 1981), pp. 271-303.

18. *See* Walter E. Rast, "Bab edh-Dhra and the Origin of the Sodom Saga," *Archaeology and Biblical Interpretation: Essays in Memory of D. Glenn Rose*, eds. L.G. Perdue, L.E. Toombs, G.L. Johnson (Atlanta, GA: John Knox Press, 1987), pp. 194-97.

19. In biblical Hebrew (written only consonants), *Gomorrah* is written as *'mr* (the mark ' representing the Hebrew consonant known as *'ayin*). The Arabic consonants are *nmr*. In the process of changing from Hebrew to Arabic, the laryngal *'ayin* was nasalized as "*n*." This is a common phenomena that is observed for initial laryngals in a word's development or when it is brought over into another language or dialect. Therefore, it is possible that Hebrew *'mr* became the Arabic *nmr*.

20. Walter E. Rast and Thomas R. Schaub, "Expedition to the Dead Sea," *American Schools of Oriental Research Newsletter* 3-4 (October/November 1975): 2-3.

21. Interview with Bryant Wood, New Orleans, November 1996.

Chapter 7—*The Exodus*

1. A.R. Millard, *The Bible B.C.: What Can Archaeology Prove?* (Phillipsburg, NJ: Presbyterian & Reformed, 1977), p. 21.

2. As cited in Charles E. Sellier and Brian Russell, *Ancient Secrets of the Bible* (New York: Dell Publishing, 1994), pp. 179-80.

3. N.P. Lemche, *Early Israel* (Leiden: E.J. Brill, 1985), p. 409.

4. G.W. Ahlström, *Who Were the Israelites?* (Winona Lake, IN: Eisenbrauns, 1986), p. 46.

5. Attempts to match gods of the Egyptian pantheon with the plagues have resulted in some of the following associations: 1) Nile gods—Hapi (Apis), Khnum, Isis; 2) Frog diety—Heqet; 3) Gnats—Set, god of the desert; 4) Flies—Re, Uatchit; 5) Livestock—Hathor, Apis; 6) Boils—Sekhmet, Sunu, Isis; 7) Hail—Nut, Osiris, Set; 8) Locusts—Nut, Osiris; 9) Darkness—Re, Horus, Nut, Hathor; 10) Death of firstborn—Min, Heqet, Isis. *See* further, Pierre Montet, *Egypt and the Bible* (Philadelphia: Fortress Press, 1968).

6. This relationship was especially connected with pharaohs Thutmose III and his son Amenhotep II (the early-date pharaohs). Both Egyptian theology and their military accomplishments gave them the status of "the sovereign god(s) of heaven and earth."

7. *See* H. Frankfort, K*ingship and the Gods* (Chicago: University of Chicago Press, 1948), p. 5; *Ancient Egyptian Religion* (New York: Columbia University Press, 1948), p. 30; I. Engnell, *Studies in Divine Kingship in the Ancient Near East* (Oxford: Basil Blackwell, 1967), pp. 4-15.

8. *See* F.W. Read, *Egyptian Religion and Ethics* (London: Watts & Co., 1925), pp. 110-11.

9. For the full documentation of this ritual, see A. Hermann, "Das steinhartes Herz," *Jahrbuch für Antike und Christentum* 4 (Munster: Aschendorffsche Verlagsbuchandlung, 1961), pp. 102-3.

10. *See* James E. Harris and Kent R. Weeks, *X-Raying the Pharaohs* (New York: Charles Scribner's Sons, 1973), p. 49 (photo).

11. For other incantations, *see* J. Zandee, *Death As an Enemy* (Leiden: E.J. Brill, 1960), pp. 259-62.

12. *See* further, E.A.W. Budge, *Egyptian Magic* (London: K. Paul, Trench, Tribner & Co., 1899), pp. 35-37.

13. For a complete analysis and defense of this position in the Exodus plague narratives see Gregory K. Beale, "The Exodus Hardening Motif of YHWH as a Polemic," Th.M. thesis, Dallas Theological Seminary (Dallas, Texas, 1976), especially pp. 46-52.

14. Leon T. Wood, "Date of the Exodus," *New Perspectives on the Old Testament* (Waco, TX: Word Books, 1970), pp. 66-87; Walter Kaiser, "Exodus," *Expositor's Bible Commentary*, 2 (Grand Rapids: Zondervan Publishing Co., 1983), pp. 288-91.

15. Edwin R. Thiele, *The Mysterious Numbers of the Hebrew Kings* (Grand Rapids: Zondervan Publishing House, 1983).

16. This has recently been revised by E.W. Faulstich (based on the research of Oliver R. Blosser) to an earlier 1461 B.C. date based on the use of new computerized astonomical and calendar conversion program. *See* E.W. Faulstich, *History, Harmony and the Hebrew Kings* (Spencer, IA: Chronology Books, 1986), pp. 196-200.

17. *See* R.A. Parker, "Once Again, the Coregency of Thutmose III and Amenhotep II," *Studies in Honor of John A. Wilson* (1969).

18. *See* Willam H. Shea, "A New Reading for Gerster's Protosinaitic Inscription No. 1 and the Identification of the Pharaohs of the Exodus," and "Findings from the Wadi Nasb in Sinai Which Illuminate Events of the Exodus," unpublished papers (Silver Spring, MD: The Biblical Research Institute, 1997).

19. *See* Cornelis Houtman, *Exodus,* Historical Commentary on the Old Testament (Kampen: Kok Publishing House, 1993), 1:175-79.

20. *See* Donovan Courville, *The Exodus Problem and Its Ramifications*, 2 vols. (Loma Linda, CA: Challenge Books, 1971).

21. J.J. Bimson, "Redating the Exodus and Conquest," *Journal for the Study of the Old Testament Supplement Series* 5 (Sheffield: JSOT Press, 1978).

22. *See* E.W. Faulstich, *Bible Chronology and the Scientific Method: The Old Testament with Secular Synchronisms* (Spencer, IA: Chronology Books, 1990), pp. 118-37. He finds that Moses saw the burning bush on September 27, 1462 B.C., called down the first plague on January 24, 1461 B.C., crossed the Red Sea on April 3, 1461 B.C., and was given the Ten Commandments on May 28, 1461 B.C.

23 E.H. Merrill, *Kingdom of Priests* (Grand Rapids: Baker Book House, 1987), p. 57.

24. John I. Durham, *Exodus,* Word Biblical Commentary (Waco, TX: Word Books, 1987), p. xxiii.

25. There are also proto-Sinaitic inscriptions dating to approximately 1500 B.C. which according to W.F. Albright, demonstrate that Semites did not lose their own language or culture even while serving as slaves in Egypt. See *Proto-Sinaitic Inscriptions and Their Decipherment* (Cambridge: Harvard University Press, 1969).

26. Charles F. Aling, *Egypt and Bible History from Earliest Times to 1000 B.C.* (Grand Rapids: Baker Book House, 1981), p. 103.

27. For the latest research see *Exodus: The Egyptian Evidence,* eds. Ernest S. Frerichs and Leonard H. Lesko (Eisenbrauns, 1997).

28. In this regard I remember the statement made by an Egyptology teacher at the Hebrew University in Jerusalem that "whoever wrote the Torah must have known Egyptian," because many unusual forms and expressions in the Hebrew text made better sense when an original Egyptian word was assumed. One example was the account of pharaoh's daughter "bathing" in the Nile. The Hebrew word translated "bathe" is strange and compares better with the Egyptian word for "wash." In this light, pharaoh's daughter went to wash her clothes at the Nile rather than take a bath (Exodus 2:5).

29. For example, the painting in Beni-Hassan of Asiatics entering Egypt in the tomb of Khnumhotep (early nineteenth century B.C.), and the report of a border guard in the eighth year of Merenpthah that Shasu were allowed entrance to save them and their flocks, see James Prichard, ed., *Ancient Near Eastern Texts*, 3d ed. (New Jersey: Priceton University Press, 1977), 259, 416ff.

30. Hershel Shanks, "An Israelite House in Egypt?" *Biblical Archaeology Review* 19:4 (July/August 1993): 44-45.

31. *See* "The Instruction of Merikare," "The Admonitions of Ipuwer," and "The Prophecy of Neferti" in James Pritchard, ed., *Ancient Near Eastern Texts*, 3d ed. (New Jersey: Priceton University Press, 1977), 416ff., 441ff., 444ff.

32. For example on the outer western wall of the Cour de la Cachette at the Karnak temple in Luxor, Egypt, Egyptologist Frank Yurco discovered a register of hieroglyphic inscriptions that portrayed a captive people called the Shasu that resemble the Israelites. *See* Frank Yurco, "3,200-Year Old Pictures of Israelites Found in Egypt," *Biblical Archaeology Review* 16:5 (September/October 1990): 20-38. For other examples, *see* Kenneth A. Kitchen, "From the Brick-fields of Egypt," *Bible and Spade* 10:2 (Spring 1981): 43-50 [Reprinted from the *Tyndale Bulletin* 27 (1976)]; K.A. Kitchen, *The Bible in Its World: The Bible & Archaeology Today* (Downers Grove, IL: InterVarsity Press, 1977), pp. 75-78.

33. Aside from the classic tale of Sinhue, there are various texts which detail the escape of slaves and publish descriptions for those who might see them and help return them.

34. *See,* for example, the Tell-el-Amarna texts and the Ipuwer papyrus, which provides an account of plagues of blood, cattle disease, fire phenomena, strange darkness similar to those described in the Exodus narrative.

35. *See* the report of Doron Nof and Nathan Paldor in the *Bulletin of the American Meterological Society* (March 1992).

36. This can be substantiated from both archaeological sources and infrared satellite photos which reveal the ancient movements of people from Egypt to Canaan (see reference below).

37. *See* John Walton, *Ancient Israelite Literature in Its Cultural Context: A Survey of Parallels Between Biblical and Ancient Near Eastern Texts* (Grand Rapids: Zondervan Publishing Co., 1989), pp. 95-107; K.A. Kitchen, *The Bible in Its World: The Bible & Archaeology Today* (Downers Grove, IL: InterVarsity Press, 1977), pp. 79-85.

38. *See* the bibliographic reference for Kenyon, Wood, and Waltke in the next chapter.

39. For a popularly written account of this discovery, *see* Trude Dothan, "Lost Outpost of the Egyptian Empire," *National Geographic* 162:6 (December 1982): 739-69.

40. Larry Williams, *The Mountain of Moses* (New York: Wynwood Press, 1990), "Epilogue."

41. *See* Stephen A. Ascough, "Santorini—Exodus—Tell el-Dab'a Project" proposal (1994). The author of the proposal may be contacted at 26 Tiffany Street West, Guelph, Canada N1H 1Y1. The proposal actually includes promise for the entire period from the time of Joseph through the period of the Judges.

42. The theory of a connection between the Santoini eruption and the Exodus has been discussed at length by Egyptologist Hans Goedicke, chairman of the department of Near Eastern Studies at John Hopkins University. *See* Charles R. Krahmallov, "A Critique of Professor Goedicke's Exodus Theories," *Biblical Archaeology Review* 7:5 (September/October 1981): 51ff.; Hershel Shanks, "The Exodus and the Crossing of the Red Sea According to Hans Goedicke," *Biblical Archaeology Review* 7:5 (September/October 1981): 42ff.; Eliezar Oren, "How Not to Create a History of the Exodus—A Critique of Professor Goedicke's Theories," *Biblical Archaeology Review* 7:6 (November/December 1981): 46ff.; Hershel Shanks, "In Defense of Hans Goedicke," *Biblical Archaeology Review* 8:3 (May/June 1982): 48ff. Goedicke believes that three eruptions of the volcano can be documented between the seventeenth and twelfth centuries B.C.

43. The A portion of the Egyptian eighteenth dynasty has been proposed based on a correlation with the late Minoan 1A period.

44. *See Nature* 382 (July 18, 1996), pp. 213-14; *see also* Associated Press article by Matt Crenson, "Evidence backs Exodus story, maverick scholars contend," *San Antonio Express & News* (Saturday, July 27, 1996), B-9.

45. Bryant Wood, "Carbon 14 Testing and the Date of the Destruction of Jericho," *Associates for Biblical Research Newsletter* 28:3 (May/June 1997), p.1.

Chapter 8—*The Conquest*

1. Paul W. Lapp, *Biblical Archaeology and History* (New York: World Publishing, 1969), p. 107.

2. John Garstang and J.B.E. Garstang, *The Story of Jericho* (London: Hodder & Stoughton Ltd., 1940), p. 172.

3. Nadav Na'aman, "The 'Conquest of Canaan' in the Book of Joshua and History," *From Nomadism to Monarchy: Archaeological & Historical Aspects of Early Israel*, eds. Israel Finkelstein and Nadav Na'aman (Jerusalem: Israel Exploration Society, 1994), pp. 222-23.

4. Interview with Amihai Mazar, Institute of Archaeology, The Hebrew University, Jerusalem, October 21, 1996.

5. *See* J. Maxwell Miller and John H. Hayes, *A History of Ancient Israel and Judah* (Philadelphia: Westminster Press, 1986), p. 83, and Bruce Halpern, *The Emergence of Israel in Canaan* (Chico, CA, 1983), pp. 98-99.

6. Interview with Bob Mullins, Jerusalem, October 20, 1996.

7. Albrect Alt, *Essays on Old Testament History and Religion*, trans. R.A. Wilson (Sheffield: JSOT Press, 1989), and D.M. Noth, *The History of Israel*, trans. P.R. Ackroyd (New York: Harper & Row, 1960).

8. *See* G.E. Mendenhall, "Ancient Israel's Hyphenated History," *Palestine in Transition*, eds. D.N. Freeman and D.F. Graf (Sheffield: Almond Press, 1983), and N.K. Gottwald, "The Israelite Settlement as a Social Revolutionary Movement," *Biblical Archaeology Today: Proceedings of the International Congress on Biblical Archaeology, Jerusalem 1984* (Jerusalem: Israel Exploration Society, 1985).

9. *See* I. Finkelstein, "The Emergence of Israel: A Phase in the Cyclic History of Canaan in the Third and Second Millennia BCE," *From Nomadism to Monarchy: Archaeology & Historical Aspects of Early Israel*, eds. I. Finkelstein & Nadav Na'aman (Jerusalem: Israel Exploration Society, 1994), pp. 150-78.

10. *See* William Dever, "Will the Real Israel Please Stand Up?: Archaeology and Israelite Historiography: Part I," *Bulletin of the American Schools of Oriental Research* 297 (1995): 61-80 (esp. p. 65).

11. Interview with Ammon Ben-Tor by Tom McCall, Institute of Archaeology, The Hebrew University of Jerusalem, November, 1996. There is some uncertainty to which destruction Ben-Tor means. The last great destruction by fire at the site was by Tiglath-pileser III in 732 B.C. Stratum IV reveals the evidence of the Assyrian destruction. His last season of excavation, during which he found the palace, was the Late Bronze Canaanite period. Since he describes burning here as well we may imply that he has this period in view.

12. Bryant G. Wood, "Did the Israelites Conquer Jericho?" A New Look at the Archaeological Evidence," *Biblical Archaeological Review* 16:2 (March/April 1990): 44-59, and rebuttal to criticisms in "Dating Jericho's Destruction: Bienkowski Is Wrong on All Counts," *Biblical Archaeology Review* (September/October 1990): 45-69.

13. As stated in his interview on the video "Jericho," in the series *Ancient Secrets of the Bible* (Group Publications, 1996).

14. For example, Tel el-Ful (Gibeah), Tel el-Jib (Gibeon), and Tel en-Nasbeh (Mitzpah).

15. This was most prevalent with Roman and Byzantine occupiers, who cleared their sites to bedrock before building, thus completely obliterating all signs of previous architecture. *See* for details David Livingston, "Khirbet Nisya Had Walls and Gates," unpublished paper (October 10, 1996), pp. 1-5.

16. Interview with Bryant Wood, New Orleans, November 1996.

17. Adam Zertal, "Has Joshua's Altar Been Found on Mt. Ebal?" *Biblical Archaeology Review* 11:1 (January/February 1985):26-43.

18. Milt Machlin, *Joshua's Altar: The Dig at Mount Ebal* (New York: William Morrow & Co., Inc., 1991):

19. Zertal follows Albrect Alt's theory of "Peaceful Infiltration."

20. Aharon Kempinski, "Joshua's Altar—An Iron Age Watchtower," *Biblical Archaeology Review* 12:1 (January/Februaary 1986):42-53.

21. The debate centers on the comparison with a similar square structure at the site of Gilo.

22. Tel es-Sultan (Jericho), et-Tell (Ai?), Tel es-Safi/Khirbet el-Qom (Makkedah), Tel es-Safi/Tel Bornat/Tel Judeideh (Libnah), Tel ed-Duweir (Lachish), Yel el-Hesi/Tel 'Aitun (Eglon), Tel Hebron (Hebron), Tel Beit Mirsim/Shirbet Rabud (Debir), Tel el-Qedah (Hazor), Tel Q Hittin (Madon), Tel Shimron (Shimron), Tel Keisan (Achshaph).

23. Hazor and Tel Beit Mirsim.

24. Jericho, Tel ed-Duwir, Tel Beit Mirsim, Hazor, Tel Quarnei Hittin, and Tel Keisan.

25. David Merling, Sr., "The Book of Joshua: Its Theme and Use in Discussions of the Israelite Conquest and Settlement and the Relationship of Archaeology and the Bible" (Ph.D. dissertation, Andrews University Seventh-day Adventist Theological Seminary, February 1996), p. 270.

26. Interview with Keith Schoville, Jackson, Mississippi, November 1996.

27. Eugene Merrill, "The Late Bronze/Early Iron Age Transition and the Emergence of Israel." *Bibliotheca Sacra* 152:806 (April-June 1995):153.

28. *See* William G. Dever, "How to Tell an Israelite from a Canaanite," *The Rise of Ancient Israel* (Washington, D.C.: Biblical Archaeology Society, 1992), pp. 26-56; Trude Dothan, "In the Days When the Judges Ruled—Research on the Period of the Settlement and the Judges," *Recent Archaeology in the Land of Israel,* ed. Hershel Shanks (Washington, D.C.: Biblical Archaeology Society, 1985), pp. 35-41.

29. For a discussion of the evidence that may be had from the ceramic record at these sites, *see* Bruce K. Waltke, "Palestinian Artifactual Evidence Supporting the Early Date for the Exodus," *Bibliotheca Sacra* 129 (January 1972).

30. Ibid., p. 47.

Chapter 9—*King David*

1. Jerry M. Landay, *The House of David* (New York: E.P. Dutton, 1973), p. 11.

2. Kathleen Kenyon, *The Bible and Recent Archaeology*, rev. ed. by P.R.S. Moorey (Atlanta: John Knox Press, 1987), p. 85.

3. See *Biblical Archaeology Review* 11:5 (September/October 1985): 26-39.

4. Terence Kleven, "Up the Waterspout," *Biblical Archaeology Review* 20:4 (July/August 1994): 34-35.

5. Eilat Mazar, "Excavate King David's Palace," *Biblical Archaeology Review* 23:1 (January/February, 1997): 52-57, 74.

6. Interview with Avraham Biran, Hebrew Union College—Jewish Institute of Religion, Jerusalem, October 17, 1996.

7. Thomas L. Thompson, " 'House of David': An Eponymic Referent to Yahweh as Godfather," *Scandinavian Journal of the Old Testament* 9:1 (1995): 74.

8. For other scholars dealing with the lack of a word divider see Baruch Halpern, "The Stele from Dan: Epigraphic and Historical Considerations," *Bulletin of the Schools of Oriental Research* 296 (1995): 67-68; E. Ben-Zvi, "On the Reading *'bytdwd* in the Aramaic Stele from Tel Dan," *Journal for the Study of the Old Testament* 64 (1994): 28.

9. One such example is in the Tel Qasile ostracon where the letters *bythrn* without a divider must mean "Beit Horon." *See* Anson Rainey, "The 'House of David' and the House of the Deconstructionists," *Biblical Archaeology Review* 20:6 (1994): 47, 68-69.

10. James K. Hoffmeier, "Current Issues in Archaeology: The Recently Discovered Tell Dan Inscription: Controversy & Confirmation," *Archaeology in the Biblical World* 3:1 (Summer 1995): 14.

11. E. Ben-Zvi, "On the Reading *'bytdwd* in the Aramaic Stele from Tel Dan," *Journal for the Study of the Old Testament* 64 (1994): 29-32, who cautions accepting LeMaire's conclusion without further investigation.

12. *See* N. Na'aman, "Beth-David in the Aramaic Stele from Tel Dan," *Biblische Notizen* 79 (1995): 19-20.

13. For further argumentation of this kind see Gary N. Knoppers, "The Vanishing Solomon: The Disappearance of the United Monarchy from Recent Histories of Ancient Israel," *Journal of Biblical Literature* 116:1 (Spring 1997): 36-41.

14. Cited in "News Briefs" in *Prophecy in the News* (September, 1993), p. 12.

15. Interview with Bryant Wood, New Orleans, November 25, 1996.

Chapter 10—*The Temple*

1. Benjamin Mazar, *The Mountain of the Lord* (New York: Doubleday, 1975), pp. 5-6.

2. Mary Curtis, " 'Bones and Stones' War Puts a City in Trenches," *New York Times,* March 1996 (Culture section).

3. Randall Price, "New Tunnel Opening," *Messianic Times* (December/January 1996-97).

4. For a more complete description of the Herodian Temple's glory and its effect on the Jews who wrongly deduced that it was inviolable and could not be destroyed, *see* Jacob Neusner, *First Century Judaism in Crisis* (Nashville/New York: Abingdon Press, 1975), p. 21.

5. For more information on the history of these Temples, *see* my book with Thomas Ice, *Ready to Rebuild* (Harvest House Publishers, 1992), pp. 39-84, and my published dissertation *The Desecration and Restoration of the Temple as an Eschatological Motif in the Tanakh, Jewish Apocalyptic Literature and the New Testament* (Michigan: UMI, 1993). For an overview of the history and theology of the Temple, *see* my articles on the same in *Premillennial Dictionary of Theology,* ed. Mal Couch (Grand Rapids: Kregel Publications, 1997).

6. *See* Benjamin Mazar, "Archaeological Excavations Near the Temple Mount," *Jerusalem Revealed,* ed. Yigael Yadin (Jerusalem: Israel Exploration Society, 1975), p. 33.

7. Interview with Amihai Mazar, Institute of Archaeology, Hebrew University, Jerusalem, October 19, 1996.

8. For a comprehensive treatment of the architecture with archaeological support, *see* Jean Quellette, "The Temple of Solomon: A Philological and Archaeological Study," Ph.D. dissertation, Hebrew Union College, February 1966, pp. 94-211.

9. *See* Volkmar Fritz, "Temple Architecture: What Can Archaeology Tell Us About Solomon's Temple?" *Biblical Archaeology Review* 13:4 (July/August 1987): 38-49.

10. Some, however, argue for a two-part or one-part Temple, depending on whether or not the entrance and the Holy of Holies should be counted as separate divisions.

11. Yohanan Aharoni, "The Solomonic Temple, the Tabernacle and the Arad Sanctuary," H.A. Hoffner, ed., *Orient and Occident: The C.H. Gordon Festschrift* (Berlin: Neukirchen-Vluyn, 1973), pp. 1-8.

12. For a popular account of Phoenician influence see Clifford Wilson, "Solomon and Israel's Golden Age: Part 1—Solomon's Temple," *Bible and Spade* 1:2 (Spring 1972): 43-47.

13. For details of this Temple see the excellent article by Sara Japhet, "The Temple in the Restoration Period: Reality and Ideology," *Union Seminary Quarterly Review* 44:3-4 (1991):195-252, which provides the most complete survey of material to date.

14. This may also be assumed from pottery models of temple-like shrines that have a porch supported by two pillars and an idol within. A good example is an Iron Age IIB model from Idalion, Cyprus.

15. *See* G. Ernest Wright, "The Archaeology of Solomon's Temple," *Biblical Archaeology* (Westminster/John Knox Press, 1962), p. 137.

16. *See* Victor Hurowitz, "Inside Solomon's Temple," *Bible Review* 10:2 (April 1994): 24-37.

17. My calculation is based on the royal cubit, which was about 20.9 inches.

18. *See* Alan Millard, *Treasures from Bible Times* (London: Lion Publishing, 1985), pp. 105-6.

19. Reported in *Dispatch from Jerusalem* (March/April 1995): 3.

20. As cited in the article "Second Temple Replica Discovered," *Jerusalem Post,* April 8, 1995.

21. For details see Bejamin Mazar, *The Mountain of the Lord* (Garden City, NY: Doubleday & Co., 1975). The field director for the dig was Meir Ben-Dov, who has also published popular pictorial books on the findings; see *In the Shadow of the Temple: The Discovery of Ancient Jerusalem* (New York: Harper & Row Publishers, 1985).

22. For the popular report of these excavations by Bahat, see "Jerusalem Down Under: Tunneling Along Herod's Temple Mount Wall," *Biblical Archaeology Review* 21:6 (November/December 1995): 30-47.

23. *See* my *In Search of Temple Treasures* (Eugene, OR: Harvest House Publishers, 1994), pp. 157-85, and my video by the same title.

24. In a conversation with Leen Ritmeyer, he suggested a First Temple period date for the tunnel.

25. Interview with Ronny Reich, Temple Mount excavations, Jerusalem, October 27, 1996.

26. Interview with Ronny Reich, Jerusalem, October 27, 1996.

27. *See* Benjamin Mazar, "The Temple Mount," *Biblical Archaeology Today: Proceedings of the International Congress on Biblical Archaeology, Jerusalem, April 1984* (Jerusalem: Israel Exploration Society, 1985), pp. 463-68.

28. Ritmeyer believes that this square platform could not have existed at the time Solomon built the First Temple, since it would not have accommodated his palace built alongside. He conjectures that it was changed from a rectangle to a square by King Hezekiah, since the first use of the Hebrew term for the square platform in Isaiah and Kings is in the time of Hezekiah's son Manasseh. Manasseh, who was an evil king, defiled the Temple and would not have re-shaped the Mount; hence, it must have been Hezekiah. We also have the prediction in the ancient sources that when the Temple Mount is made square it (the Temple) will be destroyed. Such a prediction also accompanied Hezekiah's reign *(see* Isaiah 39:6).

29. Interview with Leen Ritmeyer, Jackson, Mississippi, November 11, 1996.

30. For the most accurate description of the Second Temple, *see* Leen and Kathleen Ritmeyer, *Reconstructing Herod's Temple Mount in Jerusalem* (Washington, DC: Biblical Archaeology Society, 1991), and *A Model of Herod's Temple* (London: Ritmeyer Archaeological Design, 1993).

Chapter 11—Archaeology and the Ark

1. E.M. Blaiklock, sv. "Ark of the Covenant," *New International Dictionary of Biblical Archaeology*, eds. E.M. Blaiklock, R.K. Harrison (Grand Rapids: Zondervan, 1983), p. 68.

2. For those wanting a more precise measurement, based on a standard cubit, the dimensions were 3'9" ˇ 2'3" ˇ 2'3". Or, if the cubit was only five handbreadths (15"): 3'1.5" ˇ 1'10.5" ˇ 1'10.5". According to Rabbi Getz, who made a measurement of the inner gates within the Warren Gate, the cubit = 57.8 centimeters. If this later cubit used for the Second Temple was the same as the cubit used for the Ark, then the measurements would be 3'7" ˇ 2'2" ˇ 2'2".

3. It is a cognate with Akkadian *aranu,* which also means "box, chest." The Hebrew word is used of the Temple "money-chest" (2 Kings 12:9; 2 Chronicles 24:8-11).

4. Jerusalem Talmud, tractate *Shekalim* 6:1. Other sources say that this "layer" was only as thick as a gold *dinar* coin (*Eruvin* 19a; *Mikdash Aharon; Kreiti u'Fleiti, Yoreh De'ah* 43), although others say either a handbreadth (3"), *Yoma* 72b; Rabbi Chananel; Abarbanel (*Maaseh Choshev* 8:2), one half handbreadth (1.5"), or a fingerbreadth (.75"), *Baba Bathra* 14a; *Bareitha Melekheth HaMishkan* 6. While 3" would require far too much gold for the amount actually employed, the amount must have been sufficient to ensure the preservation of the Ark with the passage of time.

5. Cf. *Yoma* 72b; Rashi; Ralbag.

6. *See* Alan Millard, "Tutankhamen, the Tabernacle and the Ark of the Covenant," *Bible and Spade* 7:2 (Spring 1994):49-51.

7. *See* Elie Borowski, "Cherubim: God's Throne?" *Biblical Archaeology Review* 21:4 (July/August 1995): 36-41.

8. Josephus, the first-century Jewish writer who recorded an eyewitness description of the Second Temple, says of the cherubim, "No one can tell what they were like." Flavius Josephus, *Antiquities of the Jews* 8:3, 3.

9. For a discussion of these evidences, *see* Roland de Vaux, "Les chérubins et l'arche d'alliance, les sphinx gardiens et les trônes divins dans l'Ancien Orient," *Mélanges de l'Université Saint-Joseph* 37 (1960-1961): 91-124 and in English, his *Ancient Israel* 1:298-301.

10. For an example of this type cf. the illustration of King Hiram of Byblus seated on his cherub-throne (tenth century B.C.) in W.F. Albright, "What were the Cherubim?" in *The Biblical Archaeologist Reader,* 1 (Scholars Press, 1975), pp. 95-97.

11. The Old Testament, Josephus, and Philo are all unanimous in their verdict that the only items in the Ark were the tablets. The other two standard items—the jar of manna and Aaron's rod—were said to have been kept in front of the Ark (Exodus 16:33-34; Numbers 17:10; 1 Kings 8:9; 2 Chronicles 5:10; cf. Philo, *De Vita Mosis* 2.97; Josephus, *Antiquities* 3.6.5 #138; 8.4.1 #104.

12. Cf. Alan R. Millard, "Re-Creating the Tablets of the Law," *Bible Review* 10:1 (February 1994): 49-53.

13. Cf. *Baba Batra* 14a for this debate.

14. That Israel adopted practices identical with other pagan cultures is no problem to the uniqueness of God's special revelation to them as the chosen people. Some explain this by showing the reasonableness of God to accommodate His People to local customs, but with a distinct theological meaning that magnified the God of Israel by contrast. I am of the opinion that the "cultic"

(ritual) system was revealed to man from the Garden of Eden onward, and so was a part of the practice of all the separate cultures that developed after the division of the nations at Babel. Thus, even pagan cultures retained a bit of the original divine structure, though perverted and altered with the intrusion of false deities. God's purpose for Israel is to return to the original pure worship introduced in Eden, and therefore His commands concerning the establishment of the sanctuary and the sancta are in accordance with this original design.

15. Henton Davies, "The Ark of the Covenant," *Annual of the Swedish Theological Institute* 5 (1966-1967), p. 39.

16. Excerpt from recorded presentation given by Leen Ritmeyer at the annual meeting of the Near Eastern Archaeological Society, November 20, 1996 in Jacksonville, Mississippi.

17. Leen Ritmeyer, *The Temple and the Rock* (Harrogate, England: Ritmeyer Archaeological Design, 1996), pp. 24, 25, 41.

18. *See* further concerning Ritmeyer's views "The Ark of the Covenant, Where It Stood in Solomon's Temple," *Biblical Archaeology Review* (January/February 1996) and "Locating the Original Temple Mount," *Biblical Archaeology Review* (March/April 1992).

Chapter 12—Kings and Prophets

1. Amihai Mazar, *Archaeology of the Land of the Bible, The Anchor Bible:10,000–586 B.C.E.* (New York: Doubleday, 1990), p. 416.

2. Philip J. King, *Jeremiah: An Archaeological Companion* (KY: Westminster/John Knox Press, 1993), p. xxi.

3. Interview with Seymour Gittin, Albright Institute, Jerusalem, October 25, 1996.

4. Ibid.

5. Ibid.

6. *See Biblical Archaeology Review* 20:1 (January/February 1994); and for Shishak's campaign, Kenneth A. Kitchen, "Shishak's Military Campaign in Israel Confirmed," *Biblical Archaeology Review* 15:3 (May/June 1989): 32ff.

7. Interview with Amihai Mazar, The Hebrew University of Archaeology, October 26, 1996.

8. Interview with Avraham Biran, Hebrew Union College, Jerusalem, October 21, 1996.

9. For additional details about these remains see Avraham Biran, *Temples and High Places in Biblical Times* (Jerusalem: Israel Exploration Society, 1977), and for other finds from the excavations *see* Avraham Biran, *Biblical Dan* (Jerusalem: Israel Exploration Society, 1994), pp. 159-234.

10. Interview with Avraham Biran, Hebrew Union College, Jerusalem, October 21, 1996.

11. Interview with Amihai Mazar, The Hebrew University Institute of Archaeology, October 26, 1996.

12. This eighth century B.C. seal was sold at a Sotheby's auction for $80,000 and now is part of the Shlomo Moussaief Collection in London. For details see Andre Lemaire, "Royal Signature: Name of Israel's Last King Surfaces in a Private Collection," *Biblical Archaeology Review* (September/October 1996): 48-52.

13. As reported in "Archaeology in Review," *Dispatch from Jerusalem* 20:6 (November/December 1995): 3.

14. *See* Jane M. Cahill and David Tarler, "Excavations Directed by Yigael Shiloh at the City of David, 1978-1985," *Ancient Jerusalem Revealed,* ed. Hillel Geva (Jerusalem: Israel Exploration Society, 1994), pp. 39-40.

15. For complete details of these bullae *see* Nahman Avigad, *Hebrew Bullae from the Time of Jeremiah* (Washington, D.C.: Biblical Archaeology Society, 1987).

16. *See* Gabriel Barkay, "A Bulla of Ishmael, the King's Son," *Bulletin of the American School of Oriental Research* 290-291 (1993): 109-114.

17. *See* Hershel Shanks, "Jeremiah's Scribe and Confidant Speaks from a Hoard of Clay Bullae," *Biblical Archaeology Review* 13:5 (September/October 1987): 58-65.

18. First reported in a privately printed book cataloging collector's inscriptions, entitled *Forty New West Semitic Inscriptions*, ed. Robert Deutsch (Tel Aviv: The Archaeological Center, 1996).

19. For details about this discovery and others listed in the above catalog, see Hershel Shanks, "Fingerprint of Jeremiah's Scribe," *Biblical Archaeology Review* 22:2 (March/April 1996): 36-38.

20. Interview with Gabriel Barkay at Ketef Hinnom, Jerusalem, October 26, 1996.

21. Ibid.

22. Ibid.

23. Ibid.

Chapter 13—Archaeology and Prophecy

1. Thomas Urquhart, *The Wonders of Prophecy* (New York: C.C. Cook, n.d.), p. 93.

2. As stated in the article by Hershel Shanks, "Is the Bible Right After All?: BAR Interviews William Dever" (Part 2), *Biblical Archaeology Review* 22:5 (September/October 1996): 35.

3. The statistics of prophetic probability have calculated the chances of 11 prophecies finding fulfillment to be 1 in 5.76×10^{59}. This astronomical sum has been put in practical terms by Peter W. Stoner, *Science Speaks: An Evaluation of Certain Christian Evidences* (Chicago: Moody Press, 1963), pp. 95-98. For the prophetic probabilities of some of the prophecies listed in this chapter, *see* Josh McDowell, *Evidence That Demands a Verdict: Historical Evidences for the Christian Faith*, rev. ed. (San Bernardino, CA: Here's Life Publishers, Inc., 1986) 1: 318-320.

4. Appearing in this manner, the reference serves as a structural device linking the theme of the two chapters. Therefore, it cannot be regarded as a later insertion.

5. Of course the whole tenor of Isaiah is of predictive prophecy. It would be completely out of context and out of character to view this prophecy otherwise—see J. Alec Motyer, *The Prophecy of Isaiah: An Introduction & Commentary* (Downers Grove, IL: InterVarsity Press, 1993), pp. 355-56.

6. Fulfilled prophecy is not the only test, however. The prophecies of false prophets might also be brought to pass as a test of Israel's fidelity to previously revealed revelation. Therefore, if the prophecy was not in harmony with the message of true prophets or in line with the Torah, then despite its seeming authentication, it was to be rejected (see Deuteronomy 13:1-5; Jeremiah 23:16-27).

7. *The History of Herodotus Book* 1:95-216; see the Manuel Komroff edition, trans. George Rawlinson (New York: Tudor Publishing Co., 1956), pp. 16-80.

8. *Cyropaedia* 8.5:1-36; et al. in the *Loeb Classical Library* (Oxford: University Press, 1957).

9. *Ancient Near Eastern Texts,* ed. James Pritchard (Chicago: University of Chicago Press, 1978), pp. 305-6.

10. Ibid, pp. 313-315.

11. This fact was not mentioned in the Greek sources either because they may not have known Belshazzar's name or simply because they preferred to list only the first ruler, his father Nabonidus. Daniel, however, was aware of this co-regency; he notes that Belshazzar could only

bestow on Daniel the rank of "third ruler in the kingdom" (Daniel 5:29), after his father and himself.

12. Alan Millard, *Treasures from Bible Times* (Hertz, England: Lion Publishing Corporation, 1985), p. 146.

13. *Ancient Near Eastern Texts*, p. 315.

14. Ibid., p. 316.

15. Ibid.

16. However, there is no prediction that people would never live there again, as is specifically stated for Babylon's destruction. Today, there is habitation at the site of Nineveh, but, as predicted, the Assyrians vanished and the city never was again rebuilt.

17. That Tyre "never made a comeback as a real power" is the conclusion made by the most modern historical treatment of the city. *See* H.J. Katzenstein, *The History of Tyre: From the Beginning of the Second Millenium B.C.E. Until the Fall of the Neo-Babylonian Empire in 539 B.C.E.*, rev. ed. (Beer Sheva: Ben-Gurion University of the Negev Press, 1997), p. 347.

18. In the case of Babylon its final destruction has yet to occur if we take the reference to the city of Babylon in Revelation 17 and 18 as literal. For a defense of this position *see* Charles Dyer, *The Identity of Babylon in Revelation 17 and 18* (Th.M. thesis Dallas Theological Seminary, 1979), as well as his popular book *The Rise of Babylon* (Tyndale Publishing Co., 1990).

19. B.B. Warfield, *The Spiritual Life of Theological Students* (Phillipsburg, NJ: Presbyterian & Reformed, 1983).

Chapter 14—Archaeology and a Miracle

1. As cited in Howard Vos, *Can I Trust My Bible?* (Chicago: Moody Press, 1963), p. 176.

2. W.F. Albright, *The Archaeology of Palestine* (London: Pelican Books, 1954 edition), p. 255.

3. *See* John Phillips, "Miracles: Not for Today," *Moody Monthly* (July/August 1982): 72-74.

4. This relic had apparently been assumed into pagan ritualistic practices which commonly employed serpents. Several archaeological examples of serpents on Midianite ritual objects have been discovered at Timna from the thirteenth or twelfth centuries B.C.

5. For additional details *see* Jack P. Lewis, *Historical Backgrounds of Bible History* (Grand Rapids: Baker Book House, 1971), pp. 44-48.

6. This word appears on a bilingual (Assyrian and Aramaic) clay label dated to about 645 B.C. For details *see* document 30 in T.C. Mitchell, *The Bible in the British Museum: Interpreting the Evidence* (London: British Museum Publications, 1990), p. 67.

7. Recently the date of the inscription was questioned by Rogerson and Davies and said to be from Hasmonean times (Second Temple period). *See* "Was the Siloam Tunnel Built by Hezekiah?" *Biblical Archaeologist* 59:3 (1996): 138-49. Their challenge was successfully answered by Ronald S. Hendel, "The Date of the Siloam Inscription: A Rejoinder to Rogerson and Davies," *Biblical Archaeologist* 59:4 (1996): 233-37.

8. One of the better-argued proposals was that the pickmen followed a natural fissure or faultline in the limestone hill. *See* Zvi Abels and Asher Arbit, "The Digging of Hezekiah's Tunnel," in "Some New Thoughts on Jerusalem's Ancient Water Systems," *Palestine Exploration Quarterly* 127 (1995): 4-6. However, evidence of such a crack sufficient to explain the feat has yet to be discovered. For a different theory, though not conclusive, *see* Dan Gill, "How They Met—Geology Solves Long-Standing Mystery of Hezekiah's Tunnelers," *Biblical Archaeology Review* 20 (July/August 1994).

9. For a detailed account *see* Yigael Shiloh, "Jerusalem: Eighth to Sixth Centuries B.C.E.," in *The New Encyclopedia of Archaeological Excavations in the Holy Land* (Jerusalem: Israel Exploration Society, 1993), 2:704-712.

10. The first-century historian Flavius Josephus' statements about the walls of Jerusalem, especially the First Wall, helped make this determination. (*See Wars of the Jews* 5:143.)

11. Second Kings 19:35-37; Isaiah 37:36-38.

12. *The History of Herodotus*, ed. George Rawlinson, trans. Manuel Komroff (New York: Tudor Publishing Co., 1956), Book II, p. 131.

13. For discussion, *see* Siegfried H. Horn, "Did Sennacherib Campaign Once or Twice Against Hezekiah?" Andrews *University Seminary Studies* 4 (1966): 1-28.

14. For the complete translation *see* De Witt Thomas, *Documents from Old Testament Times* (London: Nelson, 1958), pp. 66-67.

15. These copies are respectively housed in the British Museum in London, the Museum of Grollenburg, and in the Museum of the Oriental Institute at the University of Chicago.

16. Hershel Shanks, *Jerusalem: An Archaeological Biography* (New York: Random House, 1995), p. 84 (top).

17. Gabriel Barkay compares these tumuli with those well known from the Aegean area, especially at Salamis in Cyprus. For a discussion of these sites *see* V. Karageorghis, *Salamis in Cyprus* (London: Thames and Hudson, 1969), pp. 151-64 and *Excavations in the Necropolis of Salamis* III [text] (Nicosia: Department of Antiquities, Cyprus, 1973), pp. 128-202.

18. Initial excavations were begun by W.F. Albright, as explained in "Interesting Finds in Tumuli Near Jerusalem," *Bulletin of the American Schools of Oriental Research* 10 (1923): 2-4, and followed up by Ruth Amiran, "The Tumuli West of Jerusalem: Survey and Excavations," *Israel Exploration Journal* 8 (1958): 205-27.

19. Interview with Gabriel Barkay, Jerusalem, October 29, 1996.

20. We should rather say there *were* 20 tumuli. Settlement building in this area has unfortunately destroyed many of these.

21. Interview with Gabriel Barkay, October 29, 1996.

22. Gordon Franz, "News from the Pits," Institute for Holy Land Studies, Jerusalem (February 22, 1983), p. 2.

Chapter 15—The Dead Sea Scrolls

1. Yadin Roman, "Scroll Work," *Eretz* (July/August 1997): 16.

2. Yigael Yadin, *The Message of the Scrolls* (New York: Simon and Schuster, Inc., 1957), p. 14.

3. *See* Shemaryahu Talmon, "Was the Book of Esther Known at Qumran?" *Dead Sea Discoveries* 2:3 (November 1995): 1-11. Talmon discusses 18 phrases in Qumran texts which are similar to, or even identical with, parallel expressions in the book of Esther. Eight of these are based on *hapax legomena* (unique expressions that occur only once) in Esther. This indicates that the authors of these texts knew at least the Esther story, but also that some were actually familiar with the biblical book. There is also additional support in the many Aramaic fragments from Cave 4 called *Proto-Esther (4Q550)*. Talmon proposes that the reason Esther was not included was because it had not yet achieved canonical status in the Qumran community. He finds some support for this in the Talmud account of a third century A.D. debate over its status (b. Meg. 7a) and the absence of any mention of the festival of Purim among the Scrolls.

4. *See* Yigael Yadin, *Tefillin from Qumran (XQPhyl 1-4)* (Jerusalem: The Israel Exploration Society and the Shrine of the Book, 1969).

5. *See* Lawrence Schiffman, "The Significance of the Scrolls," *Bible Review* 6:5 (October, 1990), p. 23.

6. For this discussion *see* Shemaryahu Talmon, "The 'Desert Motif' in the Bible and in Qumran Literature," *Biblical Motifs: Origins and Transformations, Studies and Texts 3.,* ed. Alexander Altmann (Cambridge: Harvard University Press, 1966), pp. 56-57. It may be precisely for this negative reason that the desert motif was infrequently used in the Qumran literature, even though it was of strategic significance.

7. Ibid., pp. 57-58.

8. Some accounts make Jum'a Muhammed (Muhammed edh-Dhib's older cousin) responsible for the initial find; *see* Harry Thomas Frank, "How the Dead Sea Scrolls Were Found," *Biblical Archaeology Review* 1:4 (December, 1975), p. 1.

9. Available from Harvest House Publishers (1996), pp. 536. A 60-minute companion video including on-site excavation and interviews with Scroll archaeologists and translators is also available from the same.

10. From transcript of recorded report delivered by Hanan Eshel at the Qumran Section at the American Academy of Religion/Society of Biblical Literature Annual Meeting, November, 1996, New Orleans, Louisiana.

11. From Esther Eshel's report abstract "New Ostracon Found at Qumran," given at the American Academy of Religion/Society of Biblical Literature Annual Meeting, November 1996, New Orleans, Louisiana.

12. Excerpted from a transcript made from a recorded interview with Stephen Pfann by Thomas McCall at Qumran, November 1996. Used by permission.

13. Interview with Stephen Pfann, Jerusalem, June 18, 1997.

Chapter 16—Archaeology and Jesus

1. James M. Charlesworth, *Jesus Within Judaism: New Light from Exciting Archaeological Discoveries,* The Anchor Bible Reference Library (New York: Doubleday, 1988), p. 104.

2. Rudolph Bultmann, *Theology of the New Testament,* trans. K. Grobel (New York, 1951), 1:12.

3. For the views of this group and the evangelical responses to it, *see* Michael Wilkins & J.P. Moreland, eds., *Jesus Under Fire: Modern Scholarship Reinvents the Historical Jesus* (Grand Rapids: Zondervan Publishing Co., 1995). *See also* Dale Allison, "The Contemporary Quest for the Historical Jesus," *Irish Biblical Studies* 18 (October 1996): 174-93.

4. *See* for example works by James H. Charlesworth, professor of New Testament Language and Literature and chairperson of the Department of Biblical Studies at Princeton Theological Seminary, who is a leader in interfaith dialogues in the contemporary search to establish the historical Jewish context of Jesus—see his *Jesus Within Judaism: New Light from Exciting Archaeological Discoveries* (New York: Doubleday & Co., 1988) and *Jesus' Jewishness* (New York: Crossroad Publishing Co., 1991).

5. L. Goppelt, *Theology of the New Testament,* trans. J. Alsup, ed. J. Roloff (Grand Rapids: William B. Eerdmans Publishing Co., 1981), 1:6-7.

6. *See* Jerry Varadaman, "The Year of the Nativity: Was Jesus Born in 12 B.C.? A New Examination of Quirinius (Luke 2:2) and Related Problems of New Testament Chronology," as referenced in John McRay's book *Archaeology and the New Testament* (Grand Rapids: Baker Book House, 1991), pp. 154, 385 (footnote 9).

7. *See* Jerome, Letter 58: *To Paulinus.*

8. *See* Paulinus of Nola *Epistle* 31.3.

9. *See* Bellarmino Bagatti, *The Church from the Circumcision* (Jerusalem: Franciscan Printing Press, 1971), p. 126.

10. Josephus, *Antiquities of the Jews.*

11. Interview with Ehud Netzer, Hebrew University Institute of Archaeology, Jerusalem, October 21, 1996.

12. *See* "In the Name of the King," *Eretz* 48 (September/October 1996), p. 66.

13. Ibid.

14. *See* James F. Strange and Hershel Shanks, "Synagogue Where Jesus Preached Found at Capernaum," *Biblical Archaeology Review* 9:6 (November/December 1983): 24-32.

15. *See* Stanisalo Loffreda, "Ceramica ellenistico-romana nel sottosuolo della sinagoga di Cafarnao," *Studia Hierosolymitana* 3 (1982): 313-57.

16. *See* Vasillios Tzaferis, "New Archaeological Evidence on Ancient Capernaum," *Biblical Archaeologist* 46 (December 1983): 201.

17. *See* James F. Strange and Hershel Shanks, "Has the House Where Jesus Stayed in Capernaum Been Found?" *Biblical Archaeology Review* 8:6 (November/December 1982): 26-37.

18. *See* John C.H. Lauglin, "Capernaum: From Jesus' Time and After," *Biblical Archaeology Review* 19:5 (September/October 1993): 54-63, 90.

19. For further details, *see* the first volume excavation report *Bethsaida: A City by the North Shore of the Sea of Galilee*, eds. Rami Arav and Richard A. Freund (Missouri: Thomas Jefferson University Press, 1995). The second volume of this excavation report is due to be released in November 1997.

20. These discoveries were made a few days before and during my visit to the site in June 1997.

21. For details of the discovery, *see* Zvi Greenhut, "Burial Cave of the Caiaphas Family," *Biblical Archaeology Review* 18:5 (September/October 1992): 28-44, 76.

22. *See* Zvi Greenhut, "Caiaphas' Final Resting Place," *Israel Hilton Magazine* (Spring 1993), p. 16.

23. *See* "Ossuary of Caiaphas," in P. Kyle McCarter, Jr., *Ancient Inscriptions: Voices from the Biblical World* (Washington D.C.: Biblical Archaeology Society, 1996), p. 133.

24. As cited by David Briggs, "The High Priest: Archaeologists Find Evidence of Caiaphas," Associated Press report August 22, 1992.

25. *See 4QpNah* 3-4 i 7; *11Q19* 64:6-13.

26. *See Antiquities* 12:256; 13:379-383; *Wars* 1.4.6: 96-98; 2:306-308.

27. For example, tractate Sanhedrin 43a requires the death penalty for rebels, a punishment understood after stoning as "hanging on a tree."

28. See *Life* 420-21.

29. *See* V. Tzaferis, "Jewish Tombs at and Near Giv'at ha-Mivtar, Jerusalem," *Israel Exploration Journal* 20:1-2 (1970): 18-32.

30. As deciphered by the epigraphist Joseph Naveh, "The Ossuary Inscriptions from Giv'at ha-Mivtar," *Israel Exploration Journal* 20:1 (1970): 33-37.

31. For complete details *see* V. Tzaferis, "Crucifixion—The Archaeological Evidence," *Biblical Archaeology Review* 11:1 (January/February 1985): 44-53; Joe Zias and E. Sekeles, "The Crucified Man from Giv'at ha-Mivtar: A Reappraisal," *Israel Exploration Journal* 35:1 (1985): 22-27.

32. *See* J.W. Hewitt, "The Use of Nails in the Crucifixion," *Harvard Theological Review* 25 (1932): 29-45.

33. James H. Charlesworth, *Jesus Within Judaism: New Light from Exciting Archaeological Discoveries* (New York: Doubleday & Co., 1988), p. 123.

34. *See* C. Cohasnon, *The Church of the Holy Sepulchre in Jerusalem,* trans. J.P.B. Ross and C. Ross (London, 1974), p. 29.

35. *See* Kathleen Kenyon, *Jerusalem, Excavating 3000 Years of History* (London: Thames and Hudson, 1967), pp. 153-54, and Bruce Schein, "The Second Wall of Jerusalem," *Biblical Archaeologist* 44:1 (Winter 1981): 21-26.

36. *See* Gordon Franz, "An Archaeologist Looks at the Life of Christ" (notes prepared for field trips with the American Institute of Holy Land Studies, now the Jerusalem University College, Mt. Zion, Jerusalem, revised ed. May 3, 1996), p. 21.

37. Gabriel Barkay and Amos Kloner, "Burial Caves North of Damascus Gate, Jerusalem," *Israel Exploration Journal* 26 (1976): 55-57, and L.Y. Rahmani, "Ancient Jerusalem's Funerary Customs and Tombs," *Biblical Archaeologist* 44 (1981): 229-35.

38. Gabriel Barkay and Amos Kloner, "Jerusalem Tombs from the Days of the First Temple," *Biblical Archaeology Review* 12:2 (March/April 1986): 22-39.

39. *See* James H. Charlesworth, *Jesus Within Judaism: New Light from Exciting Archaeological Discoveries* (New York: Doubleday & Co., 1988), p. 124.

40. For these requirements *see* M. Hengel, *Crucifixion: In the Ancient World and the Folly of the Message of the Cross,* trans. J. Bowden (Philadelphia: Fortress Press, 1977).

41. *See* John McRay, "Tomb Typology and the Tomb of Jesus," *Archaeology and the Biblical World* 2:2 (Spring 1994): 39.

42. *See* Dan Bahat, "Does the Holy Sepulchre Church Mark the Burial of Jesus?" *Biblical Archaeology Review* 12:3 (May/June 1986): 30.

43. Bargil Pixner, *With Jesus Through Galilee According to the Fifth Gospel,* trans. Christo Botha and Dom David Foster (Rosh Pina, Galilee: Corazin Publishing, 1992), back cover.

Chapter 17—What Can Archaeology Prove?

1. From the "Editor's Introduction," *Biblical Archaeology,* eds. Shalom M. Paul and William G. Dever (Jerusalem: Keter Publishing House, 1973), pp. ix-x.

2. Thomas W. Davis, "Faith and Archaeology: A Brief History to the Present," *Biblical Archaeology Review* 19:2 (March/April 1993): 54.

3. As cited by Jeffery L. Sheler, "Mysteries of the Bible," *U.S. News & World Report* (April 17, 1995), p. 61.

4. Nelson Glueck, *Rivers in the Desert: A History of the Negev* (New York: Farrar, Straus and Cudahy, 1959), p. 31.

5. Ibid., pp. 31-32.

6. W. F. Albright, *The Archaeology of Palestine* (London: Penguin Books, 1954 ed.), p. 128.

7. Ibid.

8. The Australian archaeologist Clifford Wilson received from Albright during a visit at Albright's home what may amount to a personal confession of faith. He reported that Albright stated, in response to his own personal relationship to Christ and the Bible: "I didn't want to die ... believing in nothing." He went on to say that Albright affirmed to him his "commitment to the Christ of the Gospels." Clifford Wilson, *Visual Highlights of the Bible* (Australia: Pacific Christian Ministries, 1993), 1:126.

9. Kathleen Kenyon, *The Bible and Recent Archaeology,* rev. by P.R.S. Moorey (Atlanta: John Knox Press, 1987), p. 20.

10. Leslie J. Hoppe, *What Are They Saying About Biblical Archaeology?* (New York: Paulist Press, 1984), pp. 96-97.

11. There are also the practical concerns of time, manpower, and money, as well as the desire to promptly publish results—all of which dictate a limitation to every dig.

12. Jacob M. Myers, *I Chronicles, Anchor Bible* 12 (Garden City: Doubleday, 1965), p. xv.

13. Cf. Robert North, "Does Archaeology Prove Chronicles Sources?" *A Light Unto My Path: Old Testament Studies in Honor of Jacob M. Myers* (Philadelphia: Temple University Press, 1974), pp. 375-401.

14. As cited by Jeffery L. Sheler, "Mysteries of the Bible," pp. 60-61.

15. Roland de Vaux in *Near Eastern Archaeology in the Twentieth Century,* ed. James A. Sanders (Garden City, NY: Doubleday & Co., 1970), p. 68.

16. Eilat Mazar, "Excavate King David's Palace," *Biblical Archaeology Review* 23:1 (January/February 1997): 52.

17. Interview with Keith Schoville, Jackson, Mississippi, November 19, 1996.

Chapter 18—Where Do the Stones Lead You?

1. W.F. Albright, *The Archaeology of Palestine* (London: Pelican Books, 1954 edition), p. 256.

2. *Sun,* May 4, 1993, pp. 20-21.

3. See *The New Encyclopedia Britannica,* s.v. "The Theory of Evolution" 18 (1986): 996.

4. *The Tennessean,* March 3, 1996.

5. William A. Dembski, "The Problem of Error in Scripture," *The Princeton Theological Review* 3:1 (March 1996): 22-28.

6. Interview with Keith Schoville, Jackson, Mississippi, November 19, 1996.

7. James H. Charlesworth, "Archaeology, Jesus, and Christian Faith," *What Has Archaeology to do with Faith?* eds. J.H. Charlesworth and Walter P. Weaver (Philadelphia: Trinity Press International, 1992), p. 19.

8. Interview with Bryant Wood, New Orleans, November 21, 1996.

9. Phone interview with Gordan Franz, March 7, 1997.

10. Robert J. Morgan, *On This Day* (Nashville: Thomas Nelson Publishers, 1997), preface.

11. Quoted in Walter B. Knight, *Three Thousand Illustrations for Christian Service* (Grand Rapids: Baker Book House, 1961), p. 31.

PERSON INDEX

Subject Index

CREDITS

The poem "The Stones Cry Out" in chapter 1 by Anne Moore was used with permission.

Charts, Diagrams, Maps

Pages 58-59: "Major Inscriptions of the Old Testament" was adapted from charts by John Walton, *Old Testament Charts* (Zondervan) and Dr. Clifford Wilson in association with Gary Stone from *Archaeology the Bible and Christ* (Pacific Christian Ministries).

Page 176: "Second Temple Jerusalem" map was adapted from map prepared by Dr. Dan Bahat for *The Carta Atlas of Jerusalem*.

Pages 202-203: Section drawing of Temple and the location of the Holy of Holies in the Temple is by Dr. Leen Ritmeyer, used by permission of Ritmeyer Archaeological Design.

Photographs

The following photographic credits indicate ownership of the original print and/or use with permission. Numbers refer to picture numbers in the text.

Cover: Photo-design by Koechel Peterson & Associates; artifacts are from the author's private collection.

1. Author, photo by Bill Dupont.

2. Author, photo by Bill Dupont.

3. Courtesy Egyptian Museum, photo by author.

4. Courtesy Ashmolean Museum, photo by Obe Hokanson.

5. Courtesy British Museum, photo by author.

6. Courtesy Shrine of the Book, Israel Museum, photo by author.

7. Courtsey Gordon Franz.

8. Photo by author.

9. Courtesy British Museum, London, photo by author.

10. Georgina Hermann.

11. Courtesy British Museum, photo by author.

12. Reproduction, courtesy Egyptian Museum, photo by author.

13. Courtesy British Museum, photo by author.

14. Courtesy British Museum, photo by author.

15. Courtesy British Museum, photo by author.

16. Jürgen Liepe.

17. Photo by author.

18. Courtesy Skirball Museum, Jerusalem, photo by Paul Streber.

19. Photo by Paul Streber.

20. Photo by Paul Streber.

21. Courtesy Associates for Biblical Research, photo by Bryant Wood.

22. Photo by Paul Streber.

23. Courtesy Smithsonian Museum, photo by Clifford Wilson.

24. Courtesy Associates for Biblical Research, photo by Bryant Wood.

25. Reproduction, courtesy Ragab Papyrus Institute, photo by author.

26. Courtesy Trude Dothan and the Hebrew University Institute of Archaeology, photo by Paul Streber.

27. Photo by author.

28. Courtesy Egyptian Museum, photo by author.

29. Photo by Paul Streber.

30. Reproduction, courtesy Avraham Biran and the Skirball Museum, Jerusalem, photo by Paul Streber.

31. Reproduction, courtesy Avraham Biran and the Skirball Museum, Jerusalem, photo by Paul Streber.

32. Reproduction, courtesy British Museum, photo by author.

33. Photo by author.

34. Photo by Zev Radovan.

35. Photo by author.

36. Courtesy Israel Museum, photo by author.

37. Photo by Paul Streber.

38. Photo by Paul Streber.

39. Courtesy of Dan Bahat.

40. Photo by Paul Streber.

41. Photo by Paul Streber.

42. Photo by author.

43. Courtesy Holyland Hotel, photo by author.

44. Courtesy Israel Goldberg, Israel Publications, Ltd., photo by author.

45. Courtesy Atara Leyoshna Temple Model Museum, photo by Paul Streber.

46. Courtesy British Museum, photo by author.

47. Courtesy of the Israel Museum.

48. World of the Bible Ministries, Inc.   Photo by Paul Streber.

49. Courtesy Seymour Gittin, Albright Institute, Jerusalem.

50. Courtesy Skirball Museum, Jerusalem, photo by Paul Streber.

51. Photo by Paul Streber.

52. Photo by Paul Streber.

53. Courtesy The Center for the Study of Jerusalem in the First Temple Period, photo by Paul Streber.

54. Photo by Zev Radovan.

55. Courtsey Gordon Franz.

56. Courtesy British Museum, photo by author.

57. Photo by Paul Streber.

58. Photo by Paul Streber.

59. Photo by author.

60. Photo by Paul Streber.

61. Courtesy British Museum, photo by author.

62. Courtesy British Museum, photo by author. *(Note: This incomplete ninth-century codex is suspected to be from Aleppo, but provenance is uncertain.)*

63. Photo by Paul Streber.

64. Courtesy West Semitic Research, photo by Bruce and Ken Zuckerman.

65. Photo by Paul Streber.

66. Photo by Zev Radovan.

67. Reproduction, courtesy Stephen Pfann and the Shrine of the Book, photo by Paul Streber.

68. Photo by Paul Streber.

69. Courtesy Man in the Galilee Museum, photo by Paul Streber.

70. Photo by Paul Streber.

71. Photo by Paul Streber.

72. Courtesy Ehud Netzer and the Hebrew University Institute of Archaeology, photo by Paul Streber.

73. Courtesy Israel Museum, photo by author.

74. Photo by Paul Streber.

75. Courtesy Israel Museum, photo by author.

76. Photo by Zev Radovan.

77. Photo by Paul Streber.

78. Courtesy Hazor Museum, Kibbutz Ayelet Hashahar, photo by Paul Streber.